Social Problems in a Changing Society:

issues and deviances

Social Problems in a Changing Society:
issues and deviances

Stephen Schafer
Northeastern University
Boston, Massachusetts

Mary S. Knudten
Richard D. Knudten
Marquette University
Milwaukee, Wisconsin

Reston Publishing Company, Inc. Reston, Virginia 22090

A Prentice-Hall Company

Library of Congress Cataloguing in Publication Data

Schafer, Stephen.
    Social problems in a changing society.
    262 p. : ill. ; 23 cm.
    Includes bibliographical references and index.
    1. Social problems. 2. Deviant behavior.
3. United States — Social conditions — 1960-
I. Knudten, Mary S., 1935- joint author.
II. Knudten, Richard D., joint author. III. Title.
[DNLM: 1. Social change. 2. Social
problems. HN58 5296s]
HN65.S37   309.1'73   75-4828
ISBN 0-87909-771-X

10   9   8   7   6   5   4   3   2

Printed in the United States of America

IN MEMORY OF

Irene Schafer

Earl L. Swedlund

Dr. Arthur C. Knudten

Contents

vi

Preface

In the history of mankind, social problems and social deviance have been common. However, what form these problems and deviances take change from month to month, decade to decade, and generation to generation. As society has developed the knowledge and capacity necessary to resolve these issues or has developed a concern for their resolution, it has taken steps to remedy the situation. Sometimes these efforts have succeeded; at others they have failed. In some instances, the deviance is redefined and made acceptable; in others it is ignored or punished. The way in which a society reacts to social problems and deviant conduct offers insight into its system of values, prevailing concerns, capacity to solve issues, and willingness to respond to its members.

The solutions offered by one generation may be different from the next. Prostitution has alternately been accepted, ignored, and proscribed throughout history. Homosexual conduct, once considered totally deviant, has not gained greater acceptance among medical or psychological professionals and to a degree among the public. Even racial and ethnic problems have been redefined as minority groups have moved to claim power and employment. The former ideal of a large family has given way to population control and efforts to restrict family size through legalized abortion.

In the pages that follow, the authors bring into focus the nature and scope of *Social Problems in a Changing Society*. Viewing twelve major areas of concern, they present the data which sets the boundaries of the modern problem and define the issues and deviances which they contain. As an evaluation of the 1970's, these chapters are subject to change and reconceptualization, too, as the dynamic of society continues the movement of social change.

As one studies these problems and issues, one is struck by the fact that there are no easy solutions—in fact, in some cases there are no likely solutions at all. Nevertheless, society—and those concerned for persons or groups living a "non-normative" existence—are charged with the never-ending task to offer answers to complex issues. Often times, these answers are unrealistic to the social climate, values, and commitments of the era. Sometimes, they are only temporary solutions to the problems they are supposed to solve. But whether they are successful or not, they continue to demand the expenditure of great amounts of energy, money, emotion, and thought. For without social problems and personal deviance, there would be little challenge to change—and without such a dynamic society could easily become static and lose its vitality.

The three collaborators on this book have had the assistance of many talented persons. Serving the role of critical analyst and editorial assistant has been Lili Schafer, the wife of Stephen Schafer. The husband and wife team of Mary S. and Richard D. Knudten compose the remaining two-thirds of the author triumvirate. In addition, Lee Nagle, Diane Willette, Margaret Ksander, Carolyn Sanders, Alison Ressler, John Goerdt, and Bruce Buxton have added their fingerprints to the debate over the problems and deviances of our day. To each the authors offer their thanks and to Stephanie Padgett for her assistance.

Stephen Schafer
Mary S. Knudten
Richard D. Knudten

CHAPTER 1

The Problem of Social Problems

The Context of Modern Social Problems

Many social problems are as old as society, but they have become more numerous and of greater concern in recent decades. This is partially due to an increased social willingness to recognize problems as problems and to seek viable solutions. Media references to social issues are now endless. Politicians argue over the need either to solve or to ignore the existence of problems. Mental illness, drug addiction, sexual aberrations, family instability, racial conflict, crime, poverty, and other community problems are forcing public reaction and demanding solutions. Most of these are not new. What is new is the general social belief that their impact must be eradicated and that the resources to solve them are available.

Even the conception of most problems has changed. In the field of mental disorder, for example, where the problem was originally conceived as the presence within the person of demons, which could be exorcised only through flogging, starving, incantations, or special prayers, the view that it is an illness dominates. In the Middle Ages, the mentally ill were tortured or burned in the name of treatment in the most severe cases, and they have been locked in chains in recent history as if they were socially dangerous criminals. Today, however, chemotherapy and outpatient treatment have largely replaced the use of sanctified ointments, heavy beatings, and personal dehumanization as a rehabilitation procedure. Current policy encourages a medical rather than a metaphysical conception of the mental illness problem and a de-emphasis of institutional care. The recent *Partlow* decision of a Federal District Court now requires minimal standards of treatment for mental retardates if they are to remain institutionalized. Similar changes have occurred in other problem areas as well.

1

Social Problems and Social Change ● Most problems have not changed as issues from one generation to another; only the perception of them has changed. A few, however, have become new problems due to an increasing recognition of the ramifications of earlier defined problems. While the contours of some problems appear blurred and obscured, others are sharp and strike at a society's conscience with an oppressing effect. In this sense history is plural.[1] In oriental societies, most of the analysis regarding social problems consisted of formulating justifications of the given social regime, "mainly centering about the sanctions of a unique revealed religion or the superior wisdom of ancestors".[2] During the Industrial Revolution, however, a different view of misery, suffering, and human poverty began to emerge. Singular religious or traditional value systems began to give way to realism, value pluralism, and a scientific conception of social reform. Currently, a new consciousness has developed. The failure of proposed solutions to problems to coincide with public attitudes has created citizen outcry concerning both the problem and the solution.[3] Because our contemporaries have associated social problems with the human rights of freedom, justice, individuality, and privacy, citizens have become more aware of the personal and political dimensions of problems inherent in their society.

Political Awareness and Social Problems ● As political awareness has grown, individuals and groups have increasingly moved to "do something" to solve a problem, despite the absence of an adequate theoretical base from which to hypothesize.[4] When coupled with the flight of concern from one problem to another, a concern related to what is "in" as a problem at a particular moment, the long-term commitment necessary to achieve solutions has been missing or only half-heartedly offered. Even in a stable society not all persons agree as to what constitutes a problem, let alone its solution. As a result, public debate over problems and solutions is often sharp and acrimonious.

The better informed, modern man is a product of the decline in illiteracy but also of widely-disseminated mass media. Unlike the relatively secluded man of the past, citizens today are public beings, unable to escape the constant barrage of data and interpretation concerning social situations and their impact upon others. Whether they are interested or not, they are pulled into an awareness of the existence and cost of these problems. Rather than perceive a problem fatalistically, today's citizens, sensitized politically, see it in more realistic terms. Aware that the economic and technological resources to solve the problem probably exist, they strive to analyze and solve, albeit not without some false starts and inadequate programs.

The Social Actuality of Social Problems

To contend that "a social problem consists of a substantial discrepancy between widely shared social standards and actual conditions of social life"[5] assumes that a chasm between actual social conditions and shared social norms exists. This discrepancy is indeed real and reflects the relative state of normative development and societal awareness at a particular time in history. It is obvious that despite the norm emphasizing the legitimization of child-bearing within marriage, many children are born out of wedlock. Also, while society expects an ethical consistency in marriage and the mutual love of husband and wife, many marriages for a number of reasons fail and are terminated by divorce. Similarly, while most societies idealistically require the observance of all laws, a large percentage of adolescents commit delinquent acts, and a sizable number of adults are involved in criminal acts, thereby undermining the prescribed social order.

Although the principle of human equality is a widely shared belief, actual racial, religious, and ethnic prejudices make this standard dubious. While education and hard work are offered as the means by which to achieve a comfortable standard of living, many persons remain poor while others live leisurely with their acquired wealth. The politically astute citizens of today are aware of these and other variances between "social standards" and "social actualities". Perceiving these variances as social problems, they often react sharply against established norms by identifying social problems with social injustice, especially if they believe that they themselves are victims of this social discrepancy. The unwed mother who resents the social stigma attached to the illegitimacy of her child, for example, may take a stand against the institution of marriage. The criminal may view conformists as members of a punitive society; juvenile delinquents may justify their deviant behavior by saying that prevailing social norms are meaningless or do not apply to their social situation. Groups set apart by racial, religious, or ethnic prejudices may demand full acceptance and equality, even when differentiated by other than racial, religious, or ethnic factors. The poor may refuse to accept poverty as their ultimate condition and demand greater economic security. Whatever the situation, modern social problems demand the concern not only of those who are personally involved but also of common citizens who have become politically sensitized to the implications of an existing problem. Both must work together if changes are to be achieved and problems solved. However, many problems will remain regardless of whether controlled or even radical adjustments are made in the social order.

Social Problems, Social Roles, and Social Organization

Social problems appear to be related inherently to social organizations and social roles. As social organizations develop roles for their members, design networks of interpretations and group relations, and proceed with the division of labor, they also inevitably create problems within both the small and large organization. The problem is even greater in a complex society composed of multiple and often conflicting social organizations. Those who control the power of the state inevitably make decisions which bear unequally on groups and individuals.[6] Since the position of a person in a modern society is always relative, his sense of deprivation or gratification is experienced in terms of being better or worse off than other individuals.[7] He perceives a tension between the actual behavior people engage in and the desired or morally demanded conduct a society says it maintains.[8]

According to the social history of mankind, the unwanted discrepancy between social standards and social actuality is not always avoidable. Problem-free societies exist only in utopian dreams, which usually assume a total homogeneity in member skills, aptitudes, interests, and capacities. Plato failed to establish his own utopian community in Syracuse; John Calvin was unsuccessful in France. Even the socialist idealist and poor shop assistant, Fourier, waited longingly in an attic room for a philanthropist who would give him the first million francs necessary to establish his utopian phalanstery, a monastic-type community in which his ideas might be realized.

However beautiful they may be, the tragic feature of these human ideals is that they are finally just dreams or utopias. Too often, the dream, largely unrealistic, is subjected to the political realities of the moment, and an alluring illusion which one runs after is lost in the battle with unalterable reality.[9] Nevertheless, while this in one sense is true, the reader should not assume pessimistically that no social problem or social injustice can be solved or alleviated, that social problems are endemic to social life and that a solution to all problems may not be easily or even finally realized.[10]

Social Roles in the Problems of Social Problems ● Desires, aspirations, and ideals, which normally motivate men to higher goals, are backed frequently by enthusiasm or a feeling of conscience. Each, however, is limited ordinarily by the boundaries of social roles which, if accepted and understood, offer persons meaningful memberships in their social groups. While the concept of role should be approached cautiously in relation to social problems,[11] the idea of roles in the problem of social problems assumes a concept of structurally or organiza-tionally designed demand, a set of expectations applied to an incumbent of a particular position.[12] An expected pattern of behavior which entails rights and duties, the role provides its possessor with a limited flexibility in aspirations and actions. It gives the person occupying the role, for example, the duty to respond to the lower limit of the defined role, while also the freedom to expand it to the upper boundary. Because role definitions provide the foundation for a division of labor, the maintenance of the role structure is a function requisite of social continuity.[13] Roles designate expected behavior patterns for the group.

No social order or social structure can exist without some form of social organization and role specification. All social organizations, therefore, are ultimately constructed on the foundation of various social roles. Role definitions essentially control the functional organization and orderly operation of the created social structure. Whether a society is organized or disorganized depends largely upon role performance. Being a mother, father, professor, student, engineer, pilot, banker, sanitary engineer, teamster, minister, or other social actor requires that the role occupant assume a position which is integrally part of some social organization and act in ways consistent with the limits of his role.

Social Roles and Deviance ● Patterns of aspirations, behavior and performance are considered and judged in relation to social standards, which are actually approved models established by those having the power to define a society's operational structure. If people fail to respond to these expectations, a discrepancy results between social standards and actual conditions. If this variance is substantial, a recognizable social problem may emerge. It is at this point that social problems and social deviance meet, inasmuch as nearly any social deviance, if substantially evident, will eventually be recognized as a social problem. However, not all persons viewing the problem do so in the same light. Therefore, the definition of deviance varies in relation to who is doing the defining.

When individuals do something which exceeds normative role requirements, they open themselves to charges of being deviant. If the number of such persons is substantial, their deviance may eventually be labeled a social problem. But deviance is not only a problem of the deviant actor. If a politically sensitized person supports these deviants, he becomes a deviant himself attitudinally, although he may be judged as a "deviant thinker" or a "potential deviant" rather than as a "deviant actor".

Although such responses to attitudes may involve the labeling of a person as a deviant or potential deviant, how quickly and to what extent an attitude or act will be labeled deviant or illegal varies from society to society and subculture to subculture. In the Soviet Union, for example, criminal deviance is evaluated in terms of the nebulous "social danger" of the act rather than the more specific "guilt" of the deviant. According to the Soviet conception, a crime is conceived without exception as a "breach of the rules of socialistic life and of workshop discipline".[14] The concept of criminality in the U.S.S.R. refers to a harm, risk, or peril to which the political and economic institutions, as representations of ideology, are exposed. Logically enough, guilt refers to a person's *otnoshenie*, his mental attitude toward his socially dangerous conduct.[15] In the United States criminality is determined in more specific terms, a violation of prescribed law.

The idea of social danger, which is a fundamental presupposition of the Soviet approach to deviance, is the pivot around which the whole system of deviant social roles is constructed. In the totalitarian notion, role-playing is primarily the duty of both the participating and observing role-player. If a substantial discrepancy between social standrads and actual conditions develops, it is considered a "socially dangerous" increase in deviant behavior rather than a "social problem". The Soviet view presumes that the person's psychic relationship with the socially dangerous deviant act determines his deviancy.

Role contents in totalitarian societies are subject to relatively frequent change as the dynamics of totalitarian ideologies demand modifications. Consequently, the role-player has to adjust accordingly. While the cultural value system of democracies may also cause numerous role modifications, the transition from one value to another is generally smoother, with the individual given sufficient time to prepare for and adjust to the change.

Socialization in the Problem Definition and Recognition Process ● Through socialization, which begins early in childhood and proceeds throughout each person's natural life, the individual is taught what he needs to know if he is to be integrated into the community and what he must learn if he is to develop his potential and achieve a level of self-satisfaction.[16] No society has been able to socialize perfectly its members or to succeed in having each participant assume a static role consistent with his position. This failure is usually due to inadequate socialization, blocked aspirations, personal inability to change roles or exposure to countersocialization which liberates the person from following social standards. All known societies demonstrate substantial discrepancies between their defined ideal norms and the actual conditions of the moment.

While socializing agencies historically have carried out role-teaching in a definitive manner, contemporary units often work against each other and support social standards less efficiently. However, many socialized persons are frequently left without necessary guidance concerning social standards, their possibility of change and the need to use their mental faculties to evaluate life conditions. Consequently, many role-players who are exposed to pluralistic and often conflicting value systems come to doubt the validity of their own roles and the content of prescribed social roles and statuses.

Frustrations as a Generating Factor of Social Problems

Roles involve a certain degree of frustration and tension. Even if role-players fully accept and understand their role, their desire to meet social standards fully exposes individuals to these challenges. However, if persons understand their role and accept the social position related to it, role stress may be lessened and serve to improve rather than impair their role performance. In this way, society may actually help individuals to understand how they may remove obstacles to their aspirations.

Frustrations may possess positive functions and may assist role-players to reach their goals. If a garbage collector (frequently referred to as a sanitary engineer) understands, for example, that his fundamental role is to contribute to public hygiene and accepts the social position that goes with this role, the tensions caused by the frustrations of personal and environmental barriers may motivate the individual to overcome these obstacles. However, if the role-player's socializing agencies have not clearly defined or have been unable to stimulate the actor to accept the prerequisites of his position, his frustrations may become severe and assume negative proportions. In such cases, the role itself may encourage the actor to develop extreme negative attitudes toward himself or the society which designed the role that he is to assume.

Those who are frustrated by personal or social obstacles and by the demand of social standards experience tension in that they lack privilege and prerogative. Inasmuch as they are inadequately socialized to an understanding of the nature and dynamics of their role, they do not comprehend, and, therefore, do not accept their position. Their reactions appear on the surface as variations of social norms. Their tensions do not usually stimulate them to positive goals and may impair their overall personal effectiveness.

Frustration and Frustration Reduction • Reactions to stress situations are not consistent and may fall anywhere on a conscious-unconscious continuum. They may be acted out "with conscious intent, with only partial awareness, or with no conscious involvement at all".[17] Many inadequately socialized role-players, having no conscious involvement in their own failure, may, as a result, be more or less unaware of tension-filled situations affecting them. They are insensitive to social reality and to the expectations of their society. In a rather passionless way they accept their situation as it is and experience minimal frustration and tension. They withdraw, as if to admit defeat in the struggle to meet social norms, seek to achieve an improved position and status, or strive to claim another role through learning. Others undergo a *relative frustration* in which recognizable tensions exist between those who support social standards and norms and those who perceive social reality as differing from that defined by the accepted standards, a recognition frequently distinguished in terms of "we" and "they".

When role-players are frustrated, the support they receive from others frequently enables them to thwart the efforts of those in power to define the content and scope of a social problem. However, those who are not consciously frustrated need to be made aware of their own frustrations before they feel or understand the implications of a tension-provoking situation.

Social Problems and Social Disorganization

Contemporary American sociologists readily utilize the idea of social disorganization as a primary explanation of social problems and problematic behavior. Traditionally, it has referred to a disintegrated or uncoordinated system of statuses and roles. It represents a condition in which social standards, as designed by those who legitimate social power, and social conditions, as experienced by those who supposedly support these standards in their daily lives, fail to mesh in a coherent pattern.[18] This understanding of social disorganization suggests not only the potential for disorganization in the community but also the probable experiencing of a substantial level of frustration by those recognizing a potential social problem. Whether a situation or condition is regarded as a social problem or not depends in large measure upon the ability or willingness of those charged with managing social discontent (e.g., police, public officials, mental health officers, etc.) to do so.[19]

Social problems and social disorganization, while closely interrelated and associated, are related only in the sense that social problems have not usually been solved or settled in one way or another. If those invoking social power are frustrated by the frustration of discontented role-players and the existing social system is unable or unwilling to manage or channel this discontent, social disorganization may become a social problem.

Anomie and Social Problems ● Although the patterns and profile of social problems have changed over many centuries, having continued to evolve since Durkheim identified them as anomic (rootless, non-belonging) situations,[20] no visible evidence suggests that they are not likely to persist or to change even more as society witnesses new power relationships. New social standards, new anomic situations and new discontents may generate, in turn, new patterns and descriptions of social problems and new forms of social disorganization. Role frustrations are an international phenomenon. In no known society are all statuses and roles perfectly or even satisfactorily integrated and coordinated. Nowhere are all human beings socialized to aspire only to realistic goals. "Wealth, income, job status, prestige, and the like," Stephen Schafer writes, "are goals sought not only by Americans and not only in our affluent if disorganized society, but by other peoples, both now and in other ages."[21]

The seeds of anomic conditions are always present in human groups. Each person has goals; some members of any group are well socialized to the limits of their roles and others are mis- or inadequately socialized. Not all aspirations may be fulfilled by any one person, but when a person finds too many aspirations blocked or unachievable, the ground is set for the intensification of frustrations and the collective expression of disorganization. From this perspective, the concept of *anomie,* a condition of blocked aspirations, used often to explain social disorganization, serves only to describe generally *how* role-frustration and social problems develop rather than *why* role-players become frustrated.

Dissatisfaction and frustration are not fully avoidable. Because of differences in goals and policy, not all individuals or social groups can achieve their desired goals simultaneously. Frequently, these goals conflict and are not attainable due to unjust social barriers or to the inability of an individual or group to formulate aspirations or goals. While the learning of skills may be encouraged, not all persons who are taught always or necessarily internalize these capacities. Many persons are inadequately socialized and, therefore, do not internalize constructive values, positive ambitions or effective means for reducing role frustrations. They often misunderstand person to person, role, and social organization relationships. Because of inadequate socialization, frustrated role-players may be unable to determine what rights, duties and choices are inherent in their given roles and, therefore, may be unable to identify with those role characteristics which they would otherwise assume. Those who are inadequately or mis-socialized often do not understand the dominant orientation of a society or its social values and norms. Their frustration, therefore, commonly surfaces as conflict rather than as non-acceptance and they react in a socially disruptive manner.

Many social problems have their origins in the frustrations brought about by rolelessness. Although Cloward and Ohlin ask how a society "persuades the poor man to accept his station in life as just",[22] they oversimplify the problem of human existence, viewing it in simple terms of distribution of wealth. Instead, the concept of adequate socialization and the idea of role-demands may provide a better explanation of the problem of social problems. In no known human society or organized group are the privileges and prohibitions evenly divided. While distribution is necessarily dependent on the division of roles, the question of distribution and the definition of roles depend for the most part upon the actions of those who legitimate power relationships.

Although social disorganization and attendant social problems are most often attributable to the fact that disadvantaged individuals and groups feel frustrated, even while privileged units enjoy their own position and find the encumbrances placed upon others completely justified, these frustrations and enjoyments in actuality are related to the degree of their understanding of the division of roles. For the privileged, the prevailing value system with its division of roles is internalized; for the disadvantaged, these values often appear as some unfair external phenomenon. While in the latter instance these values and roles seem to be products of a different culture, they are more easily accepted when the boundaries of these roles are internalized and they have lost many of their frustrating characteristics.

Whether role obstacles and limits are right or wrong, correct or incorrect, is impossible to judge objectively. Similarly, it is impossible to evaluate whether one form of social organization is better than another. Values, differentiated roles, and role definitions are neither good nor bad in an absolute sense. Rather, these values are accepted or modified, regardless of the shape and style of the accompanying social disorganization, as the relative power of variable social groups ebbs and flows.

Power Structures and Opposing Power Structures ● The operation of any power structure appears inevitably to lead to the development of opposing social structures which may take over a faltering dominant system and change its value system to some extent. If frustrated role-players do not feel the constraints imposed by the dominant power elite or if those charged with the management of discontent fail to enforce the division and definition of roles, social disorganization and social problems will take on a new profile. However, the dynamics of such change depend upon the extent of frustration and discomfort experienced by these role-players, caused by their value disagreement, and their position in relation to the power elite.

When frustrated individuals challenge successfully, a partially or entirely new value system may be formed and new limits and definitions of roles may result as former roles and values are rejected, reversed or modified. So long as the dominant power structure prevails, however, certain aspirations and goals will be blocked for those not sharing this power; roles will be kept within their original limits or slightly modified; frustrations will be accepted, neutralized or rejected; and socialization will reinforce the values of the power structure making these values legitimate. When this happens, the socialization system may become "irrelevant" to frustrated individuals who find that their roles do not relate well to what they want to learn, know or aspire to, thereby further increasing their frustration.

Frustrations, too, may arise among those conditioned to accept prescribed values as their own. Cultural and subcultural conflict, for example, can develop between the cultures of the adequately and inadequately socialized members of a society. When this occurs, two opposing groups may coexist in a society, giving an appearance of social disorganization and attendant problems. What is visualized as conflict, however, may better be understood as a problem of role socialization rather than outright culture conflict.

The criminal, the delinquent, the prostitute and the drug addict become roleless in a normative sense and are often frustrated and in disagreement with the pre-existing definition and division of roles to which they have not been adequately socialized by controlling socializing agencies (e.g., schools, churches, political parties). Their operating culture tends to conflict with the dominant normal role-designing culture. They have not been socialized to accept proper roles and values and to aspire to constructive goals. When they fail to accept a prescribed belief system, they often become alienated from their fellows. When in the condition of anomie, they associate with others in a "pointless" manner.[23] The meaning of their lives at this point is unclear; roles around which their existence should be organized are not apparent.[24] Delinquents, criminals, prostitutes, and drug addicts commonly reflect this condition.

Most deviants and offenders of this type see only the conflict with established authority but do not understand it. They recognize that opportunities for advancement and improvement are available to other people while their own aspirations appear blocked. They see a disorganized society, but they do not understand the values upon which their society is founded. They do not truly comprehend the differences between their actual role-performances and those expected by social norms. They see themselves as victims of fate. In reality, their apparent response is not due to culture conflict but rather to an inadequate socialization to cultural norms, which is often expressed as conflict with dominant norms. In this sense, social disorganization is a reflection of multiple frustrations, a picture of conflicts resulting primarily from non-understood, misunderstood or blocked social roles.

The Problem of "Rightness" and "Justice"

Every dominant power justifies its prescribed values to those it seeks to socialize. Each such unit tends to view reality in terms of this overriding worldview. But if this given system does not permit all citizens to fulfill their aspirations, or if the definition and division of roles do not reflect their views, those who are frustrated may complain about what appears to them to be social disorganization.

The assumption that these complaints are moral or ethical questions rests upon the dubious hypothesis that only one moral or ethical code possesses validity. Socially, this is impossible. Power brokers who prescribe and legitimate social norms and roles make practical rather than absolute moral judgments. They define which values, rules and roles are to be learned and indicate the rightness and wrongness of the various modes of human conduct. Whatever is defined by this legitimizing power as right or wrong must be accepted so long as those in power are able to enforce their organizational design.

Howard Becker recognizes that those classified as "outsiders" are defined as deviants because they fail "to obey group roles".[25] Therefore, before any act can be viewed as deviant, someone, Becker believes, must define a rule making the act deviant.[26] Only selected persons make rules, design social organization and social roles, and define the limits of role performance. The limits of man-performed roles depend upon a man-made role-design.[27] Because those who have the power to legislate and legitimate have the authority to decide right from wrong, ideas of what is ethical, moral or just may or may not be expressed in legal structures. How each individual responds to the established rules to fortify the given social order remains his personal life ordeal.

Morality, Immorality and Social Problems ● Most people who struggle to solve a social problem tend to conceive their crusade in moral or ethical terms. They commonly overlook the fact that multiple value and moral codes exist simultaneously and no single code dominates any modern mass society. Therefore, the support by society of one or another ethical system does not necessarily imply hypocrisy, but rather that the concepts of justice and morality are frequently expressed in pluralistic form. To defend a social issue from the perspective of one moral system and to attack it from another may be demanded by the earlier Mosaic code, Pauline moral law, Aristotelian self-realization, Thomist scholasticism, Kantian deontological ethics or Benthamian hedonism, but these can hardly be integrated into a singular value system. Those who define a normative system for a society are likely, therefore, to respond differentially and mix various conceptual presuppositions with the political realities of the moment in their formulation of an integrated system of social norms. Those who oppose what has been adopted similarly base their opposition upon selected principles of morality and justice.

In designing and defining the rules, roles and structure of a society, the legitimizing social power usually presupposes *one* moral concept and distributes responsibilities accordingly. In broad terms, it infuses its judgments with moral responsibility and respectability.[28] It encourages all social institutions to reinforce this fundamental system. Those who betray the system, then, are charged with moral irresponsibility. The values—represented by social organization, norms and the definition and distribution of roles—tend, as a result, to become moral issues, although they are largely human values and may be distinguished from ethical issues.

Although a legitimating social group usually takes a stand for a specified morality, commonly based upon its value system, and demands its acceptance as the right system, the right morality and the right justice, what is at issue is faith, mystique, belonging and belief in certain values. While the legitimating power is not the *product* of morality, it exists to enforce *a* morality.

Social Change as a Relative Answer to Social Problems

To contend that full obedience to all demands of those who define social laws can be expected from all members of a society is to ignore social reality. The fact that mankind has had so many forms of morality and justice and has experienced so much social change throughout history indicates that opposing groups have from time to time been successful in their efforts to create new normative content and structures. In some instances, those who held social power voluntarily modified their own values and redefined what they had previously specified as morality and justice. The reasons and causes of such changes, often seemingly contradictory and rather puzzling, are not well understood.

Understanding Social Change ● In order to understand social change it must be recognized as occurring in varying ways.[29] *Theories of evolution* conceive of society as a living organism that possesses the potential of smooth changes toward an ever-increasing social complexity. *Theories of equilibrium* emphasize the state of the elements that enter the system and the mutual relationships between them, presuming that any small change in one of the elements will be followed by modifications in the other elements, tending to reduce the amount of that change. *Theories of conflict* stress the mode and manner of social change, processes which are depicted as being uneven and disruptive, aimed at fundamental or structural alterations. *Theories of growth and decay,* on the other hand, mirror the social history of man in patterns or regularities of progress and regress.

A second group of explanations focuses upon the factor which causes the effect of social change. Included here are *geographic, cosmic, racial, biological, demographic, political, military, "great men," material, technological, economic* and *ideological* components.[30] A third cluster of hypotheses confuses the conditions, processes and consequences of the past and present.[31] *Theories of progress* maintain that *evolution* is an inevitable and normal process toward a better society; *socialistic and moralistic* theories suggest that ideologies stimulate change; *theories of history* attribute changes in society to some cyclical sequence; *miscellaneous theories* explain social changes in terms of geographic and biological determinism. A few others relate to *charismatic leadership, economic progress, industrialization, cultural contradictions, economic determinism* and ever-present *developmental* or *evolutionary modifications in social life.*

The Meaning of Social Change Theories ● Ordering such confusion is no easy task. Persons with differing perspectives commonly reach separate conclusions. For example, the historian moves from effects to causes while the sociologist moves from causes to effects.[32] But the problem of social change as well as the problem of social problems must be approached by the historian and the sociologist working in close cooperation. Even those within political sciences and philosophy, particularly legal philosophy, must share in this joint effort to comprehend the possible relationships of social change and social problems. Goethe's words in his *Faust*, "he who lives must be prepared for changes" dramatically indicate that change is an incessant part of human living and that all change is not necessarily for the better.

If Leo Tolstoy was correct in suggesting that most people think of changing the world and few of changing themselves, the pivot of the problem of social problems is the question of the efficiency of socialization. Those who for one reason or another are not socialized perfectly to the dominant values of a society are apt to represent other values and therefore, may be potential adherents or even advocates of social change, arguing for the need to modify, alter or change existing values. In such settings conflicts may be common with those who legitimate the existing normative system.

Whatever its actual cause and regardless of the actual conditions or how it takes place, social change always results in the partial or complete redefinition and redistribution of roles that most frequently touch upon the concepts of morality and justice and the state of social problems. These changes in a value system, role design and ultimately in the conception of morality and justice lead to changes in the conception of what is a social problem.

While change may alleviate or eliminate individual frustrations caused by blockages of personal aspirations, the pursuit of human happiness historically has not been achieved through the accumulation of goods and supplies. It is unlikely that all persons will ever be totally satisfied. Some will always remain frustrated and discontent despite the utopian beliefs which promise absolute value, absolute morality, absolute justice, and infinite happiness. Many students of social problems who propagate such beliefs and who know little philosophy might be alarmed if they were aware of the analyses and lessons of history.

Social Change and Social Justice ● Although changes in a dominant value system and alterations in definitions and distribution of roles may satisfy one role-player, they frequently negate the situation of another person. Consequently, while change may alleviate the frustration for some, it may stimulate new frustration for another. If a change from a capitalistic social and economic structure to a socialistic form of social organization, for example, causes the new factory management to replace the owner of the plant with a member of the working class, the new manager who previously viewed his role and status in terms of a social problem no longer sees it in these terms. At the same time, however, the previous owner of the factory, who may find himself in the position of a factory worker due to social change, is likely to be frustrated in his new role and perceive his new situation in problematic terms. Similarly, if the use of certain drugs is eventually legalized, the drug user, who once may have been prosecuted for marijuana usage, no longer faces the anxieties or frustrations inherent in the ban. However, the police officer who was socialized to the prosecution of marijuana users, may find himself frustrated by a new value and a new concept of justice which is inconsistent with his previous socialization.

Frustration Reduction and Frustration Creation ● How does one cure his frustrations without causing some frustration for others? Or how does one solve a social problem without creating other problems for other persons? There is no simple answer. The coexistence of multiple values, the impossibility of legislation of an absolute justice and morality, and the inherent and unavoidable differences between the limits of one role and those of another leave the cure of social problems often with a relative solution.[33] Social change may alleviate some social problems, but it may also change only the participants who face the problem frustrations. It can hardly eliminate for all persons the discrepancies between social standards and actual conditions. Even as value systems, morality, justice, and the definition of roles are relative and changing, so is the problem of social problems. From what we know from man's social history, social systems are able to set only a few feasible goals, to strive for a balance between "give" and "take" in order to minimize frustrations of role-players, to minimize person-to-person misunderstandings and to reduce the burden of the particular social problem. While many are tempted to speculate concerning the final elimination of social problems through the enactment of a variety of social changes, they ultimately must be content with substituting the reduction of social problems for their final elimination. Social change can give only a relative answer to the challenge of social problems.

Contemporary Social Problems in a Changing Society

Social change has been greater in our lifetime than in any past period of history. Definitions of values, morality, justice and roles consequently are subject to these multiple rapid changes which are demanded by an apparently increasing number of persons who claim to be frustrated by existing social norms and actual social conditions. Those sensitized to the political implications of these demands increasingly support the quest of their solution.

While these problems may take the form of problems of culture transmission, they do not end there and include values, norms, beliefs and religion commitments. Even the processes of socialization, the goals of education, the tasks of mass media, the role of primary and peer groups, the development of subcultures within the general culture, the conflicts of culture, and the significance of language have impact upon each problem area.

Problems of the individual have become increasingly prominent. Alcoholism and drug addiction, aberrant sexual practices, prostitution, homosexuality, mental disorganization, and suicide have left their mark upon the debate concerning social problems. Special and once discrete problems within primary and peer groups, including generational and sexual problems, have become public policy issues.

Crime and the issues relating to law and order have come to the forefront as social problems. Juvenile delinquency, violence, organized crime, white collar criminality, victimology and political crimes are now receiving major social attention, as are problems within the social order—overpopulation, racial and ethnic relations, poverty and such community problems as unemployment, technological change, housing and urban redevelopment. But even the ways and means of bringing about social change represent a social problem. Social movements, political propaganda, uprisings, and revolutions, democratic and totalitarian government, war, disarmament, and world peace constitute areas of new concern for man in the quest for a problem-free society.

Each problem generates frustration and conflicts. Ideologies simplify the process of reaching reasoned conclusions based upon facts. Frustrations create tensions; old social problems emerge as new and attack modern people with a fresh and often violent impact. While the problems are many, the workable analyses are few.

In a changing society any listing of social problems is necessarily incomplete. Many facts suggest that we should be pessimistic concerning our ability to solve the issues of our day; others, however, point to the optimism we must maintain if the future is to be a positive one. Recognizing human frustration and the scope of social problems is the first step toward their solution, but at the outset we must acknowledge the pitfall noted by Anatole France who contended that it is human nature to think wisely and act foolishly. As a result of human folly, scientific solutions may often take second place to solutions founded upon the emotions of the moment.

References

1. Robert A. Nisbet, *Social Change and History: Aspect of the Western Theory of Development* (New York, 1969), p. 240.

2. Harry Elmer Barnes, "Ancient and Medieval Social Philosophy," in *An Introduction to the History of Sociology*, Harry Elmer Barnes, ed. (Chicago, 1966), p. 4.
3. Lowell J. Carr, *Analytical Sociology: Social Situations and Social Problems* (New York, 1955), p. 306.
4. Robert K. Merton and Robert A. Nisbet, *Contemporary Social Problems* (2nd ed.), (New York, 1966), p. 5.
5. Robert K. Merton, "Social Problems and Sociological Theory," *Contemporary Social Problems*, p. 780.
6. Seymour M. Lipset, "Political Sociology," *Sociology: An Introduction*, ed. Neil J. Smelser, p. 441.
7. *Ibid.*, p. 451.
8. Paraphrased from Hans Kelsen, *General Theory of the Law and the State* (Cambridge, Mass., 1945), pp. 436-437; and Yehezkel Dror, "Law and Social Change," *Tulane Law Review*, Vol. 33 (1959), pp. 749-801.
9. Gyula Moór, *Bevezétes a joqfilozofiaba* (Budapest, 1925), p. 80.
10. Leon G. Cherrington and Richard Massa, eds., *Contemporary Man In World Society* (Berkeley, Calif., 1969), p. 12.
11. James W. Vander Zanden, *Sociology: A Systematic Approach,* (2nd ed.), (New York, 1958), p. 67.
12. Neal Gross, Ward S. Mason and Alexander W. McEachern, *Explorations in Role Analysis: Studies of the School Superintendency Role* (New York, 1958), p. 67.
13. Glenn M. Vernon, *Human Interaction: An Introduction to Sociology* (New York, 1965), p. 131.
14. Stephen Schafer, *Theories in Criminology: Past and Present Philosophies of the Crime Problem* (New York, 1969), p. 274.
15. M. D. Shargorodskii and N. A. Beliaev, eds., *Sovetskoe Ugolovnoe Pravo, Obshchaia Chast* (Moscow, 1960), p. 313.
16. Leonard Broom and Philip Selznick, *Sociology: A Text With Adapted Readings* (3rd ed.), (New York, 1963), p. 95.
17. James C. Coleman, *Abnormal Psychology and Modern Life* (3rd ed.), (Chicago, 1964), p. 91.
18. Merton, *Contemporary Social Problems,* p. 800.
19. William A. Gamson, *Power and Discontent* (Homewood, Ill., 1968), p. 111; the term "anomie" first appeared, it is believed, in 1893 in Durkheim's *Division of Labor in Society* (Glencoe, 1950), and in a general way refers to the discrepancy between culturally prescribed aspirations and social opportunities. Sebastian de Grazia, however, traced the use of this term back to some 2500 years before Durkheim applied it to his understanding of certain social situations.
20. Stephen Schafer, "Anomie, Culture Conflict and Crime in Disorganized and Over-organized Societies," Marvin E. Wolfgang, *Crime and Culture, Essays in Honor of Thorsten Sellin* (New York, 1968), p. 84.
21. Richard A. Cloward and Lloyd E. Ohlin, *Delinquency and Opportunity: A Theory of Delinquent Gangs* (Glencoe, 1960), p. 79.
22. Sebastian de Grazia, *The Political Community: A Study of Anomie* (Chicago, 1948). p. 6.
23. Carl G. Jung, *Modern Man in Search of Soul* (New York, 1941), p. 267.
24. Howard S. Becker, *Outsiders: Studies in the Sociology of Deviance* (New York, 1963), pp. 7-8.
25. *Ibid.*, p. 162.
26. Max Weber, *The Theory of Social and Economic Organization* (New York, 1947), pp. 324-333, 341-345, 358-363.
27. Stephen Schafer, *Theories of Criminology* (New York, 1969), Chapter III.

28. Robert Bierstedt, *The Social Order* (3rd ed.), (New York, 1970), pp. 515-516.
29. Richard P. Appelbaum, *Theories of Social Change* (Chicago, 1970), pp. 7-14.
30. Bierstedt, *The Social Order,* pp. 515-541.
31. Richard T. LaPiere, *Social Change* (New York, 1965), pp. 1-39; and Bernard S. Phillips, *Sociology: Social Structures and Change* (New York, 1969), pp. 405-423.
32. Bierstedt, *The Social Order,* p. 515.
33. Richard D. Knudten, "A Theory of Problematic Relativity." Unpublished paper presented at the annual meeting of the Society for the Study of Social Problems in New York City, August, 1973.

CHAPTER 2

Drug and Alcohol Dependency

Narcotic and Drug Dependency

Narcotic and drug involvement, already rising following the end of World War II, increased at a fast rate during the 1960's. Of the total of 57,100 opiate addicts identified in December 1965 by the U.S. Bureau of Narcotics, 52,793 were heroin addicts.[1] However, the current heroin addict population, according to U.S. Government estimates, now numbers closer to 500,000 to 600,000, including ex-addicts and temporary abstainers. A disproportionate percentage of narcotic addicts reside in New York, California, Illinois, New Jersey, Michigan, Maryland, Texas, Pennsylvania, and the District of Columbia. Largely found in urban areas, addicts are likely to be males between the ages of 21 and 30, commonly unskilled and poorly educated, members of an ethnic minority, and residents in poor housing and high delinquency areas. More than 100,000 addicts and users are now serving time in some United States jail, reformatory, or prison.[2] Since the enactment of the Controlled Substances Act of 1970 and the Drug Abuse Office and Treatment Act of 1972, which was directed to changing the drug demand through treatment, education, rehabilitation, and research and to preventing drug traffic through drug and narcotic production controls and stepped-up law enforcement, the yearly increase in addicts admitted to treatment has flattened out, suggesting that the rise in drug abuse in the 1960's and early 1970's has peaked. The Drug Enforcement Administration in July 1, 1973 subsumed the former narcotic and drug related functions of the Bureau of Narcotics and Dangerous Drugs, the Office of Drug Abuse Law Enforcement, the Office of National Narcotics Intelligence and the Bureau of Customs.[3]

The Nature of Drug Dependency • According to the World Health Organization, drug dependency, a concept that has replaced the idea of addiction, is a state of "psychic or physical dependence, or both, on a drug, arising in a person

18

following administration of that drug on a periodic or continuous basis."[4] The actual state of dependency varies in relation to the agent involved in its creation. Some produce physical dependence and a later withdrawal syndrome when their use is restricted or terminated. Many that induce dependence also encourage tolerance, making larger doses of the drug necessary to produce the earlier effect. A few may cause profound alterations in individual behavior. Because possible behavior patterns vary widely, it is necessary to differentiate drug types and characteristic forms of drug dependency.

A drug may be natural (opium) or synthetic (Demerol), have a stimulating (cocaine) or depressing (morphine) effect on the central nervous system, be highly addictive (heroin) or be totally non-addictive (marijuana).[5] While the concept of a narcotic implies that this substance induces sleep, dulls the senses or relieves pain, the word in legal practice is used primarily to describe opiates, including cocaine and opium, morphine, their derivatives, compounds, and synthetic equivalents. Within some states marijuana is classified as a narcotic, a judgment which thoroughly confuses the situation.

History of Drug Control • Drugs were not always controlled by law. An international conference on opium, called in early 1909 at the request of the United States, sought the goal of an international convention designed to limit opium production and distribution for medical purposes through legitimate channels. Even as world-wide concern over the problem mounted, pressure in the United States to control drug availability led to the enactment of the Harrison Narcotic Act on December 17, 1914. Under its terms, any one engaged in either the production or distribution of narcotics had to register with the federal government and keep records of all drug transactions. Each person handling the drugs had to pay a purchase or sales tax, and such drugs could be purchased only upon the prescription of a physician and for legitimate medical purposes.[6] A 1919 interpretation of this law by the Supreme Court in *Webb v. United States* declared that the prescription of drugs for an addict for the purpose of providing him with enough morphine to keep him comfortable and not in the course of professional treatment in the attempt to cure his habit was unintended in the original law.[7] This interpretation in 1922 eventually led to the closing of 44 U.S. Government-run narcotics clinics created to control the drug dependency problem and to the forcing of narcotic users to black market outlets. By 1920, the population of narcotic dependents shifted from the respectable to the unrespectable, with the replacement of the predominantly middle-aged and female narcotic-using population with the young and male.[8]

Legislation Concerning Drugs and Narcotics • The Bureau of Narcotics within the Treasury Department administered the Federal Harrison Narcotic Act of 1914 until recent years. Under the provisions of the Act, a tax could be imposed upon the manufacture or importation of narcotic drugs. Unauthorized possession of illegal drugs, whether intended for personal use or not, and the unauthorized sale or purchase and unauthorized importation of such narcotics was designated a criminal offense. In time, the unauthorized possession and sale became defined criminal acts in most states. In later years other efforts to control drug dependency were also undertaken.

The reported increase in post-World War II drug dependency stimulated the passage of the Boggs Amendment of 1951. It introduced mandatory minimum sentences for all narcotic and marijuana offenses; two years for the first offense, five years for the second, 10 for the third and subsequent offenses. Suspension of sentence and probation were prohibited for second offenders. By 1956, a Congress-passed Narcotic Drug Control Act permitted the application of the death penalty to minors upon conviction under specified circumstances. Mandatory minimum sentences were raised to five years for the first and 10 years for the second and subsequent offenses of unlawful sale or importation, although they remained the same for unlawful possession. Suspension of sentence, probation, and parole were prohibited for all but the first offense of unlawful possession. Distinctions were made between user and seller, a clarification which permitted greater judicial flexibility in application of sentences. State codes commonly contained comparable penalty provisions.[9]

As the problem became more acute, action could no longer be confined only to the legislative front. The 1963 statement of the American Medical Association and the National Research Council of Sciences concerning the use of narcotics in medical practice reinforced the earlier opinion that the continued administration of drugs for the maintenance of dependency is not a bona fide attempt to cure; withdrawal is most easily carried out in a drug-free environment (i.e., in specialized wards or installations for narcotic addicts); withdrawal on an ambulatory basis is medically unsound and not recommended; and ambulatory clinic plans or other forms of ambulatory maintenance are medically unsound. While it is proper ethical practice to prescribe narcotics over a prolonged period to patients with chronically incurable and painful conditions, maintain an aged or infirm addict, administer maintenance doses of methadone to a dependent person awaiting admission to a narcotic facility, and/or to administer limited and diminishing doses to such an individual during the process of withdrawal, it is improper to support persons not in one of these conditions. Not surprisingly, this viewpoint coincided with the operatonal practices of the U.S. Bureau of Narcotics, which maintained that the support of addicts on stable doses of narcotics either in a clinic or through some other medical center is generally unacceptable.[10]

Despite these definitions and codifications of law, several significant changes in the social categories of narcotic usage occurred between 1900 and 1970. Blacks composed only 10 percent of the addict population in 1900 and are believed to account for more than 50 percent of the current drug-using population. While the majority of those involved in 1900 were women, the ratio has changed currently to seven men to every one woman. In 1900, addiction was primarily a condition of the middle-aged; by 1970, youth composed the greatest number of known offenders.[11]

Drugs and Narcotics

What are now classified as drugs and narcotics take many different forms and have a wide variety of effects.

Marijuana (Cannabis) ● An estimated 20 million Americans have tried and 8 million continue to use marijuana annually. Derived from parts of the flowering tops of the female hemp plant, marijuana induces psychic changes among its users when chewed, smoked, or eaten. Commonly converted into cigarettes, it has stimulant and depressant effects upon the central nervous system. Its exact effects are not fully defined at present; it is believed to possess no known clinical value. As far as can be seen to date, the effects of marijuana usage depend in degree upon the psychic condition of the individual and the type of social environment in which it is used. Louis Goodman and Alfred Gilman report that animal experimentation indicates that there is no strong evidence that marijuana significantly affects or alters the nervous system as either a sedative or hypnotic agent.[12] However, by 1974 some researchers were reporting a possible link between marijuana usage and temporary sterility, although questions about the sample clouded the importance of this finding.[13]

Some marijuana users may feel nausea and diarrhea; however, this is not an automatic reaction. Most experience feelings of exhilaration or euphoria and frequently pleasing hallucinations. When feeling "high", the user may have a heightened sense of touch and a sense of suspended animation. Because the first-time drug user may not experience such feelings, it is probable that the social situation is important in producing the effect.[14] Tolerance, if it does develop, is minimal and physical dependency non-existent.

A series of pilot acute marijuana intoxication experiments on human subjects in 1968 by Andrew T. Weil, Norman E. Zinberg and Judith M. Nelson disclosed that in a neutral setting persons who are naive to marijuana do not have strong subjective experiences after smoking small or large doses of the drug, and the effects they report are not the same as those described by regular users of marijuana who take the drug in the same neutral setting. Even though regular users of marijuana do get high after smoking marijuana in neutral settings, they do not evidence the same degree of impairment of performance as naive subjects. Short term marijuana administration, they discovered, causes dilation of the conjunctival blood vessels, but registers no change in respiratory rate or pupil size.[15]

While the Federal Bureau of Narcotics in the late 1930's took the position that the use of marijuana led to eventual dependence upon heroin, recent research refutes this assumption. Most current evidence suggests that marijuana is less physically harmful than alcohol, which may produce psychoses, destroy body cells, and become dependency-fostering.[16] Although some evidence suggests that the majority of heroin users have smoked marijuana at some point previous to their current dependency, this does not mean that marijuana is causal to the development of opiate addiction. Goodman and Gilman state explicitly that habitual use of marijuana does not automatically lead to the use of heroin.[17] Even the President's Ad Hoc Panel on Drug Abuse found that the evidence was inadequate to substantiate a belief that marijuana incites people to anti-social acts.[18] Such evidence led 44 states by 1974 to reduce the possession of small amounts of marijuana to a misdemeanor and four to reduce it to either a misdemeanor or felony. Common prices for marijuana range from $11 to $15 per pound of regular marijuana. The Columbian brand is even greater ranging from a minimum of $35 an ounce and potentially bringing in as high as $500 per pound. The price generally varies with availability.

Heroin and Morphine ● In common usage, the "hard" narcotic problem was and is usually conceived in terms of opium and its derivatives, heroin and morphine. Opiates tend to be depressants and are dependency-producing. Because they depress the nerve centers, they are among the most effective pain killers known to man. While heroin is used occasionally in other countries for medicinal purposes, such use in the United States is illegal.

Prohibitions against the use of morphine and heroin have not always existed in the United States. At the turn of the century it was possible for an individual to purchase narcotics upon prescription by a physician at the corner drug store. Although no clear figures exist, it is estimated that between two and four percent of the American population were addicted to narcotics in 1895.[19] By 1915, however, the purchase of narcotics was defined as a criminal and even an immoral act.

For some persons *morphine* acts as a depressant, for others a stimulant. Not only does it kill pain, but morphine in moderate doses is likely to produce drowsiness and an inability to concentrate. Other side-effects include apathy, detachment, and lessened physical activity. Although the drug's impact may last from three to six hours under normal conditions, its effects for some persons may be felt for as long as 12 hours. Euphoria may be felt at first, although it may quickly be followed by a sense of sluggishness and a dreamless sleep. Morphine tolerance commonly develops after 15 to 20 days of continued use. As it occurs, the user needs ever-larger quantities in order to achieve the same level of pain alleviation originally produced with a smaller dosage. While the continued usage of morphine does not automatically cause a man to be unproductive, it may dull pain to such an extent that other physical signals of physiological danger are not felt by the subject. Morphine addicts tend to possess a decreased sexual appetite.

While the morphine dependent maintains usage at a normal level in order to prevent withdrawal, the heroin user reports a desire for euphoria as a primary motivation for continued heroin administration. Physicians and nurses are among the most frequent represented occupational groups in morphine addiction. Middle class members are most frequently found among those using this drug.[20]

Heroin, produced from a morphine base in 1898, was suspected of having addictive qualities within five years of its development. One study of Massachusetts druggists in 1889 noted that the sale of opium derivatives was highest to those of higher income.[21] A more potent drug than morphine, heroin creates an intense sense of euphoria in its users. While its effects are similar to those of morphine, heroin is more likely to have a depressant effect upon the respiratory system. Within 20 minutes of administration, heroin reaches its peak effect. As in the case of morphine, heroin produces no toxic effects nor any damage to the central nervous system.[22] The physiological problems related to heroin usage are primarily created once a dependent person has been withdrawn from the drug.[23] As long as an individual remains on the drug, it is possible to live a normal and productive life. Heroin users are likely to be one of two types. The first uses heroin in order to achieve and maintain a sense of euphoria. The second depends upon the drug primarily to stave off withdrawal.[24] A study of 925 addicts by John C. Ball and William Bates disclosed that heroin dependents are not more mobile from birth to onset of addiction than the U.S. population and that they do not lead a transient life after their initial hospitalization.[25]

As with marijuana, the cost of heroin reflects market supply and demand. A bag or packet of heroin may generally be purchased for $5 or more. The quality or purity of the narcotic, however, varies markedly. To make as much profit as possible, the distributor and the seller tend to dilute the heroin base through the addition of such ingredients as lactose and mannitol. As supply has decreased, due to increased pressures by the U.S. Government to cut production overseas, the drug has been diluted to such an extent that the typical addict does not develop excessive physical dependence, and, therefore, does not suffer serious withdrawal problems once use is terminated.[26]

Most heroin is smuggled into the United States by way of Turkey, France, Mexico, South America and some Far Eastern countries. The profits to be gained through its sale are enormous. Ten kilos of opium purchased on the black market from a Turkish farmer may cost $350 and produce one kilo of pure heroin. In turn, this kilo is cut and diluted, eventually being sold to American addicts at a total cost of $300,000 or more. The estimated 1,500 kilograms of heroin entering this country illegally each year represent less than one half of one percent of the illicit opium production in the world. The problem of control, the President's Commission on Law Enforcement and Administration of Justice surmised, "is somewhat like trying to dam a river at its widest point with much too little material."[27]

Contrary to general assumption, under *state* law addiction in itself is not a crime. A California state law making it such was deemed unconstitutional by a 1962 decision of the U.S. Supreme Court in *Robinson v. California.* Addiction has never been a crime under *federal* law. An addict cannot help but come into contact with the police if he engages in the illegal purchase, possession or sale of illegal drugs. In some states the possession of needles and syringes is punishable, in others not. Vagrancy statutes in some locations define as a punishable offense the association of known or convicted addicts with other known addicts or their presence at a place where illicit drugs are uncovered. Consequently, while addiction may not be a crime, many of the actions surrounding the actual habit may be defined in criminal terms.

Although the exact extent of involvement of drug offenders in personal and property crimes is unclear, some estimators attribute as much as 35 of all arrests for property crimes and 25 percent of crimes against the person to narcotic users.[28] It is obvious that heroin users who spend $15 to $100 per day on their habit must find money or some substitute if they are to be able to meet their physical needs. If a person turns to theft or burglary to support his habit, he commonly receives one-fifth to one-third of the value of a stolen object in cash. Others may secure the cash necessary for the purchase of drugs through prostitution, the selling of drugs to other addicts, or other methods which avoid exposure to a middleman. However, the Medical Society of the County of New York contends that there is no evidence that marijuana use is associated with crimes or violence in the United States.[29] Isador Chein believes that adolescent gangs in New York actually prohibit narcotics use among their members and that only a few gangs will use narcotics as a part of their normal operations.[30] While there is a belief that drug addicts are heavily involved in many property crimes, there is no data which supports the contention that they are responsible for 50 percent of property or other crimes.[31] The federal government even now contends that because a pattern of property crimes is common to many heroin users even before their first contact with drugs, the providing of free or cheap heroin to dependents is unlikely to affect this pattern initially.[32]

Meperidine (Demerol) and Methadone ● *Meperidine,* a synthetic pain-killer, may be addicting, but withdrawal from its use is less difficult than for morphine. As a result, it is used medically, although users may face greater problems in daily life than opiate addicts. *Methadone* is also a synthetic and nearly identical to morphine in its effects, although its users develop a tolerance more slowly. Because of its desirable characteristics, such as limiting the withdrawal symptoms of heroin and morphine addiction, methadone has been recently hailed as the answer to opiate withdrawal problems. Whether it will occupy this position in the future remains to be seen. That the actual symptoms of methadone use are milder and more prolonged when compared with opiate use is clear. For example, while heroin dependents may experience withdrawal symptoms from 12 to 16 hours after their last injection, the methadone user may go as long as 72 hours before a similar reaction sets in. During the third day of abstinence from methadone, the individual may become anxious, weak, have headaches, and remain sleepless; however, this is a minor level of discomfort in comparison to the withdrawal symptoms of narcotic users.[33] Current methadone maintenance programs are directed at making heroin dependents functional. A less well known *cyclazocine* treatment program involves the daily administration of a new drug which blocks the effect of heroin and discourages the use of opiates.[34]

Cocaine ● A powerful stimulant derived from the coca plant found extensively in South America, *cocaine* produces a feeling of excitement, hallucinations and an exaggerated belief in one's capabilities for a short time period (15-25 minutes). While the user feels greater mental and physical strength, cocaine acts to lessen the sense of physical fatigue and to permit greater physical exertion. Cocaine users can also come to feel persecuted and occasionally to show paranoid characteristics. Under certain circumstances they may become physically aggressive toward individuals they perceive as hostile to them. While the opium addict tends to be highly passive, the cocaine user often becomes crazed under its influence.[35]

Cocaine usage, rare in the United States, does not appear to create tolerance or physical dependence problems; therefore, discontinuing cocaine intake is not as difficult as withdrawal from the opiates. While cocaine in the early stages of usage is a powerful stimulant to the central nervous system, it becomes a depressant which in later stages can cause respiratory failure and even death.

LSD (Lisergic Acid Diethylamide) ● Hallucinogens in the form of LSD, mescaline or psilocybin alter the way the user views world reality. While LSD is a drug, it is not a narcotic and is most likely to be classed as an hallucinogen or psychedelic drug. It is so potent that less than 30 lbs. (14 kg.) can supply the total market in the U.S. for one year. An estimated 16 percent of college and 8 percent of high school students used LSD in the years 1970 and 1971.[36]

Early research shows that when 50 to 100 milligrams of LSD are ingested, minor changes in sensory perception occur. When 100 to 200 milligrams are taken, the person's ability to concentrate on a particular item and to see great detail is enhanced, a feeling of heaviness is invoked and new depth to color, patterns and movement are visualized. Because the drug produces a dilation of the pupils, an LSD user seeks to avoid bright lights. As far as is known at present, LSD tolerance is minimal, receding after an abstinence of a few days, and physical dependence represents no problem. However, among the dangers involved in LSD usage are the possibility of prolonged psychoses, the acting out of character disorders and homosexual impulses and suicidal inclinations, the activation of previously latent psychoses, and the reappearance of the drug's effects weeks or even months after its use.[37]

Amphetamines and Methedrine ● *Amphetamines,* which stimulate the central nervous system, are most commonly taken in the form of benzedrine or dexedrine. Their usage tends to produce increased alertness, a greater ability to concentrate, and an increased motivation for completion of boring tasks. When taken in larger doses, they may cause headaches, increased pulse rate and dizziness. In recent years the use of amphetamines has been under greater scrutiny, due to the ability of these drugs to mask fatigue and to influence individual behavior in diverse ways.[38]

Although *methedrine* is similar in chemical construction and psychological effects to the amphetamines, its effect upon the cardiovascular system is less than that of amphetamines. Nevertheless, methedrine (methamphetamine rydrochloride) is a more powerful stimulant to the central nervous system. Because it has the ability to stimulate the mind without greatly affecting the person's body, methedrine is commonly used by artists and intellectuals who are concerned with creativity. While opiates depress the nervous system and detach the user from his world, methedrine heightens the individual's awareness of his environment and stimulates him to relate to it.[39]

Barbiturates • Since the turn of the century, more than 2,500 *barbiturates* have been developed. More than 50 are now clinically in use, but they can become addictive and dangerous when taken in more than minimal dosages. Synthetics used as sedatives, barbiturates take many forms including phenobarbital, secobarbital and pentobarbital. All are depressants to the central nervous system frequently prescribed by physicians to encourage relaxation and induce sleep, but since barbiturates do not raise the threshold of pain, they are frequently unable to produce sleep for a person in pain. They may leave the user drowsy, sluggish and, within a period of time, addicted. In combination with alcohol they can cause the user's death.

Barbiturate addiction is a far greater physiological problem than heroin and morphine addiction. The speech of the addict is slow, memory poor and comprehension constricted. The person is likely to be irritable and morose and to show an exaggeration of selected personality characteristics. When undergoing withdrawal, a barbiturate dependent is likely to have hallucinations. If usage continues over a long period of time, it is possible that the dependent person will lose his ability to distinguish between perceptive and general realities.[40]

When heroin or morphine are not available to the addict, he may turn to the use of barbiturates for short-term relief. Secobarbital or pentobarbital, commonly known as "goofballs", are often used for this purpose. If a person is already addicted to one of the opiates, it is possible that its use may also lead to a second simultaneous addiction. Consequently, heroin addicts tend to use barbiturates only in cases of dire need.

Treatment of the Drug and Narcotic Dependent

Treatment for drug and narcotic dependency can be undertaken through voluntary or involuntary procedures. An addict may voluntarily work with appropriate individuals, agencies or programs, or he may be committed to a treatment facility or institution through civil commitment, most widely used in

California, New York, and areas of federal jurisdiction, in lieu of criminal prosecution, sentence or incarceration.

Efforts to treat narcotic and drug users have tended to follow one of several models. The *supervisory deterrent* approach assumes that the biochemical, psychological and social inclinations of the user can be controlled through a combination of institutional services and self-determination. The *therapeutic* model holds that drug use is related to personal and social problems. The *medical distributive* conception contends users should be given drugs under medical supervision; the *maintenance* model, a variant, relates compulsive narcotic usage to a chronic relapsing syndrome which can be controlled by ingestion of methadone, a synthetic narcotic. The *faith and dedication* conception relates drug usage to life values, structures and meaning; the *conditioning-antagonist* orientation sees drug dependency in terms of physical dependence and conditioning. The *character-restructuring, self-regulating therapeutic community* attitude presumes users are immature and cannot delay gratification. The *multimodality* conception of the problem includes multiple treatment approaches, assuming the need for many models to serve differing conditions and types of people.[41]

Early Treatment Efforts • The federal narcotic hospitals at Lexington, Kentucky and Fort Worth, Texas were first established in the middle and late-1930's to provide treatment for federal prisoners addicted to narcotic drugs. Under current policies, preference for admission is given to federal prisoners, although volunteers may be committed. Within the treatment programs of these institutions, patients are encouraged to develop and to improve the functional skills necessary for successful living within a stable environment. Voluntary patients commonly stay for less than five months and are provided no effective after-care or community supervision. Prisoner-patients on parole, however, are given greater follow-up contact. One early study of the effectiveness of these public health service hospitals revealed that as high as 94 percent of those undergoing treatment eventually relapsed.[42] A more recent study of 100 heroin addicts indicated that although 90 had used the drug at some time after their release, 46 were drug-free within the community at the time of the last contact or of their death. Those most successful had undergone compulsory supervision after discharge.[43]

A 30 year study of black admissions to the Lexington and Fort Worth hospitals revealed that a major increase in black admissions took place in 1950. Institutionalized addicts came almost entirely from northern metropolitan areas. While Negro addiction in the South was almost always found within a few big cities, white addiction was most heavily represented in southern rural areas. Black addicts were somewhat younger than white addicts in the South.[44]

Civil Commitment • Although convicted drug users have often been sentenced to special treatment facilities, alternatives for those seeking treatment as civilians are limited. The move toward the civil commitment of volunteers was strengthened by the initiation of the Civil Addict Commitment Law in California in 1961. New York followed with the Metcalf-Volker Act in 1962 and the Federal government with the Narcotic Addict Rehabilitation Act in 1966. Each was created out of the inability to solve the basic problem of addiction with traditional approaches. Later acts have expanded the treatment facilities and programs open to those seeking civil, noncriminal treatment.

In many instances, civil commitment has not been as voluntary as generally believed, because the actual commitment of the person usually takes place somewhere within the process of a criminal proceeding. Frequently, the court orders confinement in a special treatment facility with provision for release as an outpatient under supervision. Final discharge is granted upon proof of patient abstention. If the volunteer relapses, he may be returned to confinement. Civil commitment normally takes four different forms: 1) A voluntary commitment at the request of noncriminal dependents in which they request treatment and subject themselves to a prescribed maximum term; 2) The involuntary commitment of the noncriminal dependent through the law which permits the addict a jury trial on each issue of addiction; 3) Commitment on request or consent of criminal dependents who have been charged and convicted; and 4) Involuntary commitment of criminal drug dependents.

One problem with the civil commitment approach is that it assumes that the state may commit an individual to an institution for treatment in order to secure complete withdrawal. And yet, a debate still continues as to whether the withdrawal of the offender from the drug is the only legitimate goal of a narcotic treatment program. Criticisms of civil commitment programs to date focus on the demands that the drug dependent must exercise his election to undergo treatment within five days of being advised by the court of his right to elect such treatment, the inflexible term of commitment which commonly is as long as three years and an assumption within the law that the mere showing of drug dependency is sufficient for a commitment of the individual.[45]

Examples of Treatment Programs ● One example of a treatment program is located at the California Rehabilitation Center. Established in 1966 and operated by the California Youth and Adult Corrections Agency, the Center's program serves drug dependent misdemeanants and felons convicted and committed by California courts. During an average period of nearly 15 months, patients are divided into 60-person units for treatment, which includes work therapy, vocational training and even high school training. Upon completion of this phase, patients are released to outpatient status under caseworker supervision. For the first six months, they are tested for the presence of drugs five times a month on a regular or surprise basis. If the patient relapses, he will be returned to the institution for continued treatment. Those making a marginal adjustment within the community are assigned to the Parkway Center, a halfway house for assistance. After three drug-free years as an outpatient, the patient becomes eligible for final discharge.

Another attempt at treating the drug problem involves the development of the organization Synanon. Created in 1958, its approach has been to assist drug dependents to help themselves without recourse to normal professional psychiatric therapy. Based on a desire of the person to change his identity and concept of self, participants in the process use attack therapy and brainwashing in order to modify that portion of the self which has been responsible for the addict's current plight. Emphasizing a reward for good behavior, those involved in the treatment process are encouraged to equip themselves with the new tools and skills necessary to construct their own superego. Although smaller at its inception, Brooklyn's Daytop Lodge maintains a voluntary program for addicts on probation, using an approach similar to Synanon's.[46]

Recommendations for the Future • Much still needs to be learned about the drug and narcotic dependency problem. Already many of the President's Commission on Law Enforcement and Administration of Justice recommendations relating to the problem are outmoded.[47] What is known now is largely estimates. The U.S. Government, for example, believes that 80,000 heroin addicts are now on methadone maintenance programs (Figure 2.1), while only about 2,000 or fewer persons are on similar or heroin maintenance programs in Great Britain.[48] The Federal Government projects the annual need for drug and narcotic use treatment to encompass 200,000 to 250,000 persons.[49] In addition, the National Advisory Commission on Criminal Justice Standards and Goals in 1973 recommended the establishment of multimodality drug treatment systems providing comprehensive services, coordination of prevention and treatment activities through a central state and local coordinating agency and provision for drug education with special training for teachers working in this area (Figure 2.2).[50] Other suggestions have included proposals to reduce the appeal of drugs for youth by the creation of crisis centers, rap sessions, counseling outlets, alternative schools and mood alteration programs, and by the expansion of programs of employer education, remedial education, skill training, sheltered work, and job placement. Most of the approaches, however, do little to allay the major problem of barbiturate dependency which is commonly overlooked by the public.

Dependency: Alcoholism and Alcohol Abuse

The problem of alcoholism in the United States has become more severe as youth have moved in the last few years from the use of hard and soft drugs to alcohol. The National Institute on Alcohol Abuse and Alcoholism (NIAAA) claims that between 1960 and 1970 per capita consumption of alcohol in the United States increased 26 percent, an equivalent of 2.6 gallons per adult per year. By 1974, one in every 10 drinking Americans, an estimated 9½ million

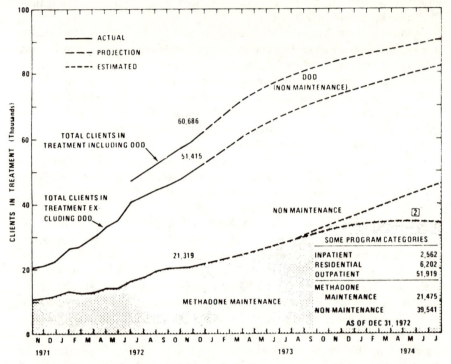

[1] The programs shown are those directly operated by Federal Government (DOD, VA, BOP) or supported with categorical grants and contracts. Programs supported indirectly through medicaid, block grants and revenue sharing (HUD, LEAA, SRS) are not shown. In addition, we estimate that in 1972, State, local and private programs were providing care to about 60,000 drug users and addicts.

[2] Significant progress in antagonist research or new techniques for withdrawal from methadone may have the effect of reducing the numbers of patients in Federally supported maintenance programs starting in early 1974.

Source: Strategy Council on Drug Abuse, *Federal Strategy for Drug Abuse and Drug Traffic Prevention* (Washington, D.C.: U.S. Government Printing Office, 1973), p. 20.

Figure 2.1 Clients in Treatment in Federally Sponsored Programs

persons, were either *problem drinkers* (persons who cause problems for themselves and society) or *full alcoholics*. The disease of alcoholism, viewed by the Cooperative Commission on the Study of Alcoholism as a condition in which an individual has lost control over his alcohol intake,[51] is found most frequently, because it usually develops slowly, among persons 35-55 years of age.[52] According to the Rutgers University Center of Alcohol Studies, an alcoholic is one who is "unable consistently to choose whether he shall drink or not, and who, if he drinks, is unable consistently to choose whether he shall stop

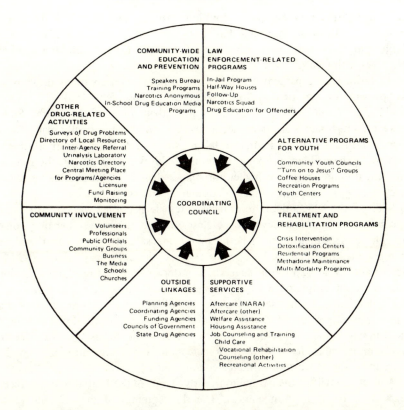

COMMUNITY-WIDE EDUCATION AND PREVENTION

Speakers Bureau
Training Programs
Narcotics Anonymous
In-School Drug Education Media Programs

LAW ENFORCEMENT-RELATED PROGRAMS

In-Jail Program
Half-Way Houses
Follow-Up
Narcotics Squad
Drug Education for Offenders

OTHER DRUG-RELATED ACTIVITIES

Surveys of Drug Problems
Directory of Local Resources
Inter-Agency Referral
Urinalysis Laboratory
Narcotics Directory
Central Meeting Place for Programs/Agencies
Licensure
Fund Raising
Monitoring

ALTERNATIVE PROGRAMS FOR YOUTH

Community Youth Councils
"Turn on to Jesus" Groups
Coffee Houses
Recreation Programs
Youth Centers

COORDINATING COUNCIL

COMMUNITY INVOLVEMENT

Volunteers
Professionals
Public Officials
Community Groups
Business
The Media
Schools
Churches

TREATMENT AND REHABILITATION PROGRAMS

Crisis Intervention
Detoxification Centers
Residential Programs
Methadone Maintenance
Multi-Modality Programs

OUTSIDE LINKAGES

Planning Agencies
Coordinating Agencies
Funding Agencies
Councils of Government
State Drug Agencies

SUPPORTIVE SERVICES

Aftercare (NARA)
Aftercare (other)
Welfare Assistance
Housing Assistance
Job Counseling and Training
Child Care
Vocational Rehabilitation
Counseling (other)
Recreational Activities

Source: National Institute of Mental Health, *Effective Coordination of Drug Abuse Programs* (Rockville, Md.: National Institute of Mental Health, 1973), p. 10.

Figure 2.2   Overview: A Comprehensive Community-wide Effort
in Drug Abuse Assistance

or not".[53] Problem drinking, described as the "repetitive use of beverage alcohol causing physical, psychological, or social harm to the drinker or to others",[54] can appear at any age. If a person's drinking interferes with his general social functioning or is harmful physically or mentally to others, he is generally believed to have a drinking problem.

The Scope and Costs of Alcoholism and Problem Drinking ● Not limited to American society, alcoholism is an especially serious problem in Ireland where drinking expresses male solidarity and serves as a substitute outlet for sexual tensions, and in France where the problem encompasses an estimated 12 percent of the population.[55] However, alcoholism is not a problem in all cultures or subcultures. Orthodox Jews, who have ritualized this experience, have historically had little problem with drinking. Among the Mormons drinking is prohibited. Although drinking has not been ritualized in Italian society, alcoholism rates have been low due to the practice of drinking alcoholic beverages with meals.[56]

An estimated 12 percent of the American population are heavy drinkers and six percent escape-oriented heavy drinkers or problem drinkers.[57] Heavy drinking is found most commonly in the urban areas of the United States; however, a high rate is also recorded among groups which normally maintain low overall drinking rates. Fundamentalists who have fallen from abstinence commonly have high drinking patterns.[58] Proportionately, alcoholism and problem drinking rates are higher for blacks than for whites; the rate for the black female is consistently higher than that for the white female.

While in the 1950's the ratio of male to female alcoholics was estimated to be 5 or 6 to 1, it is now believed to be closer to 4 to 1; however, because women are able to mask their drinking better than men, especially due to their tendency to drink at home and not be obvious at work, this ratio may be inexact. Data from Dade County, Florida suggests a ratio closer to 1 or 2 to 1. Among employees, an estimated 3 to 4 percent are likely to be "disruptive workers". Other data suggests that sons of alcoholic fathers are 4 times more likely than sons *not* having similar fathers to become alcoholics. An undefined portion of the drinking population is likely to become instant alcoholics due to a suspected biochemical imbalance problem. Non-alcoholic employees are 2½ times less likely to be absent from work than alcoholic employees.[59]

Almost one half of the 5½ million yearly arrests in the United States in recent years have been for drunkenness. The shortcomings of the criminal justice system, especially regarding the effective use of police manpower, are believed due in part to the over two million drunkenness arrests completed each year. As a legal violation, drunkenness is normally defined as being drunk in a public place or occasionally in some other location where the drunk is unable to care for his own safety. Although in many jurisdictions a drunk may be sentenced to jail for five days to six months, he is most frequently sentenced to 30 days. Slowly, this practice is changing.

The costs of alcoholism and to some degree problem drinking include a life expectancy shortened by 10 to 12 years; a disproportionate likelihood of a violent death; a higher prospect of an unhappy marriage, family impoverishment or divorce; a greater tendency toward involvement in accidents and deaths;[60] a disproportionate participation in homicides,[61] suicides and assaults; and a greater expenditure of funds ($100 million per year to process drunks and drunken drivers and $10 billion lost in work time, $2 billion in health and welfare services and nearly $3.5 billion in property damage expenses, wage losses and insurance costs). Approximately one half of all murders involve either a drinking killer or victim. Alcohol abusers are 7 times more likely to separate or divorce than the remaining non-abusing population. Over one half of the 55,500 auto deaths and the 1 million injuries due to auto accidents each year involve

Deaths per 100,000 population

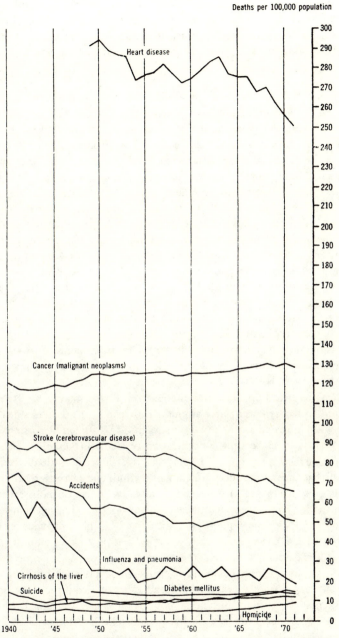

Source: Executive Office of the President, OMB, *Social Indicators, 1973* (Washington, D.C.:
U.S. Government Printing Office, 1973), p. 6.

Figure 2.3 Death Rates for Selected Causes, 1940-1971
(Adjusted to the Age Distribution of the 1940 Population)

alcohol-influenced drivers or pedestrians, many below the legal drinking age (now between 18 and 21 in most states). Some have described alcoholism as a form of suicide in which the individual unconsciously or willfully attempts to kill himself over a period of years, usually through the development of cirrhosis of the liver (Figure 2.3).[62]

Alcoholics and Problem Drinkers ● Problem drinking and alcoholism, according to David J. Pittman, involve two basic types of people: 1) Those who have a disease and need assistance, and 2) Those who are lower-class drunks or skid-rowers. The former are physiologically and psychologically ill; the latter are largely poorly educated, find interpersonal relationships difficult, generally represent an ethnic or racial minority group, are unable to fulfill productive social roles adequately and are dependent upon institutionalized living arrangements.[63] The attitudes of skid-rowers toward drinking, however, may range from total abstention to full alcohol indulgence. Interspersed on this continuum are three gradations of moderate or social drinking, sporadic excessive drinking, and heavy social drinking.[64] Many drinkers have only a drinking rather than an alcoholism problem, a condition which falls short of the alcoholic state but which nevertheless creates problems for the individual involved and those who relate to him. Persons who are problem drinkers or alcoholics are unusually susceptible to stress and frustration and commonly rely upon drinking as a solution to daily problems. Temporarily, at least, alcohol permits the user to reduce tensions, lessen anxiety, and dull sensitivity to problems confronting him. At the same time, it lessens the physiological burden normally assumed by the heart and blood vessels.

Although the ingestion of limited amounts of alcohol may cause the person to relax and to feel renewed, large amounts may lead to the drinker's death. For example, when ingested into the blood stream of a 150-pound person with an empty stomach, a .03 percent concentration of alcohol (the equivalent of one cocktail or two beers) produces limited changes in feeling; .06 percent (two cocktails or four beers) produces a feeling of warmth and relaxation; .09 percent (three cocktails or six beers) exaggerated, talkative, noisy or morose behavior; .12 percent (four cocktails or eight beers) unsteadiness or clumsiness in standing or walking; and .15 percent (five cocktails or ½ pint of whiskey) great intoxication. These effects obviously vary in relation to the amount of food eaten, the time span in which the alcohol is consumed, body size and metabolism, and the drinker's mood, attitudes, and previous drinking experience.[65] Extreme alcohol ingestion may lead to mental confusion, uncoordination, disorientation, stupor, anesthesia, coma, or ultimately death. Cirrhosis of the liver, which is increasing as a cause of death, (Table 2.1) frequently results from excessive drinking. Given these effects, most states consider a .10 to .51 percent level of alcohol in the blood to constitute legal intoxication.[66] One study of English bus drivers revealed that the more the drivers drank the more likely they were to take their buses through narrower passageways, show

TABLE 2.1

DEATH RATES FOR SELECTED CAUSES, 1940-1971 (ADJUSTED TO AGE DISTRIBUTION FOR THE
1940 POPULATION; DEATHS PER 100,000 POPULATION)

YEAR	HEART DISEASE	STROKE (CEREBRO-VASCULAR DISEASE)	ARTERIO-SCLEROSIS	CANCER (MALIGNANT NEOPLASMS)	ALL ACCIDENTS	CIRRHOSIS OF THE LIVER	SUICIDE	HOMICIDE
1940	(NA)	91.0	(NA)	120.3	72.4	8.6	14.3	6.3
1941	(NA)	87.2	(NA)	118.1	75.0	8.8	12.7	6.0
1942	(NA)	86.3	(NA)	117.7	69.8	9.1	11.8	5.9
1943	(NA)	88.7	(NA)	117.6	71.2	8.9	10.0	5.1
1944	(NA)	84.7	(NA)	118.4	68.8	8.0	9.6	5.1
1945	(NA)	85.4	(NA)	119.9	68.7	8.6	10.7	5.8
1946	(NA)	80.5	(NA)	119.1	67.0	9.0	11.1	6.4
1947	(NA)	81.3	(NA)	121.0	65.8	9.7	11.1	6.1
1948	(NA)	78.9	(NA)	122.3	63.3	10.5	10.8	6.0
1949	292.2	87.0	(NA)	125.1	57.3	8.6	11.0	5.5
1950	295.0	88.8	(NA)	125.4	57.5	8.5	11.0	5.4
1951	289.9	89.0	(NA)	124.3	59.4	9.1	10.0	5.0
1952	287.2	87.8	(NA)	125.7	58.8	9.5	9.7	5.4
1953	286.9	86.9	(NA)	125.9	57.2	9.5	9.8	5.1
1954	274.0	83.0	(NA)	125.8	53.1	9.2	9.9	5.1
1955	277.1	83.0	(NA)	125.8	54.3	9.4	9.9	4.8
1956	278.5	82.3	(NA)	126.3	54.4	9.9	9.7	5.0
1957	282.6	84.2	(NA)	126.4	53.4	10.5	9.6	4.9
1958	277.9	83.0	(NA)	124.6	49.8	9.9	10.5	4.9
1959	272.3	80.7	(NA)	124.5	49.9	10.1	10.5	5.1
1960	274.9	79.7	(NA)	125.8	49.9	10.5	10.6	5.2
1961	278.6	76.7	12.4	125.4	48.1	10.6	10.5	5.2
1962	282.7	76.8	12.6	125.6	49.7	11.0	11.0	5.4
1963	285.4	76.6	12.5	126.6	50.9	11.2	11.3	5.5
1964	276.8	73.9	12.1	126.6	52.0	11.5	11.0	5.7
1965	275.6	73.1	12.0	127.9	53.4	12.1	11.4	6.2
1966	275.8	72.6	11.9	128.4	55.6	13.0	11.1	6.7
1967	267.7	70.0	11.1	129.1	54.8	13.5	11.1	7.7
1968	270.0	71.5	9.6	130.2	55.1	14.0	11.0	8.2
1969	262.3	68.5	9.2	129.7	55.3	14.2	11.3	8.6
1970[1]	255.7	66.9	8.8	130.4	51.9	15.2	11.4	8.5
1971[1]	250.6	65.0	8.4	128.8	51.0	14.9	11.3	9.4

NA Not available.

[1] Provisional data.

Source: Public Health Service, National Center for Health Statistics, *Vital Statistics Rates in the United States, 1940-1960; Vital Statistics of the United States*, annual issues 1961 to 1968, Vol. II, Part A; *Monthly Vital Statistics Report*, Vol. 21, No. 4, Supplement (2); and unpublished data.

impaired judgment patterns and reveal patterns of overconfidence in relation to performance. However, the same amount of whiskey did not affect each driver in the same way.[67]

Drinking, Donald Horton found from his work on primitive societies, tends to be accompanied by the release of sexual and aggressive impulses. The amount of drinking in any society tends to vary directly with the level of anxiety in the society, and inversely with the strength of the counter-anxiety enlisted by painful experiences during and after drinking.[68] Others find that chronic alcoholism is partially a product of under-socialization evident in the alcoholic's inability to use a social product without abusing it, and an existing social ambiguity concerning drinking evident in the inconsistent normative standard which permits, expects or strongly sanctions drinking on some occasions while prohibiting it on others. In those groups which have a significant alcohol usage level and yet a low incidence of alcoholism, the following habits or attitudes tend to predominate:

1. The children are exposed to alcohol early in life within a strong family or religious group. Whatever the beverage, it is served in very diluted and small quantities, with consequent low blood-alcohol levels.

2. The beverages commonly, although not invariably, used by the groups are those containing relatively large amounts of non-alcoholic components, which also give low blood-alcohol levels.

3. The beverage is considered mainly as a food and usually consumed with meals, again with consequent low blood-alcohol levels.

4. Parents present a constant example of moderate drinking.

5. No moral importance is attached to drinking. It is considered neither a virtue nor a sin.

6. Drinking is not viewed as proof of adulthood or virility.

7. Abstinence is socially acceptable. It is no more rude or ungracious to decline a drink than to decline a piece of bread.

8. Excessive drinking or intoxication is not socially acceptable. It is not considered stylish, comic or tolerable.

9. Finally, and perhaps most importantly, there is wide and usually complete agreement among members of the group on what might be called the "group rules of drinking".[69]

The Development of Alcoholism • Alcoholism development normally follows a four- or five-step line of progression. In the *pre-alcoholic* phase (Phase I), which lasts from 6 months to 10 or more years, the potential alcoholic drinks to alleviate common tensions. In the *early phase of non-addictive alcoholism* (Phase II), he sneaks drinks, is preoccupied with alcohol, occasionally has blackouts and feels guilt. During the 6 months to 4 to 5 years that he inconspicuously uses alcohol, the non-addictive alcoholic tends to rationalize his drinking problem and project his sense of guilt to others. Near the end of this phase, he begins to lose personal control and becomes physically dependent upon alcohol. During the *crucial phase of addictive alcoholism* (Phase III), the now-becoming alcoholic is usually aggressive and grandiose in his actions, occasionally abstains in order to prove that he is not dependent on alcohol, changes friends and associates, and occasionally has a physical problem of some sort. At this point, he is no longer able to control his drinking activity. During the *chronic phase* (Phase IV), the alcoholic engages in drinking bouts and finds his mental abilities heavily impaired. Not only does he lose his ability to make many ethical decisions, but he begins to drink the lower grades of alcohol that his new, less desirable friends ingest.[70]

During the stage of *alpha* alcoholism, which is purely psychological, the drinker has a continuing dependence on alcohol. Within the stage of *beta* alcoholism, he engages in very heavy drinking in some sociocultural groups and develops poor nutritional habits which may produce various deficiency diseases. At the point of *gamma* alcoholism, the growing alcoholic loses control over the amount being taken in and progresses from psychological to physical dependence. During his *delta* stage of alcoholism, he becomes unable to abstain from drinking but not to control the amount he ingests on any given occasion and undergoes physical dependence without marked psychological dependence. At the final stage of *epsilon* alcoholism, the alcoholic loses nearly all control and engages characteristically in periodic drinking bouts.[71]

The Treatment of Alcoholism and the Alcoholic

To some degree, most problem drinkers and alcoholics are operational within the community. The NIAAA estimates that 95 percent are employed or employable persons living in families. Most perform more or less effectively in their jobs. Approximately two thirds of those treated for alcoholism can recover, although few will be able to abstain totally from alcoholic beverages for the remainder of their lives after recovery. Consequently, increased emphasis has been placed in recent years upon helping the former alcoholic to *control* his drinking rather than achieve total abstinence. The control effort, supporters contend, is now yielding a 60 to 70 percent apparent success rate. For those without the support of family, employer and/or therapist, the prognosis is far less optimistic.

Although alcoholism is now conceived as a medical problem, the attempt to solve it through medicine has faced many obstacles. Hospitals not only continue to discourage the admission of alcoholic patients, but most medical insurance and hospitalization plans are not prone to allow payments for treatment of alcoholism-based illnesses. Those state-sponsored programs that do provide assistance are rarely unified programs designed to solve alcohol problems. In addition, one of the most serious problems in the attempt to develop suitable treatment methods is the general unwillingness of most private and some state institutions to treat an individual who is poorly motivated and emotionally unstable, characteristics common to problem drinkers and alcoholics. Many treatment programs admit disproportionately the good risks while ignoring the poor ones, thereby inflating their success claims. Some evidence suggests that those who are admitted to hospital treatment tend to be younger patients, the highly educated, or persons who possess adequate social functioning. Acute cases of alcoholism are treated in a room or emergency ward of a general hospital, a detoxification center, a psychiatric ward of a general or mental hospital, at home, or at a private physician's office. In many instances, however, alcoholics are not treated at all but are simply jailed.

The existing 321 state hospitals provide daily some alcoholism program or services in their institutions for 37,000 patients with alcoholic diagnoses. An estimated 40 percent of those admitted to mental hospitals in some states have alcoholism problems, but only about 10 percent of the state hospitals provide alcoholism wards or special programs for alcoholics.[72] Those programs which do exist frequently operate on the concept of a therapeutic community in which the patient is encouraged to improve his personality functioning within a positive and normal environment (the concept of normalization). The alcoholic under treatment is stimulated to socialize with other patients, engage in day-to-day decision-making and participate in activities which encourage positive self-image development. Hypnotherapy, group psychodrama or even LSD therapy are used regularly or experimentally in some institutions as treatment procedures.[73]

The Need for a Unified Approach to Treatment ● If alcoholism is to be treated successfully, a unified system of alcoholism treatment resources in the form of outpatient clinics, domiciliaries, community houses, halfway houses, foster homes, and social centers must be created. The President's Commission encouraged in 1967 the establishment of civil detoxification centers as a first step to the changing of any program of processing and treating drunkenness offenders. Alcoholics or problem drinkers could be referred to these or other community resources by the center in order to assist the alcoholic overcome his problem and provide after-care services. By offering such a supportive network of agencies, the problems of the alcoholic and alcoholism within society could be sharply lessened. Criminal conduct while drunk would remain a crime, but the mere act of drunkenness would be processed as a medical problem.

Such an approach is in accord with recent court decisions which hold that the problem of alcoholism can no longer be handled through a revolving door court policy in which drunks are sentenced to a few days in jail and/or fined, are released, and are rearrested and resentenced a few days later. The *Easter v. District of Columbia* and *Driver v. Hinnant* decisions now prohibit further criminal prosecution of chronic alcoholics who have been arrested for public intoxication. The First Circuit Court of Appeals held in *Driver v. Hinnant* that it is no longer possible to stamp a person as a criminal if his drunken public display is "involuntary as a result of disease".[74] He can, however, be held for treatment and rehabilitation as long as he is not stigmatized as a criminal. In *Easter v. District of Columbia,* the District of Columbia Court of Appeals ruled that "chronic alcoholism is a defense to a charge of public intoxication" and cannot be considered a crime or a violation.[75]

The passage of the Comprehensive Alcohol Abuse and Alcoholism Prevention Treatment and Rehabilitation Act by Congress in 1970 gave impetus to the development of halfway houses for treatment and local alcoholism reception centers (LARC) for detoxification, and to the decriminalization of alcoholism problems (excepting drunken driving). Already, over 10 states have removed drunkenness from the list of criminal violations, and more are expected to follow their lead. An estimated 7,500 treatment centers existed in 1974. Models range from the Chit Chat Farms project in Reading, Pennsylvania, where patients undergo a 28-day treatment in a group therapy setting at a cost of $840, to the

Lutheran General Hospital in Chicago, which charges $1,827 for 21 days of staff-patient and patient-patient interaction and uses a medico-social rather than a psychotherapy approach to the problem; to the Seattle Schick Shadel Hospital which operates an 11-day, $1,500 program of aversion therapy. As the problem has grown in recognition, an increasing number of major firms, now over 300, have moved either privately or in cooperation with established outlets to provide company- and/or union-sponsored alcoholism treatment programs.[76]

Prevention of Alcoholism

Although prevention may involve a multitude of alternatives, most alcoholism prevention attempts have been directed toward the alteration of drinking patterns, the elimination of ambiguities concerning drinking and the integration of drinking into social life. Each of these approaches presupposes some educational program, often directed to intermediate or secondary school students. However, alcohol education, as yet, has not been widely accepted despite its potential for prevention of alcoholism and problem drinking. Some propose that alcohol education be included in driver education courses, where such knowledge can be well integrated with other personal tasks.[77] Others believe that the problem can only be prevented if discrimination against problem drinkers by prevention or treatment agencies ceases.

The attempt to prevent alcoholism by controlling the availability of alcohol has taken the forms of licensing, prohibition and state monopoly operation of alcohol sale and distribution. In some countries which have a laissez-faire system, no attempt has been made to control the availability of alcohol.[78] Overall, the mere licensing or state marketing of alcohol does little to solve the ongoing human problems of alcoholism and alcohol dependency. While many welfare agencies and organizations, such as Alcoholics Anonymous, have had many successes, their overall ability to prevent or even to treat alcoholism effectively is in doubt. Too often psychiatric clinics focus merely on the psychological aspects of the alcoholism problem and ignore its other dimensions. Private physicians, too, tend to be more willing to work with persons having temporary or short-term afflictions than those, such as alcoholics, who may need long-term treatment. The serious cases are commonly referred to state mental hospitals or hospitals having alcoholism wards.

Many of those not undergoing or released from hospitalization have been successfully assisted by Alcoholics Anonymous, an organization which encourages self-help and mutual aid and assists alcoholics to face their problems. At the outset, new members are encouraged to confess their inability to control their drinking problem and confront their inadequacy and helplessness. Working on a one-to-one basis, an organization member who has solved his problem helps a weakening alcoholic from succumbing to his craving for a drink by reinforcing his desire to abstain. The fact that this type of approach has been successful indicates the personality and peer character of the drinking problem.[79]

The Solution of the Alcoholism Problem • The solution of problem drinking and alcoholism rests with the assistance provided by traditional public health, mental health, general hospital, public welfare, vocational rehabilitation or medical services. Communities, therefore, need to provide special alcoholism treatment personnel and facilities in order to coordinate services for those in need. Detoxification centers, psychiatric health services and emergency medical care must be provided. Community mental health programs or psychiatric clinics need to make provision for outpatient clinical care for problem drinkers. Industry and unions must develop more progressive policies for the detection and treatment of alcohol problems. Further research into alcoholism, effects of alcoholism and the relationships of cultural and subcultural factors to problem drinking and alcoholism needs also to be carried out.[80]

References

1. U.S. Department of the Treasury, *Traffic in Opium and Other Dangerous Drugs* (Washington, D.C.: U.S. Government Printing Office, 1965), pp. 37-46.
2. Strategy Council on Drug Abuse, *Federal Strategy for Drug Abuse and Drug Traffic Prevention 1973* (Washington, D.C.: U.S. Government Printing Office, 1973), p. 12.
3. Drug Enforcement Administration, *Drug Enforcement,* (Fall, 1973), I, No. 1, p. 2.
4. Nathan B. Eddy, H. Halbach, Harris Isbell and Maurice H. Seevers, "Drug Dependence: Its Significance and Characteristics," *Alcoholism,* ed. Ronald J. Catanzaro (Springfield, Ill.: C. C. Thomas, 1968), p. 41.
5. Troy Duster, *The Legislation of Morality: Law, Drugs and Moral Judgment* (New York: Free Press, 1970), pp. 30-31.
6. *Ibid.,* pp. 13-14.
7. Alfred R. Lindesmith, *The Addict and the Law* (Bloomington, Ind.: Indiana University Press, 1965), p. 6.
8. Duster, *The Legislation of Morality,* p. 11.
9. President's Commission on Law Enforcement and Administration of Justice, *Task Force Report: Narcotics and Drug Abuse* (Washington, D.C.: U.S. Government Printing Office, 1967), p. 11.
10. *Ibid.,* p. 18.
11. Duster, *The Legislation of Morality,* pp. 20-21.
12. Louis S. Goodman and Alfred Gilman, *The Pharmacological Basis of Therapeutics* (New York: Macmillan, 1960), pp. 171-172.
13. *New York Times* (April 17, 1974).
14. Howard S. Becker, *Outsiders: Studies in the Sociology of Deviance* (New York: Free Press, 1963), pp. 41-78.
15. Andrew T. Weil, Norman E. Zinberg and Judith M. Nelsen, "Clinical and Psychological Effects of Marijuana in Man," *Science,* (December, 1968), CLXII, 1234-1242.
16. Lindesmith, *The Addict and the Law,* pp. 228-231.
17. Goodman and Gilman, *The Pharmacological Basis,* pp. 173-174.
18. President's Commission, *Task Force Report,* p. 13.
19. Duster, *The Legislation of Morality,* pp. 3-7.
20. *Ibid.,* p. 34.
21. Charles E. Terry and Mildred Pellens, *The Opium Problem* (New York: Bureau of Social Hygiene, 1928), p. 468.

22. Charles Winick, "Narcotics Addiction and Its Treatment," *Law and Contemporary Problems*, (Winter, 1957), XXII, 9-33.
23. Marie Myswander, *The Drug Addict as Patient* (New York: Grune and Sttatton, 1956).
24. Duster, *The Legislation of Morality*, p. 36.
25. John C. Ball and William M. Bates, "Migration and Residential Mobility of Narcotic Drug Addicts," *Social Problems*, (Summer, 1966), XIV, 68.
26. President's Commission, *Task Force Report*, p. 3.
27. *Ibid.*, p. 6.
28. Strategy Council on Drug Abuse, *Federal Strategy for Drug Abuse*, p. 14.
29. *New York Medicine* (May 5, 1966), p. 3.
30. Isador Chein, *The Road to H* (New York: Basic Books, 1964).
31. President's Commission, *Task Force Report*, p. 11.
32. Strategy Council on Drug Abuse, *Federal Strategy*, p. 32.
33. Duster, *The Legislation of Morality*, p. 48.
34. President's Commission, *Task Force Report*, pp. 15-16.
35. *Ibid.*, p. 42.
36. Strategy Council on Drug Abuse, *Federal Strategy*, p. 53.
37. President's Commission, *Task Force Report*, p. 5.
38. Duster, *The Legislation of Morality*, p. 37.
39. *Ibid.*, p. 38.
40. Goodman and Gilman, *The Pharmacological Basis*, p. 222.
41. Strategy Council on Drug Abuse, *Federal Strategy*, pp. 16-19.
42. Henrietta J. Duvall, Ben Z. Locke and Leon Brill, "Follow-up Study of Narcotic Drug Addicts Five Years After Hospitalization," *Public Health Report*, (1963), XXVII, 185.
43. George E. Vaillant, "A Twelve-Year Follow-up of New York Addicts: In the Relation of Treatment of Outcome," *American Journal of Psychiatry*, (1966), Vol. CXXII, 727.
44. William M. Bates, "Narcotics, Negroes and the South," *Social Forces*, (Summer, 1956), Vol. XXXXV, 61-67.
45. President's Commission, *Task Force Report*, pp. 17-18.
46. See Lewis Yablonsky, *Synanon: The Tunnel Back* (Baltimore: Penguin Books, 1967).
47. President's Commission, *Task Force Report*, p. 1-20.
48. Strategy Council on Drug Abuse, *Federal Strategy*, p. 33.
49. *Ibid.*, p. 20.
50. National Advisory Commission on Criminal Justice Standards and Goals, *A National Strategy to Reduce Crime* (Washington, D.C.: U.S. Government Printing Office, 1973), pp. 59-61.
51. Thomas F. A. Plaut, *Alcohol Problems: A Report to the Nation By The Cooperative Commission on the Study of Alcoholism* (New York: Oxford University Press, 1967), p. 399.
52. "Alcoholism, What It Means, What It Costs," *The Economist*, (January, 1970), CCXXXIV, 18.
53. *Time* (April 22, 1974), p. 76.
54. Plaut, *Alcohol Problems*, pp. 37-38.
55. R. F. Bales, "Attitudes Toward Drinking in the Irish Culture," *Society, Culture and Drinking Patterns*, ed. David J. Pittman and C. R. Snyder (New York: Wiley, 1962), pp. 157-187.
56. D. D. Glad, "Attitudes and Experiences of American-Jewish and American-Irish Male Youth as Related to Differences in Adult Rates of Inebriety," *Quarterly Journal of Studies of Alcoholism.*
57. President's Commission on Law Enforcement and Administration of Justice, *Task Force Report: Drunkenness* (Washington, D.C.: U.S. Government Printing Office, 1967), pp. 28-31.

58. *Ibid.,* p. 30.
59. Muriel W. Streane, David J. Pittman and Thomas Coe, "Teenagers, Drinking and the Law: A Study of Arrest Trends for Alcohol-Related Offenses," *Alcoholism,* ed. D. J. Pittman (New York: Harper and Row, 1967), pp. 71-72.
60. J. R. Carroll and W. Haddon, Jr., "A Controlled Study of Fatal Automobile Accidents in New York City," *Journal of Chronic Disease,* Vol. 15 (1962), pp. 811-826; and Melvin L. Selzer, "Alcoholism, Mental Illness and Stress in 96 Drivers Causing Fatal Accidents," *Behavioral Science,* (January, 1969), XIV, 1-10.
61. Plaut, *Alcohol Problems,* p. 49.
62. National Institute on Alcohol Abuse and Alcoholism, *Alcohol and Alcoholism* (Rockville, Md.: National Institute of Mental Health, 1972), pp. 10-12.
63. David J. Pittman, "Public Intoxication and the Alcoholic Offender in American Society," *Society, Culture and Drinking Patterns,* pp. 9-10. See also Howard M. Bahr, "Family Size and Stability as Antecedents of Homelessness and Excessive Drinking," *Journal of Marriage and the Family,* (August, 1969), Vol. XXXI, 477-483.
64. Ronald J. Catanzaro, *Alcoholism* (Springfield, Ill.: C. C. Thomas, 1968), p. 8.
65. Chauncey B. Leake, "Good-Willed Judgment of Alcohol," *Alcohol and Civilization,* ed. Salvatore Lucia (New York: McGraw-Hill, 1963), p. 19. For a discussion of the relationship of drinking and deviance, see Charles H. McCaghy, "Drinking and Deviance Disavowal: The Case of Child Molesters," *Social Problems,* (Summer, 1968), XVI, 43-49.
66. NIAAA, *Alcohol and Alcoholism,* pp. 3-4.
67. John Cohen, *Chance, Skill and Luck* (London: Penguin Books, 1960).
68. Donald Horton, "The Functions of Alcohol in Primitive Society: A Cross-Cultural Study," *Quarterly Journal of Studies on Alcohol,* (1943), IV, 199-320. Also see Don Callahan, "A Multivariate Analysis of the Correlates of Drinking-Related Problems in a Community Study," *Social Problems,* (Fall, 1969), XVII, 234-247.
69. NIAAA, *Alcohol and Alcoholism,* p. 16.
70. E. M. Jellinek, "Phases of Alcohol Addiction," *Alcoholism and Family Casework,* ed. Margaret B. Bailey (New York: Community Council of Greater New York, 1968), pp. 43-49.
71. E. M. Jellinek, *The Disease Conception of Alcoholism* (Highland Park, N.J.: Hillhouse Press, 1960).
72. Plaut, *Alcohol Problems,* pp. 57-66.
73. *Ibid.,* pp. 69-70.
74. *Driver b. Hinnant,* 356 F. 2d 761 (4th Cir., 1966).
75. *Easter v. District of Columbia,* 361 F. 2d 50 (D.C. Cir., 1966).
76. NIAAA, *Alcohol and Alcoholism,* p. 28.
77. Plaut, *Alcohol Problems.*
78. Archer Tongue, "International Responses of Alcoholism," *Alcoholism,* pp. 230-231.
79. Plaut, *Alcohol Problems,* p. 64; and Elizabeth D. Whitney, *Living With Alcoholism* (Boston; Beacon Press, 1968), pp. 80-89.
80. Plaut, *Alcohol Problems,* pp. 50-51.

CHAPTER 3

Sexual Deviation:
Prostitution and Homosexuality

The Nature of Prostitution

Prostitution is an indiscriminate commercial transaction involving the giving of one's body in sex for money.[1] The commercial dimension, among other elements, makes prostitution different from courtship which also includes intercourse. The prostitute, usually indifferent to the sexual relation that she engages in, participates in sex with those able to pay the required fare. Depending on the price, she will usually serve her client through oral, anal, or other specialized sexual acts. Frequently working under the management of a "pimp," whose affection she values, the prostitute is usually indifferent emotionally to her trysts with clients.

By defining prostitution as "the selling of sex outside of marriage as a vocation,"[2] the prostitute is differentiated from some women who exchange sex in marriage for material gains. Like many of the vices, prostitution and the prostitute operate in an area of normative ambiguity in which restrictive legal norms and the demand for such activity by a significant portion of the population make it profitable. While prostitution flourished in the past when the number of males in a population outnumbered the females, sexual outlets were severely restricted, and marriage age was high,[3] some evidence suggests these factors do not have the same effect today as they did in the past.[4]

Prostitution and Social Class ● Historically, prostitutes moved with armies and work-gangs to areas where females were in short supply. On location, they traditionally offered men domestic as well as sexual assistance. Some evidence suggests that prostitutes in early America came primarily from the lower classes. However, in later decades, middle and upper middle-class prostitutes became more common. This was especially characteristic of the Victorian period when

43

women were placed in the simple categories of good and bad and the double standard of sex for males predominated. Even in other cultures, prostitutes have been drawn from all social classes. Among those occupying a relatively high social status while serving at times as prostitutes were the *hetaerae* of ancient Greece, the *devadasis* of India, and the *geishas* of Japan. Common prostitutes, however, were drawn even in these cultures from the lower classes.

Prostitution and Social Acceptance • In the United States, prostitution has never reached the level of public acceptance noted in other countries. While opposition to prostitution in the United States was largely limited until World War I when a sharp increase in venereal disease threatened the war effort, it usually operated, frequently with police protection, outside the law. At one time, operators of an estimated 2,000 vice locations during the Chicago mayoral tenure of William Hale Thompson, paid $100 to $750 per week for police protection.[5] However, with the increase in venereal disease, the investment in houses of prostitution declined.[6] Although some now believe that houses of prostitution as accepted and clearly identifiable institutions have largely disappeared, most urban areas still have some houses in operation.[7]

During World War II, an estimated 600,000 regular and an equal number of part-time prostitutes engaged in the profession.[8] How many prostitutes operate today is unknown. However, because of the freer sexual climate, the demand for prostitutes appears to have sharply declined. Nevertheless, while prostitutes have not been officially sponsored by the American government, the armed forces go to great lengths to inform soldiers how to use prophylactics and to remain disease free. One study of venereal disease among American troops in Europe after World War II disclosed that licensed houses of prostitution represented the greatest single source of GI infection.[9] Another report, however, noted that 6 percent of the VD infections among Army members were caused by professional prostitutes, 80 percent by amateurs and 14 percent by wives.[10] Because these diseases immobilize fighting men, some armed forces medical officers have recommended the operation of houses of prostitution by the military as part of the Post Exchange (PX) system.[11]

Patrons of Prostitutes • The frequency of patronization of prostitutes by males appears to have declined markedly since World War II.[12] Most available evidence suggests that prostitution has decreased as general and sexual freedom for single, widowed, and divorced women has increased. The Kinsey research team discovered in the 1940's that male sexual intercourse rates with prostitutes had declined by one half to two thirds from the rate apparent in the previous generation.[13] While nearly 69 percent of the male population of the United States had experience with prostitutes, the majority had had no more than two contacts. Their later study of women indicated that male intercourse with non-prostitute females, however, increased conversely,[14] a growth probably due to the changes taking place in the structure and operation of the family and in sexual practices.[15] More recent studies indicate a continuing decline in commercial contacts with prostitutes.

While the Kinsey research team found that the male recourse to prostitutes was approximately one half the rate estimated prior to World War I,[16] males of grade school level who were between 16 to 20 years of age were found to have had intercourse with prostitutes 9 times as often, and males of high school level more than 4 times as often as males of college level.[17] While less than 1 percent of all extra-marital sexual intercourse was with prostitutes, more than 9 percent of the total non-marital sexual practices of males was with paid sexual partners.[18] One estimate suggests that only 4 percent of college students have had experience with a prostitute, again probably due to the greater opportunity of American males to have sexual relations with women who are not prostitutes since the marketing of birth control pills.[19]

Why Men Seek Prostitutes • Males turn to prostitutes for sexual satisfaction for many reasons. With prostitutes, males do not have to compete with other males, as is often the case in courtship, for sexual favors. The impersonality of this manner of sexual relationship frees the male from the responsibility and obligations of a potential pregnancy. His desires for a variety of sexual experience, including sadistic or masochistic, which his partner might wish to avoid, may be fulfilled through contact with a prostitute. In the transaction, males can, if they are able to mentally, be free of their inhibitions in a manner not often permitted by conventional norms.[20]

The prostitute is often highly valued because she is immediately available and must satisfy her customers to maintain her clientele. In addition, the investments of time, money and emotions by customers are much less than those necessary to reach the same sexual objective with a "nice girl". The probability, even then, of successfully attaining the sexual goal is greater with a prostitute.[21]

Prostitution and the Law • Anti-prostitution laws historically have been common in many Protestant nations while Roman Catholic countries, as a general rule, have been much more tolerant regarding this matter. Protestant attitudes toward prohibition of prostitution have been due in part to the problems commercialized sex cause business and family life and to the public's concern for the transmission of syphilis.[22] Not only does prostitution compete with marital sexual experiences, which are the binding elements of family stability, and encourage promiscuity and indifference to responsibility, it also degrades the nature of the sexual experience and is believed to have undesirable effects upon those engaging in its practice. Prostitution hastens the spread of venereal disease, undermines law enforcement, causes a public nuisance, is an affront to public morals and reduces the procreative responsibility of the population. Its existence tends to reinforce community deviant social processes, especially as prostitutes develop a special series of services and acts, barter with customers, rationalize their conduct and flout their impersonal relationships with clients.[23]

If any trend is apparent in the legal handling of prostitutes, it is toward greater tolerance in sexual activity among consenting adults with greater legal prohibitions placed upon actions which harm the public. In many places, penalties are increasing for street solicitation, the maintenance of a house of prostitution and nuisance conduct relating to the activity. In 27 states, prostitution is not defined criminally as a legal category, but its activities are processed under vagrancy or similar statutes.[24] Keeping a house of prostitution is illegal in the United States except in parts of Arizona and Nevada. In the latter state, local towns or cities may prohibit prostitution by ordinance. Where it is legal in the state, it is nevertheless unlawful for anyone to live on the earnings of a prostitute or to engage in procuring.[25] While prostitution was legal in 13 of Nevada's 17 counties in 1970, strong efforts are now being made to restrict and even prohibit the practice within the state. Nevertheless, the nearly 40 licensed houses of prostitution had an annual business of between $3 and $5 million in 1970. Each woman cleared an average of $300 per week after expenses.[26]

At present, only 8 of the 50 states sanction punishment for the prostitute's customer,[27] although as women's groups gain more political power, this will probably change. The 1974 case of a Milwaukee male dressed as a female prostitute was thrown out of court on the grounds that the law was written to control female rather than male actions. With the growing awareness of feminist issues, future court tests of prostitution laws will probably center on the sexual discrimination apparent in the laws and their traditional interpretation.[28]

The Prostitute • Prostitutes come from all class levels. The greater number enter the profession voluntarily. Despite the "white slave myth," few are coerced into prostitution. A woman becomes a prostitute because the economic rewards are greater than those in any other occupation, the work, which is unconfining and rather easy, has some element of adventure and occasional glamour attached to it, and offers immediate gratification for women with strong sex drives.[29] The apparent economic rewards gained by prostitutes have led some critics to argue that prostitution is a product of capitalism; however, other economic systems, especially communism, have also been plagued by this problem.[30]

Given this context, when an emphasis upon financial gain is part of the capitalist system and the work is so simple, Kingsley Davis asks why so *few* rather than why so *many* women become prostitutes. Answering his own question, Davis suggests that the reward the prostitute secures through her activity is not one of labor, skill or capital, but one for loss of social standing and esteem caused by moral condemnation of the prostitute. While she undergoes a public status loss, she may still occupy a relatively high status within her reference group of prostitutes, especially if she discriminates among her customers, uses her earnings in a status-approved manner, and positively relates her sexual role to her other social roles.[31]

The successful prostitute is usually between 17 and 24.[32] Although some are married, most are single. While most prostitutes come from lower socioeconomic classes and are disproportionately recruited from racial minorities, they have generally been poorly integrated into normal social groups and frequently engage in the activity in order to increase their economic power. The common prostitute today charges from a few dollars to as high as $500 per sexual act. A normal "trick" (sexual intercourse) ranges in cost from $10 to $100. The cost partially depends upon what the traffic will bear, the status of the woman involved, the type of sexual act or acts desired, the overhead involved in maintaining a location for operations and other similar factors.

While evidence suggests that women who become prostitutes are more self-sufficient emotionally than other women, the majority seem to enter the profession because of its immediate monetary rewards. Despite common folklore, prostitutes generally do not hate men. The pimp-prostitute relationship is similar to that of husband and wife. The only variation is that economic role reversal has occurred.[33]

For most women, prostitution rarely becomes a permanent occupation and is likely to be abandoned when it is no longer rewarding. While she works, however, the prostitute is able to take care of the sexual needs of a large number of perverts, strangers, physically repulsive individuals and transitory men. Prostitution performs a function which "apparently no other institution fully performs."[34]

The Classification of Prostitutes • Prostitutes vary in type and skills. The *true prostitute*, estimated to approximate 300,000 or more women in the United States, is one who makes her living primarily from offering sexual favors for money.[35] But when all types are evaluated, they may be grouped in several different ways. Robert R. Bell categorizes prostitutes into 1) *street or bar girls* and 2) *call girls*. The customer visually screens the street or bar girl before engaging her services but secures access to the call girl without previously viewing her. The street-bar girl services a lower-middle or lower-class group of customers, while the call girl relates much more commonly to middle and upper-middle class clients. As a general rule, street girls are less attractive, less educated and receive less income from their work than call girls.[36]

Other researchers have classified prostitutes into the categories of 1) *streetwalkers or prostitutes operating alone;* 2) *inmates of an organized house of prostitution;* 3) *call girls;* and 4) *high-class, independent professional prostitutes.*[37] Even more basic is a functional classification of four basic types. The *call girl* works by telephone, contacting customers and making arrangements to meet them at designated places. The *hustler* usually operates as a street-walker or tavern pickup and services her clients in taxi-cabs, nearby hotels or handy apartments. The *door-knocker* walks the halls of cheap rooming houses or small hotels soliciting customers. The *factory girl,* working under the supervision of a madame, takes on all callers. The *party girl* and the *male homosexual prostitute* represent additional types who offer sexual favors for hire.[38]

The Call Girl • Often possessed by a confused self-image, a call girl is characterized by a high sense of dependency, gender role confusion, personal aggressiveness, and incomplete internal controls. By viewing the street-walker as an undesirable, she enhances her self-image at the other's expense. Despite being a call girl, she has a tendency to distrust other call girls with whom she may be in competition. As a person on call, her status depends upon her attractiveness as a person; the visible indications of her success as seen in dress, apartment, and financial security; and the status she affords her pimp. She represents a move away from the traditional whorehouse of ten or more women and the development of mobile prostitution on a smaller scale with a greater individuality of services.[39]

In one Los Angeles study of call girls, most were between 18 and 32 years of age. All but one of those in this age range had had contact with a person professionally involved in call girl activities, whether a "pimp" or another call girl, immediately before their entrance into the trade. Nearly one half reported that their initial contact was a call girl whom they had actively sought out in order to enter into prostitution. Several women within this study became call girls in order to maintain the love of their "pimps," who generally arranged for the training of his girls. Twenty-four were initially trained by experienced call girls in local apartments, usually over a 2 to 3 month period. Their education included an orientation to the way to obtain the fee, consume drugs and alcohol, converse with clients, practice sexual and physical hygiene and solicit customers by telephone. For the most part, the call girls in this sample represented a low-level skill group, whose economic existence centered around the "pimp" or depended upon the prospect book (in which they recorded their customers' names for future contact).[40]

A Montreal study disclosed that prostitutes are slow to accept new customers into their group and to organize and develop legitimations for their conduct. They have few reliable friends and allies, tend to be mobile, or, if remaining at a single location, to be identifiable to the police. Most tend to condemn those who condemn them. Although *call-girl hustlers,* a combined category, belong to a Montreal subculture, it is rather weak and its members are tied together largely through their stigmatized occupation.[41]

Prostitutes justify their sexual activity on the grounds that they are no worse than other persons and are commonly less hypocritical; they realize financial success; others depend upon their support; and they perform an important and necessary social function. They also hold that they serve as a safety outlet by protecting society from rapes, broken marriages and sexual perverts, and by assisting aging and lonely men fulfill their sexual needs. They also contend that they are more honest in their dealings with men than most women who simply utilize sexual gifts to manipulate males to their advantage.[42]

Male Prostitution and Male Prostitutes ● Male prostitution has been known to exist for centuries, but little attention has been paid to the activity until recently. Male prostitutes are generally classified simply as homosexual or heterosexual. The *homosexual male prostitute* has been represented in history as the temple prostitute in India and the Near East and the boy prostitute of Egypt, Persia, Greece, Rome, China and Japan. In contemporary society, he is less likely to be related to a religious belief system or dominant cultural practice and to be more of an independent operator who dispenses sexual services for a fee. Some estimate that there are greater numbers of male prostitutes in the United States currently then ever before because of the tendency of male homosexuals to engage young sex partners; however, exact figures on the number of practitioners are unavailable. *Male heterosexual prostitutes,* on the other hand, have seemingly remained rather minimal in number. Bell suggests that there are probably more male heterosexual prostitutes in American folklore than in reality, although the number of "playboys" making a living by providing "companionship" to supportive women would suggest that this may not be the case.[43]

While the exact scope and incidence of male homosexual prostitution is not well defined, it is known to exist. In recent years, some gangs have encouraged younger male members to hustle homosexuals in order to get their money. This usually involves a minimum legal risk on the youth's part inasmuch as the homosexual is not too likely to report his loss to the police. However, the health risk may be much greater inasmuch as current evidence suggests that a large percentage of the venereal disease problem is related to homosexual relations.[44] Male prostitutes most highly prized tend to be between 12 and 20 years of age.

The Control of Prostitution ● The first serious efforts to control prostitution were made in sixteenth century Europe following an epidemic of venereal disease. Paris prostitutes were later required by law to register as early as 1785. Napoleon Bonaparte established the French system of segregated control in 1808 in an effort to control the activity. Under his system, brothels and solicitations for prostitution were restricted to designated city districts; houses of prostitution were licensed by the state; medical examinations were required by the government. However, most such regulation attempts proved marginally effective. By 1899, an international congress held in London sought cooperation in elimination of the "white slave" traffic. In 1919 the League of Nations set up a fact-finding body and in 1946 the United Nations took over the international effort to eliminate or severely restrict prostitution. Commercialized sex was legally banned in France in 1946, in Belgium in 1948, and in Italy in 1958. After voting rights were extended to Japanese women after World War II, legislation to suppress commercial prostitution in Japan was enacted.

Control of Prostitution in the United States • First efforts to regulate prostitution in the United States on a federal level occurred in 1910 with the passage of the Mann Act, which prohibited the interstate transportation of women for immoral purposes. By 1941, it was a federal offense to practice prostitution in designated military neighborhoods. Federal immigration laws were also modified to prohibit the introduction of alien prostitutes into the United States and to limit the participation of prospective immigrants in prostitution for a five-year period upon entrance to the country under penalty of deportation.[45]

Because prostitution has now become highly mobile, many new procedures have been adopted in the attempt to control its operation. Penalties can now be lodged against bars and other places which permit prostitutes to frequent the premises, against persons who operate employment agencies and refer women to places of commercial trade, against taxi drivers who transport customers to prostitutes, or against persons who knowingly permit prostitutes to operate on premises which they own.

City ordinance restrictions, which often overlap with state statutes, are commonly more detailed in their scope and definitions. They have been used to restrict conduct in dance halls, dance academies, massage parlors, escort agencies, Turkish baths, or other fronts for possible prostitution activity. Laws or ordinances against solicitation, loitering, and aiding or abetting prostitution are most commonly applied to those offering rather than buying the services; however, this is slowly changing.[46] Due to the difficulty in securing convictions under current prostitution statutes, laws against street-walking, loitering in bars, solicitation for acts of prostitution, and being an inmate of a disorderly house have been progressively refined in recent years.

Legal prohibitions against pandering or procuring have also been designed to control an agent who books a female into a house of prostitution and/or supervises her career. Usually, the panderer-procurer uses physical or psychological coercion to control the female in the trade. The pimp, also recognized in law, works actively for his stable of prostitutes and solicits customers for them, living parasitically from their earnings. In some states, statutes against pandering or pimping also include prohibitions and sanctions against husbands who cause or permit wives to commit prostitution or to remain in the profession.

Health laws frequently used to apply to prostitution activity. Most health departments possess the power to seek out and quarantine persons with communicable diseases until they are cured; however, such power is rarely used despite the fact that many prostitutes, seemingly free from venereal disease, may actually spread syphilis and gonorrhea. Because a heavy dose of antibiotics taken before a vaginal smear test can issue in a negative reading, periodic medical examinations are ineffective in controlling the transmission of syphilis or gonorrhea. But for the detection of herpes simplex Type 2, caused by a virus and for which there is no known cure at this moment, an examination may prove valuable.[47]

Some attempts to control prostitution under civil regulations have taken the form of "red-light abatement laws," which permit the citizen to affirm that a particular operation is a public nuisance and to request the court to issue an abatement order which directs the sale of furniture, fixtures, and other contents of the building in which prostitution occurs. Also provided for under many of these laws are the sealing of the premises for a one-year period under the supervision of the court. Other attempts to restrict prostitution operations involve the revocation of a liquor license, business license, or other state or local enabling license necessary for continued legal operations.[48]

Sexual Deviation: Homosexuality

Homosexuality, a focus of major debate in recent years, is commonly noted as a sexual relationship with a member of one's own sex. As a term, the term homosexual is used to describe "individuals who participate in a special community of understanding wherein members of one's own sex are defined as the most desirable sexual objects and sociability is energetically organized around the pursuit and entertainment of these objects."[49] As a concept and category which finds much opposition from the gay community, homosexuality involves more than active or passive partners and tensions relating to masculine or feminine roles.

The Scope of Homosexuality • Homosexuality is not new to human society. It has existed as a form of sexual outlet since the creation of man. Socrates and Plato reportedly engaged in homosexual practices as did Virgil, Horace, Michelangelo, Alexander the Great, Julius Caesar, Charles XII of Sweden, Frederick the Great, William of Orange and Lawrence of Arabia.[50] In 49 of 76 folk societies studied by Clellan S. Ford and Frank A. Beach, homosexual activities of one type or another were held to be normal and socially acceptable "for certain members of the community."[51] However, an hypothesis of general approval of homosexuality in all ancient societies cannot be supported by existing evidence.[52] Some evidence suggests that many societies tolerated homosexuality behaviorally while prohibiting it legally.[53]

While Judaeo-Christian religious groups have historically supported some sanctions against homosexual relationships, the especially puritanical and austere groups have been most pronounced in their opposition to homosexual activity. As a consequence, while it is not a crime to be a homosexual in the United States, it is criminal to engage in specific homosexual acts, whether in the form of sodomy, fellatio, or mutual masturbation.[54] As in other forms of legislated deviance, the individual homosexual must break the law in order to fulfill his homosexual desires. Homosexual acts between women are generally not prohibited by law.[55]

The prosecution of homosexuals is difficult inasmuch as consenting homosexual participants are not likely to testify against their partners. They are most successfully charged when they have used force, have engaged in disruptive homosexual activity in public, or have been victimized by others. Harsh laws against homosexuality, even when they do exist, are rarely applied to the majority of homosexual offenders. Most laws dealing with the topic are directed against specific sexual acts, public indecency, and the corruption of minors inasmuch as simply being homosexual is not a crime in its own right.

Depending upon the persons involved and the situation in which the contact occurred, penalties for homosexual conduct range from a maximum of one year in prison in New York to life imprisonment in other states. Penalties for homosexual acts range commonly up to 10 or more years in prison. Some states which have sexual deviate or sexual psychopath laws permit the commitment of an offender for treatment until a psychiatrist or other medical or mental health official can guarantee that he will not once again engage in this behavior upon release.

While laws against sodomy and other "crimes against nature" serve as the vehicles for prosecution of homosexuals, law enforcement in recent years has tended to ignore homosexuals who cohabit or fraternize in private, despite police feelings of contempt for such persons. Larger communities tend to be more tolerant of homosexual activities than smaller ones.[56] The two cities of Amsterdam and San Francisco, among others, take an obvious permissive attitude towards homosexuality, permitting the operation of many homosexual gathering places.

While homosexual acts are not considered crimes in a large part of the world, nearly every state in the United States has some prohibition, quite commonly ignored, against this form of conduct. Nevertheless, homosexuals in large cities are usually permitted to frequent "gay" bars or other locations where they are allowed to establish liaisons as long as they do not hinder or undermine public sensibility or become obvious to the general public. Frequently referred to as a "crime without a victim" homosexuality depends upon the willingness of two partners of the same sex to share themselves with each other.[57]

As with prostitution, homosexual relationships have been generally unacceptable to society, because they disrupt the family as a primary group and as an accepted locus of sexual activity. As an activity, it forces at least one partner in the homosexual relationship to foresake traditional role models and assume practices generally held to be deviant conduct.[58] Consequently, the greater the success of the homosexual in the "straight" community, the greater his anxiety is likely to be about becoming discovered[59] or being subjected to sexual blackmail. An estimated 1 in 4 homosexuals has had trouble with police, 1 in 3 has been rolled by an attacker, and 1 in 7 has been blackmailed.[60]

There are other costs of being homosexual as well. One study of venereal disease indicated that approximately 7 percent of male patients with gonorrhea admitted that they had had homosexual contact in comparison to 57 percent of those male patients with syphilis.[61] The sexual contacts of homosexuals were twice as frequent as those of heterosexual males; the venereal diseases were most commonly spread through anal intercourse largely among those between ages 15 to 29.[62] In order to contain the venereal disease problem, one major city at least issued badges to those having undergone treatment, an action which, in turn, facilitates the making of contact between homosexuals.[63]

Establishing Homosexual Contacts • Homosexual alliances take many forms, ranging from transitory to permanent relationships. The greater numbers of homosexuals are likely to engage in rather impersonal and often anonymous contacts which minimize long-term involvement and encourage "cruising" for a new liaison at a local bar or some other homosexual gathering place. Those lacking sexual appeal frequently secure the services of a homosexual prostitute, often a male youth who makes himself available for hire.[64]

Male homosexuals have been categorized as "cruisers", confirmed homosexuals who seek out partners in bars, public restaurants or other locations; homosexuals who accept solicitation while not actively soliciting homosexual partners; or situational offenders who accept the oral sex offer of a cruiser for non-homosexual reasons (e.g., curiosity, need for money, and desire for variation in sexual release).[65] While homosexuals have been commonly viewed as security and employment risks, their vulnerability rests more in their susceptibility toward blackmail than in their general social threat to others. In recent years the movement to prohibit the firing of an individual upon discovery of homosexual tendencies has been gaining support within the courts.

Homosexuals come from all social classes, intelligence levels, occupations, educational statuses, and nationality units.[66] There is some indication that homosexuals are gaining support on American college campuses.[67] While largely hidden to the untrained eye, they are sometimes identifiable in terms of their voice, walk, speech, clothing, gestures, hairstyle, or role adaptation. An English study of homosexuals disclosed that while only 17 percent possessed some obvious feminine characteristic, 66 percent of the homosexuals in the study *believed* that they could be recognized by other homosexuals.[68]

The Frequency of Homosexuality • Sixty-four percent of the societies studied by Clellan S. Ford and Frank A. Beach viewed homosexual activity as normal and as a socially acceptable form of conduct for some members of the community. The remainder held homosexuality to be either totally absent, rare, or engaged in in secrecy.[69] While the exact volume of more recent homosexuality, especially in the United States, is not well documented, the Kinsey Report of the middle 1940's disclosed that nearly 37 percent of the white male population at that time engaged in some homosexual experience to the point of orgasm between adolescence and old age. However, only 4 percent of the male population had a strong adult inclination to homosexual activity. About 10 percent had more than a casual contact with homosexuals.[70] While males were more promiscuous, engaging in homosexual acts and experiences for a greater number of years than females, homosexuality among females, studied soon thereafter, was less than one half of that of males.[71] Only 4 percent of the males within the Kinsey sample maintained homosexuality as a life pattern. Thirteen percent of white American females had had an overt homosexual experience and 4 percent were exclusively homosexual.[72] One study in Great Britain estimated homosexuals to number 1 of every 20 persons.[73]

While most homosexual relationships, according to Kinsey's findings, were situational and transitory, taking place only once or twice a year, a report of the first homosexual experience of 127 British boys who eventually became homosexual cited that the act usually occurred with a schoolboy of the same age and reflected sex play, often in a school situation.[74] However, other studies have tended to dispute this finding.[75] Nevertheless, homosexual relationships often involve "one-night-stands" in which the partners engage in sexual activity for a few minutes or for several hours or in which a homosexual couple stays overnight or spends the weekend at some location. Highly transitory relations, they rarely blossom into a homosexual affair which may last for any length of time (weeks or months).

Sometimes, homosexuals will agree to "marry," a condition of greater relationship permanence than found in the "one-night-stand" or the "affair." An even smaller number will actually exchange rings and follow the action with a honeymoon.[76] But most homosexuals engage in transitory homosexual relationships which lead to the frequent establishment of relationships with new partners. In some instances, they may run into the hundreds. For example, two thirds of the adult males in one study had had relations with over 75 different homosexual partners.[77] Other evidence suggests that not all homosexual activity is carried out between consenting adults.[78]

Because the emphasis in homosexuality is largely upon youth, individuals past the age of 30 are looked upon as less desirable partners. In order to forestall the aging process, many middle-aged homosexuals, consequently, will attempt to act and dress as their younger counterparts.[79] Because the homosexual community emphasizes youth to an even greater extent than American society in general, the aging homosexual may have to pay for the services rendered by his younger partner, even to the extent of keeping a male "mistress."[80] In some instances, delinquent gang members have served such a function.[81] However, this is not without some risk to the "master." Between 25 and 33 percent of the homosexual respondents in one research sample indicated that they had been robbed by a sexual partner.[82]

The Development of Homosexual Commitments • During the Middle Ages, the cause of homosexuality was believed to be a supernatural possession of a man by devils.[83] As a greater understanding of the problem resulted, the nature and development of homosexuality was seen in a different light. More recently, homosexual development has been viewed in terms of a four-step progression. During the *first* stage, which usually takes place in the late teens or early 20's, the homosexual begins to drift away from his friends who start to date and eventually to marry. Gradually, he becomes aware of his isolation and his dissimilarity to his former friends. During the *second* stage, he regards himself as an outcast and finds that he is unable to control his problem through will power or self-control. If he does not move on immediately to the *third* stage, the point at which he begins to meet other homosexuals, frequents their meeting places, and joins a homosexual group, he may remain lonely and feel guilty. While he does not need to mask his homosexual inclination in this group, he nevertheless must make certain that his friends in the straight society do not learn of his subterranean activity. He remains a "closet" homosexual. At this point, he is usually forced to lead two lives. If he chooses to resolve this dilemma, he may move to the *fourth* stage in which he allows the gay way of life to dominate his time and his interest. Identifying exclusively and openly with a homosexual group, he begins to defend his actions and even to attack those outside this life-style.[84]

Some question such a progression and argue that adult homosexual patterns depend upon the structures and values which surround the homosexual as he conceives of himself as a homosexual and are not consistent and similar from one person to another.[85] Because the degree to which homosexuals commit their lives to homosexuality varies markedly, simple conceptions of homosexual behavior are inadequate. Homosexuals, Evelyn Hooker suggests, are isolated men who tend to be rather invisible within the dominant society,[86] largely because of societal pressure upon them to remain invisible.

Some evaluators of homosexuality assume that men become exclusive or true homosexuals because they are unable to make normal adjustments to the obligations, performances, and network of institutionalized expectations which compose life. Because homosexual relationships are less institutionalized, they seem less complicated and permit the male greater latitude in his actions. Such analysts contend that the homosexual's problem is one of flight from females rather than attraction to males[87] and should be viewed primarily in that light. Kingsley Davis hypothesizes that the failure of homosexuality to decrease as heterosexual freedom rises is due to the increase of personal anomie which encourages males to retreat into both durable and promiscuous homosexual relations.[88]

Whatever the development process, the propensity to homosexuality varies among individuals and may be acted out in alternate ways. While homosexuals have been known to range the spectrum from exaggerated effeminacy to excessive masculinity, two extremes that tend to overstate the homosexual's condition, homosexuality for most gays is not a simple matter of dress, voice, or mannerism. It is rather an orientation to life in which the most intimate relationships that the individual enjoys are with others of the same sex.

Attempts to differentiate homosexuals from heterosexuals through psychological testing to date has generally been unsuccessful.[89] Those who propose that homosexuality is due to hormone deficiencies or genetic variance have been unable to support their contention with scientific evidence. Some evidence supports the idea that it is related to an excessive attachment to a male's mother and a weak and unsatisfying relationship with one's father.[90] But recent actions by the American Psychiatric Association have de-escalated this interpretation by removing homosexual conduct from its lists of mental disorders.[91] Nevertheless, a significant number of analysts continue to view homosexuals as troubled, emotionally upset, or neurotic individuals, characteristics shared by many married heterosexuals.[92]

The Homosexual Subculture ● The importance of the homosexual community and subculture in providing its members with defined norms and values, gathering places, and routines for relating to other homosexuals cannot be overestimated. The subculture works to protect the homosexual from a perceived hostile environment and to provide secure locations for social relationships. Such homosexual meeting places, especially bars, are typically located in residential areas with large concentrations of homosexuals, areas of high tolerance toward many forms of deviant behavior, public entertainment districts of a city, and beaches or places where homosexuals gather for recreational activities.[93] A few such bars cater to a specific gay clientele and characteristically restrict the entrance of straights or other unrecognized homosexuals.[94] Approximately 30 San Francisco and 35 Los Angeles county bars during the 1960's, for example, catered to the homosexual trade.[95] Similar outlets exist even today in nearly every major city.

A major function of the homosexual bar is to permit individuals to establish contact with potential sexual partners. To a greater extent than is true for heterosexual bars, it serves as a "flesh market" in which partners are secured and information concerning future liaisons may be obtained.[96] While heterosexual bar patrons usually sit in pairs or small groups at a bar as they relate to one another, the homosexual, given his differing goals, will commonly sit at a homosexual bar facing the room and the door, looking for a viable partner.[97] However, homosexuals who frequent bars in order to be visible and to secure a homosexual partner are a minority among practicing homosexuals.

The Tearoom Trade ● Some homosexuals make their contacts in public baths or public restrooms, also known as "tearooms." At such locations, sex is clearly impersonal and transitory. After servicing each other, they depart quickly. In the tearoom, social roles revolve around the performing and receiving of a sex act. The performer, who is generally viewed as a homosexual, performs his act on those who stop by the tearoom, known as the "trade." One performer may fellate a large number of regulars who stop by the tearoom regularly on their way to and from work. A few may be part of the homosexual bar culture.[98] Members of the trade primarily seek in their tearoom encounter a sexual release, which falls somewhere between masturbation and a love relationship. Characteristically, tearoom participants avoid conversation with their sexual partner. Most tearoom homosexuals, one study uncovered, are lonely and isolated and have had little success in marriage and in work. Because the "trade" receive rather than give in the sexual act, they do not view themselves as homosexuals, despite the fact that they may well be arrested for their actions there.[99]

Female Homosexuals ● A lesbian or female homosexual is a woman who "feels a strong and recurring need to have sexual relations within an interpersonal context with another woman."[100] As an act and category of behavior, it too is not a new phenomenon. Lesbianism is reported in the Talmud and was probably common in the harums of Egypt and India. Sappho, a sixth century poet who lived on the island of Lesbos, is generally considered the first major advocate of female homosexuality.[101] However, the medieval church condemned homosexuality, a view which has dominated public attitudes in the Western world. Only 22 percent of the cultures studied by Ford and Beach provided an indication of existing female homosexuality.[102] Only 17 percent of American Indian cultures accepted a pattern of female homosexuality.[103]

Lesbians appear to have less need for participation in a subculture and seemingly mask their lesbianism "behind a socially prepared asexuality"[104] which society permits and even expects. Few persons, for example, think anything negative about unmarried females living together; they find it normal if women kiss and touch one another affectionately or seek out one another's company.[105] Given this setting, it is not too surprising that 5 percent of the women within the Kinsey study at the time of marriage reported at least one sexual experience leading to orgasm with another woman.[106] While 2 percent of the post-married women and 19 percent of the single women had homosexual experiences with other women, none of the married women had.[107] The highest percentage (10) of sexual orgasm among women was experienced by those in college. Most evidence fails to support the belief of some analysts that younger girls are seduced into lesbian activity by older women.[108]

Few laws pertaining to the control of female homosexuality exist. Where they do, they focus on the performance of an illegal homosexual act. However, women are rarely arrested or prosecuted for such activities. For example, Kinsey reported in 1953 that no women had been convicted of homosexual activities for more than 250 years. Only 4 members of his sample had difficulty at all with the police.[109] Even then, when lesbians were arrested, they were charged most frequently for loitering and soliciting another for deviant sexual relations.

Although lesbian and male homosexual subcultures are similar, the female homosexual subculture pattern is much less frantic. While overlapping with the male homosexual subculture, the lesbian pattern is for the most part distinct. The desire of many lesbians to become emotionally and sexually attached to another woman who responds to them as women reveals, in the eyes of John Gagnon and William Simon, a commitment to nineteenth century romanticism.[110] Because the emphasis is placed upon the emotional quality of female relationships, aging does not seem to present the same problem to lesbians as it does to male homosexuals.

A sample of burlesque strippers disclosed that 26 percent of the 35 respondents had participated in homosexual activities.[111] The isolation of the girls from meaningful social relationships, the restriction posed by their occupation, and the hours they worked tended to encourage homosexual contacts. At the same time, the strippers were often disillusioned with men and viewed their customers with contempt, an attitude which reinforced the isolation of strippers from men generally.[112] Given the circumstances, burlesque strippers tended to accept lesbianism as an acceptable social response.

Female homosexuals are not restricted to the burlesque sorority. Lesbian bars, of which there are fewer than male homosexual bars, serve as social centers for many women within the lesbian subculture. Less emphasis is placed upon meeting a potential partner ("cruising") and more upon general sociability. Common activities at the bar include talking, drinking and dancing. Overall, lesbians tend to be less promiscuous and more faithful to their partners than male homosexuals. Approximately one half the single females responding to one study had homosexual relations with a single partner. Nevertheless, approximately 20 percent had had relations with 2 different, 29 percent with 3 or more, and 4 percent with more than 10 partners.[113]

Heterosexuality and Homosexuality Among Prisoners ● According to one classification system, four types of sexuality are expressed within a prison setting. An *exclusive heterosexual* is unwilling or unable to engage in homosexual acts while confined; the *exclusive homosexual,* on the other hand, finds his homosexual needs effectively gratified within confinement. The *primarily heterosexual who participates* does so because of this prison isolation, but the *primarily heterosexual but occasionally homosexual* follows a pattern common to his life outside the walls.[114]

Although studies of prison homosexuality reveal high incidence of the practice among male prisoners, prison lesbianism data disclose interesting insights into their problem. Approximately 50 percent of the inmates of the Frontera Institution for Women in California represented in one study participated in lesbian activities as a means of compensation for the loss of support and protection of parents, husband, or lover and to regain a sense of security. Non-homosexual women were forced to come to terms with the homosexual prison problem. To a large number of women, homosexuality represented a temporary adaptation to the existing environment.[115] Homosexual love affairs were forms of attempted compensation "for the mortification of the self suffered during imprisonment."[116] An estimated 30 to 40 percent of the "butch" population (male role assumers) were introduced to homosexuality for the first time while in prison. Women who "turn-out" do so not as homosexuals but as a "butch" or "femme." The choice that a woman makes speaks to her needs, her self-image, and her social and sexual commitments in the free heterosexual world. A large portion of those women who do "turn-out" expect to resume heterosexual relationships upon release.[117] While a pioneering study by Donald Clemmer of 2,300 adult male prisoners reported in 1940 disclosed that 10 percent were true homosexuals and 30 percent partly homosexual,[118] more recent assessments by Robert Bell suggest that a larger proportion of women than men have homosexual experience while in prison.[119]

Research at the Federal Reformatory for Women at Alerson, West Virginia has provided data that homosexual behavior was punished officially only if participants were found in bed together, a decision which challenged the predominant views of the custodial staff. Only an estimated 5 percent of the inmate population engaged in homosexual activities in the free community. Not only was the homosexual diad looked upon as a source of meaningful personal and social relationships by inmates, but several roles were associated with the "homosexual cluster." For example, the *penitentiary turnout* engages in prison homosexuality but differs from the lesbian who prefers homosexual relations in the free as well as the prison community. The *femme* or *mommy* takes the female role in the homosexual relationship even as the *stud* or *daddy* assumes the male. The *trick,* held generally in low esteem, fails to develop a sincere homosexual relationship and permits herself to be exploited by other inmates. The *commissary hustler* allows herself a single homosexual relationship with an inmate living in the same cottage but also establishes ties with additional tricks in other cottages for economic purposes. The *chippie* permits no stable relationship to develop and generally plays the role of the prison prostitute. *Kick-partners* participate in relatively nonpermanent physical relationships for the release of sexual tensions, while *cherries* are women who have never been initiated into homosexual practices and have never engaged in prison homosexuality. The *punk* is one who assumes the passive female role, and the *turnabout* alternately plays both male and female roles. In the female prison the homosexual diad relationship serves as a kinship system which stabilizes inmate community relationships and meets diverse interests, sentiments, and social-psychological needs.[120]

The Changing Approach to the Homosexuality Problem • Attitudes toward the acceptance or control of homosexuality are undergoing rapid change at this moment. While earlier attempts to solve the homosexual problem have generally taken the form of modification of social norms, thereby eliminating the problem of legislation, and of encouragement of homosexuals to accept treatment for their deviance, the organization of the gay counterculture has led to a challenge of former definitions of the problem. The most noticeable examples of a changing normative standard can be seen in the decriminalization of homosexual relations between consenting adults in 1967 in Great Britian and the 1974 referendum in the American Psychiatric Association authorizing the declassification of homosexuality as a mental disorder.[121] Both actions represent the elimination of the problem by a reclassification of conduct. But not all segments of society are prepared to accept this approach. Some still insist upon a treatment model, which in the past has been rather sporadic and marked by only limited success. It has not only been costly but has also demanded a lengthy treatment process.

Compounding the whole issue are public attitudes toward homosexuals and homosexuality and the attitudes of homosexuals toward themselves. Many of the negative feelings toward homosexuality, according to psychiatrist Karl Menninger, are examples of what happens when a community equates a crime (a legal category) with a sin (a theological category).[122] But the issue is not simply one of equating; it is also one of labeling and stigmatizing. Some analysts question whether the labeling and stigmatizing processes, which create a "bounded category of deviant actors" and an image of large classes of deviant persons, are truly valid. To interpret a person's actions in the framework of this homosexuality, they infer, is to admit failure to their activities within a variety of situations, while secondary participants do so in the context of their current situation.[123]

Whether homosexuality will gain full public acceptance, while unclear, appears unlikely. Although the homosexual movement has received major publicity through the news media and a degree of acceptance on some college campuses and from the public, it still represents a highly visible (for some) and yet invisible (for others) "homosexual minority." Although some legislators have sponsored bills that would permit homosexual practices between consenting adults, they have not accepted the principle that homosexuals should be permitted to marry. For example, Illinois, which has lifted penalties against private homosexual or heterosexual acts by consenting adults, has not moved in this direction. Data concerning the direction of legislation is actually mixed with at least 9 states having recently decreased the penalty for sodomy with 5 or more having increased it. It still is unsafe for gay "prostitutes", politicians, policemen, teachers, ministers and others to surface and openly express their homosexual preference.

While no one can accurately predict what the effect of liberalization of homosexual laws will be, some believe that the removal of criminal penalties will potentially lead latent homosexuals who now refrain from engaging in homosexual relationships due to their fear of the law to become overt homosexuals.[124] However, Kingsley Davis questions whether the acceptance of homosexuality as a sexual pattern can be maintained once it has been normatively regularized and institutionalized. Will not many choose to be heterosexual rather than homosexual once homosexual roles no longer serve as an avenue of neurotic escape, an expression of social hostility, or a means of protest?[125] There is, of course, no immediate scientific answer to that question.

Some analysts of homosexual patterns believe that public acceptance of such conduct for consenting and discreet adults has been increasing, but that in many places reaction is also hardening.[126] Not surprisingly, it is rare, so far, to find male homosexuality among "swingers," couples who engage in sexual relations with one or more individuals or couples.[127] However, female homosexuality among them is somewhat more common.

The Homophile Movement • Moves to lessen the stigma of homosexuality have increased with the advent of a greater social consciousness of minority rights. In the last decade, approximately 150 homosexual associations and many clubs have moved with varying success to defend homosexuality and the homophile movement.[128] While the Mattachine Society and One, Incorporated, numbering both sexes among their members, emphasize male homosexual problems, the Daughters of Bilitis focuses upon lesbian concerns. In recent years the latter has emerged as the leading association in defense of lesbian activities. Founded in 1955, it has worked to eliminate discrimination against lesbians and to seek more positive public responses toward female homosexual activities.

Most homophile organizations are composed of middle-class persons who express middle-class values. These organizations face major obstacles to group development due to the fear of later consequences, apathy caused by segmental (partial) homosexuality, and feelings of self-guilt and self-pity.[129] Nevertheless, the Daughters of Bilitis and the Mattachine Society have continued to lobby for legislative change that would permit the legalization of intrasex marriage. Several homosexual-oriented churches in major urban areas have recently advertised their services. The Metropolitan Community Church, which claims 67 affiliates, expanded into Australia in late 1974. During 1971, two Minnesota males and two Wisconsin females applied for marriage licenses as homophiles, but their applications were denied and they received only limited public support. What will occur in the future will only be known then.

References

1. Richard D. Knudten, *Crime in a Complex Society* (Homewood, Ill.: Dorsey Press, 1970), p. 183.
2. Robert R. Bell, *Social Deviance* (Homewood, Ill.: Dorsey Press, 1971), p. 226.
3. Kingsley Davis, "The Sociology of Prostitution," *American Sociological Review,* (October, 1937), II, 747.
4. Bell, *Social Deviance,* p. 227.
5. Kingsley Davis, "Sexual Behavior," *Contemporary Social Problems,* eds. Robert K. Merton and Robert A. Nisbet. (New York: Harcourt, Brace and World, 1971), p. 348.
6. Harry Benjamin and R. E. L. Masters, *Prostitution and Morality* (New York: Julian Press, 1964), pp. 21-86; and Bell, *Social Deviance,* pp. 228-229.
7. Howard C. Freeman and Wyatt C. Jones, *Social Problems: Causes and Controls* (Chicago: Rand-McNally, 1970), p. 395.
8. "Regulations of Vice," *Encyclopedia Americana,* (1945), XXVIII, 58.
9. B. J. George, Jr., "Prostitution," *Sexual Behavior and the Law,* ed. Ralph Slovenko. (Springfield, Ill.: C. C. Thomas, 1955), p. 659.
10. Benjamin and Masters, *Prostitution and Morality,* pp. 52-53.
11. Bell, *Social Deviance,* p. 232.
12. T. C. Esselstyn, "Prostitution in the United States," *Annals,* (March, 1968), CCCLXXVI, 127.
13. Alfred C. Kinsey, Wardell B. Pomeroy, Clyde E. Martin and Paul H. Gebhard, *Sexual Behavior in the Human Male* (Philadelphia: Saunders, 1948), p. 411.

14. Alfred C. Kinsey, Wardell B. Pomeroy, Clyde E. Martin and Paul H. Gebhard, *Sexual Behavior in the Human Female* (Philadelphia: Saunders, 1953), p. 300.
15. Davis, "Sexual Behavior," p. 350.
16. Kinsey, *Human Female*, pp. 249-302.
17. Kinsey, *Human Male*, pp. 599-604.
18. Marshall B. Clinard, *Sociology of Deviant Behavior* (New York: Holt, Rinehart and Winston, 1968), p. 372.
19. Vance Packard, *The Sexual Wilderness* (New York: McKay, 1968), pp. 161-166.
20. Bell, *Social Deviance*, p. 231.
21. William J. Goode, "Family Disorganization," *Contemporary Social Problems,* pp. 479-552.
22. Edwin H. Lemert, *Social Pathology* (New York: McGraw-Hill, 1951), p. 257.
23. Clinard, *Sociology of Deviant Behavior*, pp. 384-385.
24. Bell, *Social Deviance*, p. 229.
25. Knudten, *Crime in a Complex Society*, pp. 184-185.
26. *Newsweek*, March 9, 1970, p. 81.
27. Bell, *Social Deviance*, p. 229.
28. Edwin M. Lemert, "Prostitution," *Problems of Sex Behavior*, eds. Edward Sagarin and Donald E. MacNamara (New York: Crowell, 1968), p. 84.
29. Benjamin and Masters, *Prostitution and Morality*, pp. 93-94.
30. Davis, *Sexual Behavior*, p. 348.
31. *Ibid*, pp. 342-347.
32. Clinard, *Sociology*, p. 379.
33. Lemert, *Problems*, pp. 105-106; James H. Bryan, "Apprenticeships in Prostitution," *Social Problems,* (Winter, 1965), XII, 105-106, 292; and Travis Hirschi, "The Professional Prostitute," *Berkeley Journal of Sociology,* (1962), VII, 33-49.
34. Davis, *Sexual Behavior*, p. 357.
35. Clinard, *Sociology*, p. 372.
36. Bell, *Social Deviance*, p. 233.
37. Walter C. Reckless, *Vice in Chicago* (Chicago: University of Chicago Press, 1933); and Clinard, *Sociology*, p. 377.
38. Frederick W. Egam, *Plainclothesmen* (New York: Greenberg, 1952), pp. 100-104.
39. Bryan, *Social Problems*, pp. 287-297; New York Times (April 2, 1974); Harold Greenwald, *The Call Girl* (New York: Ballatine, 1958); and James H. Bryan, "Occupational Ideologies and Individual Attitudes of Call Girls," *Social Problems*, (1966), XIII, 445.
40. Bryan, "Apprenticeships," *Social Problems*, pp. 287-297.
41. H. Taylor Buckner, *Deviance, Relevance and Change* (New York: Random House, 1971), pp. 261-269.
42. Norman R. Jackman, Richard O'Toole, and Gilbert Geis, "The Self-Image of the Prostitute," *Sociological Quarterly,* (1963), IV, 150-162.
43. Bell, *Social Deviance*, p. 230.
44. Benjamin and Masters, *Prostitution*, pp. 290-303.
45. Knudten, *Crime*, p. 184.
46. George, Jr., *Sexual Behavior*, pp. 646-650.
47. *The National Observer* (May, 1974).
48. Knudten, *Crime*, pp. 185-186.
49. Erving Goffman, *Stigma: Notes on the Management of Spoiled Identity* (Englewood Cliffs, N.J.: Prentice-Hall, 1965), pp. 143-144.
50. Bryan Magee, *One in Twenty: A Study of Homosexuality in Men and Women* (New York: Stein and Day, 1966), p. 46.

51. Clellan S. Ford and Frank A. Beach, *Patterns of Sexual Behavior* (New York: Harper and Row, 1952), p. 130.
52. Kingsley Davis, "Sexual Behavior," *Contemporary Social Problems*, eds. Robert K. Merton and Robert Nisbet (New York: Harcourt, Brace and Jovanovich, 1971), p. 353.
53. George P. Murdock, *Social Structure* (New York: Macmillan, 1949), p. 317; and Otto Kiefer, *Sexual Life in Rome* (New York: Duffon, 1935).
54. "The Consenting Adult Homosexual and the Law," *UCLA Law Review*, (March, 1966), pp. 658.
55. Morris Ploscowe, *Sex and the Law* (Englewood Cliffs, N.J.: Prentice-Hall, 1951).
56. *UCLA Law Review*, p. 730.
57. Edwin M. Schur, *Crimes Without Victims* (Englewood Cliffs, N.J.: Prentice-Hall, 1965), pp. 169-178.
58. Davis, *Social Problems*, pp. 323-339.
59. Bell, *Social Deviance*, p. 279.
60. William Simon and John H. Gagnon, "Homosexuality," *Social Problems: Persistent Challenges*, eds. Edward C. McDonagh and Jon E. Simpson (New York: Holt, Rinehart and Winston, 1969), pp. 531-537.
61. E. Randolph Trice, "Venereal Disease and Homosexuality," *Medical Aspects of Human Sexuality* (January, 1969), p. 70.
62. *Ibid.*, p. 71.
63. Davis, *Social Problems*, p. 359.
64. Albert J. Reiss, Jr., "The Social Integration of Queers and Peers," *Social Problems*, (Fall, 1961), IX, 102-120.
65. *UCLA Law Review*, pp. 688-690.
66. Barbara Wooton, *Social Science and Social Pathology* (London: George Allen, 1959).
67. *New York Times* (June 5, 1974).
68. Gordon Westwood, *A Minority Report on the Life of the Male Homosexual in Great Britain* (London: Longmans, Green and Co., 1960), pp. 61-63.
69. Ford and Beach, *Patterns of Sexual Behavior*, pp. 129-130.
70. Alfred C. Kinsey, Wardell B. Pomeroy, and Clyde E. Martin, *Sexual Behavior in the Human Male* (Philadelphia: Saunders, 1949), pp. 639-641.
71. *Ibid.*, pp. 640-644; also see Alfred C. Kinsey, Wardell B. Pomeroy, Clyde E. Martin and Paul H. Gebhard, *Sexual Behavior in the Human Female* (Philadelphia: Saunders, 1953).
72. Kinsey, *Human Male*, pp. 600651; and Kinsey, *Human Female*, pp. 474-475.
73. Magee, *One in Twenty*, pp. 43-46.
74. Westwood, *A Minority Report*, pp. 24-39.
75. Paul H. Gebhard, *Sex Offenders* (New York: Harper and Row, 1965), pp. 345-636.
76. David Sonenschein, "The Ethnograhy of Male Homosexual Relations," *Journal of Sex Research*, (May, 1968), IV, 80-81.
77. Gebhard, *Sex Offenders*, p. 344.
78. Reiss, *Social Problems*, pp. 102-120.
79. Tom Burke, "The New Homosexuality," *Esquire*, (December, 1969), LXXII, 308.
80. John H. Gagnon and William Simon, "Homosexuality: A Formulation of a Sociological Perspective," *Journal of Health and Social Behavior*, (September, 1967), VIII, 177-185; and Sonenschein, *Journal of Sex Research*, p. 75.
81. Albert J. Reiss, "The Social Integration of Queers and Peers," *The Other Side*, ed. Howard S. Becker. (New York: Free Press, 1964), p. 207.
82. Gagnon and Simon, *Journal of Health*, p. 354.
83. Bell, *Social Deviance*, p. 248.

84. Michael Schofield, *The Sociological Aspects of Homosexuality* (Boston: Little, Brown and Co., 1965).
85. Gagnon and Simon, *Journal of Health,* p. 532.
86. Evelyn Hooker, "An Empirical Study of Some Relations Between Sexual Patterns and Gender Identity in Male Homosexuals," *Sex Research: New Development,* ed. John Money (New York: Holt; Rinehart and Winston, 1965), pp. 25-26.
87. Donald W. Cory, "Homosexuality," *Encyclopedia of Sexual Behavior,* eds. Albert Ellis and Albert Abarbanel. (New York: Hawthorne Books, 1961), p. 492; and Davis, *Social Problems,* p. 356.
88. Davis, *Social Problems,* p. 358.
89. Naomi Weisstein, "Woman as Nigger," *Psychology Today,* (October, 1969), III, 22.
90. Eva Bene, "On the Genesis of Male Homosexuality," *Deviant Behavior and Social Process,* ed. William A. Rushing. (Chicago: Rand McNally, 1969), pp. 163-164.
91. *New York Times* (May 2, 1974).
92. Wardell B. Pomeroy, "Homosexuality," *The Same Sex: An Appraisal of Homosexuality,* ed. Ralph A. Weltgage. (Philadelphia: Pilgrim Books, 1969).
93. Hooker, *Sex Research,* p. 95.
94. *UCLA Law Review,* pp. 689-690.
95. *IBID.,* p. 689.
96. Martin Hoffman, *The Gay World* (New York: Bantam Books: 1968), p. 51.
97. *Ibid.,* pp. 53-54.
98. Laud Humphreys, "Tearoom Trade: Impersonal Sex in Public Places," *Transactions,* (January, 1970), VII, 12-13.
99. *Ibid.,* pp. 17-18.
100. Bell, *Social Deviance,* p. 292.
101. Richard Lewinsohn, *A History of Sexual Relations* (New York: Harper, 1958), pp. 59-60.
102. Ford and Beach, *Patterns of Sexual Behavior,* p. 4.
103. Pomeroy, *The Same Sex,* p. 4.
104. Gagnon and Simon, *Journal of Health,* p. 262.
105. John H. Gagnon and William Simon, "Sexual Deviance in Contemporary America," *Annals,* (March, 1968), VIII, 118.
106. Kinsey, *Human Female,* p. 488.
107. *Ibid.,* p. 562.
108. *Ibid.,* p. 488; and John H. Gagnon and William Simon, *Sexual Deviance* (New York: Harper and Row, 1967), pp. 255-260.
109. Kinsey, *Human Female,* p. 484.
110. Gagnon and Simon, *Sexual Deviance,* pp. 265-275.
111. Charles H. McCaghy and James A. Skipper, Jr., "Lesbian Behavior as an Adaptation to the Occupation of Stripping," *Social Problems,* (Fall, 1969), XVII, 263-270.
112. *Ibid.,* pp. 265-269.
113. Kinsey, *Human Female,* p. 458.
114. Donald W. Cory, "Homosexuality in Prison," *Journal of Social Therapy,* (April, 1955), I, 137-140.
115. Richard D. Knudten, *Crime in a Complex Society,* pp. 593-597.
116. David A. Ward and Gene G. Kassebaum, *Women's Prison* (Chicago: Aldine, 1965), pp. 15-92.
117. David A. Ward and Gene G. Kassebaum, "Homosexuality: A Mode of Adaptation in a Prison for Women," *Social Problems,* (Fall, 1964), XII, 74-76.
118. Donald Clemmer, *The Prison Community* (New York: Rinehart, 1958), pp. 257-263.
119. Bell, *Social Deviance,* p. 293.

120. Rose Giallombardo, *Society of Women* (New York: Wiley, 1966), pp. 41-139.
121. *New York Times* (April 4, 1974).
122. Karl Menniger, "Committee on Homosexual Offenses and Prostitution," in *The Wolfenden Report* (New York: Stein and Day, 1963), p. 9.
123. Clinard, *Sociology.*
124. Gagnon and Simon, "Sexual Deviance in Contemporary America," *Annals,* pp. 115-117.
125. Davis, *Social Problems,* p. 360.
126. Robert V. Sherwin, "Laws on Sex Crimes," *Encyclopedia of Sexual Behavior* (New York: Hawthorne Books, 1961), pp. 626-627.
127. Bell, *Social Deviance,* p. 82.
128. Edward Sagarin, *Odd Man In: Societies of Deviants in America* (Chicago: Quadrangle, 1969), p. 345.
129. Buckner, *Deviance,* pp. 336-337.

CHAPTER 4

Mental Illness and Suicide

The Scope of Mental Illness

Although those with mental illness or disorder were described in past generations as possessed of demons and devils or as lunatics and madmen, mental problems and disorders in recent decades have been largely viewed as illnesses. The nature and scope of mental illness, however, is highly debatable. Psychiatrist Thomas Szasz, takes the position that what is commonly viewed as a mental disorder is simply an inadequate method for facing life's problems.[1] Others offer quite varied viewpoints. Regardless of their conception of the problem, however, their views represent generally an advance over the crude conceptions of previous civilizations.

The Growth of the Mental Illness-Disorder Concept ● An early modern attempt to make general approach to problems of mental illness more realistic and in line with growing scientific knowledge was undertaken by Dorothea Dix, who campaigned in 1841 for separate American institutions for the insane, and by Clifford W. Beers, who organized state mental hygiene societies and the National Committee for Mental Hygiene in 1909. Their efforts and those of affiliated mental health associations were instrumental in lessening the fear and stigma surrounding mental illness and in developing a medical interpretation of the problem. However, added momentum was given to the mental hygiene movement by the psychiatric and psychological problems resulting from World Wars I and II, the latter stimulating the creation of the National Institutes of Mental Health, designed to launch a full-scale national program to meet the challenges posed by mental illness and disorder problems. At this point, the issue could no longer be avoided. The more than 500,000 men who were rejected for service during World War II and the additional 300,000 who were discharged from the military for some form of psychoneurosis brought the issue of widespread mental illness and disorder into the open.[2]

In recent years between 2½ and 3 million persons yearly have been cared for either as outpatients or inpatients at mental health facilities in the United States. Approximately 1,200,000 persons are served yearly by outpatient psychiatric clinics and an additional 1,100,000 in county, state, federal or private mental hospitals. Some 500,000 persons also receive care at general hospitals providing psychiatric services. An estimated 400,000 adults are daily under treatment in mental hospitals in the United States. Nearly 4 in every 10 hospital beds are filled by mental patients, most are short-term. Many, however, are treated in the nearly 300 existing state and county mental hospitals.[3] Approximately one in every 12 persons will spend some time in a mental hospital before his death, although recent trends toward normalization of living relationships may reduce this ratio in the future. An overview of the distribution of patients in health-related institutions over three decades is present in Table 4.1.

The Diagnosis of Mental Disorders • A patient's treatment depends upon the adequacy of diagnosis regarding his condition. However, the more serious the mental illness, the less likely the patient is to recognize that he is ill and to seek assistance. As a result, a mental condition may go untreated or even unrecognized for months and even years. According to John Clausen, what makes mental illness the illness it is is the patient's inability to realize that he needs help for his sickness and that his problem causes disruption in interpersonal relationships.[4] Such disruption of capacity for real relationships and for pursuit of subcultural rewards is characteristic of the mentally disordered person's inner conflict, a conflict of self.[5] While this may be true, such a broad conception of the problem is itself a challenge inasmuch as a clinic evaluation of general public behavior in psychiatric terms would reveal that most people undergo periods of self-doubt and are generally selective in their relationships. David Rosenthal, however, suggests that some individuals have greater predispositions to mental illness than others.[6]

The Bases of Mental Disorders • Some mental disorders have their foundation in physical problems; others have their actual grounding in mental sources and processes. A third group involves both physical and mental dimensions. Historically, mental disorders have been classified into the three major groups of psychoses, neuroses and psychosomatic disorders. While the *psychoses* have been generally described as a major disjointment of mental processes and an inability to perceive external reality in a correct manner, *neuroses* have been conceived as entailing emotional discomfort and functional impairment without a sharp break with reality. *Psychosomatic disorders,* the third major classification, normally involve some form of organic or physical problem with a psychological overtone. Although the dichotomies of insanity and sanity are used to picture the condition of a criminal defendant in a court of law, these terms have little

TABLE 4.1

PATIENTS IN HEALTH-RELATED INSTITUTIONS: 1950, 1960, AND 1970 BY TYPE OF DISABILITY AND AGE

| | NUMBER OF PATIENTS | | | PERCENT OF PATIENTS | |
YEAR AND TYPE OF INSTITUTION	TOTAL	UNDER 65 YEARS OLD	65 YEARS OLD AND OVER	UNDER 65 YEARS OLD	65 YEARS OLD AND OVER
1950					
Mental hospitals	613,628	472,282	141,346	77.0	23.0
Homes and schools for mentally handicapped	134,189	130,005	4,184	96.9	3.1
Homes for the aged and dependent	296,783	79,247	217,536	26.7	73.3
Tuberculosis hospitals	76,291	69,699	6,592	91.4	8.6
Other chronic disease hospitals[1]	20,084	11,227	8,857	55.9	44.1
Homes and schools for physically handicapped	20,999	(NA)	(NA)	(NA)	(NA)
1960					
Mental hospitals	630,046	452,206	177,840	71.8	28.2
Homes and schools for mentally handicapped	174,727	169,965	4,762	97.3	2.7
Homes for the aged and dependent	469,717	81,764	387,953	17.4	82.6
Tuberculosis hospitals	65,009	50,811	14,198	78.2	21.8
Other chronic disease hospitals	42,476	19,312	23,164	45.5	54.5
Homes and schools for physically handicapped	24,291	(NA)	(NA)	(NA)	(NA)
1970					
Mental hospitals	433,890	320,847	113,043	73.9	26.1
Homes and schools for mentally handicapped	201,992	191,265	10,727	94.7	5.3
Homes for the aged and dependent	927,514	131,707	795,807	14.2	85.8
Tuberculosis hospitals	16,912	11,844	5,068	70.0	30.0
Other chronic disease hospitals	67,120	31,928	35,192	47.6	52.4
Homes and schools for physically handicapped	22,739	(NA)	(NA)	(NA)	(NA)

NA Not available.

[1] Identified as "Other special hospitals" in 1950 census reports.

Source: Bureau of the Census, *1950 Census of Population*, Vol. IV, Part 2C; *1960 Census of Population*, Vol. II, Part 2C; *1970 Census of Population*, Vol. II, Part 8A; *1970 Census of Population*, Vol. II, Part 4E.

Source: Executive Office of the President, OMB, *Social Judicators, 1973* (Washington, D.C.: U.S. Government Printing Office, 1973), p. 33.

validity in mental diagnosis. They represent the attempt to capture and categorize the various complex mental illnesses within simple legal categories.

The Psychoneuroses and Psychoses ● The *psychoneuroses,* which are common to large proportions of any population, are related to anxiety or disorders caused by anxiety. They commonly take the form of *anxiety reaction,* where the response pattern is diffuse or uncontrolled; *conversion reaction,* in which the neurosis causes organic dysfunctions; *phobic reaction,* where it is expressed as fear of some object, idea, or situation; *obsessive-compulsive reaction,* in which anxiety is related to morbid or unreasonable acts; and *depressive reaction,* where one appears anxious about his past failures and/or conduct. *Psychoses,* on the other hand, interrupt the ability of the psychotic person to communicate coherently with others or to follow accurately prescribed norms. Because psychoses cause deviation from general social norms, psychotic behavior is generally more serious than neurotic conduct.[7]

Schizophrenia, manic-depressive reactions and involutional melancholia are commonly classified as *functional psychoses* that have no clearly defined organic or structural cause and are believed to be psychological in character. *Schizophrenia,* which occurs frequently among young adults, involves the separation of emotion from cognitive functioning. It may include psychological withdrawal and the development of a split personality, which is revealed through delusions, odd associations, and the like. Schizophrenia is often differentiated into simple, hebephrenic, paranoid, and catatonic subtypes. About one fourth of those who enter mental hospitals over the age of 40 are institutionalized for this problem. The schizophrenic is usually identified by his inability to relate to people and by his general withdrawal from social situations. He also possesses an ability to distort communication with others and to disqualify the sources and/or the message relating to his person.[8]

The other two forms of functional psychoses tend to be more common among the middle and older-aged. The *manic-depressives,* will alternately be extremely excited and aggressive and later depressed and brooding. His disorder tends to be episodic. While the recurrence of such an illness is common, the manic-depressive is more likely to recover completely than is the schizophrenic. Those diagnosed as *involutional psychotics* have commonly undergone a physical change of life.[9]

Schizophrenia and the Schizophrenic ● As noted, schizophrenia is characterized by an individual's withdrawal from the world and his inability to assume prescribed roles. Indifferent and passive, the schizophrenic, commonly a young adult, creates an imaginary world in which hallucinations, voices, and other perceptions dominate his person. His emotional self is frequently detached from his intellectual self, revealing a split personality.

Simple schizophrenics tend to withdraw and to daydream. Becoming listless and apathetic, they forget their ambitions and lose interest in life. Rarely are they institutionalized, inasmuch as they present no threat to society or to themselves. *Hebephrenic schizophrenics,* on the other hand, may disclose symptoms of delusions, hallucinations, or odd behavior in the form of excessive smiling, silliness, and excessive gesturing as part of their disorder. *Paranoid schizophrenics* are at times both emotionally indifferent and responsive to various perceptions and noises. Their delusions of persecution are transitory and vary with their perceptions of reality. *Catatonic schizophrenics* tend to be both apathetic and impulsive, living in their own world. Common symptoms include a complete withdrawal from social consciousness, stupor, severe depressions, frenzied actions, and/or increased talking.[10]

According to Faris, the schizophrenic is a seclusive or "shut-in" person.[11] One study of 53 catatonic schizophrenics revealed that they were deficient in their ability to handle interpersonal relations with members of the opposite sex and had relatively low peer group contact.[12] While the lowest socioeconomic groups have a higher rate of disclosed schizophrenia, professional and prominent persons disclose higher rates of manic-depressant conduct.[13] The manic-depressive person experiences repression from relative- or work-associated problems, and the involutional psychotic, rejectioning retirement, gradually withdraws from social interaction. Overall, schizophrenia, manic-depressiveness, and involutional psychosis are probably related to the individual's attempt to conform to strict standards of an authoritarian parent. However, both neurotics and psychotics have fathers and/or mothers who emphasize traditional aspirations and demand perfection.[14]

Schizophrenia tends to be related in varying degrees to both hereditary characteristics and environmental stresses. Some evidence suggests that the families of schizophrenic patients are quite different in their dynamics from those of so-called normal families. If the child does not receive affection and emotional support from his family or from his relationships with others, he will be vulnerable to schizophrenia, especially if the combination of genes encouraging this likelihood are inherited. "If such vulnerability," Clausen notes, "is coupled with even a small degree of genetic vulnerability, schizophrenia may result."[15] In a more favorable family environment, the same genetic characteristic may not result in symptoms of this disorder. Genetic studies in the last few decades have uncovered that approximately 10 percent of the offspring of one schizophrenic parent and 40 to 50 percent of those from two schizophrenic parents eventually develop schizophrenia.[16] However, the assumption that schizophrenia is totally due to a genetic factor faces major criticism today.[17]

Despite the source or cause of the problem, the costs of mental illness or disorder are especially high for some persons. Under certain state laws, it is possible for a physician to have his license suspended when diagnosed as a psychotic. Some states suspend drivers' licenses. The Federal government refuses to permit such a person's induction into the Armed Forces or to grant him a security clearance. Schizophrenics who are functionally able to operate within society will be forced in some instances to undergo treatment in a mental hospital when convicted of a misdeameanor or lesser felony, while their nondiagnosed counterpart may receive probation or the light sentence commonly granted first offenders.

Disorders of the Aging ● Among older persons, mental disorders have commonly taken the forms of *senile dementia* and *psychosis with cerebral arteriosclerosis,* which are evident behaviorally in a sense of suspiciousness, confusion and loss of memory and in the inability to sustain normal body functions. Delusions, too, may be common. Approximately 25 percent of all first admissions to mental hospitals and possibly an even larger proportion of those admitted to nursing homes suffer from these forms of mental disorder. This is not too surprising inasmuch as senility or some other form of physical debilitation related to old age becomes more common as one grows older. A third form of old age mental disorder is exemplified in *paresis* or *dementia paralytica,* which results from syphilitic damage to the brain. A dated study of 35,000 cases admitted to public and private hospitals in Chicago during 1922-1934 revealed that paresis rates were highest among those living in rooming house districts in which prostitution houses were concentrated, a finding long since affected by the discovery and application of penicillin and other drugs in treatment.[18] However, paresis still results in the gradual deterioration of the brain approximately 10 years after the initial syphilitic infection. It may cause tremors, seizures and major alterations of personality. *Alcoholic psychosis,* somewhat rare among alcoholics, may cause physical and psychological deterioration, the development of hallucinations, and delirium tremens.

Sources and Causes of Mental Disorders • A comparison of 10 different societies by Joseph W. Eaton and Robert J. Weil disclosed that the variation in mental disorder rates is related to the degree of stability and integration of cultural traits, the consistency of role expectations and the strength of familial, interpersonal and community relationships.[19] Although it has been found that the stresses caused by war produced no major increase in serious psychosis in either free or occupied countries, a slight increase of neurotic complaints a week to 10 days after heavy bombing did occur.[20]

While many conclude mental illness or disorder is a product of urbanization and technological society, data from Massachusetts (between 1840-1850) and the Hutterite communities in Montana and the Dakotas suggest that this is not true.[21] Some mental disorders are not so much a reflection of mental illness as of mental deficiency. Idiocy (I.Q. of below 25) and imbecility (I.Q. of 25-50) represent two forms of such mental shortcoming which is shared by approximately 200,000 persons in state and federal institutions.[22] The more severe forms of mental deficiency are rooted in brain injury or organic deficiencies; however, others are a result of cultural deprivation.

Ultimately, the recognition of a condition of mental illness depends upon a definition of normal and abnormal human behavior, the context or situation in which the behavior takes place, and the person making the judgment.[23] Mental disorders or mental abnormality can only be understood in terms of their relationship to mental normality, which in itself is usually defined in middle class terms.[24] In interviews with 300 married women, Derek L. Phillips discovered that the rejection of emotionally disturbed persons, rather than being determined in relationship to their clinical symptoms, was founded upon the degree that they deviated from community norms. Clergymen were the least likely to reject these persons, while the rejection likelihood rose as the definition was made by physicians, psychiatrists, and eventually a mental hospital.[25]

Social Roles and Mental Disorders ● The importance of social roles in the development and maintenance of functional mental disorders cannot be underestimated. Mental deficiencies may sometimes occur when a person is unable to shift from one role to another in a normal social situation. At other times, it may be related to the individual's inability to accept and play out the contradictions inherent within any social role. Occasionally, a person will consciously or unconsciously play the mentally disordered role for reasons best understood by himself.

Thomas J. Scheff postulates that the residual rule-breaking expressed in mental disorders and illness may be due to organic difficulties, psychological deficiencies, external stresses, or defiant acts against some person or situation. The rate of unrecorded residual rule-breaking relative to the rate of treated mental illness is, he holds, extremely high. However, most residual rule-breaking is "denied" and is of transitory significance. The stereotyped imagery of mental disorder is learned in early childhood; the stereotypes of insanity are continually reaffirmed, inadvertently, in ordinary social interaction. Labelled deviants, Scheff contends, may be rewarded for playing the stereotype deviant role and thereby encouraged to remain deviant actors.[26] Scheff's theoretical model presumes that:

1. Residual deviance arises from fundamentally diverse sources, including bio-physiological, psychological, external stress and volitional, innovative or defiant actions;

2. Relative to the rate of treated mental illness, the rate of unrecorded residual deviance is extremely high;

3. Most residual deviance is "denied" and is transitory;

4. The stereotyped imagery of mental disorder is learned in early childhood;

5. The stereotypes of insanity are continually reaffirmed, inadvertently, in ordinary social interaction;

6. Labeled deviants may be rewarded for playing the stereotyped deviant role;

7. Labeled deviants are punished when they attempt to return to conventional roles;

8. In the crisis occurring when a primary deviant is publicly labeled, the deviant is highly suggestible, and may accept the proferred role of the insane as the only alternative; and

9. Among residual deviants, labeling is the singlemost important cause of the residual deviant.[27]

Mentally ill persons may unconsciously incorporate the role of insane into their personal behavior once they have been so diagnosed.[28] If they are not identified as mentally ill, they may continue to be viewed simply as an idiosyncratic member of society.

While John A. Clausen questions the presupposition that labeling a person mentally ill can make him so, he nevertheless admits that calling a person mentally ill frequently intensifies his symptoms.[29] However, Edwin N. Lemert believes that the hospitalization of anybody labeled by a family, neighborhood or community as mentally disordered depends upon the degree of stressful deviation present and the tolerance of the group towards this behavior.[30] Although commitment to a state mental institution is most complete and ritualized when a person is admitted, the stigma which is invoked upon admission is never truly removed at the time of discharge. Consequently, various researchers suggest that deviance is related to the perceptions of the deviance by the broader public.[31]

Few under the age of 15 are hospitalized for mental illness. Between 15 and 40 years of age, however, there is a sharp rise in hospital admissions. Between 40 and 60 the rate tends to remain constant, rising again in the later years of life. Youth and middle-aged persons are treated largely on an outpatient basis. Although rates vary markedly, the annual incidence rate of initial diagnosis of psychotic among Texans between 1951 and 1952 reached 73.3 per 100,000 persons.[32] In 1964, slightly more than 565,000 mental patients were institutionalized in a mental hospital; however, the number dropped sharply to 275,995 residents by December, 1972 with another 401,567 net live releases to the community.[33] Although the latter figure reflects the major changes in conception of the mental health problem realized in recent years, total admissions to mental hospitals in 1972 still numbered 390,000 persons (see Table 4.2).

Mental Illness and Urban Life ● The highest rates of hospitalized mental illness are found near the center of a city where high population mobility and low socioeconomic status are prevalent. In a study of the ecological distribution of Chicago patients admitted to public and private mental hospitals, the lowest rates were located in the stable residential areas identified by high socioeconomic status.[34] Similar findings were uncovered in New Haven. A. B. Hollingshead and F. Redlich found that schizophrenia tends to be more common among the lower socioeconomic strata members. Outpatient treatment in the form of services provided by clinics or privately by psychiatrists was more common for the upper socioeconomic strata. The initiation, type, and duration of treatment received, they discovered, vary in relationship to social class.[35]

TABLE 4.2

PATIENTS IN MENTAL HOSPITALS: 1950-1972
RESIDENT PATIENTS, ADMISSIONS, RELEASES, AND DEATHS
(STATE AND COUNTY MENTAL HOSPITALS)

YEAR[1]	RESIDENT PATIENTS AT END OF YEAR	TOTAL ADMISSIONS	NET LIVE RELEASES	DEATHS
1950	512,501	152,286	99,659	41,280
1951	520,326	152,079	101,802	42,107
1952	531,981	162,908	107,647	44,303
1953	545,045	170,621	113,959	45,087
1954	553,979	171,682	118,775	42,652
1955	558,922	178,003	126,498	44,384
1956	551,390	185,597	145,313	48,236
1957	548,626	194,497	150,413	46,848
1958	545,182	209,823	161,884	51,383
1959	541,883	222,791	176,411	49,647
1960	535,540	234,791	190,802	49,757
1961	527,456	252,742	215,596	46,880
1962	515,640	269,854	230,158	49,563
1963	504,604	283,591	245,745	49,052
1964	490,449	299,561	268,616	44,824
1965	475,202	314,020	285,760	43,964
1966	452,089	327,014	308,636	42,753
1967	426,309	348,561	335,737	39,608
1968	399,152	365,455	351,461	39,677
1969	366,815	379,838	[2]374,383	35,962
1970	338,592	393,174	394,627	30,804
1971	308,024	402,174	418,750	26,835
1972	275,995	390,000	401,567	23,282

Note: In 1970, approximately 78 percent of residents of mental hospitals were in State and
county hospitals.

[1] Data are for fiscal years, e.g., fiscal year 1950 covers the period from July 1, 1949 to June
30, 1950.

[2] Estimated from data in 1969 report.

Source: Public Health Service, National Institute of Mental Health, *Mental Health Statistics
– Current Report Series, Statistical Note,* Nos. 40, 60, and 77.

Consequently, the incidence of psychiatric care better reflects the income level
of the participant than his need for treatment.

An interview study of approximately 1,700 persons in New York City disclosed that 23.4 percent of the population was rated as impaired due to psychiatric symptoms. Nearly one half of those persons came from the lowest socioeconomic class; approximately one eighth of those in the higher socioeconomic class were so classified.[36] The midtown Manhattan study revealed that the problems related to mental distress are greater among the poor and deprived. Similar findings have been reported by Alexander H. and Dorothea C. Leighton from data gathered in a rural Canadian county.[37] However, the lower class status of a mentally ill person, Bruce Dohrenwend suggests, is not a cause of mental illness but rather a result of it.[38] One study of untreated mental illness in Kalamazoo County, Michigan, uncovered that only 34 percent per 1,000 members of the population fell into that category,[39] a finding which contrasts sharply with that of midtown Manhattan. Nevertheless, Howard Freeman and Jeanne M. Giovannoni maintain that a comparison of patient and normal groups discloses that few environmental differences are related to mental illness.[40]

The Treatment of Mental Illness and Disorder ● The treatment of mental illness, while yet involving institutionalization and shock therapy for some, has moved more to outpatient treatment. The use of antidepressant drugs and tranquilizers in treatment has become quite common since the 1950's when their use was introduced and perfected in order to overcome the shortage of space and hospital beds within mental institutions. The success of drug therapy has resulted in shorter stays within institutions and a strong movement toward outpatient care and service. As a result, insurance companies are now disclosing a greater willingness to provide contract coverage for mental illness care.

One treatment method common to both the institution and the community in order to assist the development of communication and understanding between unit members involves the use of group therapy, including psychodrama, the acting out of conflict situations by one group for a second group. A collateral benefit of this approach is that the participant is able to acquire the additional social skills necessary for adequate functioning within society. Other variations of therapy include the use of dance and music therapy, in which rhythm is used to encourage group participation.

Treatment is also accomplished in normal home settings. One of the more interesting treatment settings is found in Gheel, Belgium, where patients with mental disorders are encouraged to live normally with community members. Nearly 10 percent of the community of nearly 22,000 inhabitants have experienced some forms of mental illness. Patients work in a home or in the town, and community members strive to integrate patients into a useful social life. Mental hospitalization is used only as a final alternative.[41] Care within similar family settings has also been attempted with success in Denmark and other European countries and in the American states of Maryland and Massachusetts. Within such a context as *normalization,* every effort is made to affect treatment in a setting most similar to normal life conditions, rather than within an artificial mental hospital setting in which problems for many are reinforced rather than adequately treated.

The creation of community mental health centers, supportive of normalization, has been assisted by those who believe such care should be made widely available to the population and opposed by those who argue that in the long run it will result in infringement on individual liberty.[42] Interestingly, the radical right tends to look upon the mental health movement as a political attempt to silence government critics and part of a communist plot to take over the nation while the more moderate and liberal elements of society hail this approach as one most closely supportive of the normalization movement.

One means of assisting recovered mental patients to adjust to society upon release from a mental hospital was begun in 1937 in the form of Recovery, Incorporated. Existing currently in about 40 states, the 600 or more groups now operating emphasize self-help and mutual support in facing daily problems. Both formal and informal meetings are planned in order to assist in the community re-entry and re-integration process. Halfway houses have also been used to ease the re-entry of the hospitalized mental patient into society. Although they are more common in Europe than in the United States, an increased interest has developed recently in the United States in the creation of halfway houses for mental patients.

But the development of halfway houses has not kept pace with the quickening pattern of release of persons formerly institutionalized in mental hospitals. Patients in some state hospitals have declined by 40 to 50 percent in the last three years, while they have been forced to relocate in nursing homes, hotels, or other non-treatment centers where they become victims of the system of "normal" societal operations. Because fewer than 600 of the 1,500 to 2,000 planned mental health centers have been developed, those patients returned to the community have not uniformly received equitable treatment. Despite these shortcomings, it is evident, however, that the former "warehousing" policy of storing the mentally ill in asylums is due for a major shakeup. Legal action taken in Alabama issued in a bill of rights for mental patients under a ruling rendered by Federal Judge Frank M. Johnson, Jr. Although appealed to the U.S. Court of Appeals in New Orleans, the guarantees of treatment required by Johnson are likely to have long-term impact. They provide:

Patients have a right to privacy and dignity.

No person shall be deemed incompetent to manage his affairs, to contract, to hold professional or occupational or vehicle operator's licenses, to marry and obtain a divorce, to register and vote, or to make a will, solely by reason of his admission or commitment to the hospital.

Patients have a right to be free from unnecessary or excessive medication.

Patients have a right to be free from physical restraint or isolation.

Patients shall have a right not to be subjected to experimental research without the express and informed consent of the patient, if the patient is able to give such consent, and of his guardian or next of kin, after opportunities with independent specialists and with legal counsel.

Patients have a right to opportunities for physical exercise, religious worship, and 'interaction with members of the opposite sex.'[43]

Much of this argument is based upon the 14th Amendment which holds that no state shall deprive any person of life, liberty, or property without legal due process, frequently not the case in commitment to a mental institution.

The Scope of Suicide

Suicide has been simply defined as the "intentional taking of one's life or the failure, when possible, to save one's self when death threatens."[44] Whatever its definition, the contemplation of suicide is quite common to humanity. What is uncommon is the actual completion of the act. Nevertheless, suicide has both an individual and a collective dimension. It results not only in individual death but the termination of one's involvement within the general society.

The number of suicides in the United States in recent years has numbered close to 25,000, per year. The rate in 1971 was 11.3 per 100,000 population as compared to 9.4 for homicides, a rate that has largely remained consistent since 1943.[45] Inasmuch as many suicides are undoubtedly not reported, it is probably more likely that an estimated 40,000 persons commit suicide yearly. At least 125,000, and possibly as many as 225,000 persons attempt some suicidal act annually.[46] Attempted suicide rates are generally 6 to 8 times higher than the actual number of suicides in a given year.[47] Nearly one half of all suicides occur among married persons between the ages of 15 and 65. The suicide volume in Great Britain is about one fourth and in Japan two thirds that of the United States.

The Criminal and Emotional Aspects of Suicide ● Most states of the United States do not consider suicide a crime. Fewer than five do. Only rarely are criminal penalties inflicted for attempted suicide. In Great Britain, where criminal law against suicide existed until 1961, fewer than one tenth of the attempted suicides were even sentenced to prison in a criminal action. Nevertheless, when the anti-suicide law was revised, penalties were still prescribed for those who would assist, counsel, or participate in the suicide act of another.

Suicide is commonly viewed as a bizarre act of an emotionally disturbed person, a product of unsatisfactory social relationships, or a result of aggressive impulses.[48] Suicidal persons usually feel isolated and are often unable to establish regular social friendships and relations. Many attempted suicides appear to want to live rather than die and seek an acceptance and an acknowledgement of their achievements and a clearly defined relationship involving love and work.[49] However, some suicides are probably situational or spontaneous responses and other escapist acts. *Situational suicides* are commonly impulsive and unpremeditated, frequently taking the form of juvenile suicide over a broken love relationship, punishment, or withholding of some privilege. The loss of friends or the discovery of poor health may also lead to situational suicide. *Escapist suicides,* on the other hand, are frequently carried out to avoid life responsibility. For example, a murderer who later takes his own life engages in escapism.[50]

Karl Menninger maintains that suicide is the ultimate form of self-destruction which people share in every day to some extent. He argues that persons who engage in alcoholism and precipitate automobile accidents by their irresponsible driving are in effect participating in "partial suicide."[51] Although other factors, including mental illness, may be involved, Austin L. Porterfield predicts a positive correlation between motor vehicle accidents and suicide-homicide rates in the United States.[52]

Some investigators maintain that approximatley 15 percent of all completed or attempted suicides involve persons with a mental or emotional disorder of some sort.[53] Emile Durkheim, who believed that suicide rates exist in inverse proportion to the innovation of the social group of which the individual forms a part, differentiated suicide into the three types: anomic, egoistic, and altruistic. As an act, suicide is primarily a measure of the degree of anomie existing in a society. The *anomic* suicide is a person who is not closely bound to society due to weak or faulty socialization. The *egoistic* suicide is one who is not thoroughly integrated into the society due largely to his self-centered focus and his own belief that he should remain unintegrated. The *altruistic* suicide is the person who is so well integrated into society that he is willing to die in order to preserve its essence.[54] Whatever its type, suicide, according to Durkheim, represents a positive or negative act by the victim which he knows will eventually kill him.[55]

Passing beyond Durkheim's analysis, M. D. W. Jeffrys adds a fourth type, *samsonic* suicide. An individual in this context takes his life as a result of an institutionalized belief that the spirits of the dead can return and wreak vengeance upon the living.[56] Despite the widespread emphasis given Durkheim's theory of suicide and the complementary distribution of homicide and suicide, African data dealing with the problem do not support his hypothesis.[57]

A study of 768 successful and 5,906 attempted suicides in Los Angeles County by Edwin S. Shneidman and Norman L. Farberow in 1957 disclosed that those who typically attempt suicide are female, caucasian, either married or single, generally housewives, commonly between 20 and 30, native-born and disposed to depressions or marital problems. Women usually attempt suicide by the ingesting of an excessive number of barbituates. However, those who *complete* the suicide successfully are typically caucasian males, skilled or unskilled workers, married, native-born, and facing depression, ill-health or marital discord. Typically, males complete their suicides through hanging, exposure to carbon monoxide, or by shooting.[58] Nearly three fourths of the successful male suicides in Los Angeles County, they found, have threatened or attempted previously to take their own lives.[59]

Suicide in World Cultures ● International suicide patterns and attitudes vary markedly. The Indian act of *suttee,* the publicly encouraged ritual suicide of the widow upon the death of her husband, ended only in the Nineteenth century.[60] In many places in the Far East, suicide is a socially approved way of maintaining or regaining one's honor. Yet the Koran, especially dominant in Middle East cultures, prohibits suicide among Muslims.

While suicide tends to be highest in technologically advanced countries north of the equator, this is not completely true. Suicide rates vary extensively among the Finns, Swedes and Norwegians and among the technologically advanced nations of Great Britain, the United States, Australia, New Zealand and Canada.[61] The Eskimo suicide rate in Canada has been generally higher than that of the rest of the Canadian population (41.7 to 12.2 per 100,000 persons).[62] During the last century, urban suicide rates exceeded the rural rates in nearly all countries and provinces. In the United States the former difference between these communities has diminished.

The suicide rate for males generally exceeds that of females. However, the exact rate differs markedly by country. A study of 1,000 reported *attempted* suicides in 1933 revealed that the female rate per 100,000 persons was nearly twice as high as that for males.[63] However, more recent data indicate that the range of male dominance in suicide ranges from 1.1 to 1 in Luxenbourg (1964) to a high of 23 to 1 in Nicaragua (1965).[64] The suicide rate per 100,000 population until the age of 60-69, when a slight decline appears, tends to increase directly with age for American males and slightly with age for American females. Similar tendencies are found among most European populations. In Japan, the rate for both Japanese males and females rises sharply up to the age of 24, lessens between 30 and 50 and increases from 50 until over 80. While blacks in the United States maintain a low suicide rate, some black tribes in Africa possess high rates.

Problems to be noted in any type of study of suicide include the recognition that suicide rates vary widely from 4.4 suicides per 100,000 in Chile to 20.5 in Japan, that many countries have a vested interest in covering up suicide rates and that data concerning suicide are generally inconclusive.[65] The suicide rates in 1960 per 100,000 population ranged from a low of 0.1 in Jordan to a high of 29.6 in Hungary. At the same time, the rate in the United States was 10.8, in France 15.0, and in Austria 23.1.[66]

Reliability of Suicide Statistics ● The reliability of statistical data concerning suicide is open to question. Gregory Zilboorg argues that the variable interpretation of the nature of suicide by those who define the act makes the validity of such data suspect.[67] Others simply argue that most official statistics are unreliable.[68] In a study of deaths in New Zealand between 1946 and 1951,

Jack P. Gibbs uncovered 955 cases of suicide, a record which compared favorably with the 1,036 cases reported in official statistics. Nevertheless, Gibbs concludes that the debate concerning the reliability of suicide statistics remains open.[69]

The Hindu religion permits suicide if it is a religious end. Buddhism accepts voluntary suicide. In Viet Nam the burning of oneself in gasoline became an effective means of Buddhist protest against religious persecution and the continuing war in the 1960's.[70] However, suicide receives no support in Christian, Jewish or Muslim cultures. Both Judaism and Christianity openly condemn suicide. Christians are encouraged to endure suffering and poverty and to utilize adversity as a means for preparing oneself for eventual salvation. While in its early days as a minority religion Christianity did in essence support suicide for the faith through martyrdom,[71] it soon held suicides to involve the murder of an innocent man.

Suicide Rates • Contrary to the situation in most Asian countries, the suicide rate in Japan remains high. The Japanese pattern of suicide is unique in that it has high incidence rates among those 20 to 25 and 65 or over. In that nation, rural areas and females have high suicide rates. Highest incidences occur during night hours. Manoru Iga hypothesizes that the high suicide rate of Japanese youth may be attributed to their "weak ego," strong and uninhibited impulses, sense of obligation, guilt and shame, and a favorable attitude toward suicide, with a basic sense of personal insecurity.[72]

Factors Influencing Suicide • Religion seems to have some influence over suicide proneness. Protestant suicide rates are higher than those of Jews or Catholics, although exceptions to this rule can readily be found. Austria, which is a predominantly Catholic country, has a high rate of suicide in contrast with the normally lower rates found in Catholic territories.[73] While the Catholic suicide rate is less than the Protestant or Jewish, it is higher than the Mormon rate.[74] Similarly, married persons are somewhat less prone to suicide than widowed, divorced or single persons. Although the overall Muslim suicide rate has remained close to 2 per 100,000, the Christian rate during the same period has been 1.5 and the unmarried rate 10.8. The rate has been even higher for the divorced (21.5) and the highly educated (36.6).[75]

Suicides in Ceylon are strongly committed to the cultural norms of the nation. A large portion of the suicides among those of relatively high status is due to the stress they feel as they seek to gain an outstanding position.[76] In general, if custom and tradition accept or condone suicide, many people will terminate their own lives. If, on the other hand, it is strongly condemned by Church and/or State, it will be less common.[77] Austin L. Porterfield believes the relationship between secularization and suicide is close.[78]

Suicide and Economic Life • Suicide rates tend to be higher during economic depressions and lower during periods of economic prosperity. During the 1908, 1923, 1929-1933 and 1937 economic crises, for example, suicide rates among white males increased dramatically. At the time of the Depression, suicide rates for white men were nearly double the rates of the previous periods.[79]

Unemployment increases the tendency to suicide among low-income groups, while employment may do so among high-income groups.[80] A study of white male suicides in New Orleans by Warren Breed showed that substantial work problems are involved among those committing suicide. Downward mobility, reduced income, unemployment, and other job and business difficulties permeate the suicide decision-making process.[81] Although data on the occupational involvement of most suicides is incomplete, the rate for pharmacists was 24 times that of carpenters in Tulsa County in the 1950's.[82]

A study of the suicide and homicide rates in 48 countries suggests that suicide rates tend to be high and homicide rates low in countries of high economic development, and that suicide rates tend to be low and homicide rates high in countries of low economic development.[83] Suicide rates tend to drop sharply among soldiers during wartime, although many warriors may be in fact committing suicide as they fight.

Suicide, Social Disorganization, and Socioeconomic Status • Some investigators suggest that the suicide rate varies directly with the extent of social disorganization.[84] However, others argue that the rates of suicide are unrelated to or actually vary inversely with the other alleged effects of social disorganization.[85] Peter Sainsbury found the relationship in London to be somewhat inconsistent inasmuch as suicide rates were closely related to rates of divorce and illegitimacy but not to those of juvenile delinquency.[86] However, the lower the socioeconomic status, the higher, Ronald W. Maris hypothesizes, is the suicide rate. Restraint deriving from being in a subordinate status (a vertical restraint) tends to aggravate suicide. Suicide appears to vary inversely with social integration; mental illness seems to be disproportionately high among suicides; and alcoholism, racial, and physical factors have some effect upon the suicide rate.[87] In New Zealand, upper class fathers produce a high proportion of suicidal sons. Suicide rates there are significantly higher among persons of high prestige; and victims of suicide, born at whatever level, frequently change position on the prestige scale between generations.[88]

Some analysts maintain that the suicide rate varies inversely with the degree of status integration of the population,[89] a viewpoint not held by all. Those societies characterized by a high degree of status integration, they theorize, tend to have a low suicide rate. Those status configurations that are infrequently occupied within a society, however, tend to have a high suicide rate. However, opponents of this thesis suggest that the contention is questionable inasmuch as the idea of status integration has logical weaknesses, the utility of its operational definition is unclear, and other data tend to contradict the theory.[90]

Suicide and Homicide • If a youth internalizes harsh parental demands and discipline during adolescence, a *high* psychological probability of suicide and a *low* psychological probability of homicide can be expected. On the other hand, strong external adult restraints may produce a *high* sociological probability of homicide consequent to frustration and a *low* probability of suicide related to frustration.[91] Suicide within a population, according to Andrew F. Henry and James F. Short, Jr., is related to the strength of the relational system, which varies in relation to the external restraints placed upon the behavior of the population, and the external restraints placed upon the behavior of its members, which vary inversely with their status position. Married persons generally have lower suicide rates because they are involved in stronger relational systems than single, divorced, or widowed persons. Consequently, the suicide rate of any population, they hypothesize, varies inversely with the strength of the relational system of its members; the strength of the relationship system varied directly with the external restraints placed upon the members' behavior; and the external restraints placed upon the members' behavior vary inversely with the members' status.[92]

Murder Followed by Suicide • Nearly one third of all murderers in England and Wales completed suicide after committing their crimes. While many were mentally ill at the time, others disclosed normal conduct patterns or were overcommitted to normative concepts and values. In New South Wales, nearly 22 percent of the murder offenders (115 males and 41 females) killed themselves after their acts, and another 4 percent (17 male and 14 female) attempted suicide unsuccessfully. In Denmark, over a 28-year period involving 545 cases, slightly more than 42.2 percent of Danish killers eventually took their own lives, while an additional 9.6 percent attempted suicide. Nearly 64 percent of the female homicide offenders killed themselves, with another 16.1 percent completing a serious suicide attempt. D.J. West uncovered that the murder-suicide offender is most likely to be representative of the general community, often married and living in a conventional family setting.[93]

The Prevention of Suicide • The prevention of suicide is most difficult and involves much more than the punishment of a potential violator. Some prisons or service agencies attempt to prevent suicide through custodial care, counseling, and/or psychiatric treatment. Usually, these take the form of suicide prevention centers, "hotlines", or some type of emergency organization designed to talk potential suicides out of committing the act. Recognizing that suicides often result from depressions, feelings of despair, accident proneness, or some other psychological physiological problem, these programs attempt to motivate the individual to social participation rather than to life termination. In 1969, nearly 40 suicide prevention centers were in operation within the United States with some hope that an even greater number would be in operation two decades later.[94] Even though the modern approach to suicide prevention emphasizes a therapeutic concern for the would-be suicide, the difficulty of containing the problem or predicting its occurrences makes it largely impossible to prevent suicide from occurring despite what measures are taken.

References

1. Thomas S. Szasz, *The Myth of Mental Illness* (New York: Hoeber-Harper, 1961).
2. R. H. Felix and Morton Kramer, "Extent of the Problem of Mental Disorders," *Annals,* (March, 1953), CCLXXXVI, 8.
3. John A. Clausen, "Mental Disorders," *Contemporary Social Problems,* eds. Robert K. Merton and Robert Nisbet. (New York: Harcourt, Brace and Jovanovich, 1971), p. 29.
4. *Ibid.,* p. 33.
5. Robert W. Winslow, *Society in Transition* (New York: Free Press, 1970), p. 307. Also Richard J. Bord, "Rejection of the Mentally Ill," *Social Problems,* (Spring, 1971), XVIII, 496-509.
6. David Rosenthal, *The Genain Quadruplets* (New York: Basic Books, 1963).
7. Clausen, *Social Problems.*
8. Jay Haley, "The Family of the Schizophrenic: A Model System," *Journal of Nervous and Mental Disease,* (1959), CXXIX, 357-374.
9. Norman Cameron, *The Psychology of Behavior Disorders* (Boston: Houghton-Mifflin, 1947), p. 513.
10. M. Greenblatt, B. Levinson and R. Williams, *The Patient in the Mental Hospital* (New York: Free Press, 1957), pp. 438-526. For more detailed information about schizophrenia, examine the *Schizophrenia Bulletin.*
11. R. E. L. Faris, "Cultural Isolation and the Schizophrenic Personality," *American Journal of Sociology,* (September, 1934), XL, 155-169.
12. S. Kirson Weinberg, "A Sociological Analysis of a Schizophrenic Type," *American Sociological Review,* (October, 1950), XV, 600-610.
13. Roman Hall and Harrison N. Trice, *Schizophrenia and the Poor* (Ithaca, N.Y.: Cayuga Press, 1967), pp. 18-41; and Frank Reisman, Jerome Cohen and Arthur Pearl, *Mental Health of the Poor: New Treatment Approaches for Low Income People* (New York: Free Press, 1964).
14. Winslow, *Society in Transition,* pp. 311-312.
15. Clausen, *Social Problems,* p. 60.
16. David Rosenthal and Seymour Ketz, *The Transmission of Schizophrenia* (London: Pergammon, 1969), Part II; and Leonard I. Heston, "Psychiatric Disorders of Foster-Home-Reared Children of Schizophrenic Mothers," *British Journal of Psychiatry,* (1966), XII, 819-825.
17. Don D. Jackson, "A Critique on the Literature on the Genetics of Schizophrenia," *The Etiology of Schizophrenia* (New York: Basic Books, 1960), pp. 37-87.
18. R. E. L. Faris and H. Warren Dunham, *Mental Disorders in Urban Areas* (Chicago: University of Chicago Press, 1939).
19. Joseph W. Eaton and Robert J. Weil, *Culture and Mental Disorders* (New York: Free Press, 1955). Also H. B. M. Murphy, "Culture and Mental Disorder in Singapore," *Culture and Mental Health,* ed. Marvin K. Opler, "Cultural Differences and Mental Disorders: An Italian and Irish Contrast in the Schizophrenias–U.S.A.," *loc. cit.,* pp. 425-442.
20. Donald D. Reid, "Precipitating Proximal Factors in the Occurrence of Mental Disorders: Epidemiological Evidence," *Causes of Mental Disorders: A Review of Epidemiological Knowledge, 1959* (New York: Milbank Memorial Bank, 1961).
21. Herbert Goldhamer and Andrew Marshall, *Psychosis and Civilization* (New York: Free Press, 1953); and Eaton and Weil, *Culture and Mental Disorders.*

22. Clausen, *Social Problems*, p. 43.
23. Frederick C. Redlich, "The Concept of Health in Psychiatry," *Explorations in Social Psychiatry*, eds. Alexander H. Leighton, John A. Clausen and Robert N. Wilson (New York: Basic Books, 1957), pp. 145-146.
24. Kingsley Davis, "Mental Hygiene in the Class Structure," *Psychiatry*, (February, 1938), I, 55-64.
25. Derek L. Phillips, "Rejection of the Mentally Ill: The Influence of Behavior and Sex," *American Journal of Sociology*, (October, 1964), XXIX, 679-687; and Derek L. Phillips, "Rejection: A Possible Consequence of Seeking Help for Mental Disorders," *American Journal of Sociology*, (December, 1963), XXVII, 963-972.
26. Thomas J. Scheff, *Being Mentally Ill: A Sociological Theory* (Chicago: Aldine, 1966), pp. 40-84.
27. Thomas J. Scheff, "The Role of the Mentally Ill and the Dynamics of Mental Disorder," *Sociology*, (December, 1963), XXVI, 436-453; and "The Labelling Theory of Mental Illness," *American Sociological Review*, (June, 1974), XXIX, 444-452.
28. Scheff, *Being Mentally Ill*, pp. 43-82.
29. Clausen, "Mental Disorder," *Social Problems*, p. 48.
30. Edwin M. Lemert, *Social Pathology*, (New York: McGraw-Hill, 1951), p. 406.
31. Kai Erickson, "Notes on the Sociology of Deviance," *Social Problems*, (Spring, 1962), IX, 307-314; and Jack P. Gibbs, "Rates of Mental Hospitalization: A Study of Societal Reaction to Deviant Behavior," *American Sociological Review*, (December, 1962), XXVII, 789-792.
32. E. Gartly Jaco, *The Social Epidemiology of Mental Disorders* (New York: Russel Sage Foundation, 1960).
33. Department of Health, Education and Welfare, *Trends* (Washington, D.C.: U.S. Government Printing Office, 1965), pp. 2-29.
34. Faris and Dunham, *Mental Disorders*.
35. A. B. Hollingshead and F. Redlich, *Social Class and Mental Illness* (New York: Wiley, 1958).
36. Leo Srole, *Mental Health in the Metropolis* (New York: McGraw-Hill, 1962).
37. See Alexander H. Leighton, *My Name Is Legion* (New York: Basic Books, 1959); Dorothea C. Leighton, *The Character of Danger* (New York: Basic Books, 1963); and Walter R. Gove and Patrick Howell, "Individual Resources and Mental Hospitalization," *American Sociological Review*, (February, 1974), XXXIX, 86-100.
38. Bruce P. Dohrenwend, "Social Status and Psychological Disorder: An Issue of Substance and an Issue of Method," *American Sociological Review*, (February, 1966), XXXI, 15-34; also see H. Warren Dunham, Patricia Phillips and Barbara Scrinivasan, "A Research Note on Diagnosed Mental Illness and Social Class," *American Sociological Review*, (April, 1966), XXXI, 223-277.
39. Jerome G. Manis, Milton J. Brawer, Chester L. Hunt and Leonard C. Kercher, "Estimating the Prevalence of Mental Illness," *American Sociological Review*, (February, 1964), XXIX, 84-89.
40. Howard E. Freeman and Jeanne M. Giovannoni, "Social Psychology of Mental Health," *Handbook of Social Psychology*, eds. G. Lindsey and E. Aronson (Cambridge: Addison-Wesley, 1969).
41. Opler, *Culture*, pp. 4-5.
42. For arguments on this matter see Gerald Caplan, "Some Comments on 'Communities, Psychiatry and Social Power,' *Social Problems*, (Summer, 1966), XIV, 23-25; and Ronald Leifer, "Community Psychiatry and Social Power," *Social Problems*, (Summer, 1966), XIV, 16-22.
43. A. A. Low, "Recovery Incorporated: A Project for Rehabilitating Post-Psychotic and

Long-Term Psychoneurotic Patients," *Rehabilitation of the Handicapped,* ed. W. H. Soden (New York: Ronald Press, 1949), pp. 213-226; and *The Milwaukee Journal* (July 5, 1974).

44. Ruth S. Cavan, *Suicide* (Chicago: University of Chicago Press, 1928), p. 3.

45. Executive Office of the President, Office of Management and Budget, *Social Indicators* (Washington, D.C.: U.S. Government Printing Office, 1973), p. 7.

46. Ronald W. Maris, *Social Forces in Urban Suicide* (Homewood, Ill.: Dorsey, 1969), pp. 5-6. For a discussion of suicide among youth, see Joint Commission on Mental Health of Children, Task Force III, *Suicide Among Youth* (Washington, D.C.: National Clearinghouse of Mental Health Information, 1969).

47. Erwin Stengel, *Suicide and Attempted Suicide* (Baltimore: Pelican Books, 1964), p. 75.

48. Howard E. Freeman and Wyatt C. Jones, *Social Problems: Causes and Controls* (Chicago: Rand-McNally, 1970), p. 520.

49. Margarethe von Andics, *Suicide and the Meaning of Life* (London: William Hodge and Co., 1947), p. 173. Attitudes toward suicide attempters are discussed in Edward Ansee and Richard McGee, "Attitudes Toward Suicide Attempters," *Bulletin of Suicidology* (Fall, 1971), pp. 22-28.

50. Ernest R. Mowrer, *Disorganization: Personal and Social* (Philadelphia: Lippincott, 1942), pp. 357-365; and David P. Phillips, "The Influences of Suggestion on Suicide," *American Sociological Review,* (June, 1974), XXXIX, 340-354.

51. Karl Menninger, *Man Against Himself* (New York: Harcourt, Brace and World, 1938).

52. Austin L. Porterfield, "Traffic Fatalities, Suicide and Homicide," *American Sociological Review,* (December, 1960), XXV, 900.

53. Peter Sainsbury, *Suicide in London: An Ecological Study* (New York: Basic Books, 1956).

54. Emile Durkheim, *Suicide,* trans John A. Spaulding and George Simpson (New York: Free Press, 1951).

55. *Ibid.,* pp. 44-45.

56. M. D. W. Jeffrys, "Samsonic Suicide or Suicide of Revenge Among Africans," *African Studies,* (1952), XI, 118-122.

57. Paul Bohannen, "Theories of Homicide and Suicide," *African Homicide and Suicide,* ed. Paul Bohannen (Princeton: Princeton University Press, 1960), pp. 3-29.

58. Edwin S. Shneidman and Norman L. Farberow, *The Cry For Help* (New York: McGraw-Hill, 1961), pp. 22-46.

59. Edwin S. Shneidman and Norman L. Barberow, *Clues To Suicide* (New York: McGraw-Hill, 1957), p. 9. Female suicide is discussed in John F. Newman, Kenneth R. Whittemore and Helen G. Newman, "Women in the Labor Force and Suicide," *Social Problems,* (Fall, 1973), XXI, 220-230.

60. Upenda Thakur, *The History of Suicide in India* (Delhi: Munshi Ran Manohar Lal, 1963).

61. Jack P. Gibbs, "Suicide," *Contemporary Social Problems,* eds. Robert K. Merton and Robert Nisbet (New York: Harcourt, Brace and Jovanovich, 1971), p. 288. Ethnic variations in suicide patterns are traced in Richard A. Kalisk, "Suicide: An Ethnic Comparison in Hawaii," *Bulletin of Suicidology* (December, 1968), pp. 37-43.

62. G. C. Butler, "Incidence of Suicides Among Ethnic Groups in the Northwest Territories and Yukon Territory," *Medical Services Journal,* (1966), XXI, 252-256.

63. *Demographic Yearbook,* 1967.

64. F. C. Lendrum," "A Thousand Cases of Attempted Suicide," *American Journal of Psychiatry,* (1933), XIII, 479-500.

65. Arthur E. Hippler, "Fusion and Frustration: Dimensions in the Cross-Cultural Ethnopsychology of Suicide," *American Anthropologist,* (December, 1969), LXXI, 1077.

66. *Demographic Yearbook,* 1967, Table 24.
67. Gregory Zilboorg, "Suicide Among Civilized and Primitive Races," *American Journal of Psychiatry,* (May, 1963), XCII, 1350.
68. George Simpson, "Methodological Problems in Determining the Aetiology of Suicide," American Sociological Review, (October, 1950), XV, 660; Jack D. Douglas, *The Social Meanings of Suicide* (Princeton: Princeton University Press, 1967); and S. Gargas, "Suicide in the Netherlands," *American Journal of Sociology,* (March, 1932), XXXVII, 699.
69. Gibbs, *Social Problems,* p. 278.
70. Allie Mazrui, "Sacred Suicide," *Atlas,* (March, 1966), XI, p. 165.
71. *The Demographic Yearbook,* 1967.
72. Manoru Iga, "Cultural Factors in Suicides of Japanese Youth With Focus on Personality," *Sociology and Social Research,* (October, 1961), XLVII, 75.
73. Gibbs, *Social Problems,* p. 288.
74. Robert W. Winslow, *Society in Transition* (New York: Free Press, 1970), pp. 321-322.
75. Markam Samaan Khalil, "Suicidal Behavior in Cairo," *National Review of Criminal Science,* (1962), V, 14-20.
76. Arthur L. Wood, "A Socio-Structural Analysis of Murder, Suicide and Economic Crime in Ceylon," *American Sociological Review,* (October, 1961), XXVI, 752.
77. Louis I. Dublin and Bessie Bunzel, *To Be Or Not To Be* (New York: Harrison Smith and Robert Haas, 1933), p. 15.
78. Austin L. Porterfield, "Suicide and Crime and Secular Society," *American Journal of Sociology,* (January, 1952), LVII, 331-338.
79. George Allen and Edward Ellis, *The Traitor Within* (Garden City: Doubleday, 1961), pp. 20-30.
80. William A. Rushing, "Income, Unemployment and Suicide: An Occupational Study," *Sociological Quarterly,* (Autumn, 1968), IX, 493-503.
81. Warren Breed, "Occupational Mobility and Suicide Among White Males," *American Sociological Review,* (April, 1963), XXVII, 179-188.
82. Elwin H. Powell, "Occupation, Status and Suicide: Toward a Re-definition of Anomie," *American Sociological Review,* (April, 1958), XXIII, 132.
83. Richard Quinney, "Suicide, Homicide and Economic Development," *Social Forces,* (March, 1965), XLIII, 401.
84. Mowrer, *Disorganization;* Mabel A. Elliott and Francis E. Merrill, *Social Disorganization* (New York: Ronald Press, 1948); and Ruth S. Cavan, *Suicide.*
85. Austin L. Porterfield, "Suicide and Crime in the Social Structure of an Urban Setting: Fort Worth, 1930-1950," *American Sociological Review,* (June, 1952), XVII, 341-349.
86. Sainsbury, *Suicide in London,* p. 41.
87. Maris, *Urban Suicide,* pp. 159-166.
88. Austin L. Porterfield and Jack P. Gibbs, "Occupational Prestige and Social Mobility of Suicides in New Zealand," *American Journal of Sociology,* (July, 1960), LXVI, 147.
89. Jack P. Gibbs and Walter T. Martin, *Status Integration and Suicide: A Sociological Study* (Eugene, Ore.: University of Oregon Books, 1964).
90. William J. Chandliss and Marion F. Steele, "Status Integration Suicide: An Assessment," *American Sociological Review,* (1966), XXXI, 531; and Robert Hagedorn and Sanford Labovitz, "A Note on Status Integration and Suicide," *Social Problems,* (1966), XIV, 84.
91. Andrew F. Henry and James F. Short, Jr., *Suicide and Homicide* (New York: Free Press, 1965), p. 44.
92. *Ibid.,* pp. 44-47.

93. Donald J. West, *Murder Followed by Suicide* (Cambridge, Mass.: Harvard University Press, 1966), pp. 113-130.
94. Maris, *Urban Suicide*, p. 6; Edwin S. Shneidman, "Some Current Developments in Suicide Prevention," *Bulletin of Suicidology* (December, 1967); pp. 31-34; Anson Haughton, "Suicide Prevention Programs in the United States—An Overview," *Bulletin of Suicidology* (July, 1968), pp. 25-29; Edwin S. Shneidman, "Preventing Suicide," *Bulletin of Suicidology* (December, 1968), pp. 19-25; and Charlotte P. Ross and Jerome A. Motto, "Implementation of Standards for Suicide Prevention Centers," *Bulletin of Suicidology* (Fall, 1971), pp. 18-21.

CHAPTER 5

Family Disruptions: Unhappy Families, Parent-Youth Conflict, Broken Homes, Divorce

Disruptions in the Traditional Family Patterns

A well-known thesis states that the family is an integral part of society and is one of the strongest and most significant social pillars. The happier and better its families, the happier and better, the thesis continues, is the total society. For centuries social philosophers have maintained and continue to profess, as William J. Goode points out, that the family is a major element in the social structure.[1] For example, Bernhard J. Stern calls attention to the fact that throughout man's social history there has been a close and intimate relationship between the family and other social institutions, because those who make up the family also participate in the economic, religious, political, and other social activities of the community.[2] Consequently, a well-functioning family institution is a prerequisite to the operation of an organized, well-integrated, and well-functioning society. When it does not function adequately, the family may pose a social problem. However, since most families do not always function efficiently, deficiencies in family functioning do not automatically mean that a social problem has developed. The basic issues relating to the problematic aspects of the family are what does well-functioning mean, what precipitating factors cause these disruptions, and to what degree do disrupted families exist and affect social life? In other words, what social problems derive from problems of the family, and/or what social problems cause problems in the family to develop?

The Function of the Family • The family is probably the most important of the human relationship networks devised to meet personal and group needs.[3] Because these networks are bound together with the family structure, and because the family "performs a vital part of the functions necessary to individual life,"[4] crises in the family structure may easily lead to other crises within society. Consequently, when the dismemberment and demoralization of the

88

family occurs, it endangers both personal and social stability. Such a realization gripped Pitirim A. Sorokin before his death when he predicted that family instability would reach the point of total disintegration within the not too distant future.[5] While accepting the idea that the American family is losing its traditional functions, W.F. Ogburn, on the other hand, also contended that the family is declining in its relative importance as a social institution.[6] But despite these evaluations of contemporary trends, the family still continues to be a critical element in social life. The degree and extent of family life disruptions still unavoidably influence whether human needs are met and satisfied or not. For in spite of the fact that we usually think of the family in kinship terms, the problematic aspects of family life focus on the commitments and attachments of persons differentiated along the axes of age and sex.[7] The success of the socialization process, the progression of economic standards, the maintenance of social control, and the continuance of group harmony and group peace depend crucially upon stable family clusters.

Although the family influences society, the conditions of society also exert influence upon the family.[8] While some factors in society are coincident with the family structure and, thus, supportive, others are not or are even missing. Frequently, certain external and internal factors cause the development of stress or some other emotional derangement which disrupts family functioning and leads to a family crisis. For example, poverty, poor housing, unemployment, war, economic depression, or social disorganization are often equally as responsible for family disruptions as diminishing love, marital disappointment, mental cruelty, drinking, in-law difficulties, sexual incompatability, parental neglect, infidelity, illness, generational disagreement, or the like. A multiplicity of interlocking factors may disrupt the equilibrium and harmony within the family, and inadequate family functioning may effect far-reaching social consequences. As a result, family problems can be clearly understood only in relation to the operations of the total society. Because they have a disruptive effect upon the larger society, unhappiness in the family caused by generational divisions, broken homes, desertion, separation, divorce, and other disruptions cannot usually be contained within a small family group.

Unhappy Families

Unhappy families, regardless of whether they represent an incomplete family unit or not, almost always become a social problem. Composed of a husband and wife who live together even though they have minimal contact and communication, have strong emotions for each other even if hostile or quarrelsome, and fail to live up to their original role obligations and to offer each other mutual support, they compose "empty shell" families. Because they represent only a legal skeleton of what a family is meant to be, they are destructive not only to other family members, but also to a certain degree to the larger society.

Although, "unhappy families" are usually complete families that are characterized by a degree of husband-wife unhappiness, the term does not exclude the possibility of physical disruption of the household. However, when family members stay together in spite of disruptive relationships, maladjusted, delinquent, or at least dissatisfied children may result. While children in a one-parent or no-parent family may have as great an opportunity to develop as youth in a happy two-parent family do, children within an unhappy family, whether two-parent or less, may cease to learn and function in a normal manner and may even engage in deviant conduct.

A variety of factors, mostly those which lead to desertion, separation, or divorce, are involved in the emergence of family happiness. Fading or disappearing love, unsatisfying sex relations, attention paid to another person, difficulties with in-laws, mixed religious commitments, differences in social backgrounds, variable role interpretations, disappointments with one's partner, mental and/or disabling physical illness, and a decline in family economic prosperity may serve as the foundation of a spouse unhappiness which almost unavoidably may spread to the child members of the family. In such cases, family members live in depressive unhappiness without mutual understanding, usually seeking emotional satisfaction outside the family unit. Even though the unhappy family continues to be a small group of persons bound together by marriage and blood relationships, each family member leads his own life.

Why unhappy family members stay together instead of trying to free themselves from their deficient relationship and to establish a new and happy family is not clear. No statistical table or research project records the true volume of unhappy families which continue their instrumental obligations and their formal cohabitation even though the family as a unit no longer has substance. While the husband holds a job and provides for the family, the wife takes care of the house and meals, and the children go to school and attend to chores in the home,[9] they all still have little in common. Their care for each other is instrumental or functional rather than emotional or sentimental. While each member probably has some desire to escape from this unhappy and undesirable situation, they rationalize the problem and avoid the dissolution of their "family."

Some spouses explain that they do so for the sake of their children, believing that their children's future is better guaranteed if they grow up in a "full" family circle in which the seriousness of the original marital pledges and obligations are continued. Frequently, they strive to save the children from the almost unavoidable social stigma of living in an incomplete family. However, some marital partners remain married because they think separation or divorce may undermine their respectability, as blame is assessed for the violation of traditional societal rules which divorce or separation imply. Still others continue the family relationship because of religious beliefs which oppose the dissolution of marriage even though it does not meet the ideal conceived in religious dogma.

Nevertheless, whatever their reasons for continuing their unhappiness within the family, the unhappy family not only deprives its members of a satisfying family life but also becomes a social problem. Apart from the destructive fact that family members in these circumstances cannot serve the total society as they ought and the children cannot receive the kind of socialization which is supposed to make them happy, healthy and valued members of their social group, unhappy family members may be tempted to invoke a double standard. In the one, family members coexist in unhappiness secretly; in the other, they may conceal the happiness they have with others outside the family because it is socially unacceptable. In either situation public morals are somewhat compromised.

Disagreement Between Young and Old ● Disagreements between age groups have existed in every generation. From the beginning of group living to the creation of modern society the coexistence of different age clusters has been a social necessity. Discrepancies in their views have always been a prominent feature in their mutual coexistence. Consequently, the so-called "generation gap" is truly not an entirely new phenomenon. Conflicts between parents and children have ranged historically from simple incorrigibility of children to parracide (the killing of one's parent/s) and between young and old, from violent attacks against the adult value system to total withdrawal from family relationships. However, these disagreements and conflicts have recently become far more visible, more widespread, deeper and more painful, and higher in social cost than ever before. The loosening of the former close relations between parents and their children and the permitting of greater freedom to the young have seemingly led youth to reject the values of their elders. Their parents in turn have refused to accept many of the life conceptions of the young. The modern confrontation of ages, therefore, has made an existing problem much more serious, and contributes to the problems of unhappy families.[10]

Kingsley Davis' contention that the "decelerating rate of socialization" is one of the major factors in parent-adolescent conflicts in contemporary western civilization[11] actually points to a significant historic cause of disagreements between young and old and explains much of the modern conflict. The "modern" parent is unable to understand the "modern" youth in part because the rate and scope of socialization generally diminishes as one ages. At the same time, the amount of knowledge and experience about the world in which both groups live increases, thereby creating a slowdown of learning despite the fact that socialization is a lifelong process and every member of society learns something new every day. It is also obvious that the time in one's life when one experiences events has an impact on one's perception of such events. For example, the effect of the Vietnam war was quite different for young persons than for older persons. Many of these older persons had during their early life experienced a major depression followed by a World War, thus, their perception of the Vietnam war was somewhat different from that of young people who had enjoyed relative prosperity and peace up to that point in their lives. Mannheim speaks to this point in an essay "The Problem of Generations."[12]

The differential ability or willingness of each group to understand and to learn has created new problems between the generations. Many issues exist because both groups do not learn the same things. After gaining the necessary knowledge and participating in prescribed experiences prerequisite to the acceptance of planned and meaningful social roles, the adult tends to decelerate the rate of his continued learning and focuses his attention on those roles which are part of his daily functioning. The more he knows and experiences within his field of endeavor, the less information he generally needs to gain through further learning. As he secures even greater knowledge and experience with the passing years, he comes to know more about his immediate field of concern but less about others. However, his growth in general knowledge has commonly been slowed or even stunted. On the other hand, the youth has yet to make his choices or to accept his future social roles. Thus, he proceeds to gather the information and experience necessary for anticipated role success. As a result, some youths learn and experience more in the limited time they have lived to date than adults experience in their lifetime.

Most of the discord between young and old stems from the youth's exploration of what has already been examined by adults. Their disagreements are products of the differences which require acceleration of the rate of socialization for one age group (youth) and which permit the deceleration of the rate of another (adult). The decelerating rate of socialization for adults, however, is not a cause of the conflicts or disagreements between age groups, but usually is a symptom of a person's inability or failure to accumulate vast stores of knowledge and experience in his youth. This difference, which is not the fault of either the youth or the adult, inevitably leads to differing viewpoints, disagreements, and occasional conflicts. However, the young also eventually arrive at that point in life where they decelerate the rate of their further socialization. As they advance in age, they are the ones who face similar challenges from the new generation of youth. Biologically and sociologically, this is a perpetual process. All young eventually become old; new young always emerge. The disagreements and conflicts between young and old, therefore, are inherent to social life; only the actors change in the continuum of passing years.

Factors in Parent-Youth Conflict

The difference in the amount of information and experience the young and old are exposed to does not explain fully the disagreement between the generations. These variances are colored by the idealism of youth and by the realism of the adult. Both perceptions of reality largely stem from the differential choices and roles available to each group. While youth has yet to decide which opportunities to experience in the future and to differentiate for themselves the best alternatives for their lives, the adult has already made his choices, recognized the limits of his future, and made a realistic appraisal of his relationship with others.

Differential Role Opportunities ● During the adolescent and early adult period in one's life, each person acquires various levels of skill and competency necessary for adult living.[13] However, even before a youth develops these abilities through the socialization process, he is exposed to a wide variety of social opportunities. Having failed to this point to develop an ability to evaluate opportunities as they really are, the youth is intrigued by their glamour and not their drudgery. He may see the physician, for example, as a warm-hearted person concerned with other people's health and fail to see him as an ordinary person who cannot avoid being involved in the financial aspects of a medical practice. He may also see a gray-haired and black-robed judge as impersonified justice and wisdom and not realize that he is often bored with petty cases and frequently administers law rather than justice. While he may conceive of the police officer as a brutal social oppressor, he may fail to understand that the policeman works endlessly for community peace and security within the defined and administered limits of law. Seeing the variety of social roles as they "should be" rather than as they "are," the youth may live in an idealistic world which does not and cannot exist.

Experience and knowledge often limit the future choices and opportunities of the adult. Reality, tempered by many years of experience, has taught the adult to exist in the world as it is and to accept the behavioral limits contained in social roles. While the adult may be more competent than the youth to measure the advantages, disadvantages, possibilities and barriers of particular acts, he is usually less idealistic inasmuch as his idealism has been corroded by experience. This does not mean the adult loses all idealistic impulses but rather that he gives up attempting to reach idealistic goals. The aspirations and goals the adult seeks are perceived more realistically.

While youthful idealism is commonly uncontrolled and oftentimes innocent, adult realism is influenced by an understanding of the ramifications of an action pattern. Aristotle recognized centuries ago that the young are socialized to social ideals, while the adult has reconciled his ideals with the limits imposed by group living. It is largely inevitable, therefore, that the youth holds adults' standards to be faulty and inadequate, even as the adult holds the judgments of the young to be unrealistic. Their roles, statuses, opportunities, and frames of reference are different.

Differential Political Belief ● The realism versus idealism dimension is a fundamental element in the differences between generational political beliefs. While the "adult political man" speculates on social issues and problems, the "youthful political man" speculates on social issues and attacks them with a massive and sometimes utopian activism. The socio-political history of man abounds with examples in which youth have rallied for change while adults have remained reserved and restrained. Leaders of demonstrations, protests, uprisings, and revolutions have historically taken advantage of the idealistic readiness of the young to act and have used them as prime movers for change and in social combat. In our society, the problem is somewhat different. It is tied to the passive attitudes of adults and the more informed and activistic commitments of the young to the world in which they live.

As the modern adult looks back to the adult of past generations and resents the latter's relative disinterest in social problems, so today's young resent the disinterest, inaction, static views, and faulty understanding which adults possess concerning what should be done in order to improve society. While it may be true that the adult is wrong but realistic and the youth is right but unrealistic, the adult is usually reluctant to admit that he is hesitant to approach the problems of his society, and the youth persistently refuses to concede that his approach to social problems may be unrealistic. A disagreement or conflict between political beliefs of the young and old, therefore, is inevitable, although a reconciliation of the two would help to make society peacefully dynamic and progressive.

While differences in political belief have existed between generations in the past, "there is something about today's world," Kenneth Keniston writes, "that seems to give the young a special restlessness" and "an increased impatience with hypocrisies" of the past world.[14] There are wide variations in political beliefs among youth. While many may oppose the existing political situation, their opposition may range from an attempt to change the system from within to complete giving up on the system. Among the latter, some will work to overthrow the system, while others simply "turn off" and become apathetic. Many contemporary youth who wish to overthrow the system have assumed a political belief that is exclusively theirs and excluded adults from any participation or contribution to its operation. Some have become so exclusive that they have even excluded many youths in the same age categories from involvement. They have become a "youth political subculture."

It is the latter subculture which makes present-day youth "different" from the political youth of past decades. It is this group of *youth within the youth* which is especially restless and "impatient with hypocrisies." However, this group has never fully disclosed what makes it uneasy nor fully purged itself of its own hypocrisy. While the members of the youth political subculture use violence as a means to "change *from* what," they do not encourage "change *to* what and *how*." While members of this subculture are different from political youth of the past, they are also different from other contemporary political youth.

This does not mean that all youth should agree politically with all adults, for such a goal is largely impossible. Studies[15] have shown, for example, that a significant portion of youth not only oppose but rebel against their parents' political views. In their reaction, they move to the radical left rather than accept the moderate or conservative rightest viewpoints of their parents. Although this may not be a new trend, what is new in this youthful dissent is the degree of the disagreement and the style of its expression. While all social movements in which youth participate, Lewis S. Feuer contends, "have been characterized by the highest degree of selflessness, generosity, compassion, and readiness for self-sacrifice," at times "the idealistic spirit has done violence to itself and to others" and "has been transmuted into a destructive force in human history."[16] This is the *new* facet of youthful dissent.

However, these features not only characterize differential political beliefs, but also appear in all forms of youthful alienation from adult society. Such estrangement is not really new except in its degree and in its more uninhibited expressions. The extent to which other forms of youthful alienation contribute to political disagreements and vice versa is difficult to measure, but all such phenomena coexist and are a part of the total parent-youth conflict scene.

Differential Value Structure ● One of the major sources of conflict between parents and youth stems from the different value systems to which the two generations adhere. In fact, it is a fear of losing validation of their values on the part of parents and a fear of having their values controlled on the part of youth that is at the heart of intergenerational conflict.[17] Especially as it relates to drug and alcohol use and to sexual behavior, generational differences occur. Although alcohol usage is prevalent in the United States as well as in many other countries, and such usage is generally regarded by all segments of the population as being reasonable and allowable, the use of drugs, especially marijuana, is primarily a youthful phenomenon. A 1972 National Commission on Marijuana and Drug Abuse nationwide survey of incidence and attitudes toward the use of marijuana estimated that 24 million Americans over 11 years of age, approximately 11 percent of the population, have tried the drug at least once. It concludes that age is the most important corollary of marijuana use, almost half of marijuana users being between 16 and 25 years of age. Of the 18 to 21 age group, about 40 percent used marijuana at least once. Among the high school population, 30 percent of juniors and seniors and 17 percent of freshmen and sophomores indicated that they had tried the drug. With respect to the college population, 44 percent have tried marijuana.[18]

At least two other reports support the accuracy of these estimates. In response to the 1972 Gallup Poll, 51 percent of a national sample of college students reported that they had tried marijuana at least once.[19] A nationwide four year panel study of the male class of 1969 by Lloyd Johnston uncovered that 21 percent of the respondents had used marijuana sometime during their high school years. The incidence figures increased to 34 percent in 1970, the group's first year out of high school. Johnston concluded that the relatively high usage in the college population and the observed higher conversion rate of college-bound when compared with civilian employment-bound youth will probably mean an even greater relationship in the future between education and marijuana use.[20] For although marijuana usage is increasing particularly among those 21 years of age or older and among high school students, usage among adults is especially pronounced among those with higher educational backgrounds.

As might be expected, the differentiation in usage between youth and adults results in a difference of opinion regarding the legalization of marijuana. The 1972 Gallup Poll survey indicates that more than 80% of the adult population is opposed to marijuana legalization. A 1970 nationwide Harris Poll of those between the ages of 15 and 21 found that 63% of these respondents opposed legalization. Seventy percent of those between 15 and 17 years of age opposed such decriminalization.[21] While it is clear that the majority oppose legalization of marijuana usage, the distinction between the attitudes of youth and that of adults is nevertheless evident.

Knudten and Meade, in a survey of existing legislation, show that most "progressive" legislation regarding marijuana possession has excluded the non-adult population from legal sanction. Despite the hesitancy of the general public to endorse the legalization of marijuana, a practice of lenient and haphazard enforcement of the law, resulting in the present tactic of *misdemeanorization*, has ensued. Thus, in spite of adult opposition to marijuana usage, a compromise enforcement policy has frequently been engaged in whereby possession will not result in a major sanction. At the same time, however, legislated criminal penalties for marijuana violations have usually increased in severity for subsequent convictions and the penalty for a sale conviction is consistently more severe than is the case for possession. Such practices within society seem to indicate that the adult population, that group which is normally involved in enacting legislation, is willing to recognize the value structure of youth in that it has generally lessened the sanction for use of marijuana while still maintaining more severe controls over what it regards as the more severe violations of drug abuse, continued usage and sale.[22]

Another area of variation in belief between youth and parents concerns the extent of sexual behavior, especially sexual intercourse before marriage. Sorenson reports that only one third of all adolescents believe that they hold common attitudes with their parents about sex. As they grow older, agreement with their parents' opinions on matters of sex diminish. In fact, adolescents have less respect for their parents' opinions on sex (65%) than for their opinions in general (80%).[23]

While a majority of adolescents (60%) oppose having sex for physical pleasure alone, they feel that adults assume physical pleasure is the main or only reason adolescents engage in sexual intercourse before marriage.[24] All told, two thirds of all adolescents agree that if two people love each other and are living together, getting married is just a legal technicality with which they should not be required to comply. However, such adolescents also recognize that their parents have different views, 72% believing that their parents think that sexual intercourse before marriage is immoral while only 12% think their parents would want them to live with their prospective marriage partner before marriage.[25]

Adolescent perception of parental views is apparently fairly accurate. Reiss found that 77% of a national sample of adults 21 years and older viewed premarital coitus as a violation of a norm. Many of these individuals held this view with sufficient intensity to place such behavior outside their tolerance level.[26]

Parental values of love, responsibility, and future orientation, which dominate the question of premarital sex relationships, are not necessarily negated by youthful sexual attitudes and activities. The emphasis is more on love and responsibility, however, than future orientation. Sorenson found that 21% of all American adolescents and 40% of those who had sexual intercourse are serial monogamists without marriage. A serial monogamist is an unmarried non-virgin who is having a close sexual relationship with a partner and who rarely or never has sex with another person during the life of the relationship. The code of serial monogamy requires that neither party enter into the relationship with the unspoken assumption of marriage. However, 55% of all serial monogamists answer "yes" or "probably" to the question "do you plan to marry your partner?" In contrast to the serial monogamist, only 15% of all American adolescents are sexual adventurers, those who seek mates without interest in initiating or maintaining a sexual relationship.[27]

The Differential Concepts of Authority • Perhaps a cause of the generation gap, indeed with far-reaching consequences, is the different way in which parents and children or adults and youth conceive authority. Power and authority are no longer vested within the father alone. Social life has passed well beyond the Roman period when the power of the father (*patria potestas*) was legally absolute and his rights included not only the maintenance of home discipline (*ius leviter castigandi*) but also decision-making in regard to his child's life (*ius vitae ac necis*). Although the rights of children and youth are rather limited, and their father can legally demand that any money they make be turned over to them until they have reached the age of legal responsibility (between 18 and 21 in the United States), the authority of the father has clearly diminished. Rather, what Feuer calls "generalized equilibrium" exists, a condition in which no generation frustrates another's energies and intelligence, deprives the other of its proper place in society solely because of its years, or forces another generation to carry an "undue portion" of society's burdens.[28]

Until the sixties, the American father, in cooperation with the mother, exerted home discipline and directed his child's life without provoking a significant disequilibrium and without arousing dominating feelings on the child's part of being oppressed, denied or blocked in his ambitions and aspirations. Parental authority was exercised rather smoothly; youth accepted this authority without *significant* resentment or rebellion against it. During this period, children understood parental authority to include a kind of societal assignment to direct and to shape their lives according to established cultural models and a right to guide, teach and train them so that they might function properly in their future life. Although the authority of the parents within the internal organization of the family and of adults within the structure of society to some extent limited the freedom of youth, they accepted it in most instances as if it were the "truth" imposed upon them in their own interest. This was true in urban, suburban, or rural communities, among all social classes, and in patriarchal and other family types.

The protest of the sixties has changed much of this. Both the youth and his parents have developed a different conception of adult authority and their own social roles. Youth are no longer bound to the family and to the larger society by traditional authority ties. They have assumed greater independence and in many instances more adult social roles. Society, which has been traditionally stratified according to wealth, occupation, social class and other factors, now finds that the factor of age is also an important variable in the ensuing differentiation of social classes. While in the past, and to a limited extent even now, parents commonly looked forward to the day when their children would be adults and had a reasonable chance of having their desires and expectations for their children fulfilled,[29] their current anticipations are only hopes, not expectations, of what may happen in the future. Parents are no longer able to exercise full authority and define what their child's future shall be. This does not mean that adults still want to keep youth subordinate, but rather that the principle of self-determination reigns supreme. Even conservative parents strive to "establish love-ties with their children" but use such ties of emotional dependency to force children gradually toward independence and family-leaving.[30]

While youth still accept the general authority of parents and adults, they do so only insofar as it is necessary to reach that point in life where they as adolescents decide their own intellectual commitments and personal-social values. At this point, the extent of their emotional attachment to their parents and their respect for their elders remains unclear. How much of this is related to the youth's economic needs? This is difficult to determine. Nevertheless, the concept of authority that once was understood and interpreted by adults and youth somewhat uniformily now has two rather different meanings. While the adult understanding is broader and more comprehensive, the youth's perception of adult authority is narrower and time-limited and is frequently conceived in terms of adult duties and obligations to youth.

This conflict between the two concepts of authority, which actually developed within the American family decades ago and was widely expressed in the sixties, tends to be resolved in favor of the young. Only future evaluators of parental and youth roles will be able to discern whether resolution of generational conflict in this manner benefits or hinders social coherence. However, it is clear that parents and adults tend to "give in" to their children and to give up portions of their traditional authority, formerly used to promote the youth's interest. Not only has the father's Roman-style patriarchal rule become a relic of the past, but his authority and ability to influence his children's values have declined. Even the strict discipline of Charles Dickens' day remains only an example within his novels of past relations between generations; teachers are no longer able to exercise authority in the same manner as they once did.

The Changing Concept of Educational Authority ● The conception of authority in the field of adolescent education, no less significant or more important than the changes apparent in parental power, is also undergoing change. In the late sixties a long series of demonstrations, first only at universities but later expanding even to high schools, occurred at commencements as well as in the course of the academic year. Many campus protests were political in nature; others were directed against educational authorities by students who wanted more power in the management of their institutions. Convinced that they were being "shortchanged" and that they did not receive the kind of education necessary for adequate personality development and for eventual entrance into functional social roles, students demanded change and a voice in the change process. Feeling cheated educationally, especially at the larger institutions, "they were ripe," Andrew Hacker suggests, "for any demonstration against authority in general and campus officialdom in particular."[31]

The demand for "student power" included the right to influence management of a school, determine modes of operation, decide what and how professors teach, and pass upon on-going policy. Students demanded the right to participate in deciding curricular content, the timing of classes, faculty employment strategy, admission policies, examination procedures, commencement speakers, and other campus and off-campus problems which affect students. In many cases, they achieved these goals. While students claimed that their reform movement, sometimes accompanied by violence, would establish democracy and introduce quality into American higher education, many administrators and academic personnel, in turn, argued that such an approach could only bring about a gradual decline in educational quality. Only the future can tell who is correct. But it is clear that student protests and administrative reactions have had their effects and have been based upon the different conceptions of educational need and the different conceptions of authority relationships which each party possesses.

The Disagreement Between Young and Young ● It is incorrect to assume that all youth are against all adults and the so-called generation gap monolithically divides the generations. Neither all old nor all young fully agree with the dominant posture taken by leaders of their own group. Consequently, the so-called generation gap is not always supported by every member of each group against the members of the other group. While many contemporary youth hold that the adult world they are being invited to join is completely irrelevant and hostile to their own ambitions and desires, other youth see it as a meaningful society which offers major satisfactions and rewards. Although these youth agree that there is a generation gap, they disagree with the contention that the adult society is always asking the wrong questions and is never right. They remain open to reason. Similarly, not all adults see youthful idealism and desire for change as a threat, but rather welcome the input which youth can make for society.

The questions of who belongs to one youth group and who to another depends largely upon the youth's self-concept and his understanding of roles which may cause him to deny adult society and to join the camp of social dissenters or may direct him away from these peers and help him to bridge the generation gap. However, both his self-concept and his role understandings are shaped by the two competing socializing agencies, elders and peers. Therefore, his self- and role-concept are products of the merger of these forces, which may differ for each person.

Although parental desires are of great importance to children in a long-range sense, they attempt to win the approval, admiration, and respect of their peers in their everyday activities.[32] While parents in past generations were able to transmit their values, habits, skills, and life styles to their children without being significantly disturbed by the value system of their children's peers, now the transmission of values often falters, fails, or is forced to compete with counter-influences, including those provided by youthful peers within a rapidly changing industrial society. The diminished access of adults to their children exposes youth more forcefully to peer socialization, the person-to-person peer interaction which encourages them to defy adults, parental values, and the values of adult society in general. In this way, the "inner-directed" and "tradition-directed," described by David Reisman, gave way to "other-directed" youth.[33]

Although the youth's peer group increasingly influences the life of the youth, "parents are still," Arnold Rose maintains, "the main influence in establishing the child's relationship with these groups."[34] The parents' denial of generational differences, an act no less detrimental than the parents' so-called permissive or "don't care" attitude, may force the young to join peer groups that deny the adult world. If parents and the general adult world, on the other hand, help youth to determine their relationship toward other socializing agencies and assist them in the forming of their self-concept and role aspirations, this will make generational interaction a progressive process.

Parent-youth conflict is, of course, only one factor involved in the total picture of family disruptions. While it may be a major cause of unhappiness within the family setting, it usually occurs within the framework of an intact household. Seldom does a family "break up" because of conflict between generations of the household. However, other types of family disruptions do involve the breakup of the home.

Broken Homes

A concern for the broken home has persisted for decades, especially as it has related to family wholeness as a juvenile delinquency preventative.[35] Generally, the idea of the broken home refers to the absence of one or both parents due to death, desertion, separation, or divorce. Although the implications of broken home life differ for children in relation to the cause of parental absence, past studies have largely minimized these differences and frequently included all types of parental absences under the umbrella term "broken home." As now utilized, the concept not only describes a disruption in the unity of the family, but also places a stigma upon the children within the broken home.

Delinquency and Broken Homes ● The Census Bureau estimated in 1923 that nearly one half of all children in institutions for delinquents came from broken homes. Even the Children's Bureau at the time of its beginnings in 1928 indicated that about one third of the delinquent boys and about one half of the delinquent girls within its study were not living with both parents. Studies dealing with the family status of children incarcerated in institutions show that most of the inmates, especially the girls, come from broken homes.[36] In their extensive 1929 study of 7,278 families of boys between 10 and 17 years in the Chicago area, holding the age and ethnic groups constant, Clifford R. Shaw and Henry D. McKay found that the ratio of broken homes among the delinquent and nondelinquent school population was 1.18 to 1. However, they concluded that it was not the broken home which caused adolescent deviance but rather the accompanying cumulative effects of family discord.[37] Similarly, Thomas P. Monahan concluded from his 1954 Philadelphia court study of some 9,000 juvenile delinquency cases that one third of the white boys and three fourths of the black girls came from broken homes.[38] However, despite these findings, the methodological shortcomings employed within these studies make it impossible to determine or confirm a causal relationship between the broken home and delinquent or criminal deviance.[39] Nevertheless, public opinion still holds that broken homes tend to produce delinquent children more frequently than any other element or factor. As a consequence, children of broken homes who have not displayed any kind of deviant behavior are often labelled juvenile delinquents.

Although it is logical to assume that children socialized and raised in a complete family would have a better chance to develop into healthy and happy adults, it would be an error to assume that the broken home is a predictive and major factor in the maladjustment of children. Of greater importance are the emotional and economic costs of the broken home upon the spouse who is left alone with the responsibility of caring for herself/himself and the children. This spouse, who began with a complete family, is now left unaided in the completion of family responsibilities. The lone spouse has to change major aspects of life style and adjust to a new personal, family, and social situation regardless of the cause of the broken home.

As with duties, the single parent's social status may also change. Emotional ties to the children, relationships with in-laws and friends, type and time of work, selection of leisure time activities, economic position, and availability to build a new complete family structure are also affected. In the one-parent broken home the remaining parent has to understand and accept a new and often burdensome role which may require the mobilization of more extensive physical and intellectual energies. As a result, whether this spouse and the children of the broken home will be useful and constructive members of society or whether they will become unhappy and maladjusted persons depends in large measure upon their ability to comprehend the changes which have occurred in their social roles and to mobilize the energy necessary to meet these changing demands. Even though the broken home poses a serious problem for every family member, as a mere fact it is itself not necessarily a social problem.

Separation and Divorce

When the broken home is a result of marriage partners terminating legally their cohabitation, a different dimension is added. While *separation* usually implies the informal but factual departure of one spouse from the marriage with or without the tacit or expressed agreement of the other spouse, it may be formalized by a court of law. *Desertion*, on the other hand, is a type of separation in which the deserting spouse not only leaves the other member but also attempts to hide his whereabouts, if only temporarily, by avoiding all contacts or communications with the marriage partner, children, and relatives he left behind. *Divorce*, often following the separation, is that final point at which a marriage is terminated through legal action. While the actual volume of separations and desertions is unknown, the number of divorces can be secured from a review of recorded court statistics. However, because attitudes toward divorce have varied considerably over time, divorce statistics are not as readily available as one might expect. It was not until 1960 that national data was collected from state records in the United States. In 1968, forms certifying divorce and annulment were adopted by the Division of Vital Statistics of the National Center for Health Statistics and recommended for use by all states. Compilations of such data are not yet available.[40]

High divorce rates traditionally signify that the family system is not functioning well or that marriage is not fulfilling its expected role. However, because all separations do not lead to divorce, the dysfunctional or malfunctional nature of the family is significantly more severe than indicated by official divorce rate statistics. Current figures, it has been estimated, should be increased by at least 25 percent if a true understanding of the divorce rate is to be gained. While the urban nonwhite population has traditionally utilized separation, often in the form of desertion, to terminate a marriage, a 1960 Health, Education, and

Welfare Department study revealed that the total rate per 1,000 of disrupted marriages for males was 3.6, separated 1.5, and divorced 2.1, and for females 4.8, 2.0, and 2.8 respectively.[41] The divorce rate per 1,000 married couples in the U.S. has varied from 7.8 in 1935 to a high 14.4 in 1945. After decreases to 9.2 in 1960 the rate in 1964 had increased again to 10.7.[42] Divorce rates vary according to the spouses' social class, urban, rural or small town residence, economic situation, age, length of marriage, age of children, and a number of other factors which contribute in some degree to the decision to seek divorce. While nearly everywhere throughout the world divorce rates are increasing, American society has the dubious honor of having the highest divorce rate. Since the turn of the century, the American divorce volume has roughly quadrupled, increasing especially after World War II. But the situation is quite similar in other societies.[43] For example, England, France, Sweden, Germany, and other Western countries also give evidence of increasing marriage failures; unofficial sources report similar trends even in the Socialist nations. Even though the number of divorces decreased in Japan at the beginning of the twentieth century, it increased in the post-World War II period. Despite these findings, much more research and comparative analysis is needed before those factors which play a decisive role in the development of divorce rates can be isolated. Since 1960, nearly 258 divorces have occurred in America for every 1,000 marriages, a figure which indicates that every third or fourth marriage in the United States fails.[44]

William J. Goode questions what changes in our social structure have caused this effect within the family system.[45] Undoubtedly the increased tensions, conflicts, aspirations, and ambitions that affect people and the pace of a hectic and competitive life style which has emerged primarily since the post-war period are involved. The exhaustive work demands placed on the husband, the wife's decision to enter the employment marketplace, the effect of parental work schedules on their children, the intervention of parent substitutes, the fluctuating economic situation, and the permanent stress and strain that are part of world affairs also take their toll.

But the most striking change, Goode believes, has occurred in the general values relating to marriage and subsequently to divorce. While no majority philosophy would characterize marriage as bad and divorce as good, both marriage and divorce are now taken more lightly than before. For many, marriage is no longer viewed as a life partnership which contains heavy duties and role obligations for each partner as well as for the forthcoming children. Similarly, divorce is likewise no longer perceived as something socially shameful which creates a sense of guilt for one or both spouses. The denunciation of divorce has become gentler and milder; and the denunciators, should they come even from the Church or from some highly respected secular source, often cannot compete with the pressures placed upon the marital participants by the family crisis itself. Because the traditional social consequences of divorce have largely been eased both by those who have divorced as well as by society generally, many legal jurisdictions have made the obtaining of a divorce an easier process.

Divorce is not a self-contained action. Its evaluation cannot be isolated from the analysis of the institution of marriage. Thus, when marriage has generally less value attached to it, less resentment or disapproval follows divorce. Similarly, the more divorce is accepted or approved, the more lightly is marriage likely to be taken, a situation which supports the increase in divorce. The movement away from the single "wife-and-mother" role, with its comfortable social and economic security and its subordinating and rather boring domestic duties, to the "companion" and "partner" roles, anticipated by Clifford Kirkpatrick some two decades before the women's liberation movement started to publicize its revolutionary visions, has to some extent assisted the increase of the divorce rate. Both roles have presupposed a rather extensive revaluation of both marriage and divorce.[46] The "companion" role is based largely upon the expectation that the wife wants to share her husband's ego and libido satisfactions; the "partner" role assumes that both the husband and wife shall carry equal burdens and enjoy equal privileges as if a marriage is simply a business proposition negotiated by future partners. Both are products of a new cultural definition of marriage. While both are generally measured in terms of the potential monetary rewards available to the partners, the changing marital and world situation may cause the informal renegotiation of the terms of the original contract. Such an approach is at odds with the traditional concept that marital cohabitation continues to the death of one spouse and that marital partners need to adjust as they are able to unforeseen situations and changed conditions.

Without acquitting or relieving the male population of its responsibilities for the increasing number of marital conflicts and divorces, attention must nevertheless be given to the fact that since World War II females have assumed new roles, gained greater independence and accepted fewer restrictions upon their actions. The traditional female obligation to children and the household has been significantly modified by many women, thus destroying any semblance of traditional marriage and even family life. Rising female aspirations have changed many of the original role definitions which have guided mate selection and marital arrangements and have generated in many homes the new conflict leading to divorce. Having agreed to the traditional "wife-mother" role at the time of their marriage, many men have been unable to adjust to a changed marital situation brought about by the wife's new ambitions and have responded in a manner leading to divorce. If the new feminism continues to influence young women to remain single and encourages already married women to transform marriages, the former will reduce (by not being married at all) and the latter will increase (by being married on clearly different basis) the divorce rate. Inevitably, this will lead to a new definition of and new role conceptions within the institution of marriage.

References

1. William J. Goode, "Marital Satisfaction and Instability: A Cross-Cultural Class Analysis of Divorce Rates," *International Social Science Journal,* (1962), XIV, 507-526.
2. Bernhard J. Stern, "The Family and Cultural Change," *American Sociological Review,* (1934), IV, 199-208.
3. Floyd M. Martinson, *Family in Society* (New York, 1970), pp. 9-10.
4. *Ibid.,* p. 10.
5. Pitirim A. Sorokin, *The Crisis of Our Age* (New York, 1941). The interpretation of the theme of his work.
6. W. F. Ogburn, *Recent Social Trends* (New York, 1933), pp. 661-708.
7. Donald W. Ball, "The 'Family' as a Sociological Problem," *Social Problems,* (1972), XIX, 295-307.
8. Paul H. Glasser and Lois N. Glasser, *Families in Crisis* (New York, 1970), p. 4.
9. William J. Goode, "Family Disorganization," *Contemporary Social Problems,* eds. Robert K. Merton and Robert A. Nisbet (New York, 1966), p. 533.
10. Alfred Adler, *What Life Should Mean to You,* ed. Alan Porter (New York, 1931). Adler dedicated his book to the human family "in the hope that its members may learn. . . to understand themselves better."
11. Kingsley Davis, "The Sociology of Parent-Youth Conflict," *American Sociological Review,* (August, 1940), V, 523-535.
12. Karl Mannheim, *Essays on the Sociology of Knowledge* (New York, 1952), pp. 276-320.
13. James C. Coleman, *Abnormal Psychology and Modern Life* (Chicago, 1964), p. 140.
14. Kenneth Keniston, "Youth, Change and Violence," *The American Scholar,* (Spring, 1968), XXXVII, 227.
15. Among others see Russell Middleton and Snell Putney, "Student Rebellion Against Parental Political Beliefs," *Social Forces,* (October, 1962), XLI, 377-383.
16. Lewis S. Feuer, *The Conflict of Generations: The Character and Significance of Student Movements* (New York, 1969), p. 3.
17. Vern L. Bengston and Joseph A. Kuypers, "Generational Difference and the Developmental Stake," *Aging and Human Development,* (1971), II, 249-240.
18. National Commission on Marijuana and Drug Abuse, *Marijuana: A Signal of Misunderstanding* (New York, 1972).
19. George Gallup, *The Gallup Poll* (New York, 1972).
20. Lloyd Johnston, *Drugs and American Youth* (Ann Arbor, 1973).
21. Louis Harris and Associates, *The Harris Survey Yearbook of Public Opinions—1970* (New York, 1971).
22. Richard D. Knudten and Anthony Meade, "Marijuana and Social Policy," *Addictive Diseases: An International Journal* (forthcoming, 1974).
23. Robert C. Sorenson, *Adolescent Sexuality in Contemporary America* (New York, 1973). p. 83.
24. *Ibid.,* p. 115.
25. *Ibid.,* p. 358.
26. Ira L. Reiss, *The Social Context of Premarital Sexual Permissiveness* (New York, 1967).
27. Sorenson, *Adolescent Sexuality,* pp. 219-245, 280.
28. Feuer, *Conflict of Generations,* p. 318.
29. Daniel R. Miller and Guy E. Swanson, "The Changing American Parent," *Studies in Marriage and the Family,* ed. Robert R. Bell (New York, 1968), pp. 165-166.

30. William J. Goode, *The Family* (Englewood Cliffs, N.J., 1964), p. 78.
31. Andrew Hacker, "The College Grad Has Been Short-Changed," *Social Profiles: USA Today, A New York Times Book* (New York, 1970), p. 178.
32. James S. Coleman, *The Adolescent Society* (New York, 1961).
33. David Riesman, Reuel Denney and Nathan Glazer, *The Lonely Crowd* (New York, 1950).
34. Arnold M. Rose, *Sociology: The Study of Human Relations* (2nd rev. ed.), (New York, 1965), p. 231.
35. Sophia M. Robison, *Juvenile Delinquency: Its Nature and Control* (New York, 1960), pp. 108ff.
36. Negley K. Teetors and John O. Reinemann, *The Challenges of Delinquency* (Englewood Cliffs, N.J., 1950), p. 153.
37. Clifford R. Shaw and Henry D. McKay, "Social Factors in Juvenile Delinquency," *Report on the Causes of Crime by the National Commission on Law Observance and Enforcement* (Washington, D.C., 1931), pp. 276ff.
38. Thomas P. Monahan, "The Delinquent Child and the Broken Home." Paper presented to the Eastern Sociological Society meetings in New York City on March 25, 1956, cit. Robison, *Juvenile Delinquency*, p. 110.
39. Travis Hirshi and Hanan C. Selvin, *Delinquency Research* (New York, 1967), pp. 114-141.
40. Hugh Carter and Paul C. Glick, *Marriage and Divorce: A Social and Economic Study* (Cambridge, Mass., 1970), pp. 1-13.
41. Hugh Carter and Alexander Plateris, "Trends in Divorce and Family Disruption," *Health, Education and Welfare Indicators* (September, 1963), pp. v-xiv.
42. Cater and Glick, *Marriage and Divorce*, p. 31.
43. See among others, *United Nations Demographic Yearbook, 15* (New York, 1963).
44. Bureau of Census, *Statistical Abstract of the United States, 1964* 85th ed. (Washington, D.C., 1964), p. 64.
45. Goode, *The Family*, p. 503ff.
46. Clifford Kirkpatrick, "The Measurement of Ethical Inconsistency in Marriage," *The International Journal of Ethics*, (1935-1936), XLVI, 445-446.

CHAPTER 6

Sexual Intercourse:
Problems Outside and Inside Marriage

Is Sex a Social Problem?

Human interest in sex from the beginning of personal and social history has extended far beyond the level of physical and intellectual curiosity. From the romantic myths of preliterary history through the classical dramas and bucolic poetry, the piquant Decameron of Giovanni Bocaccio and the spicy memoirs of Giacomo Girolamo Casanova, to modern literature and arts, more has been written and pictured about sex than about any other aspect of human interaction. Modern-day interest has expanded to include cheap pornography, misleading pseudo-scientific literature, so abundantly available in the fast-growing number of "adult" bookstores, and the "X-rated" films or "stage shows" which possess neither artistic merit nor elements of decency. Each panders to lewdness and obscenity, causes sexual excitement or lust, and attracts an unparalleled number of persons regardless of their sex, age, and social position. But the problematic aspects of sex do not end at this point. The desire to secure sexual materials has been joined by a more openly expressed want to participate in sexual pleasures, a desire which has sometimes significantly influenced the outcome of human history. Sex has shaped human interaction and events, whether in the form of family quarrels or devastating human wars and whether among ordinary men or well-to-do personalities, those who live in rural districts or urban areas, crowded slums or ornate palaces.

Although the interest in sex is as old as man, the scientific evaluation of the question is rather new. In a long series of works, Sigmund Freud held sex to be a major stimulus in determining and directing human behavior. Whether the Englishman Henry Maudsley in claiming that social advancement is founded upon sexual feeling, the German Baron Richard von Krafft-Ebing in condemning all sexual practices other than heterosexual intercourse, or perhaps various branches of the Freudian school in making feelings about sexual intercourse responsible for nearly every kind of human conduct, including criminal and delinquent acts, were correct is questionable. However, each correctly presumed that sex is an accentuated and often decisive feature in interpersonal and social interaction.

In the past ordinary men thought largely about the role of sex in human affairs in terms of their narrow social circle or their personal lives. Most men were hardly aware that sex had become influential in crucial incidents that concerned the population as a whole. If some were aware, they treated it discreetly and rarely discussed it publicly in an inopportune fashion. The role of sex in human decision making and general living are now discussed both orally and literarily in an exaggerated and sensational manner, sometimes attributing a role to sex even in cases where it has no real role. Today men are almost obsessed with sex in all of its forms and expressions. Consequently, a centuries old personal problem has become a social problem; the personal and the discreet have become common and public. In our liberated age, when the leading or participating in a movement of liberation has become a fad and when our free society has made freedom a fetish, sex too is liberated—not merely in practice, where it has always been somewhat free and in marriage even obligatory, but in public discussion where sexual matters have traditionally been handled in a more discreet, private, and traditional manner.

The Public Discussion of Sexual Questions ● The unfettered discussion of sexual problems and the less inhibited participation in a variety of sexual practices and relationships are reflections of the decline in importance of general social relationships and an increase in the desire for bodily pleasures.[1] Not only have the clan and extended family shrunk in size, but bonds within the nuclear household have also become loose, inactive, and neglected. Visits of adult children and aging parents have become less and less frequent. Individualism has challenged the character and quality of man's relationships and the nature of his ties with his own community. Restless social mobility, long commuting distances, and ever-increasing bureaucratic duties imposed upon each member of society by the continually expanding bureaucracy leave little time and provide minimal motivation for a person to share in communal or intellectual interests. Such pressures force the common man to withdraw to a small social circle which is ruled by hedonistic goals, empty intellectualness, and irresponsible sexual interests which offer instant satisfactions without involving one in long-term efforts or commitments that promise rewards only at a later date.

While sex in itself is not a social problem per se, the public style and open engagement in sexual practices are what create the difficulty. Although without sex most social institutions would collapse and traditional forms of organized society would come to an end, it is the valuation of sex rather than sex itself which has become problematic. The preoccupation with personal gratification and the decline in male and female willingness to assume the laborious social responsibility involved in maintaining lasting social relationships provide the foundation for this aspect of social problems. In this era when many men hold nothing sacred or private, the realm of sex has also suffered. What makes sex a social problem is that free and guiltless sex is now glibly recommended to modern man as a "natural" ambition to such an extent that much of his physical and intellectual energy, which might have been exerted toward world better- ment, has now been diverted to personal pleasures nowhere related to constructive communal interests. Modern sexual freedom, it now appears, includes the tendency to seek sexual gratification irresponsibly, even offensively, outside traditional institutions and social roles. Even "the concept of marriage as a meal ticket and a license to copulate, prefixed by a brief spell of euphoric romance,"[2] one observer concludes, is nearly on its way out.

Sex and Venereal Disease ● This excessive emphasis upon the practice and enjoyment of sex not only pulls many ordinary men away from their social responsibilities and attacks social institutions but also creates new or expands old social problems. The accelerated growth in sexual freedom, the general changing of moral and ethical standards, and the introduction of the contraceptive pill and similar devices into social practice, for example, have been decisive factors in the sudden resurgence of venereal disease. Whereas reported cases of primary and secondary syphilis dropped to 6,516 in 1955, 20,186 cases were reported in 1970, a rate of 10 cases for every 100,000 in the population. Gonorrhea occurs even more frequently, being the most prevalent of *all* communicable diseases reported in the U.S. In 1955 almost 240,000 cases were reported. By 1970 573,200 cases, a rate of 285.2 per 100,000 population, were reported to State Health Departments.[3] The increasing prevalence of gonorrhea is attributable primarily to rising promiscuity.[4] Cohen discovered that the percentage of gonorrhea cases diagnosed among women increased from 14.06 percent in 1965 to 20.05 percent in 1968, while the proportion of infected females using the "pill" rose from 23.8 percent to 40 percent during the same period.[5] A. Boulton Hewitt confirmed this finding in his discovery that the gonorrhea rate among women who use oral contraceptive agents is three times the rate for the total fertile female population.[6] In addition, the transmission of venereal disease through homosexual acts is also increasing. Because one out of three homosexuals is sexually promiscuous and because he usually fails to take precautions to prevent infection, the homosexual's freedom is a serious threat to public health.[7]

While rapid increase in the incidence of syphilis and gonorrhea are alarming, these are treatable diseases. Both diseases are caused by bacteria and, if treated promptly with strong doses of antibiotics, almost always can be cured. However, another venereal disease, until recently almost unrecognized by doctors and the general public, has become evident. This disease caused by a virus, *herpes simplex* Type 2, is resistant to all known medication. The virus is similar to herpes simplex Type 1 which causes cold sores or fever blisters, but Type 2 is almost always acquired through sexual contact and is highly contagious.

The disease may be second to gonorrhea in prevalence but no one knows for sure because reporting of cases is not required by the Public Health Service. Dr. William E. Josey, associate professor of gynecology and obstetrics at Emory, estimates there has been a three- to fourfold increase in the past 10 years.[8]

Venereal disease rates are rising especially among teenagers who are participating increasingly in coital promiscuity and noncoital transmission. The rising incidence of sexually transmitted diseases is attributed mainly to radical modifications of sexual behavior, resistant gonococcal strains, increased mobility, packaged holidays, antisocial behavior, and the overconfidence caused by the "pill." "Looked at dispassionately it almost appears," Catterall contends almost pessimistically, "as though mankind is plagued with a built-in desire for destruction ... the biological evolution of man seems to have come to a standstill."[9] It is this impact of sexual freedom in self and public health victimization that makes sexual liberation an aspect of current social problems.

Premarital Sexual Relations

Although contemporary sexual freedom embraces the interest and most often the actual action of nearly all age groups, social strata and sexes, nothing illustrates the scope of this social problem more clearly than the spectrum of premarital sexual relations, by definition the sexual behavior of unmarried youth. What complicates this aspect of the problem is that contraception for the nonmarried young female, a major instrument upon which sexual libertarianism depends, is a special problem within the problematic aspects of sex, not only for moralists but also for many sexual liberals. For example, the physician who prescribes the pill or contraceptive device for an unmarried teenage girl may groan inwardly at the same time. Even if the question of the morality of the situation does not bother him, other ramifications of uninhibited sexual intercourse may. In some instances, he may feel that the providing of his service is justified, especially where the prospect of future marriage is present; in others, he may view the premarital sexual relationship as little more than an unrestricted swing toward copulation outside of marriage, as if it were a harmless natural part of the normal life conduct. At this point the problem within the problem of sex becomes apparent. Copulation has various ramifications, such as the spreading of venereal disease mentioned earlier, which go beyond the act itself. When feminists support this age group in their claim for equal opportunity for sexual enjoyment, it is questionable whether they are demanding equality or a dangerous privilege.

A New Social Norm? ● Whether the massive involvement of modern youth in excessive and free premarital sexual relationships is due to a genuine desire to enjoy sex or to a newly developed social norm which, if not followed, would make the young person a kind of deviant, is a crucial question. If the former, it is difficult to understand why this almost irresistible drive has emerged only now and not centuries ago. Of course, it may be explained chiefly in terms of the encouragement offered by various liberation movements which brought the awareness of biological drives into the open. If the latter, then Ira Reiss offers an explanation when he suggests that sexual permissiveness is learned in a social setting in the same formal and informal ways as other attitudes, which are acquired in the course of participating within a social group.[10] Sexual norms, Reiss contends, are not really different from other group norms in the sense that not only are they endorsed but they are also expected to be followed.

Sexual norms develop through the values youth gain from their parents, friends, and the social groups to which they are exposed in the course of their maturation.[11] The pace of response to permissive pressures, most often coming from the peer group and promoted by the individual's biological sex drives, depends upon the strength of the basic values instilled in the youth through parental upbringing and reflects in part the social position of the young person's family. However, the general liberality and adventurousness of the American youth culture places family cultural training in jeopardy. The peer system seems to support values regarding sexual practices which may represent deviancy from society at large.[12]

Although both Reiss and Robert R. Bell hint that "rebellion" as a response to a functional subculture and its value system often represent conformity from the point of view of the subgroup, it is not necessarily true that premarital sexual relations are regarded as deviance by the larger society. While the majority of American society does not approve of or openly endorse premarital sexual relationships, most members seem to accept the practice; therefore, to call such practices sexual permissiveness may be incorrect. It could be that the term "disinterested" or "tolerated" more clearly express what adults and the larger society think about this aspect of American youth culture. The somewhat hesitantly intervening parental attitude, often simply neglect, coupled with the fast-growing interest and involvement of the adult society larger in sex facilitate the acceptance of youth's premarital sexual interests and its participation in premarital sexual relationships. While the situation in the sixties may have been as described by Reiss and Bell, the issue of sex is no longer, if ever, confined to youth. This explains in large measure why young persons' premarital sexual relationships have gained "nonapproved acceptance."

Premarital Sexual Alternatives ● Premarital sexual relationships may be classified into four categories.[13] *Abstinence* is a state in which premarital intercourse is regarded as wrong for both sexes. It represents conservative values and causes guilt feelings when violated. Although this attitude has been losing social support, it nevertheless retains strong influence. However, once the abstinence value has been violated, "recidivism," despite feelings of guilt, is likely to result. *Permissiveness with affection,* according to Reiss, emphasizes an equalitarian standard that permits conditional premarital coitus for both men and women. This type of relationship is likely to be common where an established relationship may carry into the future, as for example, in engagement or strong affection, and/or the guilt feeling is rationalized or neutralized. However, the relationship is susceptible to a decrease in love emotions or an increase in love disappointments which may undermine the affectional sexual relationship.

Permissiveness without affection refers to a total disregard of affectional stability due to physical attractions which dominate the premarital relationship. Although not necessarily based upon promiscuity, it nevertheless emphasizes a growing indiscriminate belief in sexual freedom. Its essence is the seeking of sexual pleasure unrestricted by marriage, cohabitation, deep and lasting emotions, or other types of permanent projections. The *double standard* refers to the restriction of women and the right of men to engage in premarital sexual relationships. A traditional belief, the double standard has some following in American society and is common to nearly all foreign cultures. Although the so-called "orthodox" double standard in rare situations makes allowances for sexual relationships by females who are engaged or who are in "true" love relationships which include a justifiable hope for engagement. Regardless of which of these variable attitudes is expressed, it is generally clear that little is done socially to prepare adolescents for future sexual relationships. Although sex education is gaining support, it is evident that the momentum for the movement has come from a public demand to respond to growing sexual problems rather than to a clear desire to prepare youth adequately for marriage.

Premarital Sex and Sex Education ● The frequency of premarital sexual relationships is not due to the emergence of sex education programs but rather to the revolutionary increase in desire to engage in premarital sexual contacts. Sex education, where it is taught, is usually very rudimentary and far from what it should be. Often it is purely technical, although it also tends to convey attitudes. At other times, it may be more idealistic and somewhat devoid of helpful physical knowledge. While the teaching of physical facts is relatively simple, knowing what attitude to convey in teaching and how to teach are far more difficult. To inform youth about the physical aspect of sex as if it were simply a thrill, a supreme pastime, or a sport represents one extreme. To teach that sexual intercourse should be restricted to persons mutually bound to each other by a superior affinity in the form of a rite or sacrament represents the other end of the continuum. Although it is easier to teach the former than the latter, the rapid lifting of virtually all limits concerning the public discussion and display of what has, hitherto, always been regarded as a private matter makes accurate and wise sex education extremely difficult. While some books, films, or educational courses seriously attempt to respond to the problem, most are still produced and distributed for commercial purposes under the guise of public service.

At a time when movies, television, advertisements, and cheap literature bombard youth and when attitudes toward sex outside of marriage change so swiftly, it is the lack rather than the superabundance of information which is at least partially responsible for the alarming increase in rates of venereal disease and for the high number of illegitimate and premaritally conceived babies who now compose about 25 percent of all births. While many parents believe they should offer sex education to their children, others admit that they are incapable of completing the task and want the job done by the schools. However, well-intentioned educators generally talk only about the mechanics of sex and not about that which lifts sex above the biological level. In their desire to be free from criticism, they tend to simplify the relationship and compare human relationships to sex lives of animals.

Thomas Carter contends that while there is nothing false in teaching that men and women, when aroused, rub against one another just like chimpanzees or other animals, the termination of the discussion at that point is inadequate and therefore misleading.[14] Man, he notes, is unique among living creatures; after all, he was able to build the Parthenon, compose the B minor Mass, and give a higher meaning to the word "love." As opposed to Reiss' and Bell's somewhat simpler and descriptive "sociological" orientation, Carter argues essentially that in teaching the proper physical procedures and experienced sex customs, we should necessarily impart a mental attitude concerning it. Mating behavior, including premarital sex, should contain, he maintains, not only a social context but also an emotional significance and dignity.

There is considerable evidence that there is increased sexual permissiveness among the young before marriage. Not only is premarital intercourse on the increase, but such activity is beginning at younger ages.[15] Other sexual activities, such as masturbation, are also carried out increasingly at younger ages and by both sexes.[16] Nevertheless, one has to be aware of the fact that the female's emotional involvement and commitment in sexual relations, mainly before marriage, tends to be deeper than that of the male. As a consequence, the current and rapidly continuing trend toward making premarital sexual relationships a custom or even a norm is not necessarily a move toward a free and greater pleasure for all. It may result in an increased emotional affliction or problem for many young women. However, cultural changes may also condition the emotional makeup of women and eliminate many possible psychological problems that could result from premarital sexual relationships, consequences which have biological imports and genetic-behavioral implications. Although the women's liberation movement seeks to persuade the public that women are not really so different from men, at least in terms of their right to sexual satisfaction, psychological differences between men and women can only be eliminated by genetic and biological changes in the sexes. Because complex behavior patterns inevitably stem from complex socio-cultural and bio-genetic patterns, women seem to be immutably different from men.

The Problem of the Unwed Mothers and Illegitimacy

For centuries, customs and laws have been oriented to procreation within legitimate marriage, and illegitimacy has carried a social stigma. While the former has emphasized the protection of the family as the most important basic institution of organized society, the latter has sought to reinforce a value which encourages sexual contact only between husband and wife. Man's social history testifies that laws, customs, and the public favor the functional and structural legal continuity of the "whole" family, even to the point that a child who is able to "display" two living parents who live together in a legitimate marriage receives greater social acceptance than one whose family is broken either by divorce or by death. About 10 percent, if not more, of American children, however, share the fate of living with only one parent, most often the mother. The seriousness of this problem is evident in the fact that most of the tasks for which a family is responsible rest upon both rather than one parent. Providing for the physical, emotional, and social needs of all the family members, Paul Glasser and Elizabeth Navarre contend, is a full-time job for two adults, and thus, "structural characteristics of one-parent families" do have their undesirable consequences.[17]

Although modern society is now witnessing a trend toward the acceptance of a one-parent family, the unwed mother and the illegitimate child are still exposed to societal disapproval. Should they belong to the upper strata of the society or be better known through professional performances, their condition may be publicized in news media gossip columns. This is so because "the generic social issue in illegitimacy is that illicit births are regarded as a threat to the family as a social institution."[18] Perhaps cynically, Kingsley Davis suggested that the best way to eliminate illegitimacy is to abolish marriage;[19] but it is obvious that social problems cannot be solved merely by changing attitudes, social customs or laws. Any such attempt indicates only that the society does not want to solve this social problem or to remove the stigma it attaches to illegitimacy, largely derived from the perceived promiscuity of the unwed mother.

Licit and Illicit Births ● Illicit births receive greater attention than do unwanted pregnancies. However, not all illicit births are unwanted; and not all licit births are desired. Illicit births, Vincent contends, represent only a fractional portion of the total number of annual unwanted pregnancies.[20] The estimated 350,000 annual illicit births compose only about 10 percent of those pregnancies which occur despite the wishes of sexual partners. About three quarters of all first pregnancies among U.S. women between the ages of 15 and 19 occur before marriage.[21] The number of abortions, pregnant brides, married couples who relinquish children by offering them for adoption, and married fathers and mothers who continue to keep their children although they do not want them far exceed the number of unwed mothers. While children born to unwed mothers may pose a painful social problem, the other aspects of the problem are often more visible and more challenging to the moral values of society, especially if the unwed mother is young.

The rate of illegitimate births has increased significantly since World War II. According to an estimate of the U.S. National Center for Health Statistics, the number of illegitimate births per 1,000 unmarried women in the age group of 15 to 44 increased markedly between 1940 and 1960 and has continued a slight increase to this day.[22] While the rate in 1940 was 7.1, it increased by 1960 to 21.8, a threefold enlargement. By 1968 the rate was 24.1. Among the youngest group, under 15 years to 24 years, the number of illegitimate births increased almost fourfold. In the age group of 25 to 29 years, the number in 1940 was 10,500 which rose to 35,200 in 1968. While the rate for blacks and other minority groups has always been higher than for whites, 89.5 compared to 12.5 in 1967, the rate has increased in greater proportion for whites than for blacks. Although enlarged use of hospital maternity facilities may account for some of the growth in the number of recorded illegitimacies, much of this growth may also be due to a reduced use of contraception and to a higher rate of women engaged in premarital coitus. There is some evidence that fertility rates among unmarried women follow patterns similar to those of married women.[23] Thus, the upward trend may be paralleling the general increase in fertility evident during this time period. However, modern youth culture has been more tolerant of illegitimacy and has lessened, Ira L. Reiss believes, former social pressures which often led an unwed mother to seek an abortion.[24]

Who are the Unwed Mothers ● Answers to such questions as who are the unwed mothers, from what cluster of people or social stratum do they come, and is it possible to predict who will have a child out of wedlock are not easily offered without some reference to changing sexual morality. Four familiar answers have been given to these questions.[25] The *mentality* answer associates illegitimacy with low intelligence or even mental derangement and encourages the sending of unwed mothers to psychiatric clinics for testing and treatment. The broken home response assumes that illegitimacy is a product of such a condition, often of deficient or missing moral and social controls over the actions of the young female. The *geographic mobility* analysis sees illegitimacy in terms of inadequate controls coupled with social change. The *disturbed parent-daughter relations and emotional disturbance* explanation finds illegitimacy to be an attempt to establish substitute emotional ties. But the problem is far greater than these explanations would indicate.

Because each of these factors has been attributed historically to lower class members, unwed mothers until recently have often been restricted to jobs requiring few skills, have not been encouraged to gain an adequate education, and have been largely relegated to low socioeconomic status.[26] As the public has become more aware that mental derangement, broken homes, emigration and immigration, and disturbed parent-daughter relationships are not exclusively lower class problems but appear equally among middle and upper class members, although better hidden, many of the sanctions surrounding illegitimacy have broken down. While some illicit births, as Ruth Cavan suggests, occur among girls who hold jobs in bars, restaurants, dance halls, and hotels which cater to men expecting sexual relations with their female employees, another major portion of the total aggregate are from middle and upper-class unwed mothers. To explain illegitimacy, therefore, in terms of the exploitation of the poor, emotional disturbance, and the subordination of females by better educated and more sophisticated higher class males can only misconceive the existing problem and misidentity the couple producing the child.

The rise in the rate of unmarried mothers within the general population cannot be detached from the problem of and increase in the frequency of premarital relationships and the almost limitless sexual freedom which modern contraception offers. While a certain number of illicit childbirths by unwed mothers is due to emotional or other "exploitation" or to criminally forced sexual relations, at least as many premarital pregnancies and illegitimate births are by-products of liberated female sexual morality which does not prohibit the birth of a child before or even outside of wedlock.

The Care of Illegitimate Children • Children born outside of marriage and without a father not only continue to face a social stigma, despite the liberated context of their birth (inasmuch as those who tend to attach the stigma are in themselves not liberated), but also may not be exposed to the care, socialization, or qualities necessary to equip them to be functional members of society. If it is true that the care and socialization of the child is a full-time job of both parents and the child's success or failure rests largely upon their joint efforts, an illegitimate child is born into a structurally crippled one-parent family. Those who oppose this view and argue that successful children often come from broken homes or that unsuccessful youths are frequently products of whole but unhappy homes fail to recognize the rule for the exception.

The so-called illegitimate child has to enter the society not only without a father, but often also without even knowing who the father is. The mother, too, may not be aware of who her male partner in conception is, or if, as frequently happens, she does know, refuses to reveal his name even to their child. While this may be due to shame, it may also be because of the desire to protect her lover. However, the chief reason for attempting to locate the "disappeared" or "lost" father is usually not to give the child information about his father but "to establish paternity and exact medical costs or support for the child."[27] As a result, little is known about the unmarried father in comparison to the unmarried mother. While many unmarried fathers evade all responsibility for the child they have helped to produce, most accept some financial responsibility but do not play the father role or participate in their child's care.

In such circumstances the total burden and responsibility for raising the child falls upon the mother. Unless she lives on welfare or receives satisfactory financial support from the child's father, the unwed mother is forced economically to take or continue a job in order to live, thereby leaving some of the task to others and giving up a substantial part of her parental responsibility to raise the child. When this occurs, the illegitimate child grows up and is socialized not as a functional family member but rather as an individual having a maximum of one parent and a minimum of none.

While group or day centers, philanthropically oriented neighbors, or other "third persons" may assume some of the childrearing responsibilities of the working unwed mother, the child may be exposed to haphazard care. Because the partially participating working unwed mother's value system agrees largely by chance, if at all, with the one represented by the given care center, nursery, or "third person," the illegitimate child, as a rule, faces serious problems in reconciling the frequently conflicting values to which he has been exposed by the varying socializing agents. Neither public attitudes nor public policy, however, offer the unwed mother sufficient assistance to solve her problems or to care for her illegitimate child. Even if they did, the problem would probably remain, because many unwed mothers who willingly become pregnant outside of marriage unfortunately either do not care about the fruit of their premarital sexual relationship and/or cannot or do not want to understand that their pleasure-seeking sexual activity may cause emotional problems for their children at a later date. Unwed mothers rarely have expertise in the physical and emotional aspects of contraception, hygiene, disease, sexual performance,[28] and in costs of premarital pregnancy. Seldom do they realize that their illegitimate child poses a highly important and most difficult social problem.

Marital Sex Difficulties

Ambrose Bierce, the nineteenth century author, defined marriage as a small group that consists of a master, a mistress, and two slaves, "making in all two." His definition has been no less attacked than the traditional twentieth century description which sees marriage in terms of only two persons; the husband, the master, and the wife, the slave. Both definitions of marriage are bitterly and resentfully challenged by modern feminists and members of various female liberation movements who demand changes in the married partnership, not only in terms of the general rights and duties of married partners, but also in their sexual relationships. These ambitious changes would not only alter psychological relationships and the purpose and style of love-making, but would also modify the legal rights and duties of monogamic marriage, especially as they apply to the married couple's regular private sexual activities.[29] What contemporary feminist liberators attack is what Thomas Carter has described as a private affinity between two persons bound to each other in a permanent and exclusive marital association, which is fully realized between husband and wife not only in the physical and psychological excitement of sharing the same bed over the years, but also in the living through of the inevitable life struggles together in ways that complement each other.[30]

Married partners, preferably before they complete their nuptials, should be aware of the crucial issues of legal cohabitation, for if problems arise in the marriage, it may fail, and the nuptial tie may be broken. Frequently, it is the physical, sexual relationship which fails and undermines the other aspects of the marriage. The extensive sexual and marital literature published for public usage suggests quite clearly that sexual problems underly a large percentage of marital problems. Not only does such literature discuss questions of mate choice, the economics of home management, and relations with in-laws, but also sexual relationships of marital life partners. Although these materials in the past emphasized sex as a means to an end (i.e., producing children), the more recent publications have encouraged marital sex as a goal in itself. In the nineteenth century such publications warned against the excessive expenditure of sexual energy, discussed the dangers of intemperate sexual behavior, and examined the grave consequences of sexual indulgence and the abuses of conjugal privileges. In general, they conceived of marital sex as something neither to be approached lightly nor to be engaged in with an anxiety-free mind. While the older sex and marriage manuals made marital sex an integral part of all other affectionate marital rights and duties, many similar contemporary publications depict marital sex as a kind of vacuum, emphasizing sexual satisfaction and ignoring many of the more general relationships of the married male and female.[31]

The Transition From the Past to the Present • This transition in attitude occurred at the turn of the century when a more positive and sophisticated attitude toward sex in marriage developed.[32] Nonproductive marital sex received greater acceptance. The physician William Lee Howard, for example, argued that only "happy and joyous sex relations can keep the world moving and progressing,"[33] and William J. Robinson acclaimed the independence of marital sexual behavior, noting that "the sex instinct has other high purposes besides that of perpetuating the race."[34] By the early 1900's, greater attention was being given to mutual orgasm as a requisite to sexual satisfaction and marital gratification. In this period and until the 1940's, women increasingly expanded their sexual rights within marriage, and husbands increasingly agreed to the assumption that they had a responsibility to enable their wives to exercise this right and "to make certain she experiences sexual satisfaction."[35] During this period, Sigmund Freud impressed the world with his insights regarding the significance of sexual attitudes on social and emotional behavior patterns.

Although the having of a sexual relationship remains the ultimate legalized norm and procreation the eventual sexual goal within marriage, the tie has been expanded to include the personal gratification of biological sex drives. Fulfillment by both partners has become a legitimate expectation of the marital experience. Where a successful sexual adjustment is not made, the marriage may be strained or crippled, leading potentially to separation or divorce and to the ruination of an otherwise happy and healthy relationship. While some marriage participants are able to overcome dissatisfying sexual relationships and maintain marital stability because of the other satisfactions marriage offers, others are unable to overcome their sexual difficulties and terminate their marriages. What direction the marital relationship takes depends largely upon the total configuration of assets or debits which the marriage includes and the personality characteristics of the marital partners. While their premarital sexual experience may be an important determinant of this outcome, it may also be an obstacle to long-term marital stability. However, if the participants did become aware of the emotional and physical costs and benefits of living together and/or of the emotional problems caused by separation before marriage, this experience may help them remain faithful to each other even if their sexual relationship were to fail at a later date.

Although still far from universal approval and acceptance, apparent drastic changes have occurred in marital sexual morality. Whether these practices will become the new norm or not will be determined in the future. If they do, many of the sexual problems inherent in marriage may disappear. Although these norms may undermine and even destroy marital and family relationships as a by-product of their fulfillment, this may occur only in extreme cases in which sexual commitments are not restricted to the marriage itself. Nevertheless, adultery, regardless of man's social history, is still often legally prohibited and socially resented. A married person engaging in a voluntary sexual relationship with a person other than his or her lawful spouse has generally been treated as a social outcast. However, in some forms of extramarital sexual response, this has not been the case.

An Emancipated Marital Sex Form ● One of the most emancipated forms of marital and extramarital sex is called "swinging" or "mate-swapping." Swinging presupposes, according to Carolyn Symonds, a willingness of acquainted or unacquainted individuals or couples to swap sexual partners and favors and/or to go to a swinging party for the sake of having sexual relations or intercourse with strangers.[36] Not all swingers are married; in fact, one study finds that more single persons than marrieds are involved in group sex.[37] While both single persons and unmarried couples may swing at these parties, among married participants both husband and wife actively share in the orgiastic festivities. Although most mate-swapping or swingers are introduced to the idea before they desire or are given the opportunity to engage in its practice, those who are recruited tend to be married couples with abnormal sexual inclinations or without traditional moral attitudes and persons who have had sexual failures in marriage.[38] Swingers are commonly introduced to the practice through mass media advertisements, friends, or acquaintances. Customarily, the husband and wife agree to accept the invitation.

Although mate-swappers or swingers may be aware that they are deviants, they tend to view themselves as emancipated persons who are pioneering a sexual revolution that is aimed at the elimination of marital sexual restrictions or to excuse their actions on the grounds that it solves their sexual problems within marriage. In order to reconcile their deviant conduct and enforced moral and legal norms, they define "swinging behavior in positive terms, as the appropriate behavior to meet whatever needs they have."[39] They do not necessarily consider group sex a substitute for one-to-one sexual contact, but more a supplement. Actually, they neutralize their guilt and avoid seeing themselves as participant actors in a social problem. Both their marital difficulties and their efforts to solve their problems are in themselves problems for society.

An Alternative Marriage Form ● Group marriage has apparently been reasonably common throughout human history and definitely exists today.[40] Such an arrangement usually consists of a group of adults living in a single cooperative community and having at least theoretically sexual access to all other members of the same community. While group marriage affords a considerable degree of sexual variety, widens and enhances love relationships for many individuals, and provides economic and social advantages for many individuals, it is often difficult to find four or more adults who can live harmoniously together. Selecting a suitable group of several individuals with whom one would like to have a group marriage arrangement apparently is a problem similar, but compounded, to selecting a single marriage partner. As a result, most such arrangements break up after several months or several years, particularly for nonsexual reasons.[41]

Although group marriage may provide a logical alternative to a monogamic relationship for some and provide a means whereby the sexual difficulties which may arise between two individuals can be dispersed, such an alternative is apparently only for a select few. Although sexual deficiencies represent one of the most significant tensions within marriage, they are not the only tensions possibly present. While sexual compatibility is one of the pillars of the meaningful marriage, it is far from being the only pillar. The importance of sexual difficulties in deciding the fate of a marriage usually depends upon how personality and human interaction are expressed. Such problems may only be exaggerated in group marriage. Consequently, extramarital sex interests, Herman C. Lantz and Eloise C. Snyder believe, may be due to a breakdown in both the interpersonal and the erotic aspects of marriage. Therefore, swinging and group marriage alternatives represent failures of individuals to be socialized and to accept conventional norms regarding sexual relationships as well as other interpersonal activities.[42]

Abortion and Contraception

Abortion, and generally contraception, is a subject about which almost everyone is considerably confused.[43] A devious problem, it conceals much misery under its many continuing arguments. Few problems involve more dimensions. Abortion includes elements of crime, sin, scandal, conflict, and even tragedy. One could probably assume that if women dominated the legislatures, the punishment sanctioned for abortion would have been abolished long ago and many tragedies would not have resulted. But abortion is an old problem, and the search for a logical solution which meets the demands of all parties, if it is possible, is still in the future. In spite of the Supreme Court decision in 1973 allowing abortions early in pregnancy, the argument rages on. While "family planning," as it is tactfully called, has become as respectable as gardening and socially approved organizations are ready to advise married couples about the spacing of children and the artificial limitation of families, abortion is often utilized as a last resort to terminate a pregnancy when planned methods fail, and is not given the same acceptance as other family planning methods. Although criminal prohibitions have been reduced, many individuals still regard abortion as a form of murder.

The validity of assuming that abortion is really a form of homicide depends upon a formal definition of the time when life begins and a decision concerning what definition of life is to be protected in criminal law. Does life begin at the time of actual birth, a certain stage of pregnancy, or conception? The debate still continues. Some, however, present a reverse viewpoint and maintain that the prevention of an unwanted conception today is really a social protection for tomorrow. Regardless of these viewpoints, the confusion and complete arbitrariness which surround this problem pose hazards for the future.

Abortion is not a cure for a disease; rather, it is an answer to a pressing personal and social situation. But while it can help keep the population from growing too large, abortion may undermine or hinder the development of a strong nation. For example, it may relieve men of the burden of the birth of unwanted children and alleviate the problem of illegitimacy, but it does not do so without some consequences. If the death rate exceeds the birth rate, the population will decline and the decrease will cause aftereffects. Consequently, even though there is no simple answer to the problem of abortion, the time has come to lift this practical health and social problem out of the fog of idealistic hopes and theoretical abstractions and to place it into the arena of constructive realism.[44]

From the point of view of law and prevailing moral standards, abortion *is* a kind of deviance. From a medical point of view it is, to some extent, a health hazard. This is one reason why, as James M. Henslin has pointed out, affected parties place neutralization processes into operation as they make a decision to abort.[45] Most persons involved in abortion attempt to protect their self-concept from any moral recrimination caused by their action. However, some women, according to Henslin, are unable to neutralize the societal norms which they have internalized and are burdened with guilt feelings after the abortion has been completed. In order to avoid such feelings, the majority of the sex participants, therefore, turn to other birth control devices designed to prevent unwanted pregnancy, illegitimacy, or the consequences of an abortion.

Because birth control practices, other than abortion, are as old as humanity itself, the intent of avoiding pregnancy, at least in its essence, is not a new social problem. Even the Old Testament refers to *coitus interruption,* withdrawal before ejaculation.[46] The ancient Egyptians used leaves or cloth to make barriers to the cervix; the Greeks encouraged male homosexual relationships in order to prevent conception. In the Middle Ages, members of the clergy mainly advocated abstention, but during the same period, the condom, or penis sheath, made of linen or fish skins, maybe the oldest birth control device, came into wide usage. However, modern family planning and the development of campaigns for female sexual rights has assisted the growth of more contemporary contraceptive methods. The diaphragm, or in its other form the cervical cap, essentially a rubber instrument designed to fit over the cervix and to be inserted into the vagina before intercourse or left in place for a longer period of time, is one such product. Another method, sanctioned even by the Roman Catholic Church, is not a product but is simply a periodic abstention from sexual relationships during those days of the month when a woman is capable of conceiving. Also among the modern methods is sterilization, in the form of vasectomy for males and salpingectomy, or tubal ligation for females, used mainly by those couples who have completed their families or who wish to avoid the use of contraceptives and to make childbirth impossible.

Many other future contraceptives in the form of progestin, nonsteroid chemical methods, and other devices are under development and testing. Nevertheless, "the pill" is one contraceptive that enjoys presently the greatest popularity and is used primarily by those who believe in the separation of procreation and the right to have unlimited and unconsequential sexual pleasures. Composed of the female hormone estrogen and of progestin, a synthetic substance that is chemically similar to the natural progesterone produced by a woman's ovaries, the pill acts to suppress ovulation.[47] Next to sterilization, it now seems to be the safest contraceptive method, although its possible side effects are not yet fully known. Inconclusive studies, however, warn that the pill may be instrumental in causing strokes and even cancer among women.

Although still imperfect, the use of contraceptives has reinforced the trend toward the legalization of abortion as a means of avoiding the birth of unwanted children, even at the risk of causing injury to the presumptive mother. Social views regarding premarital and extramarital sexual relations add further incentive to provide a means to forestall unwanted children. It is unlikely that the social problems which result from the sexual act will be eliminated even by the most perfect means of birth control, however. Sexual intercourse has wide ranging ramifications.

References

1. Elizabeth Janeway, "Are We Making Too Much of Sex?" *Boston Sunday Globe* (November 21, 1971), pp. 28-34. (Based on her study on "Man's World, Woman's Place.").

2. *The Observer* (London), (December 13, 1970), p. 7.
3. *Today's VD Control Problem—1971,* American Social Health Association, p. 53.
4. R. R. Willcox, "The Essence of Gonorrhea Control," *Acta Dermato-Venereologica,* (1965), XLV, 302-308.
5. L. Cohen, "The 'Pill', Promiscuity, and Venereal Disease," *British Journal of Venereal Disease,* (April, 1970), XLVI, 108-110.
6. A Boulton Hewitt, "Oral Contraception Among Special Clinic Patients," *British Journal of Venereal Disease,* (April, 1970), XLVI, 106-107.
7. Michael Schofield, "Social Aspects of Homosexuality," *British Journal of Venereal Disease,* (1964), XL, 129-134.
8. *The National Observer* (May 11, 1974).
9. R. D. Catterall, "The Venereal Diseases," *Nursing Times,* (August, 1968), LXIV, 1041-1043.
10. Ira L. Reiss, *The Social Context of Premarital Sexual Permissiveness* (New York, 1967), pp. 164-168.
11. Arthur M. Vener, Cyrus S. Stewart and David L. Hager, "The Sexual Behavior of Adolescents in Middle America: Generational and American-British Comparisons," *Journal of Marriage and the Family,* (1972), XXXIV, 696-705.
12. Robert R. Bell, *Premarital Sex in a Changing Society* (Englewood Cliffs, N.J., 1966), pp. 159-160.
13. Ira L. Reiss, *Premarital Sexual Standards in America* (New York, 1960), pp. 80-144.
14. Thomas Carter, "Where the Sex Revolution Fails," *The Observer* (London), (February 6, 1972).
15. Melvin Zelnick and John F. Kanter, "The Probability of Premarital Intercourse," *Social Science Reserach,* (1972), I, 335-41.
16. Cunter Schmidt and Volkmar Sigusch, "Changes in Sexual Behavior Among Young Males and Females Between 1960-1970," *Archives of Sexual Behavior,* (1972), II, 27-45.
17. Paul Glasser and Elizabeth Navarre, "Structural Problems of the One-Parent Family," *The Journal of Social Issues,* (1965), XXI, 98-109.
18. Clark E. Vincent, "Teen-Age Unwed Mothers in American Society," *The Journal of Social Issues,* (1966), XXII, 22.
19. Kingsley Davis, "Illegitimacy and the Social Structure," *American Journal of Sociology,* (1939), XLV, 215-233.
20. Vincent, *Social Issues,* pp. 23-24.
21. Zelnick and Kantner, *Social Science Research,* pp. 335-341.
22. U.S. National Center for Health Statistics, *Vital Statistics of the United States,* 1973.
23. Etienne van de Walla, Edward Shorter, and John Knodel, "The Decline of Non-Marital Fertility in Europe, 1880-1940," *Population Studies,* (1971), XXV, 375-93.
24. Ira L. Reiss, *The Family System in America,* (New York, 1971), pp. 347-350.
25. Elizabeth Herzog, "Unmarried Mothers: Some Questions To Be Answered and Some Answers To Be Questioned," *Child Welfare,* (October, 1972), XLI, 339-350.
26. Ruth Shonle Cavan, *The American Family* (4th ed.), (New York, 1969), pp. 477-480.
27. *Ibid.,* pp. 480, 468-469.
28. Elaine C. Pierson, *Sex Is Never an Emergency* (Philadelphia, 1971), p. 1.
29. See among others, "New Marriage Styles," *Time,* (March 20, 1972), XCIX, 12, 56.
30. Carter, *The Observer.*
31. Michael Gordon, "From an Unfortunate Necessity to a Cult of Mutual Orgasm: Sex in American Marital Education Literature, 1840-1940," *Studies in the Sociology of Sex,* ed. James M. Henslin (New York, 1971), pp. 53-77.
32. *Ibid.,* pp. 60-64.
33. William Lee Howard, *Facts for the Married* (New York, 1912), pp. xii.

34. William J. Robinson, *Woman: Her Sex and Love Life* (New York, 1929), pp. 286-287.
35. Gordon, *Sociology of Sex,* pp. 67-68.
36. Carolyn Symonds, "Sexual Mate-Swapping: Violation of Norms and Reconciliation of Guilt," *Studies*, p. 81.
37. George C. O'Neill and Nena O'Neill, "Patterns in Group Sexual Activity," *Journal of Sex Research*, (1970), VI, 101-112.
38. Symonds, *Studies,* pp. 81-109.
39. *Ibid.,* p. 108.
40. Albert Ellis, "Group Marriage: A Possible Alternative?" *The Family in Search of a Future,* ed. Herbert A. Otto (New York, 1970), p. 85.
41. *Ibid.,* p. 89.
42. Herman R. Lantz and Eloise C. Snyder, *Marriage: An Examination of the Man-Woman Relationship,* (2nd ed)., (New York, 1969), pp. 270-273.
43. Stephen Schafer, "Rethinking the Abortion Problem," *Criminologica,* (February, 1967), IV, 5.
44. Richard D. Knudten, *Criminological Controversies* (New York, 1968), pp. 51-79.
45. James M. Henslin, "Criminal Abortion: Making the Decision and Neutralizing the Act," *Studies in the Sociology of Sex,* ed. James M. Henslin (New York, 1971), pp. 120-134.
46. Paul R. Ehrlich and Anne H. Ehrlich, *Population Resources Environment: Issues in Human Ecology* (San Francisco, 1970), pp. 211-231.
47. *Ibid.,* p. 216.

CHAPTER 7

Aging and Dying

The Socio-Biological Problem of Aging and Death

Human aging and dying are unavoidable and irreversible life processes. Until a few decades ago society simply accepted the biological truth that people age and ultimately die. No analytic attention was paid to the fact that men spend about one quarter or more of their lives growing up and preparing for mature participation in human groups, approximately one half engaging in a variety of activities and social roles in their attempt to gain happiness, and the final quarter in a progressive process of lessened activity, possible physical decline, followed by inevitable death. Since the establishment of the species approximately 600,000 years ago, an estimated 77 billion persons have passed through these cycles of life and death. A proportion of them never experienced an extended process of aging because their lives were terminated suddenly by disease, famine, accidents, warfare, capital punishment, crime victimization, sudden heart-attacks, or other "unusual" or "abnormal" circumstances. This type of dying, while it may be traumatic for those close to the individual, is not a social problem. However, the process of decline which occurs in the later years may be a problem, not only for the person undergoing the process and for those close to the individual, but also for society as a whole.

In many societies, old age brought only respect and honor. In rural America and in most European agrarian countries the aged person was accepted as a useful farm worker, even when hard physical labor was no longer possible. Among the ancient Hebrews, Greeks, and Romans, those entering the last phase of their life cycles were believed to possess mystical power, dominating wisdom, and recognized authority. "Gerontocracy," government of old men, was customary in the majority of ancient and early societies. The aged served as chieftains, peacemakers, and judges. Even in modern societies the old are often preferred for such positions. The practice of keeping the aged in the highest regard and of utilizing their sagacity, experience, and knowledge with esteem and reverence has been maintained for thousands of years, regardless of the fact that all aged persons have not been worthy of such honors. Longish grey hair, a bushy beard, slow walking and talking, and the carrying of a cane, stick, or other items associated with aging readily disclosed the presence of the old and attracted respect. While respect for the aged has not been eliminated today, the emphasis within society on youth and youthful activity has lessened the extent of concern and respect for the elderly. It has only been in recent years that human aging, a "sometimes terrifying and depressing subject,"[1] has emerged from under the veneer of superficiality, the real problems that older people face have been recognized, and an understanding of dying and death have evolved from fear, mourning and mysticism.

Perhaps one reason for the expanding interest in the elderly and their problems is the increasing numbers of older persons in society. Since the turn of the century, the elderly have been constantly increasing as a percentage of the total population. While in 1900 persons over the age of 65 comprised 4.1 percent of the population, by 1970 this percentage increased to 9.9. This increase, along with the fact that the elderly are increasingly choosing to live alone, have low incomes, and are less likely to be working than they were in the past, means that a sizeable segment of the population face new problems and that society must deal with them.[2]

The Rise of Gerontology ● Gerontology, based upon the findings and methodologies of biology, genetics, biochemistry, physiology, medicine, psychiatry, psychology, economics, and the social sciences is a relatively new science. As a field, it seeks to give the aging and dying as well as society generally a better understanding of the character of the phenomena which affect them. In the early stages, gerontological investigations took the form of a few studies in the nineteenth century. After World War I an even greater concentration of research, mainly on the evaluation of the psychological characteristics and the intelligence of the aged, appeared.[3] While Edmund V. Cowdry pioneered such investigations,[4] V. Korenchevsky worked before World War I to organize an international interdisciplinary organization for the scientific investigation into the problems of aging in Britain. Gerontology really developed after World War II when the American Psychological Association in 1946 established its Division of Later Maturity and Old Age. The first issue of the *Journal of Gerontology*, published by the American Gerontological Society, was soon followed by the European *Gerontologia*. Otto Pollack published the results of his Social Science Research Council study on social adjustment in old age.[5] In 1950 the first American Conference on Aging convened and in the same year the International Association of Gerontology, which later held challenging international conventions in the United States, Italy, Denmark, Austria, and other countries, was formed. *A Classified Bibliography of Gerontology and Geriatrics* was published in several always enlarged editions.

In the United States a White House Conference on Aging was convened. A Senate Sub-committee undertook hearings on the problems of the old; the Department of Health, Education and Welfare established its Administration on Aging and proposed medicare in an attempt to help the aged maintain their health; and literature pertaining to the field was published in great quantities. By the 1960's the field of gerontology was well established and the problems of the aging were increasingly being recognized. Correspondingly, the former emphasis upon respect for the aged and mourning of the dead shifted to one of understanding aging and dying as social problems. Society began to realize that "today's aged are socially and culturally (if not organically) different from the old people before them, just as today's children are different from those of yesterday and tomorrow."[6]

The Biological Aspects of Aging

Although senescence (growing old) is a personal physical condition that leads to dying and death, "the fundamental mechanisms in biological aging," D. B. Bromley notes, "are not known for certain."[7] Some theories of senescence suggest that human cells are "designed" to work only for a certain period of time after which they become weakened and unable to protect the organism. Other researchers contend that no protected environment is able to insulate the human organism from life hazards which are bound to kill it after causing one or more vital organs to malfunction for awhile. Every death has a clinically recognizable cause which preceeds dying; every death, if the person is successful enough to reach the last cycle of his life, is precipitated by the aging of the organism. Although it is sometimes argued, mainly by medical men, that nobody has ever died of old age, it is beyond argument that aging hastens or brings about the clinical cause of death.

Anatomy and physiology offer information about the aging process.[8] In growing older, bones change their chemical composition and become more easily broken; the loss of teeth affects eating and speaking efficiency; posture and muscular coordination decline; and physical strength is gradually lessened. Certain body cells are renewed at a slower rate; certain other tissues, mainly in the nervous system, are not replaced at all. The skin loses elasticity; wrinkles appear as the underlying fat disappears. The hair thins, becomes gray, and even baldness ensues. The digestive system functions with greater difficulty. One's appetite lessens. The presence of aging becomes evident even to the lay observer as senses reveal a decline or a faulty operational pattern. Reduced vision and loss of hearing are followed by lessened sensitivity to taste, touch, and smell and greater intolerance of pain, reaction to exterior phenomena, and problems of imbalance. Perhaps the most important deficiency relates to the circulation of blood. When flow is restricted, fatal structural damages in the aging organism may occur.

However, not all aging symptoms develop at the same time or even at the same rate. The central nervous system, which in one's youth organizes and regulates behavior harmoniously, may later permit the aging process to proceed rapidly in one physiological organ or mechanism while still protecting the others. However, this possibility varies from man to man. One person may maintain a high level of physical strength into his late years (one Swedish king, for example, played tennis even in his 80's), while another may need a wheelchair at 70 years. Although some people are capable of delivering worthwhile intellectual products almost to the end of their lives (Sir Winston Churchill, for example, reached the peak of his career and fame when most people are expected to retire), others display senile thinking rather early. Some individuals with greatly limited physical capability are known to possess impressive mental agility and clarity, while at the same time others in relatively good physical health disclose a marked mental decline.

When and to what extent neurological disorders, respiratory diseases, hearing and vision defects, heart and blood vessels diseases, and emotional and mental illness will develop cannot be fully predicted. When a terminal illness and death will occur and to whom it will happen is difficult, if not impossible, to determine. As Moss and Kent suggest, "Medically speaking, aging is not a single process, but a series of overlapping and interlocking events."[9] Chronological, mental, and physical age do not proceed hand-in-hand. The number of years of age are at times denied by the person's mental state; his intellectual productivity may contradict his physical condition in one way or another.

Although it is often true that the aging process is "disorganized" in the sense that one part of the human organism may decline earlier than another, no part of the human organism can escape from the decline caused by aging. The aged organism displays biological characteristics that are not pathological or morbid but rather that reveal normal aging profiles. Although Goethe's old Faust was transformed into a young man by the creative force of Mephistopheles' magic brew, we still do not know in actuality how an old human organism may be successfully regenerated. The present knowledge of biology and medicine cannot prevent aging and dying. Although it has been suggested that methods to delay age changes will soon be available,[10] this may only put off or prolong the inevitable. Modern "elixirs of life" are not aimed at rejuvenation but rather at getting men to the point of old age[11] where gerontology takes over.

The Psychiatric Aspects of Aging

A physiological or biological regression of the human organism usually includes the decline of mental capacities. Even if mental problems do not appear at the same rate as the biological, they do develop generally as aging results. While there are few mental illnesses that occur typically in old age, some psychic disorders or mental degeneration may develop which are not recognized clinically. Although they are mental abnormalities, they are "normal" as opposed to "abnormal" abnormalities.[12] Among the *normal abnormalities* are the impairment of memory, including a lessening ability to remember recent events; a reduced rate of learning, particularly of languages and all kinds of skills; difficulty in integrating new information with old, mainly as social change continues; decline of flexibility and creativity, often displayed in lower tolerance to psychological stress; and a lessened capacity to cope with seemingly pressing life situations.[13] The tendency of older people to show anger and hostility and to blame others for their own failures and circumstances is also included in the same category. Frequently, they react enviously. However, as many aged persons develop a narrowing of their interests, gradually focusing upon their own personal or health affairs and their fear of death, they are possessed by self-hate, a form of hostility against themselves, and by pessimism, an ambivalent psychological state which sometimes leads to suicide attempts.[14]

One of the most important manifestations of a normal abnormality is the decreased rate, the declining speed, and the disorganized character of the aged person's responses to outward stimuli and to earlier internalized values. An old man who continues to walk in the rain with a rolled umbrella on his arm rather than over his head is an example of this problem. As opposed to a younger person's quick and immediate action to open the umbrella, the older person stops, looks at the sky, determines that raindrops are falling, and only then opens his umbrella.

Occasionally, tardy and often confused responses by the old result in crimes or behavior generally regarded as deviant. Certain crimes, such as sexual deviance or embezzlement, may be a result of aspirations unreachable due to old age. Others, on the other hand, may be a product of deficient response-functioning in which the prohibitions taken for granted in youth are understood only after the act is committed (i.e., shoplifting). On the other side of the coin, many old people are easily victimized because their physical weakness does not permit them to defend themselves or their slow reflexes do not allow them to escape harm or to thwart crime.

The Abnormal Abnormalities • The *abnormal abnormalities* are quite different from the normal abnormalities. Among these are senile brain damage (dementia senilis) and cerebral arteriosclerosis, two major psychotic disorders which account for the overwhelming majority of mental disorders in later life.[15] In these, pathological aging processes are quite evident. *Senile dementia* tends to appear at about 70 years of age, although it is difficult to find the mean age of onset. As happens with most psychoses at all ages, many mental patients are cared for at home for some time before the family decides to turn to hospitalization for assistance. More common among women than men, senile brain disease develops slowly among the aging. While its symptoms vary from one patient to another, they often resemble the common normal abnormalities which develop as one grows old. The aged person tends to retreat into himself. He withdraws from his social environment, becomes increasingly self-centered, and resists new ideas and changes in his routine even if they are in his interest.

Because his memory impairment is more marked than in normal senility, his comprehension of facts and concepts is generally accompanied with confusion and disorientation. Restlessness, agitation often with screaming or shouting arguments, delusions, and hallucinations lead the old person to a variety of antisocial conduct. Senile dementia, which may be rather simple and not much different from the symptoms of normal aging, may be compounded with paranoid reactions, evidenced primarily in serious suspicions, with delirious response, expressed in combative and incoherent behavior, or with severe depression, accompanied by hypochondriachal and nihilistic responses. Many aged people inflicted with dementia senilis ultimately become unmanageable. Because their mental problem is so frequently and so closely coupled to their physical deterioration, their recorded mortality rate is high.

Cerebral arteriosclerosis, the other major mental illness of old age, displays symptoms similar to those of senile dementia. Yet, they develop faster, fluctuate in severity, and even show temporary improvement. Caused by blockage or rupture of a main or small blood vessel somewhere in the brain, it is a small or mild stroke, which causes the degeneration of brain tissue. Headaches, convulsive seizures, and emotional outbursts often torture aged patients who react to their condition with morose pessimism and frequent weeping, behavior which is looked upon as abnormal by society. Partial paralysis, tremor, sensory losses, and speech defects are also common symptoms of the problem. While senile dementia usually runs a long course, cerebral arteriosclerotic brain disease usually travels a shorter one to a fatal end. Death is not necessarily caused directly by arteriosclerosis; it may be due clinically to heart failure or pneumonia.

The possibilities of treatment for both diseases are limited because the general biological decline brought about by aging hinders efforts to retard the progress of these psychoses. This may be even more true of the so-called presenile dementias (Alzheimer's disease, Pick's disease, Hunington's chorea, and others). While they are rare mental illnesses of more or less unknown origin, they develop in middle age and continue to the last part of the life cycle. Although the normal abnormalities of senescence are at least to some extent understood and accepted by laymen, the psychotic mental disorders of the aged, which members of the old person's family and the general public frequently misunderstand, create special social problems.

The Sociological Aspects of Aging

Since it is an immutable truth that "the ultimate cause of death is birth, and aging is a process that starts at conception,"[16] a recognition of this fact must be included in a systematic study of social systems. Because man is mortal, the necessity of recruitment, Wilbert E. Moore points out, is a crucial issue in social organization.[17] Society is composed not only of biological beings but also of role-players who are biological beings. When a role-player ages and becomes unable to carry out the duties of his expected role, or if he dies, the problem of role succession arises inevitably inasmuch as society cannot afford any discontinuity of roles. While biological reproduction is necessary to maintain the social organism, recruitment for the various role-positions, renewed division of labor, and reassignments to roles are virtually indispensable to societal continuity. Consequently, the aging and dying of the members of a society pose critical problems that require continual demographic observation and social attention. Their replacements must be anticipated and socialized in order for society to maintain its continuity in the face of social change.

Although a social system does not usually change at a very fast rate, the executors of the system do. Streetsweepers, professors, mailmen, plumbers, bookkeepers, policemen, and other workers keep society functioning and carry the burden of keeping it organized. Eventually, each leaves his role-position and it is occupied by another. Therefore, replacement streetsweepers, professors, mailmen, plumbers, bookkeepers, and police officers have to be found and socialized to these and all other necessary roles in order to replace those who have reached old age or have died. Streets still must be kept clean, students must be taught, mail must be delivered, broken pipes have to be replaced, credits and debits must be entered in a variety of record books, and laws must be enforced.

At a designated age, all persons begin to produce and to contribute to the continuity of society. After a number of years their production and contribution reach their peak. However, it is some time before they lose their function within society. Yet, people think of a specific set of roles as the culmination of their personal existence and they fear old age because it means abandoning these roles without the prospect of significant replacement roles.[18] Their achievements lessen and they ultimately become obsolete and even "useless" (or better, unuseable) to the functioning of society. But such definitions of "uselessness" are narrow. While adult occupational roles may be abandoned, old age contribution roles may be expanded. In "successful aging,"[19] Marvin R. Koller writes, achievement may continue or other contributions may be made. Aging can be successful when the aging person remains fully involved with others and continues his valuable contributions to the social order as his replacement is delayed. But it also can be successful at times when an older person withdraws from close interaction with others, disengages from demanding social duties, and is replaced by another. In the first instance, aging is successful because it serves the needs of the total group, in the last because it may bring the person happiness and personal gain. The one represents the macro-view and the other the micro-view of the social impact of aging.

The Macro-view of Aging • Numerous factors contribute to the social macro-view of aging. Each has some consequences for planning and organizational continuity. The life chances of a member of any given society are not exclusively dependent upon the person's biological inheritance but are significantly affected by social conditions. While biological needs may cause society to think in terms of replacing the person, the social needs of society may determine the probability and timing of the change. Factors of sex, class, occupation, public health, medical care, war, economic life, crime, fertility, and many other social variables shape the patterns of normal biological expectancy, either by extending man's productivity and delaying his aging and death or by cutting short his contributions and hastening an early life end.

To some extent society defines which age groups should be charged with which responsibilities in order to maintain a functioning society. Society even partially defines when aging begins. Certain roles are made available only to designated age groups. For example, marriage cannot be made, votes cast, entry into the labor market permitted, and a variety of offices held if a person is underage. On the other hand, once one has arrived at a specified later age, usually about 65 years, retirement may be mandatory. In short, the actual biological potential of a man, even if untrue physiologically, is determined in large degree by those holding social power. Nevertheless, early maturity and late aging are not rare phenomena.

Social history provides many individual examples of persons who have defeated societal age restrictions. William Pitt, for example, became the Prime Minister of Great Britain at the age of 24, and Paul Dudley White successfully directed the treatment of his own coronary ailment while well past normal retirement age. They are only two of the many who found such social restrictions obsolete. Nevertheless, society often is reluctant to adjust to this fact and continues to force a large number of persons into premature aging. Because biological and social aging do not occur simultaneously, many who are biologically young and chronologically aged need to remain productive. Consequently, a society which forces retirement upon all its members because they have reached an arbitrary, predetermined age limit tends to lose a measure of productivity and experience which it does not need to lose. Oftentimes, biology is more flexible than social policy. The rigid macro-view of aging may result in a self-defeating formalism. Medico-biological facts and socioeconomic assumptions frequently conflict.

The Micro-view of Aging • Whether by choice or by social decision, people tend to disengage as they age from certain interactions within society. "Disengagement" represents the micro-view of aging and a change in lifestyles, social roles, and social relationships. According to the general theory of disengagement usually attributed to M. Elaine Cumming,[20] and a product of a five-year study in an American city of 275 persons between the ages of 50 and 90 who had shown good health and some financial independence, normal aging "is a mutual withdrawal or 'disengagement' between the aging person and others in the social system to which he belongs."[21] It is brought about by the aging person or by the decision of others in society. In Cumming's proposition, disengagement is a change in the equilibrium that existed in the middle cycle of life between the individual and his society. While the patterns of disengagement vary from person to person and depend largely upon the previous engagement of the given individual, they usually involve the growth of a greater distance between the parties to the equilibrium. "The depth and breadth of a man's engagement," Cumming notes, "can be measured by the degree of potential disruption that would follow his sudden death."[22] The process of disengagement, therefore, commences before aging begins.

Not all agree with this conception, however. Critics argue that little attention has been paid by Cumming·or others to the idea of "mutuality" in retreat or withdrawal. These are not always clearcut actions. In many cases, the aging person disengages not because he really wants to, but because he is aware of the fact that he is expected to withdraw (mutuality). In any event, the withdrawal that occurs is from the principal social roles that define adult identity, not from all activity and social relationships. The reason the term disengagement is used is that social roles that might compensate for retreat from occupational and other adult identity roles have not yet been institutionalized.[23]

Whenever disengagement begins, aging persons start to interact less, thereby decreasing the scope of their social roles. The reduction of role-obligations due to disengagement results in a relative freedom from duty. However, this freedom is relative inasmuch as intensity of devotion to the "engagement" decides whether it is really freedom or deprivation. Many elderly persons will resist cultural and family pressures to reduce their work and responsibilities. Except if forces to disengage by ill health, they are even likely to resist the idea of giving up an independent life and private home for the possible advantages of a nursing home. In such contexts disengagement is a form of deprivation rather than freedom.

Disengagement involves a shrinkage in the activities and relationships of the aging person, a separation from associations that necessarily causes a decrease in his emotional interest in others and an increase in his interest in his own problems. Ultimately, the aged person's self-interest may develop to the point where his interest is almost exclusively in his own security and physical health. As a by-product, the self-centered old person may resent those who are not familiar with the process of disengagement in aging, most often his family or persons in the social environment. Disengagement is not an abrupt and sudden abandonment of roles and interaction or a swift disruption of emotional ties, but rather is a gradual, ever-increasing process. It starts with the selection of activities which the aging person regards as important and worth retaining. Seeing his time running out, he tends to concentrate on what he feels is a "must" before he leave his earthly life. Gradually eliminating many of those choices as he ages further, his final interests and aspirations are reduced to a self-concern for his physical being.

Social Policy and the Aged

While bureaucratic cultural norms and social rules urge the beginning of disengagement as one grows older, gerontology, on behalf of the individual as well as society, seeks to delay the disengagement process. When society puts pressure upon people to withdraw and retire, and when rules rather than individual physical condition determine the beginning of aging, society actually creates a mass of useless persons by depriving them of useful social roles. Consequently, gerontology has developed as a field dealing with such problems. It includes a concern not only for medical assistance and the physical well-being of the individual, but also for the happiness of socially rejected aging persons. It seeks to put disengagement in its proper perspective, slowing down the process for those able to remain active, and to assist in the development of a social policy that permits such persons to maintain valued roles within the social system. While some progress has been made in providing the aged with various social services, a fully developed gerontological social policy has yet to emerge. Even when the younger members of society express concern for the aging, they are not expressing a concern for social policy but rather the need to improve the environment that they will have to live in in their later years.[24]

The nature of the problems the aged face can be seen by examining income levels. Although retirement is seen by some as a time to enjoy life and live on the savings obtained during working years, retirement for many is not the joy that it is made out to be. Nearly 50 percent of those 65 or older have insufficient income. In the early 1960's 55 percent of the persons in this age group had incomes of less than $1,000 per year, 23 percent $1,000 to $2,000, 9 percent $2,000 to $3,000 and 13 percent $3,000 or more. Fifty percent of those households 65 and over in which incomes were combined had annual incomes of less than $2,830 per year and 25 percent less than $1,620 per year. For the nine million widowed, divorced, separated, or never married aged who live on approximately $1,000 a year, the problem of subsistence was especially serious.[25]

Because individuals approaching old age commonly have only a home, moderate life insurance coverage, and cash or assets of less than $2,000, they must depend in large measure upon Social Security benefits.[26] In 1965 the median liquid assets in checking accounts, savings and bonds for persons 65 years of age and older amounted to $1,200. For those between 45 and 64, the median was close to $8,000, mostly tied up in a home equity. Although the median has increased slightly in the last few years, it has not kept up with the rate of inflation.[27]

Nearly 50 percent of the aged who live in families and 80 percent of those aged living alone have incomes below a *modest but adequate* standard ($2,800 for a couple and $2,000 for an aged person living alone). About 42 percent of the older couples and nearly 75 percent of single aged have incomes that do not even cover the *low cost* living plan ($2,500 for married couples and $1,800 for singles). Twenty-five percent of the couples and 60 percent of the single aged have incomes below that of the *economy* plan ($1,800 for aged couples and $1,300 for an aged single person).[28] The economy budget permits an expenditure of only $0.90 per day per person for food and $4.84 per year for snacks away from home. Under the economy budget, the aging couple will be able to purchase an upholstered chair every 11 years, an overcoat for the husband every nine years, two pairs of nylon stockings and one wool dress for the wife every three years, and movie tickets once a month.[29]

Major textbooks in social welfare and social work barely focus upon the problems of aging and the services provided the aged.[30] Part of the reason is the paucity of material and programs dealing with these problems. The White House Conference on Aging in 1961 recommended the adoption of a "Senior Citizen's Charter"[31] which spelled out the rights of the aged as well as their obligations and which delineated social policy and social services for elderly Americans. According to this Charter, the essential rights of every senior citizen are to be useful; be able to obtain employment; be free from want; have a fair share in recreation, education, and medical care; have decent housing; have the moral and financial support of his family; be free to live independently; live and die with dignity; and have access to available information about how to improve the later years of his life. At the same time, his obligations, according to this Charter, are to remain active and useful, apply sound principles to physical and mental health, seek avenues of service in post-retirement years, make the benefits of his experience and knowledge available, make himself adaptable to the changes added years will bring, and maintain relationships with family, neighbors and friends. While the Charter suggests an ideal which older citizens should follow, their ability to exercise these responsibilities and rights and to perform their duties depends upon whether society provides the possibility for their realization. The rejection of the old, for example, most often comes from the immediate family, itself a repudiation of a Charter recommendation. However, society also rejects elderly persons, although not entirely because the old are not wanted or because society is impatient with the aged. Rather, the rejection is related to the heavy emphasis which a competitive society places upon performance. Those unable to respond fully to these expectations find their position and value challenged by youthful or middle-aged persons capable of doing the job. The President's Conference on the Aging in 1971 probed many of these problems more fully.

Perhaps the most significant step toward providing services to the aged was taken in the passage of the Social Security Act of 1935, since then amended several times, which provides limited financial support to those who have reached retirement age. Since then, Medicaid and Medicare, which help the elderly to obtain essential health care, have been devised and put into operation. However, only incidental and minor community efforts have been made to alleviate the remaining problems of the aged. The fact that most penal institutions house "prison aspirants," aged persons who commit crimes in order to get into prisons where they find more security and care than normally available to them in the free society, only illustrates the community failure to provide for those in such need. The deterrent atmosphere of many nursing homes, the scarcity of clubs and community centers for old people, the limited development of housing projects suitable for the aged, the difficulties in obtaining employment after retirement, the resourcelessness of counseling agencies, and the observable indifference of charitable and sectarian agencies, save some praiseworthy exceptions, demonstrate that the issues surrounding aging are burning social problems.

The Social-Psychological Aspects of Dying

If aging has now been recognized as a social problem, it is perhaps due to a new awareness of the conditions awaiting the aged person and to a growing resistance to accepting these conditions in later life. Increasingly, young workers are arranging for some form of retirement insurance that will secure financial comfort in old age. The number of those who realize that aging and its problems are inevitable is growing. Few think in terms of death following old age, however. Most simply live for momentary personal happiness without thinking of their inescapable end. This is why dying and death are not generally considered major social problems. While John Hinton raised the challenging question of "who cares for the dying?,"[32] he does not provide an adequate answer.

Dying, however, is a social problem at three levels. It has a different effect on society than it has on the individual undergoing the process. Therefore, dying is a problem for the individual, for those caring for the individual, and for those who remain. How individuals react to the realization that they are, in fact, dying has been studied in some detail by Elizabeth Kuebler-Ross.[33] She finds that a dying patient goes through several stages, assuming the process is at all prolonged. These stages include a rejection of the idea, feelings of pity and sorrow both for themselves as well as for those who will remain, and, eventually, acceptance of death. The greatest fear of death stems from the accompanying sense of hopelessness, helplessness, and isolation, not so much from the event itself.

Dying also has an impact on those who are immediately caring for the dying patient, nursing home staff or hospital personnel. Within a nursing home setting, dying may be a "career" with various stages. Success is then defined as moving or appearing to move from one stage to the next as slowly as possible.[34] David Sudnow, studying death in a hospital, found that the staff develops systematic means of handling most deaths. Those who are frequently confronted with the task of communicating the fact of death develop the skill and ability to respond to a variety of standardized responses on the part of the bereaved.[35]

The effect of death on those remaining, both the immediate family as well as society as a whole, is the third level at which dying is a social problem. When a person has died, a variety of emotions are expressed by those who remain alive. Grief, most common among those who were closest to the deceased, is frequently accompanied by self-criticism, self-doubt, and a questioning of whether one had done enough for the deceased during his lifetime or in the course of his terminal illness. Simple sorrow, another well known feeling, is sometimes associated with a sense of relief based on the assumption that death is better for the deceased than the prolonged agony of his final sickness. However, apathy and "social mourning" are the most common reactions of those outside the immediate family and of those within the circle of close friends who join the congregation of genuine mourners out of social obligation. In nearly all cultures of the world, a formal participation in grief is minimally expected. Sometimes, hostile feelings and anger are also evident. Such reactions are most frequent, E. Lindmann[36] and C.M. Parkes[37] believe, if the case involves an unexpected death, if a relatively young person has died, if the death was caused by an accident, or if the person had been "acutely" diseased before death. Occasionally, animosity towards doctors or clergymen is expressed in the form of criticism of the deceased's treatment or the denouncing of God.[38]

Society's Responses to Death • Reactions to death are not confined to the close family or friends. Society also responds to the fact of death. Upon death, Hinton notes, a man's "life story is not allowed to come to an abrupt conclusion, but must be rounded off with an appropriate after-death ceremonial."[39] Such events not only offer comfort and support to the deceased's family, but they also demonstrate that the person is dead and that the social group accepts its occurrence. But the effect of such ceremonies is different in each case. Society's reaction to death is based partially upon an evaluation of the deceased's "engagement" or position within the social system during his lifetime. The reaction of society to the death of an American President or a British Prime Minister, for example, is clearly different from that expressed following the death of a streetsweeper or an unknown college professor. The societal reaction to one's death is determined by the social definition of one's life.

Mourning over the deceased has declined in social importance and is due to man's general refusal to face the fact of his eventual mortality.[40] "Modern society," R. Fulton and G. Geis contend, "rejects death in the most formidable and paradoxical fashion."[41] While the deceased's rank, wealth, occupation, or social significance are still reflected within contemporary funerals and interments as they also were in ancient Egypt and Rome, they no longer require months of mourning, the closing of temples or other places of worship, or the completion of some elaborate mysterious and superstitious rites.[42] Death ceremonies have been reduced to simple, practical, and rational rituals which do not hinder the survivors' completion of their normal social roles. But the cutting short of the time given to ceremonials and mourning may be a rationalization designed to avoid thinking about the inevitable end each man must face.

The idea of death arouses a variety of emotions, including the most common, fear. Because men do not know what to expect after leaving this earth, they are afraid of the unknown. Many try to explain that it is not so much death they fear as the dying process; this too may only be a rationalization of the fear of death itself. "Dying," David Sudnow writes, "seems to be an essentially predictive term."[43] The realization that they are dying causes some men to avoid such a fearful thought. Liking comfort, they feel discomfort at the idea of death. Consequently, they tend to do everything possible to protect themselves against it. However, most people think it is important to make some plans for death.[44]

"If our present society," John Hinton suggests, "were a sincerely Christian one, there would be a general conviction that death has been vanquished."[45] Inasmuch as this is not the case, the idea of dying raises fears and uncertainty for many. Although religious beliefs are not always reassuring, the belief in life after death and a heavenly reward for earthly effort may alleviate this problem. Similarly, the idea that those who fail to follow prescribed social norms will be punished after death may prompt many to lead a fuller and more meaningful life. Clearly, religious belief in life after death has a positive effect on the aged as they are placed in a dying situation.[46]

References

1. D. B. Bromley, *The Psychology of Human Aging* (Baltimore, Md., 1966), p. 17.
2. U.S. Department of Commerce, Bureau of the Census, *We the American Elderly* (Washington, 1973).
3. Among others see, C. C. and Walter R. Miles, "The Correlation of Intelligence Scores and Chronological Age from Early to Late Maturity," *American Journal of Psychology*, (1932), XLIV, 44-78; D. Wechsler, *The Range of Human Capacities* (London, 1935); and L. M. Terman and Maud A. Merrill, *Measuring Intelligence: A Guide to the Administration of the New Revised Stanford-Binet Tests of Intelligence* (London, 1937).
4. Edmund V. Cowdry, *Problems of the Aging* (Baltimore, Md., 1939).
5. Otto Pollack, *Social Adjustment in Old Age* (New York, 1948).
6. Bertram B. Moss and Fraser Kent, *Caring for the Aged* (New York, 1966), pp. 3-4.
7. Bromley, *Human Aging*, p. 65.
8. *Ibid*, pp. 38-65; and see Robert C. Atchley, "The Aging Individual," *The Social Forces in Later Life: An Introduction to Social Gerontology* (Belmont, Calif, 1973), pp. 43-95.
9. Moss and Kent, *Caring For the Aged*, p. 9.
10. Alex Comfort, "The Prolongation of Vigorous Life," *Impact of Science on Society*, (1970), XX, 307-319.
11. Stephen Schafer, "Old Age, Mental Abnormality and Crime," *Preparatory Papers, II/4.* Fourth International Criminological Congress, The Hague (1960), p. 1.
12. *Ibid.*
13. James C. Coleman, *Abnormal Psychology and Modern Life* (3rd ed.), (Chicago, 1964), p. 499.
14. John Hinton, *Dying* (Baltimore, 1967), p. 33.

15. *Ibid*, pp. 499-505; H. H. Marks, "Characteristics and Trends of Cerebral Vascular Disease," *Psychopathology of Again*, eds. P. H. Hoch and J. Zubin (New York, 1961), pp. 69-99; Bromley, *Human Aging*, pp. 129-143.

16. Wilbert E. Moore, "Aging and the Social System," *Aging and Social Policy*, eds. John C. McKinney and Frank T. deVyver (New York, 1966), p. 24.

17. *Ibid.*, pp. 25-30.

18. Zena Smith Blau, *Old Age in a Changing Society* (New York, 1973), p. 177.

19. Marvin R. Koller, *Social Gerontology* (New York, 1968), p. 51.

20. Elaine Cumming, L. R. Dean, and D. S. Newell, "Disengagement, A Tentative Theory of Aging," *Sociometry*, (1960) XXIII, 1; Elaine Cumming and W. E. Henry, *Growing Old* (New York, 1961); J. Cumming and E. Cumming, *Ego and Milieu* (New York, 1962); M. Elaine Cumming, "New Thoughts on the Theory of Disengagement," *New Thoughts on Old Age*, ed. Robert Kastenbaum (New York, 1964), pp. 3-18.

21. Cumming, "New Thoughts," *Old Age*, pp. 3-4.

22. *Ibid.*, p. 4.

23. Blau, *Changing Society*, p. 151.

24. Donald P. Kent, "Social Services and Social Policy," in McKinney and de Vyver, *Aging*, p. 215.

25. Staff Report to the Special Committee on Aging, *Basic Facts on the Health and Economic Status of Older Americans* (Washington, D.C.: U.S. Government Printing Office, 1961), pp. 16-17.

26. Mark S. Gordon, "Aging and Income Security," *Handbook on Social Gerontology*, ed. Clark Tibbits (Chicago: University of Chicago Press, 1960).

27. George Kotone, Charles A. Lininger and Eva Mueller, *1963 Survey of Consumer Finances, Monograph No. 34* (Ann Arbor: University of Michigan Survey Research Center, 1964), pp. 98-101.

28. Gresham M. Sykes, *Social Problems in America* (Glenview, Ill.: Scott, Foresman and Co., 1971), p. 182.

29. Sykes, *Social Problems,* and Margaret F. Stotz, "BLS Interim Budget for a Retired Couple," *Monthly Labor Review,* (November, 1960), LXXXIII, 1141-1157.

30. See among others Elizabeth A. Ferguson, *Social Work: An Introduction* (Philadelphia, 1963); Arthur E. Fink, Everett E. Wilson and Merrill B. Conover, *The Field of Social Work,* (4th ed.), (New York, 1963); and Walter A. Friedlander, *Introduction to Social Welfare,* (3rd ed.), (Englewood Cliffs, N.J., 1968).

31. *The Nation and Its Older People* (Washington, D.C. 1961), p. 118.

32. Hinton, *Dying*, p. 147.

33. Elizabeth Kuebler-Ross, *On Death and Dying* (New York, 1969).

34. Elizabeth Gustafson, "Dying: The Career of the Nursing Home Patient," *Journal of Health and Social Behavior,* (1972), XIII, 226-235.

35. David Sundow, *Passing On: The Social Organization of Dying* (Englewood Cliffs, N.J., 1967).

36. E. Lindmann, "Symptomatology and Management of Acute Grief," *American Journal of Psychiatry,* (1944), CI, 141.

37. C. M. Parkes, "Bereavement and Mental Illness," *British Journal of Medical Psychology,* (1969), XXXVIII, 1.

38. Hinton, *Dying*, p. 169.

39. *Ibid.*, p. 7.

40. Gwynn Nettler, "Review Essay: On Death and Dying," *Social Problems,* (Winter, 1967), XIV, 336.

41. R. Fulton and G. Geis, "Death and Social Values," *Death and Identity*, ed. R. Fulton (New York, 1965), p. 73.

42. Death and rituals or funeral practices in the past and in non-Western societies are treated mainly by the anthropological literature. Durkheim, Evans-Pritchard, Malinowski, Radcliffe-Brown, and others significantly contributed to this area of knowledge. From the more modern literature see E. Bendmann, *Death Customs* (New York, 1930); Jack Goody, *Death, Property and the Ancestors* (Stanford, 1962); Thomas T. Jones, "Thanatology," *The Church's Ministry to the Homebound,* ed. Richard A. Goodling.

43. Sudnow, *Passing On,* p. 64.

44. John W. Riley, Jr., "What People Think About Death," *The Dying Patient,* ed. Orville G. Brim, Jr., *et. al.* (New York, 1970), p. 37.

45. Hinton, *Dying,* p. 37.

46. David O. Moberg, *Spiritual Well-Being, Background and Issues* (Washington, 1971).

CHAPTER 8

Crime

Crime in America

The 1967 Report of the President's Commission on Law Enforcement and Administration of Justice, known popularly as the President's Crime Commission, noted that the causes of crime are "numerous and mysterious and intertwined," and "no one way of describing crime describes it well enough." The report concluded that "there is much crime in America, more than ever is reported, far more than ever is solved, far too much for the health of the Nation."[1] Crime, the Commission presumed, is a prominent social problem for which, according to our present state of knowledge, no panacea can be proposed, no definitive answer offered, and no solution claimed to rest on the horizon. Although society has improved its defenses against crime, technological developments have enriched detection methods, and the treatment of offenders has been advanced and promoted by uninterrupted theoretical and research efforts, crime control has not yet been achieved.[2]

Crime and Crime Statistics ● In the United States crimes have been officially recorded only since 1930 in Federal Bureau of Investigation's *Uniform Crime Reports*. Not until 1958 were the crime rates of rural areas and two other important crime categories, rape and larceny, included. When compared with official European measurement efforts, this represents a rather belated American entry into the objective evaluation of the crime volume. In France regular yearly criminal statistics have been published since 1825.[3] Austria started to release criminal statistical tables with Hungarian data in 1828; England began its data gathering in 1856.[4] Hungary instituted independent recording in 1874, Italy in 1890, and nearly all European states in the years following. Canada established a criminal statistics program in 1876 and Japan in 1882.

The official American crime rate investigation did not begin until much later.

141

Although vigorous efforts have been made to improve the American reporting system since 1930, the recency of the *Uniform Crime Reports* makes the scientific evaluation of American criminality difficult. If Emile Durkheim correctly hypothesized that crime is a "normal" phenomenon,[5] only an extensive historical and retrospective statistical analysis can reveal whether contemporary American crime is truly normal, below normal, or above normal.

When Durkheim contended the "normality" of crime, he did not mean that it is normal "in the sense of being desirable;"[6] rather, he implied that criminal action is a logical part of social life. Crime, according to Durkheim, is a social problem which will persist as long as organized human groups possess normative rules. The normality of crime, therefore, is related to the cultural, organization, and developmental state of a given society. The crime rate is "normal" in the Durkheimian sense only if it does not pass below or above this level. Because we do not know what is the "normal" scope of crime in the United States, reports which demonstrate increases in criminality often alarm the public and stimulate elected officials to do something about it, even when their actions may have little effect upon the actual problem.

The reliability of the current crime data are open to question. Accuracy in crime statistics is often undermined by the emergence of temporary, current, or short-term "topical" crimes, variations in the body of legally defined criminal offenses, unintegrated definitions of law enforcement tasks, differing court practices, uneven public prosecutor policies, public insensitivity to law enforcement problems, inaccurate reporting, and the limited visibility of "white collar" crimes. Then too, the American data which are available through the *Uniform Crime Reports* (see Table 8.1) are based on voluntarily submitted police statistics. From the outset, users of the *Reports* are cautioned against drawing conclusions from direct comparison of crime figures between individual communities or between one year and another without first considering the variety of factors that influence criminal conduct.[7] Yet, even with these reservations, the public is frightened to hear that a burglary is committed in America every 12 seconds, a larceny every 7 seconds, an automobile theft every 34 seconds, and a violent crime (murder, forcible rape, robbery, or assault to kill) every 36 seconds.[8] Even if this were normal in the Durkheimian sense, it poses a grave social problem that demands an answer. It is far too simple to recommend travel by horseback in order to reduce automobile thefts and to deprive bank robbers of a fast means of escape, to abolish air travel to make air hijacking impossible, to advocate the wearing of chastity belts to lessen rape, or to close department stores to eliminate shoplifting. Negative responses to these crime forms may alleviate the symptoms, but they rarely help to solve the problem or to treat the offender.

The Meaning of Crime Statistics • Although crime statistics do have their shortcomings, they do serve as an index of the problem.[9] Table 8.2 illustrates the scope of the crime problem as defined in 1973. Among the crimes of

TABLE 8.1

INDEX OF CRIME—UNITED STATES, 1973

AREA	POPULATION[1]	TOTAL CRIME INDEX	VIOLENT[2] CRIME	PROPERTY[2] CRIME	MURDER AND NONNEGLIGENT MANSLAUGHTER	FORCIBLE RAPE	ROBBERY	AGGRAVATED ASSAULT	BURGLARY	LARCENY-THEFT	AUTO THEFT
United States Total...........	209,851,000	8,638,375	869,465	7,768,910	19,509	51,002	382,683	416,271	2,540,907	4,304,363	923,640
Rate per 100,000 inhabitants	....	4,116.4	414.3	3,702.1	9.3	24.3	182.4	198.4	1,210.8	2,051.2	440.1
Standard Metropolitan Statistical											
Area.............[3]	152,853,000										
Area actually reporting[3].....	96.8%	7,231,583	758,778	6,472,805	15,396	43,385	363,880	336,117	2,112,775	3,522,049	837,981
Estimated total	100.0%	7,372,041	768,771	6,603,270	15,665	44,146	366,687	342,273	2,156,213	3,594,019	853,038
Rate per 100,000 inhabitants .	....	4,823.0	502.9	4,320.0	10.2	28.9	239.9	223.9	1,410.6	2,351.3	558.1
Other Cities..............	22,774,000										
Area actually reporting	90.2%	694,525	45,141	649,384	1,130	2,516	9,030	32,465	173,732	437,311	38,341
Estimated total	100.0%	762,616	50,255	712,361	1,285	2,765	9,939	36,266	191,662	478,439	42,260
Rate per 100,000 inhabitants .	....	3,348.7	220.7	3,128.0	5.6	12.1	43.6	159.2	841.6	2,100.8	185.6
Rural	34,225,000										
Area actually reporting	80.1%	421,497	38,897	382,600	1,925	3,262	4,701	29,009	163,220	196,224	23,156
Estimated total	100.0%	503,718	50,439	453,279	2,559	4,091	6,057	37,732	193,032	231,905	28,342
Rate per 100,000 inhabitants .	....	1,471.8	147.4	1,324.4	7.5	12.0	17.7	110.2	564.0	677.6	82.8

[1] Population is Bureau of the Census provisional estimate as of July 1, 1973.

[2] Violent crime is offenses of murder, forcible rape, robbery, and aggravated assault; property crime is offenses of burglary, larceny-theft and auto theft.

[3] The percentage representing area actually reporting will not coincide with the ratio between reported and estimated crime totals since these data present the sum of the calculations for individual states which have varying populations, portions reporting and crime rates.

Source: Federal Bureau of Investigation, *Uniform Crime Reports—1973* (Washington, D.C.: U.S. Government Printing Office, 1974), p. 58.

TABLE 8.2

TOTAL ESTIMATED ARRESTS, UNITED STATES, 1973

Total[2]	9,027,700
Criminal homicide:	
Murder and nonnegligent manslaughter	19,210
Manslaughter by negligence	4,030
Forcible rape	25,720
Robbery	127,530
Aggravated assault	208,100
Burglary—breaking or entering	434,000
Larceny-theft	858,900
Auto theft	155,800
Violent crime	380,560
Property crime	1,448,700
Subtotal for above offenses	1,833,300
Other assaults	383,700
Arson	14,600
Forgery and counterfeiting	56,400
Fraud	142,800
Embezzlement	12,400
Stolen property; buying, receiving, possessing	90,100
Vandalism	169,300
Weapons; carrying, possessing, etc.	155,400
Prostitution and commercialized vice	55,800
Sex offenses (except forcible rape and prostitution)	65,500
Narcotic drug laws	628,900
Opium or cocaine and their derivatives	88,000
Marijuana	420,700
Synthetic or manufactured narcotics	33,400
Other—dangerous nonnarcotic drugs	86,800
Gambling	68,300
Bookmaking	6,100
Numbers and lottery	11,600
All other gambling	50,600
Offenses against family and children	70,200
Driving under the influence	946,800
Liquor laws	272,000
Drunkenness	1,599,000
Disorderly conduct	720,400
Vagrancy	62,300
All other offenses (except traffic)	1,196,600
Suspicion	67,100
Curfew and loitering law violations	151,200
Runaways	265,600

[1] Arrest totals based on all reporting agencies and estimates for unreported areas

[2] Because of rounding, items may not add to totals.

Source: Federal Bureau of Investigation, *Uniform Crime Reports—1973* (Washington, D.C.: U.S. Government Printing Office, 1974), p. 121.

violence, *murder and other willful killings,* the gravest of all offenses against the person, naturally invite most attention, although they comprised only two percent of the total number of violent crimes committed in 1973. With an approximate 157 percent increase in crime since 1960, nearly 20,000 murders in the United States are committed in a year. About half (44 percent) are committed in the Southern states. Most take place in the last third of the year, commonly in December. The majority of the murderers use handguns (67 percent); cutting and stabbing appear as the next most favorite methods. Males outnumber females as victims by more than 3 to 1, but, although the difference is not significant, more wives than husbands are victims in cases involving married partners. The racial distribution of victims is roughly 47 percent whites and 53 percent non-whites. Slightly less than half of the murder offenders have lately come from those younger age groups under the age of 25. Only 79 percent of the murders known to the police were cleared by the arrest of an alleged offender (see Figure 8.1).

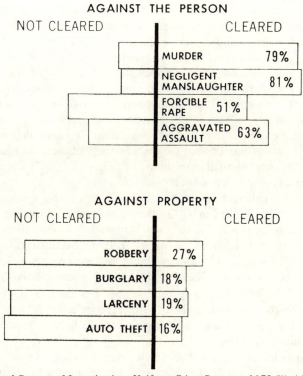

Source: Federal Bureau of Investigation, *Uniform Crime Reports—1973* (Washington, D.C.: U.S. Government Printing Office, 1974), p. 29

Figure 8.1 Crimes Cleared by Arrest 1973

Aggravated assaults, attacks against the person involving the infliction of severe bodily injury, comprise five percent of the identified serious offenses, 48 percent of the crimes of violence, and now number more than 416,270. The Southern states lead in this category (37 percent). The *Uniform Crime Reports* suggest that most aggravated assaults occur within the family and among neighbors and acquaintances. As an offense category, both the criminal-victim relationship and the nature of the attacks resemble the characteristics of homicide. The arrested males outnumber females by 7 to 1. *Forcible rape* violations increased to 51,000 in 1973 and compose nearly six percent of the volume of crimes of violence. However, this is probably the most under-reported serious crime due to the understandable reluctance of the victim to identify herself as a victim. The victimization risk is significantly higher in larger cities than in suburbs and rural areas. The Southern states possess the highest rate. Although it has been observed, especially in rape cases, that individual law enforcement departments develop localized methods to deal with various kinds of cases, Gilbert Geis and Stephen Schafer find that forcible rape rate is higher in a social setting which has a relatively permissive sexual ethos than in one which culturally restricts heterosexual contacts.[10] Males in the age group 16 to 24 represent the most frequently arrested group for this offense. Fifty-one percent of all arrested rape offenders were white in 1973. An estimated 15 percent of the reported rapes were determined by investigation to be unfounded.

Robbery, a face-to-face crime in which the victim is frequently injured, and which occurs most frequently during December, has increased by 46 percent since 1968. Of the estimated 382,680 robberies reported in 1973, most occurred in cities, commonly in the Southern states. The rates were 571 victims per 100,000 persons in cities over 250,000 population, 76 in suburban areas and 18 in rural areas. About one third of the robbers, many of them armed, were under the age of 18; over one half were under 25 years of age. Of the arrested, 35 percent were white and 65 percent non-white.

Burglary, the unlawful entry of a structure to commit a felony or theft, reached 2,540,900 offenses in 1973. This, too, is predominantly a city crime, occurring mainly in the Southern states. Although burglars still favor activity under cover of the darkness of night, daytime burglaries of unattended residences are increasing. The average dollar loss per burglary is $337. During 1973, property owners lost about $543 million; nonresidential losses added another $313 million, making a total of $856 million. The overwhelming majority of burglars are young; about 84 percent are under 25; over one half of all burglars (54 percent) are under the age of 18. In this crime type, white outnumber black offenders 2 to 1.

After burglaries, *larceny-theft* shows the highest volume. It now accounts for 4,304,400 offenses per year. The Western states reported a 1973 rate of 3,032 offenses per 100,000 inhabitants, while the North Central states had a rate of 2,132, the Southern states 1,792, and the Northeastern states 1,579. Larcenies are more common during the summer months and cause a yearly loss of over

$603 million. Pocket picking, purse snatching, shoplifting, and thefts from automobiles represent leading theft forms. Thirty-seven percent of the arrests for this crime are made among youth under 18; a relatively large number of female offenders are involved. White offenders outnumber black in this crime category. *Automobile thefts* numbered 923,600 in 1973. Most were stolen within large cities. Most common in the Northeastern states, car thefts engage few female participants. Nearly three-fourths of those arrested persons are under the age of 21; 56 percent are under the age of 18. Two thirds of those arrested for auto theft are white.[11]

Fundamental Ideas of the Crime Problem

Perhaps the oldest of all social problems, crime may be the most serious due to the social disruption it brings. Its volume is without doubt even larger than its officially recorded visibility. Whatever its scope, the problem of crime and its solution has been marked by five consecutive developmental stages which range historically from: 1) Private revenge, emphasizing individual solution of the problem; 2) Divine revenge, stressing superstition or a belief in supernatural justice; 3) Absolutism of the sovereign, including the despotic control of deviance; 4) Humanitarianism, emphasizing the dignity and rights of man; and 5) Social defense, extending more recently to a scientific concern for juvenile delinquents, crime victims, organized criminals, white collar violators, and violent offenders.

Private Revenge and Individualism • In primitive and rudimentary communities, the idea of *revenge* dominated the popular approach to what are now called crimes. While crimes committed against the total community (*e.g.,* treachery or treason) were punished collectively, all other violations were judged problems to be resolved by the individual victim. The revenge idea encouraged a victim to get even with his attacker on his own. However, his attempt to avenge himself usually prompted the attacker to defend aggressively his own person, leading to a continuing conflict between the criminal and his victim. Socially, this approach to the crime problem was little else than a mutual effort to secure power.[12] While both attack and revenge represented expressions of a struggle to secure desired goals, perpetual revenges and counterrevenges, involving individual and group blood feuds, hindered the peace of a community.

Divine Revenge, Superstition, and Supernatural Intervention • The consolidation of religious ideas and institutions (*e.g., the asylum,* which provided safety for hunted criminals, and the *treuga dei,* which prohibited crimes for a period of time to serve the peace of God) modified the feud concept and led to the notion of *divine revenge.* Most criminal acts were regarded as an attack against the deity or some supernatural force which would react to human actions through floods, earthquakes, pestilence, or plague. Demonology, mysticism, magic, and witchcraft became the dominant features of criminal justice; crime as a social problem was understood in theological and quasi-theological terms. Irrational revenge dominated the social control system. Punishments were bloody and cruel. "The sinner," spokesmen of the period claimed, "must not only pay a debt to society; he must get right with God."[13]

Absolutism of the Sovereign and Despotism ● Ruling sovereigns, during the third period, used their unlimited power, recently acquired, to create the idea that the ruler possessed total authority to judge and to control offenders. Criminal acts were defined as attacks against the ruling sovereign; punishment was the ruler's legitimate response to these threats. Although this era began with a system of "composition," an appeal to avoid private and blood revenge by monetary or economic compensation, and an effort to reduce criminal violence, the idea of despotic deterrence still predominated. As commerce and urban life developed, new types of crimes and criminals also arose. The public received only limited protection against political corruption, judicial miscarriages, and autocratic rule. During this period, statutory criminal law was more fully developed.[14]

Humanitarianism and the Rights of Man ● The Period of the Enlightenment saw the introduction of the *humanitarian ideas* of human dignity and the rights of man and reduced some of the previous horrors. Cruelty was replaced by humanistic ideals, deterrence by care and correction, arbitrariness by moderation, and despotism by some guarantee of individual freedom. By the end of the eighteenth century, the machinery of criminal justice was entirely in the hands of the state; crime was defined as an act against the public interest. Many favored the radical reform of criminal law and spoke against corporal punishment and in support of the reformation of the penal system. The ancient understanding of crime and its treatment was rejected. Voltaire and the Encyclopedists prepared the ground for the reorientation of criminal law. Cesare Beccaria's published monograph *On Crimes and Punishments,*[15] which proposed new principles for judicial and penal action, stirred European criminological thought. Crime was made a purely legal category and punishment was defined as a means for equalizing guilt. The administration of criminal justice, dominated by a belief in free will, was conceived as merely the application of the demands of the printed law.

Social Defense and Scientific Approach ● As men began to question the concept of free will, new assumptions concerning the problem of criminal deviance emerged. The search for crime causes led to the *application of the scientific method* to crime problems. The focus began to change from the evaluation of the criminal act to an examination of the problems of the criminal actor. The belief grew that society could defend itself only by getting at the root causes of crime. Cesare Lombroso, Raffaele Garofalo, and Enrico Ferri pioneered theoretical and empirical efforts to direct attention to the joint responsibility of the criminal actor and his society for crime.[16] While Lombroso, Garofalo, and Ferri differed in the etiologies they proposed,[17] they sowed the seeds found in many modern crime explanations. Lombroso related criminality to biological or anthropological causes and emphasized a concept of "atavism," which assumed that criminals are a reversion to a primitive or subhuman type of man, a "born criminal." Garofalo took a more legalistic or moralistic approach and made efforts to find a definition of "natural crime." a type of deviation to be found historically in all cultures. Although Ferri, a lawyer, proved to be the most sociological of these early theorists, he stressed "social responsibility" and social protection (defense).

Understanding Crime

The work of Lombroso, Garofalo, and Ferri in the last quarter of the nineteenth century gave birth to three major approaches to the search for crime causes. The *bio-psychological school* directed its investigation to the criminal man, exploring his physical, psychic, somatological, and constitutional characteristics in order to propose strategies for combatting criminal conduct. This orientation assumed that the criminal is partially or totally abnormal, a condition which significantly determines his criminal behavior. Some theorists within this school found a "criminal diathesis," a constitutional proclivity potent enough to determine man's crime,[18] or concluded that criminals by nature are organically inferior.[19] The German Ernst Kretschmer[20] and the American William J. Sheldon[21] proposed classifications of body types in relation to criminal inclinations. Johannes Lange anticipated the criminal destiny of twins.[22]

Other branches of the bio-psychological school emphasized psychological and psychiatric models. An emphasis upon crime due to mental degeneration and numerous defective "family trees" emerged from an extension of Lombroso's concepts. Psychoses, mental defects, shortcomings of the central nervous system, neurasthenia, and subintelligence, measured by various mental tests, were eventually blamed for actual criminal conduct. Sigmund Freud related crime to personality repression,[23] while more recently, members of this school have tried to relate crime to the variable structure of human sex chromosomes (*e.g.,* the XYY factor).

The *sociological school,* an orientation favored in the United States, contends that the criminal is a product of his society. Criminal ecology, one of its branches, relates deviant behavior to the special influence of the physical and social environment, maintaining that the criminal is "a puppet of time and space."[24] Several early investigators saw juvenile delinquency in terms of city "delinquency areas."[25] However, the most popular unit of the sociological school contended that criminal conduct originates in the abnormalities of the offender's social life. Different socially from those whose behavior is proved "normal" by their conformity to the law, they represent a variant within the socialized human group. Criminal conduct to these analysts is a form of antisociality. The offender, the French anthropologist Leonce Manouvrier noted in the nineteenth century, is simply an instrument on which society plays.[26] J.A.E. Lacassagne held that the social environment is the "bouillon for culturing criminals."[27]

Not all theorists within the sociological school followed the same tack. Some emphasized the social interaction to which a man is exposed. Benoit A. Morel was among the first to point to the impact of "moral contagion."[28] Gabriel Tarde offered the clearest insight into the importance of interaction in proposing his "laws of imitation" which he believed had a definite effect upon human criminality.[29] Edwin H. Sutherland presupposed Tarde's ideas in his theory of "differential association."[30] Just as a person can acquire the patterns of conformist behavior, he can also internalize, Sutherland theorized, patterns favoring law-violating conduct. Crime, he assumed, is a learned behavior which depends upon the extent and intensity to which individuals share conforming and deviating group relationships.

Still others in the school explain crime in terms of culture, its values and norms, and their conflict. The Belgian Adolphe Prins pioneered this viewpoint,[31] but it was the American Donald R. Taft who chose to understand crime in terms of the conditions, dynamics, and complexities of a given culture.[32] Thorsten Sellin explains crime as an expression of conflict in conduct norms. Those theorists focusing on "social existence," the system of the society, find crime to be a product of structural disturbance; they contend that inconsistencies in the social structure and the uneven distribution of values, norms, goals, and rewards cause crime. Emile Durkheim, the French student of social organization, traced crime to anomie, the lack of rules and the absence of norms, lawlessness, or weakened norms that may lead to deviant behavior.[33]

Some crime analysts find the causes of criminal deviance within economic conditions or structure and demand basic socio-structural modifications. William Adriaan Bonger, for example, contended that the structure of a capitalist society exerts varied pressures of different social classes and causes crime.[34] The historical understanding of economic conditions, the significance of class struggle, the idea of surplus value, and other issues known to Bonger were later articulated in what is now described as Marxist ideology. Since the development of the Marxian synthesis, which views crime as an economic product, such explanations have been presupposed in the reformation of criminal law in the Soviet Union and other socialist societies.

More recently, Richard D. Knudten has proposed a middle range Theory of Relativity, relating delinquency and crime to culture, social organization, small group, and personality factors. In an extensive formulation, Knudten maintains that delinquency and crime are relative and depend upon the situation in which criminal norms and action are located as defined by the cultural environment, the person's tendency to ignore or to neutralize limits placed upon his actions by his social class and social status, his ability to resist pressures which call for violation of laws placed upon him by his group roles, and his tendency toward action as determined by his individual personality.[35] In his "power-theory," Stephen Schafer contends that criminal conduct can be understood only through the examination of "dual responsibilities," which are interrelated and cannot be disconnected. The first responsibility refers to the command of a recognized social power, should it be a one-person dictator or a democratic parliament. It is the only source that defines legally human behavior and decides what is legitimate and illegitimate. The power in this decision makes use of its value system and forces other persons to follow it. Each person is made responsible for his own conduct under threat of infliction of punishment should he not obey. The second responsibility refers to those factors, which, despite the power's threat, lead men to take a stand against the power's command by committing a crime. Therefore, crime and the crime rate are dependent upon the efficiency and success of the dominant power's ability to socialize others and to get them to believe, or at least to accept, that the power's command is right and justified for the total social group.[36]

The *multifactor approach,* an effort to reconcile the findings of the bio-psychological and sociological schools, represents the third major orientation. Its pioneer, the German Franz von Liszt, wanted to mediate the discrepancies between the other two major schools by proposing that the causes or factors of crime are "multiple," not exclusively biological, psychological or sociological. Many contemporary theorists who claim membership in the sociological school in fact propose a multifactor approach to the problem of crime.

What Makes a Man a Criminal?

Despite the admirable efforts of current theorists and researchers, none can truly claim they know what makes a man a criminal. This is probably why the crime problem is described so negatively to the public; stay off the streets at night, leave lights on in your residence from sunset to dawn, avoid speaking to strangers, install brighter street lights, keep away from "criminal areas," lock your cars, use detection mirrors in department stores, purchase bank and home alarm systems, make policemen more efficient by paying them better, redevelop slum areas, and create a neighborhood network for reporting suspicious persons. Each is a defensive measure undertaken against those who are believed to be potential offenders or who have already developed criminal careers. But no *definitive* scientific explanation as to what causes one man to turn against another or his property is yet in sight. Most are still hypotheses open to further testing.

Each theory of crime attempts to fathom why laws are both obeyed and violated. Inevitably, this effort leads to the question "what is criminal justice?"

This is not easily answered. Some hold that "justice" means only what those who use the term agree to make it mean; therefore, the concepts of crime and justice are relative. While membership in one category of society promises only a low risk of criminal conduct, belonging to another may make a man susceptible to a higher crime risk, a "categoric risk," which offers a greater chance of being arrested. While the "categoric risk," actually a kind of public prejudice, exposes certain persons to those crimes enumerated in criminal statistics, the "punishment of public opinion," another type of public prejudice, prevents these people from leaving the criminal world and from re-entering the society of law-abiding citizens.

Although the law limits the scope of court judgments and sanctions, public opinion knows no such bounds. Once a person becomes a cipher within official criminal statistics, public opinion stamps the criminal stigma upon him and fortifies his categoric risk in a manner similar to the Roman *capitis diminutio maxima,* which kills morally.[37] Its "punishment" adds to the conventional judicial sentence. Most often it is a "life sentence" if the criminal, who has already paid his debt to society, cannot gain release from the tight rein of public prejudice and stigmatization.

The Ordinary Criminal

Traditional or ordinary criminals represent the bulk of law violators. They are the ones the public fears as criminals and who compose the "crime problem." Apart from the group of psychotics and psychopaths who commit crimes caused by the stimulation or pressures of their delusions or hallucinations, many of whom are being cared for by mental hospitals or correctional institutions, ordinary criminals in the broadest sense of the term can be classified as: 1) occasional criminals; and 2) professional criminals.

The Occasional Criminal • Although *occasional criminals* appear to represent the simplest form of criminality, they in fact exemplify the most difficult. In contrast to all other criminal types, their life style is similar to the noncriminal elements of society.[38] They are likely to live decent lives, participate in regular recreational outlets, follow useful career patterns, and even practice their religious faith. When it occurs, their crime is only an episode in their lives and has no distinct or continuing pattern. For the most part, they follow social requirements and reflect normative aspirations.[39] Frequently, their criminal acts are stimulated by a particular situation (*e.g.,* drunkenness, an opportunity to steal, or the like). They usually resist criminal tendencies, although sometimes they weaken in the face of pressure to commit criminal acts. Their crimes, as a consequence, are nearly totally unpredictable and cover a wide range of charges. No one knows when and under what circumstances occasional criminals will commit a murder, an embezzlement, an automobile theft, a rape, or another criminal act.

Persons in this category often justify their criminal conduct in terms of unusual or unexpected pressure. They may argue that the special characteristics of the situation excuse the violation of law and assume a philosophical position that the overwhelming force of criminal pressure, usually need or emotion, did not allow them to settle their problem through legitimate or conventional procedures. If this pressure toward crime is especially powerful, they may feel that the right to redress the situation is theirs alone. If they are hungry, only they can determine, so they claim, that they "must" steal; if they are jealous, only they know that they "must" kill. Occasional criminals tend to act, therefore, on the assumption that in a given situation they alone can and must decide right and wrong and execute the decision.

The occasional criminal's justification of crime commonly reveals the immediate pressures of a given situation, but necessarily the absence of alternative ways to achieve the desired goal. In some situations, occasional criminals may simply be unable to conform to the norms of their group successfully; at other times, their poorly socialized personality has little chance to relate their criminal conduct, which is prompted by the given situation, to social values adequately. In each instance, situational pressures force occasional criminals to deviate from their conventional reactions and provide justification for criminal actions taken.

As a result of their continuing socialization, occasional criminals usually develop normal ethical attitudes as they mature. Their inner control, their socioethical ability to resist wrong, learned through the socialization process, functions according to the value system common to their social group. Essentially, they know what their role is within their society. However, their occasional crime—crime "on occasion"—is the result not of shortcomings in their socialization but of inadequacies in the specific social situation that neutralize and cause them to betray their learned values.[40] Their activity is likely to be due to their unpreparedness to face all possible emotions or needs and unexpected occasions or opportunities.

The popular belief that occasional criminal conduct is similar to professional criminal behavior, which is essentially profit oriented, is unfortunate.[41] It tends to confuse the crime problem and make resolution of the problem highly difficult. However, some occasional criminals do become professional criminals or even participants in organized crime.

Professional Criminals ● *Professional criminals* violate law for profit. Whereas the occasional criminal acts under the pressure of need or emotion, professional criminals seek a monetary reward. If the occasional criminal achieves financial gain, it is incidental to some other primary end. Professional criminals, however, seek financial advantage or economic profit as a primary goal. Because professional criminals reveal an inadequate transmission and socialization of norms, they are not equipped with normal socioethical attitudes. Their personalities are products of faulty or totally unsuccessful socialization procedures. While the occasional criminal is a good *citizen,* the professional criminal is a good *criminal.* Professional criminals function in ways comparable to the work and life of other professionals in legitimate occupations.[42] Generally speaking, they have a "full-time job" and usually establish a locus of operation away from their home environment. Frequently, they cut their family ties.

Although the common cliche states that juvenile delinquency is the first certain step toward professional crime, no available evidence "proves" a probable cause-and-effect relationship. Juvenile delinquency *may* or *may not* lead to professional criminal conduct. A professional criminal career, however, necessarily begins with "amateur" crime. Training, practice, and experience are required for graduation to true professionalism. Professional criminal accomplishment and identity occur as the individual develops appropriate skills to reach profitable goals. Professional criminality is directed not only toward obtaining conveniences and pleasures, but also, and possibly first of all, toward gaining a living. Once individuals become true professional criminals, they are likely to remain such unless their socioethical personality is remobilized.[43]

Organized and White Collar Criminals

In the last decade, interest concerning organized and white collar crime has grown. Many contend that both forms are ultimately more harmful to society than the more personal forms of traditional crimes represented in occasional and professional criminality due to their tendency to corrupt normal social processes and organizations.

Organized Crime ● A significant crime form because it involves multiple and organized criminal participants and victims who are exposed to some harm, organized crime has been seen as a serious problem by the public only in recent years. Organized crime is not simply a loose or casual group of criminals who seek to complete one or more offenses successfully, but represents a functional organization designed to commit continuous crimes and sometimes to engage in legitimate business activities. Whereas the individual professional criminal may associate and cooperate with others due to the specific requirements of the planned crime, the specific crime in "organized crime" is a by-product of an organization formed for general criminal purposes. The organization is a primary rather than secondary group and commands the total individual. In general terms, the nature and character of organized crime include:

1. *A permanent association of criminals in which many participants are "tenured" members.* They share a "moral" commitment to a comparatively permanent or lasting association. If the interest of the organization (i.e., the need for secrecy or for special skills) necessitates the continued involvement of an associate despite his desire to withdraw, he may be

forced by threats or other methods to continue his membership and participate in further crimes.

2. *Organizational goals and aspirations designed for profit.* Although the criminal organization or its members may engage in activities which seem to minimize the profit motive, financial gain is always the ultimate goal of the criminal confederation.

3. *A large number of participant members.* Even though the exact number of persons in organized crime cannot be defined or stated with certainty, organized crime, as criminal organizations go, is a substantial organization.

4. *The profitable existence of the group.* Individual and professional criminals outside organized crime may decide to engage in a specific criminal act before engaging in the violation; such collusion to determine a general area of profitable activity is characteristic of organized crime.

5. *As association or cooperation with others in order to achieve intended criminal ends and predetermined organizational goals.* This effort may include the establishment of economic or social monopolies in an entire geographic area. Coexistence with other criminal groups is commonly filled with conflict.

6. *A clear-cut criminal organization structure.* As a part of a functional group designed to meet the goals of its leaders and the needs of its members, each participant engages in a variety of activities and occupies a specific social role commonly accepted by group members and generally coordinated through the leadership and discipline of one or more persons. While females may fulfill designated roles in the predominantly male organization, the leaders are nearly always males.

While the efficiency and complexity of the group generally depend upon the size of the membership, every organized crime unit presupposes preparation for criminal conduct, action, and immunity from arrest insofar as possible. Because the life of the group depends upon the dependable performance of duties and responsibilities, performance is rewarded and failure to perform punished ruthlessly.

7. *A high priority given to organizational planning.* The goals of the group and its interest in survival require a continuing maximum effort by all members. While planning is recognized as essential to group success, it is characterized by a high degree of flexibility and imagination. In each instance, the goal of the moment governs the decision to use a particular technique.[44]

Two Conceptions of Organized Crime ● The two dominant conceptions of organized crime offer differing explanations of its major characteristics. One perceives organized crime in general terms, a group which covers and controls nearly all aspects of society, and commits nearly all types of crimes. According to this view, members are ruled by a few criminal families. The second conception understands organized crime in more *specific terms,* as if it were a special crime form which covers and controls only small areas and involves only certain sorts of crimes. This specific group is normally ruled by one person or a small coalition of professional criminals who do not necessarily belong to a single "family." Such an outlook presupposes the functional operation of multiple dependent criminal organizations which act on a relatively small scale. While the first type is usually identified by the name "Mafia" (or "Maffia") and "La Cosa Nostra," the latter is named and classified by the terms "gangs," "syndicates," and "rackets," depending upon the type and orientation of their activities.

General-Type Organized Crime • When the *general* type of organized crime first emerged is not known. In all likelihood, it was not much before the nineteenth century. Even then, it probably was an outgrowth or refinement of an historically older special type of organized crime. The European origin of *special*-type organized crime appears to rest with the beginnings of urbanization, the first decades after the Middle Ages, when vagabonds, adventurers, and other new types of criminals made their appearance and banded together to make their criminal activities more efficient and successful. For example, Gabriel Tarde mentions in his *Penal Philosophy* that a "society of brigands" developed "special associations" and "great professional syndicates of crime."[45] The "maffia," according to Tarde, was just one of these criminal groupings, "a band of Sicilian brigands," similar to the Neopolitan "camorra" which, in turn, resembled the associations of high class thieves of Paris.

The roots of "family leadership" and "social influence" in contemporary general-type organized crime rest in the original "maffia" in Sicily. The "maffiosi" operated as a clan which conspired to obtain political power over other clans. At the time, the "maffias" amounted, however, to hardly more than large-scale special-type criminal organizations. Their ambition to possess political influence was motivated by a desire to gain supremacy over competing criminal bands. Not only was the "maffia" one representation of the many existing special organized crime groups, but its overall power was much less than that assumed by contemporary students of organized crime.

Generally, it was this type of "maffia" that was imported to the United States from Sicily near the end of the Nineteenth century, when many immigrants, coming from the southern parts of Italy and Sicily, brought to the new country their home culture and customs, including clan spirit and a tendency towards violence. They also carried elements of the "Maffia" and "The Black Hand" in their midst.[46] Whether this "Maffia" (or "Mafia") extended its activites in the new country into a nationwide criminal organization or to a form of criminal confederation of a limited number of large-scale organizations given a name like "La Cosa Nostra" ("Our Thing") is still open to argument.[47]

Similarly, whether these allegedly powerful criminal organizations actually absorbed smaller-scale special-type organizations, such as gangs, syndicates, and rackets, and made them operational subdivisions is not fully clear. Even whether this special-type organized crime exists independently or whether its continuance depends upon the good will of such organizations as the Cosa Nostra is not fully documented. However, since World War II, crime experts and the public have been willing to accept the idea of the existence of a Mafia or Cosa Nostra sort of general-type organized crime and to neglect the problems created by special-type criminal organizations.

The President's Commission on Law Enforcement and Administration of Justice accepted the general-type explanation of organized crime in its 1967 report, noting that organized crime "is a society that seeks to operate outside the control of the American people and their governments" and involves thousands of criminals working in a complex structure with intricate conspiracies in order to amass huge profits.[48] Sociologist Donald R. Cressey further affirms that in the United States criminals have managed to put together an organization which is at once a nationwide illicit cartel and is dedicated to securing millions of dollars through extortion, usury, fraud, corruption, violence, and murder.[49] Organized crime, Cressey believes, has begun to undermine basic economic and political traditions and institutions. To what extent this has occurred remains unsubstantiated.

Danilo Dolci, an Italian idealist and devoted social reformer, found in Sicily that a mutual relationship and possible alliance, at least, exists between political leaders and organized crime. Native politicians who compromise with the mafia, Dolci suggests, can be classified into four categories: (1) those who have no principles and do not care how they get the votes or with whom they are dealing; (2) those who consciously and purposefully enter into mutual exploitations with organized criminals; (3) those maffiosi who want to be elected to influential positions; and (4) those who are young and, therefore, seek ways to adapt themselves to the given system.[50]

Organized Crime in the United States • In the United States, organized crime has attempted to establish illegal gambling and monopolies, dictate the action of some congressmen or other political leaders, amass a fortune by importing narcotics, buy immunity from prosecution for murder, use a union to extort a small businessman's livelihood, bribe city officials in order to get a license or a contract, and demand a share of a businessman's profits.[51] What organized crime wants, the President's Crime Commission maintained, is money and power. What makes it different from law-abiding organizations and individuals with those same objectives, "is that the ethical and moral standards the criminals adhere to, the laws and regulations they obey, the procedures they use are private and secret ones that they devise themselves, change when they see fit, and administer summarily and invisibly."[52]

The operations of these Maffias or Cosa Nostras so alarmed the President's

Commission that it proposed a national strategy against organized crime and recommended an annual investigative grand jury, legislation dealing specifically with wiretapping and electronic bugging, special protection for potential witnesses, special police intelligence units, a permanent joint Congressional committee on organized crime, the development of citizens' crime commissions, the creation of preventive strategies by private business associations, and a number of other measures designed to combat such criminal organizations.[53]

To what extent the belief in a general-type organized crime is confused or equated with a widely extended form and conception of white collar criminality or with large-scale public immorality that dominates profitmaking practices, often using criminal methods or instruments which are tolerated and/or even adopted by many members of our competitive society, is indefinite. There is some evidence to suggest that these groups are really powerful and are influenced, if not controlled, by 24 tightly knit "families" which are believed to be master-minding and ruling organized crime in the United States.

Patterns of La Cosa Nostra • The structure, hierarchy, family spirit, and internal discipline of the general-type "La Cosa Nostra" resembles those of Sicilian Mafia clans.[54] At the top of each of the 24 criminal organizations constituting "La Cosa Nostra" is the *boss,* who is aided by a *consigliere* (*counselor*) who plays the role of a counselor or advisor. Next in rank is the *underboss,* a deputy leader. Under him are positioned the *lieutenants* (*caporegima*), who are served in turn by the soldiers (*soldati*), assigned to one or another lieutenant, according to the activity to be completed. Actually, these soldiers enforce discipline over group "fronts" and members, responding to orders of the boss by the use of threat, assault, and murder. However, the boss is only a leader of a group. The highest ruling body of the total confederation of 24 families is the *commission* (*commissione*), a type of "judicial" board, representing the ultimate authority in organizational disputes, consisting usually of 9 to 12 men. Although the total organization is highly sophisticated and is decentralized with delegated authority, New York City, the locale of the most powerful criminal families, is regarded as the unofficial headquarters of the entire crime organization.

The most influential and perhaps wealthiest families, outside of those in New York, operate in New Jersey, Illinois, Florida, Louisiana, Nevada, Michigan, and Rhode Island. While the bosses know each other and are interrelated through the decision-making power of the commission, they identify with the total Cosa Nostra-type crime organization. Those who are positioned under the boss tend to identify with the given "family" to which they actually belong. This helps to enforce "the code," an informal and unwritten set of rules of discipline, which stipulates that no member of the organization may interfere with the leader's interest or may seek protection from organized crime decisions by seeking assistance from law enforcement agencies. The "code" expects unconditional discipline and absolute loyalty from its adherents, even to the extent of going to prison for a boss who exploited all his subordinates. The authority of the boss, subject to the possibility of being overruled by the Commission, is "absolute within his 'family,' geographical area, and any sphere of influence which does not bring him into conflict with another boss,"[55] The so-called "gangland murders" indicate that ruthless discipline is being enforced by the leader of a criminal organization of the Cosa Nostra type within his territory.

Specific-Type Organized Crime: Gangs, Syndicates, and Rackets ● Special-type organized crime, taking the form of criminal gangs, syndicates, and rackets are usually disinterested in social or political power and motivated by a goal of criminal profit. While the general-type organization seeks social and political influence in order to reach criminal goals, the *gang's* crime method depends primarily upon the use of physical force.[56] Some evaluators identify the gang with the deviant associations of juvenile delinquents. Despite their similarities, they are strikingly different. For example, while the juvenile gang is usually composed of friends sharing similar sentiments and motives, the adult criminal gang is based upon reason. Friendship among gang members may develop later on. The juvenile delinquent gang frequently imitates adult models and engages in activities that provide a feeling of thrill; the adult criminal gang is formed for profit and is guided by crude realities. Although the juvenile gang prepares the act and carries it out, the adult criminal gang not only plans the event, but also defends and protects its members following the criminal incident.

Although the juvenile gang is a rather loose organization, using humiliation or corporal punishment as a means of disciplining errant members, the adult gang has a sophisticated and tight structure in which discipline is often a matter of life or death. The juvenile delinquent gang is rather "immobile," staying for economic reasons within a certain geographical area, often close to the home of its members. The adult criminal gang, on the other hand, is quite "mobile," moving within the city or even to another state or country to pursue the most productive criminal activities.[57] Bank safes, large firm payrolls, jewelry of wealthy people, and the like are the favorite targets of adult criminal gangs; kidnapping for ransom, burglary, robbery, breaking and entering, automobile theft, and similar offenses represent preferred crimes. Since their method involves the use of physical force, they often engage in additional instrument crimes, such as assault or homicide. The problems of the gang is a part of the general crime problem.

The *criminal syndicate,* a name often mistakenly used to identify the Cosa Nostra-type organization, is a special-type criminal association which provides illegal gambling, smuggling, narcotics, prostitution, and other services to the public. While the unity of the gang is based on fear, the syndicate takes advantage of one's desires. While the gang only "takes," the syndicate also "gives." The syndicate's victims are also its "clients." Inasmuch as they, too, enter into criminality by buying illegal services, they are willing criminal victims. As a result, the syndicate applies physical force against its victims infrequently and restricts the use of violence largely to conflicts between competing syndicates. Consequently, less public hatred or anger is expressed against syndicates than against a gang. Criminal syndicates nearly always enjoy a degree of public tolerance, if not approval, in their operations. As opposed to the gang, the criminal syndicate needs capital to acquire its facilities and stock and to establish a locale for providing or selling services to willing and possibly eager purchasers. The "owner" or the "financier" of the syndicate is almost always invisible. Because the syndicate strives to maintain some type of economic monopoly in a given geographic area or type of business, its members are usually reluctant to tolerate the operation of competitors.

The syndicate is primarily an urban organization. Although small towns are also familiar with their services, syndicates prefer to work in big cities or metropolitan areas where a great number of prospective victim-clients reside. As a result, syndicates, as opposed to the gangs and rackets which do not really need an "establishment," are relatively immobile. Although among all special-type criminal organizations, the syndicate stands the closest to the Mafia-style La Cosa Nostra-type, it shows little interest in social or political power, except, of course, if bribery or similar activities are necessary to establish a monopoly or to maintain a peaceful criminal operation.

Rackets, on the other hand, revolve around extortion or coercion. A form of organized blackmail, they are founded upon the oldest of all methods used by any organized crime group. As Jacob extorted Esau's birthright, so man has historically gained illegal ends or immoral advantages through a method of extortion and coercion. While racket victims are traditionally recruited from among those necessarily required to conceal some crime or immoral act, skillful racketeer techniques can easily make anyone a victim.

Although the gang is part of the general crime problem, the Mafia and Cosa Nostra-type criminal organizations, the syndicates, and the rackets pose more serious social problems and involve more than a criminal attack by an inadequately socialized and roleless person against another. Each of the latter forms are founded upon the inadequacies of its victims, who need to be socialized against being easy prey for such operatives and against being functional contributors to the varied forms of organized crime.

White Collar Crime ● *White collar crime* has been committed in every society since wealthy and respectable members of the upper socioeconomic classes began to engage in questionable activities related to their occupations.[58] Even the ancient Greeks and Romans experienced the phenomenon. However, modern white collar crime is more virulent and disturbing. As a concept, white collar crime refers to a wide range of criminal and near-criminal offenses committed in the use of one's socioeconomic resources. It is an unanswered question whether the criminal's socioeconomic power, an absolute condition for white collar crime, refers exclusively to the upper strata of society, or whether, as it was suggested to Sutherland by Stephen Schafer,[59] to the criminal's social and/or economic power, which can be interpreted in a relative sense. This latter concept may be applied to any social group in which the criminal, regardless of his wealth and social respectability, possesses social or economic power over other members of a given group.

Despite these problems, a white collar crime is generally conceived in terms of an offense that is committed by someone who has social or economic power over his victim and who uses this power not only to facilitate the successful commission of the offense, but also to help the powerful perpetrator avoid the ordinarily expected penal sanctions, legally prescribed for such violations. White collar crimes are most often committed by a member of the upper socio-economic classes against victims of a lower social class.

When the President's National Crime Commission undertook its monumental task of examining the state of crime in America and attempted to provide solutions to the crime problem, the bulk of its work dealt with "street-crimes,"[60] White collar crimes, however, are hardly even seen on the streets. They are committed more or less invisibly, from within the fortresses of the economically and socially powerful. The powerless are exposed to their power but cannot really see it exerted.[61] In the broadest sense, the "power" used by the white collar criminal is the power of knowledge which permits the violator to operate successfully within society. He acquires this information by virtue of his social circumstances and he exercises it through his social position. His knowledge allows him to use clever and ingenious means for achieving success and for taking advantage of the less developed knowledge of the less powerful, his victims.

Due to its character, white collar crime statistics are largely unavailable. Consolidated statistics comparable to the FBI's *Uniform Crime Reports* concerning traditional crime do not exist regarding white collar crime.[62] Nevertheless, the information that is published indicates that extreme social and economic harm is caused by this crime type. Hardly any part of our social life, including the medical and legal professions, is excluded from the problem. Edwin Sutherland's pioneering study, for example, noted that 90 percent of the 70 largest corporations in the United States were habitually criminal in their operations. Even now, many of the articles in general social use are distributed and sold by corporate groups in violation of the law.[63] Nearly one half of a 1961 sample survey of executives who subscribed to the *Harvard Business Review* cited their belief that the American business executive tends to ignore ethical laws. Because he is preoccupied with profitmaking, he will violate a code of ethics whenever he thinks he can avoid detection.[64] Other evidence suggests that persons in the legal and medical professions, operatives of drug companies, mass media, automobile repair agencies, watch and radio repair shops, and many other economic "powers" which have the ordinary "powerless" man at their mercy, display periodic white collar criminality. A great many automobile garages charge for work not needed or not completed, watch repair shops bill for a complicated job instead of recognizing and repairing a minor clock fault, or medical doctors will send bills for unnecessary services or for services already paid for by insurance policies. Because daily needs expose the powerless to the powerful and the scope of white collar crime is ambiguous to begin with, no accurate reporting system concerning this activity can be designed, and no reliable statistics have been developed.

However, white collar crime may cause different types of harm.[65] In one form, it may result in economic damage to individuals, companies, and even to the consuming public. For example, tax fraud is believed to cost the government a minimum yearly loss of $25 to $40 billion. Financial harm through securities fraud is conservatively estimated to be in the neighborhood of $500 million to $1 billion yearly. Close to $500 million is annually spent on worthless or misrepresented drugs. In addition to an assumed financial loss, actual and possible physical harm may also be potentially caused by white collar criminality through food, health, and drug law violations. The sharp rise in the number of medical malpractice suits suggests that the public is now demanding higher physician accountability of actions taken. Some persons are even asking if certain doctors should not be jailed for their violations.[66] Yet, because of many unknown factors, losses brought about by white collar crime remain only estimates.

The chief type of harm produced by white collar crime is its tendency to reduce the level of public morality. When those who have difficulty in achieving financial success see otherwise respectable persons taking advantage of laws designed to protect the public interest, they find justification for making their own social adjustments.

Types of White Collar Crime ● In its broadest sense, white collar crime embraces nearly all segments of society, permitting a relatively easy classification of offenders in terms of their professions, occupations, and businesses. Under this conceptualization, it is possible to view the white collar offender as a lawyer, a watch repairman, a plumber, a doctor, a car dealer, an automobile serviceman, or even a supermarket manager. However, such an approach may ultimately lead to an overall accusation of the total society by dividing it into white collar criminal and victim categories. Even the victim may be conceived as a white collar criminal within his context if he possesses social or economic power over others and uses it dishonestly against them in order to achieve financial gain.[67] But such an approach does not differentiate adequately the various forms of power at work. One typology that strives to overcome these shortcomings and to narrow the scope of white collar offenses offers the following categories:

1. White collar criminals who use their *economic power.*
2. White collar criminals who use their *social power.*
3. White collar criminals who use their *power of profession.*

4. White collar criminals who use their *power of persuasion.*

1. White Collar Criminals Who Use Their Economic Power • Edwin H. Sutherland, who had such persons primarily in his mind when he proposed the concept, located white collar violators in the upper socioeconomic strata of society. Due to their economic position, they are highly influential in shaping and guiding social life. The so-called "robber barons" of the last half of the nineteenth century, for example, are now regarded as white collar criminals. They built their power in the economic areas of banking, the stock exchange, oil development, real estate, insurance, public utilities, and other economic operations.

This form of white collar crime is a product of corporate growth, economic penetration of foreign markets, industrial and technological espionage, formation of monopolies, and monetary competition.[68] It represents a type of business corruption in which the "corruptor" is a highly influential and economically powerful actor. Criminal prosecution of this violator, due to his economic power, is difficult, if not impossible. In view of his respectability, which is founded upon his economic success, he is able to corrupt not only his business opponents, but also to disarm the machinery of criminal justice. His offense is not a "crime" in the legal sense because his skill in using his power makes it possible for him to operate on the extreme limits of tolerated corruption. His financial success is not the fruit of diligent work or extraordinary economic knowledge, but rather an exploitative use of his financial resources at the expense of others.[69] In one case of electrical equipment price-fixing, those charged ranged from the president of the local Chamber of Commerce to a hospital board member, chief fund raiser for the Community Chest, bank director, director of the taxpayers' association, and organizer of the local Little League. All held respectable social positions which may have been acquired through the respect paid to their economic power. As their defense attorneys contended, they were "fine" men who should not be incarcerated "behind bars" with common criminals convicted for "serious" crimes, although the electrical conspirators had been charged with flagrant criminal offenses in patent contradiction of the Sherman Antitrust Act of 1890.[70]

2. White Collar Criminals Who Use Their Social Power • While they are similar to the first type, they operate in *social* situations which do not primarily involve the world of business and which mask potential power or financial rewards from public view. Unethical or dishonest political practices, whether carried out daily in national politics or in the political manipulations of a department, an association, or any other group, fall into this category. Operationalized from the fortress of the social power against the powerless members of given groups, these acts of violation may not bring such white collar criminals financial rewards as directly, immediately, or greatly as may outright economic white collar crimes, but they do permit their participants to gain indirect financial and "moral" advantage at the expense of their powerless "victims." This type of offense uses the formalities of roles, rules, and ethics to affect personal gain and power.

"Crimes committed under cover of official position,"[71] to use Manuel Lopez-Rey's term, constitute probably the greatest number of unreported crimes, immoral or dishonest acts, and unethical practices. They cause an unbelievable volume of human unhappiness, not to mention the large total of financial losses, and only benefit the socially powerful white collar criminal and his associates. Such exploitative deeds increase the offender's power, facilitate the furthering of his questionable activities, and often brutally increase the volume of victim losses and unhappiness. Because knowledge of their crimes are largely limited to those who actually are their "victims" and who are reluctant to report such information due to fear of further victimization, these white collar criminals, too, enjoy outwardly the respect of the general public.

3. White Collar Criminals Who Use Their Power of Profession ● These offenders take advantage of the skill, knowledge, or expertise which they possess but which others need.[72] Increasingly, those who have traditionally had the responsibility of helping the helpless are now using their abilities to take advantage of the helplessness of others for unethical or dishonest financial gain. This aspect of white collar "criminality" appears to be a contemporary product dependent upon a high degree of individualism that lessens or eradicates the sentiments professionals have traditionally had for others. Among those who use the power of their profession or their expert knowledge to exploit the lack of information of others for their own financial advantage are not only watch, radio, and television repairmen, automobile servicemen, contractors and architects, plumbers, electricians, appliance servicemen, and pharmacists, but also medical doctors, lawyers, and persons in other service professions.

One area of "white collar criminality" in which the power of the profession is used to victimize those whose power of knowledge lags behind the expertise of the "culprit" is that of automobile repair. First mass produced in the United States, the automobile has now become a necessity not only for pleasure, but primarily for transportation to work, school, shops, and many other places unaccessible by public transportation. Those who make and service cars, therefore, have a captive audience. As car owners in America trade their vehicles every two, three, or four years for new or used models, they frequently face the problems of purchasing, financing, and maintenance. Because most are mechanically inexperienced, their limited knowledge of cars is easily used against them.

Another area of white collar crime involving the power of profession can be seen in the doctor who sends his heart patient to a hospital by ambulance while he drives after the vehicle to be certain that his patient was really taken to the hospital. He then not only charges for his unnecessary check on the ambulance but also claims an amount in addition to what he gets for such services from the patient's medical insurance. In other instances, he may perform a series of unnecessary examinations and charge special fees for each test. The growing tendency of doctors to protect themselves from patient malpractice suits by the ordering of extra laboratory tests has made the detection of unnecessary medical services more difficult.

The problem of unnecessary medical assistance is not that much different from the action of a plumber who solves the problem of a momentary insufficiency of hot water by warning his victim-customer that his work insures only temporary relief and that either a new water tank will have to be installed or some other major changes in the pipe system made if the customer wants to avoid further trouble. And the plumber is not really different from the automobile service station attendant who recommends changes in a car's wiring or the purchase of new tires after first suggesting to the driver that his car may not be safe. Frequently, this kind of threat is used in order to intimidate the "victim" to surrender himself to the expert knowledge of the white collar "criminal."

The dishonest or unethical selling of health, life, or safety insurance, as with other areas of white collar crime operations, unavoidably undermines the public's trust in honest and ethical professional advice. As distrust is generalized and extended to legitimate businessmen or professionals, patients or customers are not only alienated from the sincerely helpful doctor, plumber, or car repairman, but are often led by their tendency to disregard all advice to substantial damage or real danger.

4. White Collar Criminals Who Use Their Power of Persuasion ● Although they are similar to those who use their power of profession, they do not prey upon the victim's lack of expert knowledge, but rather upon their human desire for a better, safer, or more pleasant life. The victim is attacked through persuasion and dishonest or unethical selling practices. In this form of white collar crime, it is not that the victim does not get what he pays for or that he gets and pays for something unnecessarily, but that he does not get what he originally wanted because some elements he thought were present are missing or other elements he thought were absent are present. In other words, the victim is persuaded to believe in the honesty of an offer that turns out to lack integrity. Hair dye, for example, may work as advertised and yet the fact that it may cause skin irritation or even blindness if used on eyebrows is concealed from the public in the persuasive advertising which brings the virtues of the commodity to the purchaser's attention. The twenty-four hour mouthwash does not last the expected time; even the effectiveness of tooth toughener and tooth brightener pastes depends upon the consumer going regularly to a dentist. Contrary to the assumption of imaginative advertising, the habituation of an individual to a certain cigarette brand in itself will not attract beautiful girls to the side of the smoker. Even many detergents which are advertised as being the solution to all wash problems are commonly not as good as advertised and may not even be new products.

Through television, newspaper, and other mass media, the public is daily persuaded to believe that unless it buys the items advertised, its members will have bad breath, be unable to sleep, have nervous tension, be unable to avoid ulcer pains, have ugly or disorderly hair, be constipated, be in a bad mood, have slow growing children, have a dirty kitchen, have an unhappy visiting employer, or some other general deficiency. Overall, the emphasis is upon the need to buy the suggested product if people want to lead happy, healthy, and appropriate lives. Some insurance agents even make every effort to persuade men that they are heartless and wicked husbands unless they sign a mortgage insurance policy. After all, they reason, an American man must be prepared to drop dead at any moment and must not fail to leave his wife with at least a roof over her head.[73] A similar accusation of "heartlessness" is also used to motivate dog owners to buy foods their pets "deserve" or to stimulate citizens to give to some charities which never receive the money collected.

In the majority of the cases, no technical criminal offense, as in many other white collar crimes, can be established against the persuader. Yet, the gap between persuaded illusion, imagination, and belief, on one hand, and reality, on the other, refers to dishonest and unethical practices which potentially may cause various forms of damage and encourage distrust of honest and ethical businessmen. If it is true that white collar criminality is growing, it is due to the moral weakness of the dishonest and unethical man who learns in a highly competitive society how to succeed "without really trying."

The Political Criminal

Although *political criminals* are not a new phenomena, they are now receiving special international attention in view of the development of the contemporary "political man" and the numerous revolutions, upheavals, and violent social movements of this century. Often called *convictional criminals,* because they are usually "convinced" about the just character of their political cause, they promote their goal through crime.[74] While the more conventional "occasional" criminals may steal food when hungry, shoplift a gold ring if overcome with desire, or kill another out of jealousy, they are stimulated by their own individualistic personal need, desire, or emotion. When professional criminals burglarize a bank or embezzle another's money, they act for their own personal gain. Convictional criminals, on the other hand, have an altruistic as opposed to an egoistic motivation which may be related to a political, social, moral, or religious ideal or commitment. Believing unconditionally in their altruistic goal, they act upon their beliefs. Consequently, this crime, which serves their altruistic commitment, is not strictly a form of ego fulfillment. From origin to completion, the offense is a communal or nonpersonal experience.[75] Ideals and convictions dominate their being, giving their crimes secondary importance in their eyes. In past decades, suffragettes who broke the law in order to fight for women's liberation, members of the Resistance who injured others to hamper the invader, and counterrevolutionaries who killed to preserve their ideology committed convictional crimes in order to realize their defined ideals. More recent examples can be found in the Weathermen and the Symbionese Liberation Army efforts to influence the direction of society.

Although their ideals stand in the forefront, the convictional criminal does not necessarily discount the implications of crime and punishment. Genuine convictional criminals inevitably face a tragic internal clash between their social loyalty to law and order and their altruistic ideals. This creates a major psychic and ethical strain and represents a nearly insoluble and almost catastrophic clash between moral and socioethical demands. While they struggle to reconcile these two ideals, convictional criminals ultimately commit the crime out of a sense of obligation of commitment to an altruistic cause. Due to the power of their conviction, they cannot refrain from committing the crime even at the sacrifice of their own life or freedom.

The overwhelming pressure of their ideals causes convictional criminals to commit the criminal act. Inasmuch as they view their conduct as disobedience or disloyalty to the laws of their society, they are not deterred by fear of penal consequences or personal socioethical resistance factors. They have some feelings of anxiety and agitation, but they are not directly caused by the crime itself. Their crimes are not dominant concerns but are viewed merely as acts that intervene between convictional decisions and ultimate ideals.

Ordinary conventional, not convictional, *criminals* undergo minimal internal struggle before committing their crimes. Their anxiety is confined mainly to careful planning, the maintenance of security, and the successful accomplishment of their deviant act. Convictional criminals, on the other hand, are generally less concerned with the actual mechanics of their crime and are frequently restless after the commission of their crimes, possibly due to pangs of conscience, fear of arrest, or other conditions that may upset their psychic equilibrium. Their consciences satisfied, convictional criminals are relieved by their crime and their previously upset balance is restored.

Because every breach of secrecy may jeopardize their success and future, conventional criminals place great importance upon security. By contrast, convictional criminals with their altruistic attitudes and ideology place less emphasis upon secrecy and even seek publicity for their cause. They hide and disguise their activities only to guarantee their success. Their motivation, their antagonism toward certain aspects or the totality of society's value system, and their propagation of their ultimate aims are communal in character and generally serve their final objective, the promotion of a similar communal ideal. Dramatic publicity designed to maximize public understanding of their actions, therefore, is almost a necessary part of the convictional criminal's plan of action. Publicity, however, leads frequently to further deviance inasmuch as the convictional criminal summarily rejects much of the established political, social, moral, religious, or economic order and encourages others to do likewise. As they succeed in disseminating their ideals to the broader population, the number of convictional crimes increases. Their crimes, as a result, serve as an example to would-be followers. Because convictional crime may even be supported by public opinion, punishment of convictional offenders may fail to deter later convictional crimes. Punishment may serve only to interest others in the movement's ideals and to recruit members for other convictional crimes.

Not all convictional criminals are genuinely convinced about the just nature of their cause. Everyone who claims to be a convictional criminal may not be in the true sense. Some may be attracted by the publicity stimulated by convictional crime; many others simply use the convictional ideal as an excuse for their own deviant acts. Moved by love of adventure, kick or thrill, psychopathic deviation, or hope for gain, the *pseudo-convictional offender* may join forces with the true convictional criminal although motivated by selfish interests. Any aggressive idealistic movement is likely to have both convictional and pseudo-convictional criminal participants. However, pseudo-convictional criminals reveal several typical characteristics, including an absence of any moral basis for their crime and of any altruism in their "conviction." Dominated by their personal gain, they simply take advantage of the convictional crime context to steal, rob, or murder. They are not engulfed by the tragic dilemma between their loyalty to the general principles of law and order and to the criminal representation of their just cause. For the pseudo-convictional criminal, the convictional crime is simply an opportunity for crime, not really different from any other criminal opportunity.[76]

The Social Problem of Rehabilitation

Of the various types of criminals mentioned to this point, the occasional criminal, seemingly the most simple, poses the most difficult problem to crime control and treatment. In part, this is due to the fact that the other criminal types—professional, organized, and political—are committed so much to their activity that they are unlikely to change their conduct pattern. While social change may gradually eliminate convictional criminals as the goals they work toward are reached, and treatment agencies may be able to resocialize some professional offenders to legitimate social roles and opportunities, the occasional criminal's acceptance of what social roles mean and demand make the control of his behavior much less promising. Little, if anything, can be done to anticipate the spontaneous crime of occasional or situational offenders. Their conduct cannot be adequately anticipated or even protected against. This does not mean that convictional or professional offenders can easily be rehabilitated and the occasional cannot, but simply that the convictional criminal's rehabilitation requires a major social change. If this does not occur, this offender's reaction to ordinary punitive measures, except if persuaded that his commitment is mistaken, may even fortify his former convictions. Although the professional criminal should be the easiest to rehabilitate, the high rate of recidivism among this type signifies just how difficult it is to resocialize this type of offender.

However, most significant factors in unsuccessful rehabilitation are not only the current lack of clear insight into the causes of crime, but also the inadequacy of contemporary knowledge about efficient "cause-eliminating" treatment methods.

The continuing increase in the rate of reported crimes suggests that modern efforts to prevent crime and rehabilitation processes are still unsuccessful. Its solution is not really in sight, although new programs of coeducational prison development, work release, diversion of offenders away from court action before they enter the correctional prison system, and community-based corrections represent potential success areas. Penologists even now continue to change the old formulas of punishment to ones of "correction," "reformation," "rehabilitation," and "community-based treatment," methods not always appreciated fully by the public. Many are ready to extrapolate known processes into hypotheses, although their viability and implications are undefined. We are still far from an answer to the ultimate question: Which are the right ways to rehabilitate? Despite continuing experimentation, the greater number of offenders participate in a prison and treatment system which emphasizes the isolation and punishment of the offender within a prison-type setting. Both systems are still heavily punitive in nature, suggesting that those who use the term "punishment" rather than the misleading phrase "rehabilitation" are more correct in describing what actually is taking place.[77] Although "punishment" has been replaced by newer ideas of "correction," "rehabilitation," and "community treatment," this does not change their implied disapproval of criminal conduct, whether rooted in political conviction, an occasional pressing situation, organized criminality, or professional criminal profit-seeking. Whether they are called punishment or some other term, the official social consequences of crime are still punitive and expiatory or deterrent and preventive.

Crime has always been disapproved and will remain so indefinitely, even if it is the product of social injustice or a sick criminal mind, a factor which creates insurmountable difficulties in rehabilitating offenders. Once violators have been labelled criminal, it is most difficult to delabel them. Karl Menninger's proposal to pit "love against hate," charging society with "the crime punishment," is just another admirable attempt to abolish centuries old punishment and replace it with the "message of the new psychiatry."[78] Even this, however, cannot avoid a sense of demandingly punitive "disapproval."

Attempts to Rehabilitate • American jails, penitentiaries, prisons, and correctional facilities rarely follow adequate rehabilitation techniques. Not only are most institutions of this type understaffed, but jails, which most offenders first come into contact with, usually have no programs or treatment personnel associated with them. Those institutions that do have programs tend to follow one of two rehabilitation models: total organization or individual treatment. *Total organization* stresses its function and applies its procedures to all inmates; *individual treatment* attempts to develop a closer relationship with individual offenders within the institution. While both approaches are present in every sizable institution, more often than not the total organization concept, due to cost, efficiency, and theoretical factors, dominates penal practice.

The prison, a name used to describe all institutions which deprive a man of his liberty, is a *total institution* that has a general custodial and rehabilitative function. A self-existing entity theoretically designed to secure changes in the inmates behavior, it regulates the life of each inmate, including his range of choices, through its administrative and custodial staff who remain legally and factually superior to the prisoners, those whom they are supposed to correct.[79] Although the two groups of custodians and prisoners attempt, despite their differing goals, to live together in relative peace, these feelings of superiority and inferiority hinder the rehabilitation process, which is already marginal due to the apparent lack of proven treatment methods. If prisoners for one reason or another resist the rehabilitative efforts of the staff and feel the disciplinary measures in the form of solitary confinement, dietary restrictions, loss of yard privileges, deprivation of the rights of visitors and correspondence, transfer to another institution, and other harsh measures against those who refuse to comply, this marginality becomes even more pronounced. At this point, any pretense of rehabilitation becomes submerged in the maintenance of discipline and the protection of the "rights to rehabilitation of other inmates." However, these procedures are usually enacted for the benefit of the staff and administration rather than for offender behavioral change. It is highly unlikely that the threat of institutional punishment, which is a form of punishment upon punishment, does much to bring about rehabilitation; it is just as likely to encourage embitterment and deepen antisocial attitudes. The negation of prisoner interests and a continual reminder of inmate powerlessness merely lessens the possibility that the total institution will be able to reform inmates successfully.

When the prison emphasizes total institutional concepts, it stresses rules, which are designed for the mass handling of offenders, and security, which isolates the offenders within a concentration of violators he would normally not come into contact with on the outside. In such a context, mail is usually censored, family member visits limited, privacy nearly impossible to achieve, and mass eating and marching emphasized. However, to mitigate some of this harshness and to promote the rehabilitation of all inmates, counseling services are simultaneously made available, religious services and medical care are provided, and vocational training and work programs are operated in order to promote the rehabilitation of all inmates. At many institutions, educational and recreational facilities are also offered under the rubric of treatment.

As the trend toward individualized treatment has grown within penal practice, efforts have been increased to lessen the isolation of offenders from their communities.[80] Speakers, volunteer visitors, and entertainers are permitted increasingly within institutions in order to bring the "normal" society closer to the inmate. Prisoners with low recidivism risk are being given work or study releases, home furloughs of designated lengths, mainly on special holidays or occasions, such as Thanksgiving, family weddings or funerals, and other opportunities to maintain contact with home and community. One of the most dramatic rehabilitative efforts has focused on work-release, a program which allows the prisoner to work outside the walls for salary during the day and to return to the prison for lock-up during the night. The President's National Crime Commission found that the work-release program has been largely effective. At some institutions, inmates are eligible for work-release after they have served as little as 15 percent of their sentence and at others immediately upon entrance. Recent efforts to shut down some existing juvenile and adult institutions and treat offenders in the community have also produced results while stimulating major public debate.

Not all groups of offenders can be treated effectively through an incarceration approach. Mentally sick or retarded criminals, sex offenders, alcoholics, violent and habitual escapees, females, those under death sentence, and other "special" violators cannot be well integrated into overall institution programs. They not only pose a custodial threat but also a rehabilitation problem as well. Their treatment necessitates a more sophisticated classification program and individualized special rehabilitative programs, which have been developed sporadically.

Although the basic idea of classification is not controversial, what is meant "has varied widely among criminologists and prison administrators alike."[8][1] In fact, little has been done to design and execute programs tailored to the different types of criminals within the sentenced population. Except for what is called "seriation," the division of the prison population into natural inmate groups (on the basis of sex, mental states, dangerousness, and the like), not much has been accomplished in refining generalizing rehabilitation programs for specified groups or types of criminals.

An overall discrepancy appears between punishing and punishment. In most legal and penal systems, including those in the United States, the sentence is passed first; only then is the offender classified. Consequently, the sentence is enacted without any classification and the classifying work of rehabilitation is necessarily limited to the orders of the sentence. For example, if a bank robber receives a five-year prison sentence, his penalty is inflicted without any typing of the offender. Normally, he will be classified at an institution in terms of his maleness rather than his bank robbing act. The prison system, therefore, will receive him as one of many thousands of male criminals and will enroll him in the prison's general rehabilitative program, regardless of the diagnosis of his condition or criminal characteristics, unless he belongs to one of the mentioned "special offender groups." General institutional rehabilitative programs are unable to deal adequately with the needs of the common offender.

Within the general program of most penal institutions, individual treatment methods are not numerous. Those that do have them tend to apply them poorly. Usually, they are geared to the nonpunitive, therapeutic approaches as exemplified by psychiatric social work, psychological group therapy, psycho-drama, psychoanalysis, and other clinical-type efforts.[82] They are hampered by the indefiniteness of the success potential of these clinical methods and the inadequate staffing provided for these programs by governing administrators.

Because of these limitations, it is highly doubtful whether the problem of crime will ever be solved fully. Penologists generally hold that "many offenders are sentenced to imprisonment not because this is in itself the sentence of choice, but, in effect, for lack of any more appropriate alternative."[83] It is generally clear that American correctional programs in their present state cannot perform their assigned work. They need to be upgraded substantially and encouraged to relate their efforts to the eventual return of the vast majority of offenders to their home community. For example, the English Advisory Council on the Penal System emphasized the need for innovation, proposing new or improved noncustodial and semi-custodial penalties, including the "day fine system," which would equalize monetary penalties for the rich and poor, the improvement of community services, disqualification for certain occupations, forfeiture in depriving the offender of an article of property, and intermittent custody in the form of weekend imprisonment.

The operation of adult criminal institutions costs more than $500 million annually with the total yearly correctional expenditure probably reaching above $1 billion. The average annual cost of institutionalizing a felon, depending upon who is doing the estimating, is $9,000 to $12,000. Despite these expenditures, and not counting the amount spent on research, a successful solution to the problem, demanded by the public, has not been achieved. The American correctional system handles 1.5 million offenders or more on an average day and has about 2.5 million admissions in the course of a year. While the federal, state, county, and municipal governments operate a great variety of programs, no substantial success has been achieved in the control of recidivism and the commission of further offenses. While crime and corrections are well publicized in the mass media, it is a world that has remained largely unknown to law-abiding citizens and to those others who mostly offer simplistic solutions to this problem.

Recommendations of the President's Advisory Commission

How can the trends in criminal offenses and victimization be turned around and the crime rate reduced? An effort by the government to establish priorities in this area led to the formation of the National Advisory Commission on Criminal Justice Standards and Goals. In its wide-ranging 1973 report, the Commission recommended many commonplace and controversial steps. By 1983, homicide, forcible rape, and aggravated assault, it proposed, should be reduced by 25 percent; robbery and burglary by a minimum of 50 percent. Priority must be given to preventing juvenile delinquency and to the minimizing of young offender contact with the criminal justice system. Public and private services to citizens, victim, and witnesses should be improved. Delays in adjudication and disposition of criminal cases must be reduced. Citizen involvement in crime control must be increased. In the area of police, the Commission recommended the consolidation of all departments employing fewer than ten officers, the redefinition of the policeman's role with a stronger emphasis upon crime prevention, the diversion of cases involving drunks and the mentally ill to other outlets, the increased employment of minorities and the enactment of legislation permitting the authorization of warrants over the telephone. In speaking to the courts, it proposed the trying of all cases within 60 days of arrest, the requiring of judges to hold full days of court, the unification of all courts within each State, the restriction of review appeals per case to one, the elimination of plea bargaining, the screening of criminal cases coming to the attention of the prosecutor to the diversion of inappropriate cases from the criminal justice system, and the elimination of grand juries and arraignments. Regarding corrections, priority, the Commission noted, should be given to restriction of construction of major State institutions for adult offenders, the phasing out of all major juvenile offender institutions, the elimination of disparate sentencing practices, the establishment of community-based correctional programs and facilities, the unification within each State of all correctional functions and the expansion of education, salary and training for all levels of correctional personnel. Other recommendations stressed the establishment of permanent criminal code revision commissions in each State, the decriminalization of vagrancy and drunkenness, and the elimination of importation, sale, and private possession of handguns by 1983.[84]

References

1. President's Commission on Law Enforcement and Administration of Justice, *The Challenge of Crime in a Free Society* (Washington, D.C., 1967), pp. 1-18.
2. *Ibid.*, pp. 245-291.
3. *Compte general de l'administration de la justice criminelle en France.*
4. *Tafeln zur Statistik der osterreichischen Monarchie.*
5. Emile Durkheim, *Les Regles de la methode sociologique* (Paris, 1895).
6. Talcott Parsons, *The Structure of Social Action* (New York, 1968), Vol. 1, p. 375.
7. Federal Bureau of Investigation, *Uniform Crime Reports—1973* (Washington, D.C., 1974), p. viii.
8. *Ibid.*, p. ix.
9. Alvin Rudoff, "The Soaring Crime Rate—An Etiological View," *Journal of Criminal Law, Criminology and Police Science,* (December, 1971), LXIV, 543-546.
10. Gilbert Geis and Stephen Schafer, "Forcible Rape: A Comparative Study of Offenses Known to the Police in Boston and Los Angeles." Paper presented to the meetings of the *American Sociological Association* in San Francisco, 1968; later in an expanded form published with the co-authorship of Duncan Chappell and Larry Siegel.
11. Federal Bureau of Investigation, *Crime Reports,* pp. 26-28.
12. Stephen Schafer, *Theories in Criminology: Past and Present Philosophies of the Crime Problem* (New York, 1969), pp. 97-110.

13. Donald R. Taft, *Criminology* (3rd ed.), (New York, 1956), p. 357.
14. Schafer, *Theories,* pp. 97-110.
15. Cesare Bonesana, Marchese de Beccaria, *Trattato dei delitti e delle pene* (Tuscany, 1764).
16. From the time of Aristotle, Socrates, and the Roman physician Galen, many attempted to understand crime; man's skull, face, and mind were the targets of investigation. See details in Schafer, *Theories.*
17. Cesare Lombroso, *L'Uomo deliquente* (Milan, 1876); Raffaele Garofalo, *Criminology,* trans. Robert Wyness Millar (Boston, 1914); Enrico Ferri, *I nuovi orizzonti del diritto e della procedura penale* (Turin, 1881).
18. Charles B. Goring, *The English Convict: A Statistical Study* (London, 1913).
19. Ernest A. Hooton, *The American Criminal: An Anthropological Study* (Cambridge, Mass., 1939).
20. Ernst Kretschmer, *Physique and Character*, trans W. J. H. Sprott (London, 1925).
21. William H. Sheldon, *Varieties of Delinquent Youth: An Introduction to Constitutional Psychiatry* (New York, 1949).
22. Johannes Lange, *Crime and Destiny,* trans. Charlotte Haldane (New York, 1930).
23. Among the numerous well-known works of Sigmund Freud, see *A General Introduction to Psychoanalysis* (New York, 1920). More recent variants of personality explanations of criminality are expressed by P. K. Burgess, "Eysenck's Theory of Criminality: A New Approach," *British Journal of Criminology,* (January, 1972), XII, 74-82.
24. Hans von Hentig, *Das Verbrechen, I. Der Kriminelle Mensch in Kraftspiel von Zeit und Raum* (Berlin, 1961).
25. Clifford R. Shaw, *Delinquency Areas* (Chicago, 1929); with Henry D. McKay, *Social Factors in Juvenile Delinquency* (Washington, D.C., 1931); *Juvenile Delinquency and Urban Areas* (Chicago, 1942).
26. Leonce Manouvrier, "La genese normal du crime," *Bulletins de la Societe d'Anthropologie de Paris,* (Paris, 1893), IV, 405-458.
27. Lacassagne made this statement in the course of a discussion at the first international criminal-anthropological congress in 1885 in Rome; see *Actes du Premier Congres International d'Anthropologie Criminelle, Biologie et Sociologie, Rome, 1885* (1886-1887), pp. 165-167.
28. Benoit Augustin Morel, *De la contagion morale: du danger que presente pour la moralite et securite publique la relation des crimes donnee par les jounaux* (Marseille, 1870).
29. Gabriel Tarde, *La Philosophie Penale* (Paris, 1890).
30. Edwin H. Sutherland, *Principles of Criminology* (3rd ed.), (New York, 1939).
31. Adolphe Prins, *Criminalite et repression* (Brussels, 1886).
32. Donald R. Taft, *criminology*, (3rd ed.), (New York, 1956).
33. Emile Durkheim, *De la division du travail social* (Paris, 1893), *Le Suicide* (Paris, 1897).
34. Willem Adriaan Bonger, *Criminality and Economic Conditions,* trans. Henry P. Horton (repr. New York, 1967). Bonger's theoretical construction calls to mind Leon Radzinowicz's comment (*Ideology and Crime,* New York, 1966, p. 90) that Merton's notion of class vulnerability, a dimension Merton added to Durkheim's anomie theory, was "in some ways curiously reminiscent of Bonger."
35. Richard D. Knudten, *Crime in a Complex Society* (Homewood, 1970), pp. 5-6.
36. Schafer, *Theoreis,* pp. 6-14.
37. See Stephen Schafer and Richard D. Knudten, *Juvenile Delinquency: An Introduction* (New York, 1970), pp. 297-299.
38. Ruth Shonle Cavan, *Criminology* (3rd ed.), (New York, 1962), p. 96.
39. Schafer and Knudten, *Juvenile Delinquency*, pp. 109-110.
40. See Hans J. Eysenck, *Crime and Personality* (Boston, 1964).

41. Carl Werthman, "The Function of Social Definitions in the Development of Delinquent Careers," in President's Commission on Law Enforcement and Administration of Justice, *Task Force Report, Juvenile Delinquency and Youth Crime* (Washington, D.C., 1967), pp. 155-170.
42. Edwin H. Sutherland and Donald R. Cressey, *Principles of Criminology,* (6th ed)., (New York, 1960), p. 232.
43. For a study that attempts to isolate delinquent or criminal subcultures and the opportunities open to individuals as their criminal careers develop, see Irving Spergel, *Racketville, Slumtown, Haulberg* (Chicago, 1964), where Racketville, Slumtown, and Haulberg refer to organized racketeering, gang fighting, and professional thievery, respectively.
44. George B. Vold, *Theoretical Criminology* (New York, 1958), p. 224.
45. Gabriel Tarde, *Penal Philosophy*, trans. Rapelje Howell (Boston, 1912), pp. 254-5, 277-292.
46. Donald R. Cressey, *Theft of the Nation: The Structure and Operations of Organized Crime in America* (New York, 1969), pp. 8-9.
47. "La Cosa Nostra is a Criminal Fraternity." Testimony of J. Edgar Hoover, Director of the Federal Bureau of Investigation, *Hearings Before the Subcommittee on Departments of State, Justice, and Commerce, the Judiciary, and Related Agencies Appropriations of the House Committee on Appropriations,* 89th Congress, 2nd Session, 1966, p. 272; cited also by Cressey, *Theft of the Nation,* p. 10.
48. President's Commission, *Task Force Report,* p. 187; President's Commission on Law Enforcement and Administration of Justice, *Task Force Report: Organized Crime* (Washington, D.C., 1967), p. 1.
49. Cressey, *Theft of the Nation,* p. 1.
50. Danilo Dolci, *The Man Who Plays Alone: The Story of One Man's Fight Against the Sicilian Mafia* (New York, 1970), pp. ix-x. The original published in Italian under the title *Chi Gioco solo* in 1966; in English first in 1968.
51. Cressey's examples, *Theft of the Nation,* p. 2.
52. *Task Force Report,* p. 1.
53. *Ibid.,* pp. 16-24.
54. Based on descriptions in *The Challenge of Crime in a Free Society,* pp. 193-196, and Cressey, *Theft of the Nation,* Chapter VI, "The Structural Skeleton," pp. 109-140.
55. Cressey, *Theft of the Nation,* p. 113.
56. Eric Partridge, *A Dictionary of the Underworld: British and American* (London, 1950), p. 278.
57. See also Alan J. Puffer, *The Boy and His Gang* (Boston, 1912); Hans von Hentig *The Criminal and His Victim, Studies in the Socio-biology of Crime* (New Haven, 1948), pp. 192, 195; Ruth Shonle Cavan, *Criminology,* (2nd ed.), (New York, 1957), p. 151; and Donald R. Taft, *Criminology,* (3rd ed.), (New York, 1956), pp. 222-227.
58. Thirty-fourth Annual Presidential Address delivered at Philadelphia, Pa., on December 27, 1939, in joint meeting with the American Economic Society. Published in the *American Sociological Review* (Feburary, 1940), V, 1, 1-12.
59. Stephen Schafer's book-review on Gilberg Geis, ed., *White-Collar Criminal: The Offender in Business and the Professions* (New York, 1968), in *The Journal of Criminal Law, Criminology and Police Science,* (March, 1970), LXI, 1, 90-92.
60. President's Commission on Law Enforcement and Administration of Justice, *Task Force Report: Crime and Its Impact—An Assessment* (Washington, D.C., 1967), p. 102.
61. Donald R. Cressey, "Foreward," in Edwin H. Sutherland, *White Collar Crime* (New York, 1961), p. xii.
62. President's Commission, *Task Force Report: Crime and Its Impact,* pp. 103-104.
63. Edwin H. Sutherland, "Crime of Corporations," in Albert K. Cohen, Alfred Lindesmith,

and Karl Schuessler, eds., *The Sutherland Papers* (Bloomington, Indiana, 1956), pp. 78-96.

64. Raymond C. Baumhart, "How Ethical Are Businessmen?", *Harvard Business Review,* 39 (Jul.-Aug., 1961), pp. 6-19, 156-176.

65. President's Commission, *Task Force Report: Crime and Its Impact,* pp. 103-104.

66. Howard Whitman, "Why Some Doctors Should be in Jail," *Collier's,* 132 (Oct. 30, 1953), pp. 23-27. 1974 Congressional Hearings on Consumer Interests have provided similar insights into this problem.

67. For an excellent selection of various white-collar crimes, see Geis, *White-Collar Criminal;* some of the examples used here are cited from his book of readings.

68. Manuel Lopez-Rey, *Crime: An Analytical Appraisal* (New York, 1970), p. 16.

69. Geis, *White-Collar Criminal,* p. 103.

70. *Ibid.,* pp. 104-105.

71. Lopez-Rey, *Crime,* p. 39.

72. *Ibid.,* p. 34.

73. One of the co-author's personal experiences within twenty-four hours after he arrived in the United States.

74. Although this expression may be open to criticism, it was used in the original formulation of the concept; Stephen Schafer, "Juvenile Delinquents in 'Convictional' Crime," *International Annals of Criminology,* I (Paris, 1963), pp. 45-51.

75. See Schafer and Knudten, *Juvenile Delinquency,* pp. 165-168.

76. Stephen Schafer, *The Political Criminal* (New York: Free Press, 1974).

77. See Schafer, *Theories,* pp. 291-302.

78. Karl Menninger, *The Crime of Punishment* (New York, 1966).

79. See, among others, Erving Goffman, "On the Characteristics of Total Institutions: The Inmate World," in Donald R. Cressey, ed., *The Prison* (New York, 1961), pp. 16-22; Stanton Wheeler, "Socialization in Correctional Communities," *American Sociological Review,* (Oct., 1961), XXVI, 699-712; Don C. Gibbons, *Changing Crime in a Complex Society* (Homewood, Ill., 1970); for the historical development of the correctional system of our time, see Harry Elmer Barnes and Negley K. Teeters, *New Horizons in Criminology* (New York, 1944).

80. See The President's Commission on Law Enforcement and Administration of Justice, *Task Force Report: Corrections* (Washington, D.C., 1967), pp. 56-57.

81. Committee on Classification and Casework, American Prison Association, *Handbook on Classification in Correctional Institutions* (New York, 1947), p. iii.

82. Donald R. Cressey, "Professional Correctional Work and Professional Work in Correction," *National Probation and Parole Association Journal,* Vol. 5 (Jan., 1959), pp. 1-15.

83. Report of the Advisory Council on the Penal System, Home Office, *Non-Custodial and Semi-Custodial Penalties* (London, 1970), p. 3.

84. National Advisory Commission on Criminal Justice Standards and Goals, *A National Strategy to Reduce Crime* (Washington, D.C.: U.S. Government Printing Office, 1973), pp. xvi-xix.

CHAPTER 9

Juvenile Delinquency

The Problem of Juvenile Delinquency

Hardly any aspect of the crime problem causes so much confusion or disagreement as does juvenile delinquency. Since the middle of the nineteenth century, when protests against cruelty in criminal justice prompted a world-wide movement for the separate processing of children and adolescents by juvenile courts, laymen and specialists have tried to develop a general consensus regarding the concept and definition of delinquency, its causes, and effective treatment policies, programs and methods.[1] Because juvenile delinquency is somewhat schizophrenically defined as both a crime and a non-crime, it presents a most difficult problem. It is a crime in the sense that if committed by adults, it is a criminal offense, but it is a non-crime because the category was theoretically established to assist children to overcome their problem rather than try them as criminal offenders.

The emotional involvement of parents with their children aggravates this special offense category. The issue is confused by well-meaning adults who contend that the delinquent of today will be the criminal of tomorrow. In a context where everyone contributes his home remedy to the problem, contradictory, inconsistent, and often mutually exclusive opinions of parents, teachers, psychiatrists, social workers, ministers, sociologists, and judges yield an excess of approaches to the issue. Although these critics often attribute all "undesirable" conduct, including disobedience, resistance to discipline, disrespect, incorrigibility, smoking without permission, hawking stolen merchandise, or scavenging cigarette butts to single causes, it is difficult to discover the true link between delinquent conduct and the often presumed factors in the youth's life causing his "delinquency."[2] Too often, mischief and delinquency have been intertwined and children made responsible for acts that bring no criminal penalty if committed by adults.

177

Whether through ignorance or choice, laymen tend to minimize the principles of "care, protection, and prevention" that theoretically govern the current approach to juvenile delinquency. Unaccustomed to the idea of providing help to those who cause societal disruptions, they call for punishment as a means to control delinquent acts. By so doing, they distort the problems seriously and actually encourage its expansion. They fail to realize that only a fractional minority of the juvenile population is "technically delinquent" and that the overwhelming majority of those who are referred to the juvenile court need society's care and protection more than its hatred and condemnation. While urging that energetic measures be taken against juvenile delinquency, the laymen forgets a portion of his own adolescent conduct that probably could today be labelled "delinquent."

Delinquency and Self-Reporting ● The more perceptive students of delinquency generally recognize their own previous delinquent conduct. In an informal classroom experiment conducted over a four-year period in which students answered research questions pertaining to delinquency, Stephen Schafer discovered that no more than 3 of 50 college students in an average juvenile delinquency class denied having participated in some delinquent activity; only one, however, had ever been brought before a juvenile court. Although the vast majority of these students admitted to such delinquencies as shoplifting, petty theft, restaurant and hotel "souvenir collecting," truancy, disobedience to parental or scholastic authority, and early drinking, few had ever been arrested or brought to the attention of the court.

A comparison by Austin L. Porterfield of the delinquent behavior of 337 Texas college students and of 2,000 delinquent boys brought before the Fort Worth juvenile court confirmed these findings.[3] Others have discovered that court statistics are wholly inadequate to measure the volume of illegal youthful conduct within the community. Adolescent misconduct is, in fact, so frequent that even a moderate increase in arrests for delinquency could create the semblance of a "delinquency wave" without the slightest change in adolescent behavior. James F. Short, Jr. and Ivan F. Nye found little difference in quantity between the delinquent activities of high school boys in general and those sent to training schools.[4]

The serious disparities between the official reports of delinquency rates and the volume of delinquent conduct admitted by the person himself raises serious doubts about the accuracy of current official delinquency statistics. Admittedly, all known delinquencies are not detected by the police or reported to the Federal Bureau of Investigation for tabulation with its *Uniform Crime Reports* or other collections of delinquency data.[5] Consequently, information provided by self-reporting procedures are important sources of data concerning the actual volume of juvenile delinquency.

The discovery of many former undetected delinquents who have become successful citizens in later life raises the troublesome but persistent question:

"At what point and why did our present respectable friends decide to mend their ways?"[6] Not all professional students of delinquency are prepared to answer this question.

The Concept of Delinquency • Although crime and delinquency are basically similar concepts, they differ with respect to the age of those who can be regarded as lawbreakers, the range of behavior that is defined as violations, the treatment reserved for offenders, the method of defining illegal conduct, the type of behavior prohibited, and the reasons for such definitions of deviance. As most crimes are also delinquencies in the sense that they are acts of which society disapproves, the nature of crime must be comprehended before delinquency can be understood. However, not every delinquency is a crime, and some crimes cannot be termed delinquencies. According to criminal law, a crime is a conduct or an action that is defined and codified in law as a criminal violation. It may involve a failure to do what the law demands or to refrain from an action that the law prohibits. The former legal definition of crime upholds the principle that no crime exists unless it is so defined by the law (*nullum crimen sine lege*). This, however, is not true in defining juvenile delinquency.

The term "delinquency" is basically similar to the term "criminality." Both express relationships between the existing structure of law and the violations of law by some members of society. Although the main distinction is largely quantitative rather than qualitative, the term *delinquency*, an offense commonly committed by a juvenile between the ages of 7 and 16 to 18, depending upon the state, is used as a convenient category to differentiate offenders by age from ordinary adult criminals. Actually, delinquency is an extension of the concept of crime. Without an adjustment in the definition of criminality, the illegal acts committed by juveniles and adults would be considered equivalent. The delinquency concept, however, permits a distinction between levels of responsibility. As a result, a murder committed by juveniles and adults will have similar results but are processed, if the juvenile is judged as a juvenile, separately. The delinquency concept permits a distinction between levels of responsibility. As a result, a murder committed by a twelve-year-old boy may be regarded as a delinquent act, whereas, if committed by a fifty-year-old man, or even an eighteen-year-old girl, is held to be a criminal act. Similarly, shoplifting by a forty-year-old man is defined as criminal conduct, whereas the same activity by a fourteen-year-old female is viewed as a delinquent act. The two terms also involve radical distinctions in preliminary investigation procedures, court proceedings, and penal consequences.

Variables in Individuals Responses • The relations among pressures toward criminality and one's ability to distinguish between right and wrong differ for a variety of reasons. Age differences alone result in markedly different conduct, exposure to criminal pressures, and ability to resist. Because adults supposedly have been more thoroughly socialized and have become more mature personalities, society assumes that they should automatically be held responsible for their offenses. The complete concept of juvenile delinquency as distinguished from adult crimes, however, depends upon an age differential and an additional aspect of criminality, which the authors call crime-"plus." The "plus" refers to additional dangers that may lead juveniles into criminal conduct. For example, if an adult does not report to his job, he may be fired without penal consequences; if a juvenile does not attend school, he may be processed through the juvenile courts. Crime-plus suggests the fundamental necessity of society to protect and care for juveniles, who stand in greater danger of succumbing to crime pressures because of their inexperience and age. Because the juvenile represents an incompletely developed physical, psychological, physiological and ethical organism, his perception of moral standards and socioethical values has not necessarily reached the level of maturity necessary to resist even ordinary crime pressures. Therefore, he needs and deserves extra protection, ordinarily not available to adults, to insulate him against these pressures.

The term delinquency implies not only a specific age group but also variable responses to the challenges and influences that impinge upon the youth's ability to resist. For this reason, the period of the juvenile's life before he has committed a delinquent act is sometimes referred to as "predelinquency" or "potential delinquency." These terms, however, often seem inappropriate, for they actually refer to the delinquent act itself.[7] Nevertheless, because the vast literature on crime and delinquency generally assumes that "precriminal" delinquency covers practically anything that may happen in a child's or juvenile's life, the concept ultimately "contributes to the inflation of the problem."[8]

The Crime Zone and the Danger Zone ● If the juvenile enters into the *crime zone,* which includes all punishable criminal offenses, the youth's violation triggers a form of legal intervention designed to prevent further crimes and to enlist care and protection. Conversely, if he has entered only the *danger zone* (i.e., becomes truant), an area of delinquency which is not specifically defined in law as a criminal offense, society intervenes in order to prevent the possibility of crime. Under current laws, the state may intervene in juvenile affairs even if no formal criminal offense has been committed. Contrary to the general prohibitions surrounding the prosecution of adult offenders, the state may intervene in the interest of the juvenile's welfare in order to defend him against his own presumed inability to resist criminal pressures. Through the juvenile court, the state extends its paternal care for the juvenile instead of or in addition to the concern and protection offered by natural parents. The late 1960's Gault and Kent decisions of the U.S. Supreme Court have clouded this distinction, however. As the juvenile is presumed to be less responsible and more "salvageable," he is treated differently from the adult who commits the same crime, a basic principle that these decisions probably cannot and will not change.

Juvenile Delinquency and Youth Crime in the United States • In the late 1960's, the President's Commission stated that America's best hope for reducing crime is to reduce juvenile delinquency and youth crime,"[9] a position strongly supported by statistical data. Although present knowledge of the volume of delinquency is limited by the absence of extensive and dependable data, the available facts are enough to understand the seriousness of this social problem (see Table 9.1). National juvenile delinquency and youth crime statistics on a national scale, collected only by the FBI's *Uniform Crime Reports,* register the number of juvenile arrests and referrals to juvenile courts. A few other agencies record juvenile referrals to various social agencies for other purposes. However, these do not provide detailed information about the vast number of unsolved

TABLE 9.1

TOTAL ARRESTS OF PERSONS UNDER 15, UNDER 18, UNDER 21, AND UNDER 25 YEARS OF AGE, 1973

[6,004 agencies; 1973 estimated population 154,995,000]

OFFENSE CHARGED	GRAND TOTAL ALL AGES	NUMBER OF PERSONS ARRESTED				PERCENTAGE			
		UNDER 15	UNDER 18	UNDER 21	UNDER 25	UNDER 15	UNDER 18	UNDER 21	UNDER 25
TOTAL	6,499,864	614,716	1,717,366	2,654,516	3,586,283	9.5	26.4 1	40.8	55.2
Criminal homicide:									
(a) Murder and nonnegligent manslaughter	14,399	216	1,497	3,607	6,426	1.5	10.4	25.1	44.6
(b) Manslaughter by negligence....	2,996	83	363	876	1,397	2.8	12.1	29.2	46.6
Forcible rape	19,198	813	3,772	7,500	11,633	4.2	19.6	39.1	60.6
Robbery	101,894	11,015	34,374	56,678	77,773	10.8	33.7	55.6	76.3
Aggravated assault	154,891	8,200	26,270	47,293	73,724	5.3	17.0	30.5	47.6
Burglary–breaking or entering	316,272	73,139	170,228	227,280	266,969	23.1	53.8	71.9	84.4
Larceny–theft	644,190	146,910	310,452	414,954	492,783	22.8	48.2	64.4	76.5
Auto theft	118,380	17,736	66,868	87,925	101,339	15.0	56.5	74.3	85.6
Violent crime[1]	290,382	20,244	65,913	115,078	169,556	7.0	22.7	39.6	58.4
Property crime[2]	1,078,842	237,785	547,548	730,159	861,091	22.0	50.8	67.7	79.8
Subtotal for above offenses	1,372,220	258,112	613,824	846,113	1,032,044	18.8	44.7	61.7	75.2
Other assaults	275,105	21,013	53,044	89,245	136,626	7.6	19.3	32.4	49.7
Arson	11,096	4,420	6,491	7,625	8,588	39.8	58.5	68.7	77.4
Forgery and counterfeiting	41,975	729	4,657	12,329	22,732	1.7	11.1	29.4	54.2
Fraud	85,467	686	3,159	12,575	31,316	.8	3.7	14.7	36.6
Embezzlement	5,612	87	429	1,212	2,360	1.6	7.6	21.6	42.1
Stolen property; buying, receiving and possessing	70,238	7,121	23,738	38,423	50,430	10.1	33.8	54.7	71.8
Vandalism.....................	121,011	51,377	83,428	95,743	104,396	42.5	68.9	79.1	86.3
Weapons; carrying, possessing, etc. ...	115,918	4,756	18,635	36,085	57,077	4.1	16.1	31.1	49.2
Prostitution and commercialized vice ..	45,308	150	1,769	12,066	28,497	.3	3.9	26.6	62.9
Sex offenses (except forcible rape and prostitution)	48,673	3,698	9,784	15,566	23,012	7.6	20.1	32.0	47.3
Narcotic drug laws	484,242	16,222	127,316	275,553	391,251	3.3	26.3	56.9	80.8
Gambling	54,938	270	1,544	4,168	8,991	.5	2.8	7.6	16.4
Offenses against family and children ..	42,784	222	994	7,098	15,109	.5	2.3	16.6	35.3
Driving under the influence	653,914	242	9,026	61,780	149,713	(3)	1.4	9.4	22.9
Liquor laws	183,813	7,178	74,690	132,789	146,748	3.9	40.6	72.2	79.8
Drunkenness....................	1,189,489	4,207	34,722	117,141	237,364	.4	2.9	9.8	20.0
Disorderly conduct	461,553	36,114	103,556	184,088	268,529	7.8	22.4	39.9	58.2
Vagrancy	50,310	1,272	6,016	14,385	29,411	2.5	12.0	28.6	58.5
All other offenses (except traffic)	848,835	87,475	231,018	371,517	515,808	10.3	27.2	43.8	60.8
Suspicion	40,927	4,383	13,090	22,579	29,845	10.7	32.0	55.2	72.9
Curfew and loitering law violations....	118,003	33,651	118,003	118,003	118,003	28.5	100.0	100.0	100.0
Runaways.....................	178,433	71,331	178,433	178,433	178,433	40.0	100.0	100.0	100.0

[1] Violent crime is offenses of murder, forcible rape, robbery and aggravated assault
[2] Property crime is offenses of burglary, larceny and auto theft
[3] Less than one-tenth of 1 percent.

Source: Federal Bureau of Investigation, *Uniform Crime Reports–1973*(Washington, D.C.: U.S. Government Printing Office, 1974), p. 130.

and unknown deviant and illegal acts of youth. The available data suggest that the majority of offenses against property are committed by young people under the age of 21, the age group also responsible for a substantial volume of major crimes against the person. The number of recidivists in this age category is higher than in any other age group. Arrest rates are highest for youth between the ages of 15 and 17. The "criminal age," once between 35 to 45, is now dominated by teenagers. Because youth between 14 and 17 years increased numerically by nearly 1.5 million between 1966 and 1970 and will increase by an additional million by 1975, 2.5 million by 1985, and three million by 1990, the American crime picture will be rather grim if the adolescent delinquency and crime rate continues at the same level. Some studies indicate that nearly 90 percent of all youth in the United States have committed at least one act for which they could have been labeled delinquents or young criminals.[10] A large portion of offenders, however, have never been detected, arrested or brought to the attention of the juvenile court.

The officially recorded juvenile delinquents are predominantly male, outnumbering girls by about 3.5 to 1 (see Table 9-2). But this figure is misleading inasmuch as fewer girls are likely to be picked up by the police. Adolescent male delinquencies or crimes are often larcenies, burglaries, auto thefts, and drug law violations; young females usually are referred to courts for larcenies, simple assaults, drug abuse, and disorderly conduct. In general, delinquents seem to be concentrated in the larger cities as opposed to rural areas where their offense rate is lowest. Many come from broken homes and tend to do poorly in school. Demographic data indicate that delinquents are commonly products of social and economic deprivation, actually coming from families which have a lower than average income and status. In recent years arrests of juvenile females for sex offenses have declined.

New Forms of Juvenile Delinquency ● Although the concept of juvenile delinquency is relatively new and youth crime is an old social problem, it has taken at least five new directions since World War II. First, crimes against the person, sex offenses, and the illegal use of liquor and drugs show a marked increase. Second, delinquencies and crimes with violence, including homicide, assault, vandalism and hooliganism, often committed without apparent reason or only for fun, thrill, or kick, have become increasingly signficiant. Third, the age of those becoming involved in deviant activities is declining. Fourth, delinquents in the upper and middle classes are showing greater visability. Fifth, significant growth has occurred in the number of associational and gang delinquencies.[11]

Although these phenomena have not been well documented, many contrasting explanations have been offered to explain their presence. For example, while poor living conditions have in the past been blamed for the rise in delinquency and crime and poverty believed to be an important causative factor, higher living standards, as experienced in the United States, United Kingdom, Sweden or

TABLE 9.2

TOTAL ARREST TRENDS BY SEX, 1960-73

Offense Charged	Males						Females					
	Total 1960	Total 1973	Percent Change	Under 18 1960	Under 18 1973	Percent Change	Total 1960	Total 1973	Percent Change	Under 18 1960	Under 18 1973	Percent Change
TOTAL [1]	2,891,354	3,695,870	+27.8	397,862	889,333	+123.5	351,220	686,068	+95.3	68,312	248,713	+264.1
Criminal homicide:												
(a) Murder and nonnegligent manslaughter	3,761	9,048	+140.6	312	1,098	+251.9	780	1,581	+102.7	25	99	+296.0
(b) Manslaughter by negligence	1,580	1,469	−7.0	123	201	+63.4	186	191	+2.7	9	15	+66.7
Forcible rape	6,857	13,823	+101.6	1,185	2,753	+132.3						
Robbery	29,710	77,264	+160.1	6,993	27,265	+289.9	1,487	5,748	+286.6	359	2,071	+476.9
Aggravated assault	43,141	93,097	+115.8	5,668	16,435	+190.0	7,261	14,979	+106.3	638	2,871	+350.0
Burglary—breaking or entering	113,227	199,718	+76.4	53,497	107,009	+100.0	3,857	11,311	+193.3	1,652	5,597	+238.8
Larceny—theft	158,733	291,645	+83.7	78,222	143,789	+83.8	31,710	139,861	+341.1	13,153	61,124	+364.7
Auto theft	52,128	82,679	+58.6	31,640	46,614	+47.3	2,074	5,296	+155.4	1,299	3,133	+141.2
Violent crime [2]	83,469	193,232	+131.5	14,158	47,551	+235.9	9,528	22,308	+134.1	1,022	5,041	+393.2
Property crime [3]	324,088	574,042	+77.1	163,359	297,412	+82.1	37,641	156,468	+315.7	16,104	69,854	+333.8
Subtotal for above offenses	409,137	768,743	+87.9	177,640	345,164	+94.3	47,355	178,967	+277.9	17,135	74,910	+337.2
Other assaults	103,892	157,831	+51.9	10,173	28,844	+183.5	11,264	25,154	+123.3	1,765	7,443	+321.7
Forgery and counterfeiting	17,807	20,538	+15.3	1,153	2,173	+88.5	3,522	7,637	+116.8	349	908	+160.2
Fraud and embezzlement	26,015	38,911	+49.6	643	1,786	+177.8	1,914	7,297	+281.3	136	590	+333.8
Stolen property; buying, receiving, possessing	8,348	43,139	+416.8	2,355	14,580	+519.1	799	5,002	+526.0	176	1,345	+664.2
Weapons; carrying, possessing, etc.	29,114	78,675	+170.2	6,166	13,161	+113.4	1,751	7,074	+304.0	187	789	+321.9
Prostitution and commercialized vice	6,796	10,188	+49.9	119	409	+243.7	17,535	30,166	+72.0	294	1,186	+303.4
Sex offenses (except forcible rape and prostitution)	33,635	33,030	−1.8	6,311	6,203	−1.7	5,947	2,663	−55.2	2,427	875	−63.9
Narcotic drug laws	25,605	280,407	+995.1	1,488	67,776	+4,454.8	4,284	48,263	+1,026.6	237	14,564	+6,045.1
Gambling	96,244	40,175	−58.3	1,190	1,145	−3.8	9,363	3,808	−59.3	40	94	+135.0
Offenses against family and children	33,006	21,709	−34.2	483	368	−23.8	2,899	2,354	−18.8	214	155	−27.6
Driving under the influence	134,000	383,019	+185.8	1,066	5,234	+391.0	8,698	30,818	+254.3	59	406	+588.1
Liquor laws	70,180	92,604	+32.0	14,863	34,669	+133.3	11,555	16,788	+45.3	2,344	8,660	+269.5
Drunkenness	1,117,121	778,421	−30.3	10,963	19,731	+80.0	98,434	59,130	−39.9	1,246	3,228	+159.1
Disorderly conduct	314,416	256,316	−18.5	39,326	57,394	+45.9	49,873	61,215	+22.7	6,945	12,470	+79.6
Vagrancy	117,138	25,409	−78.3	6,327	3,366	−46.8	10,505	15,099	+43.7	824	723	−12.3
All other offenses (except traffic)	348,900	666,755	+91.1	117,596	287,330	+144.3	62,899	174,633	+177.6	33,934	120,367	+254.7
Suspicion (not included in totals)	108,785	26,431	−75.7	19,651	7,998	−59.3	14,411	4,445	−69.2	3,000	1,432	−52.3

[1] Based on comparable reports from 1854 cities representing 79,540,000 population and 524 counties representing 14,711,000 population.

[2] Violent crime is offenses of murder, forcible rape, robbery, and aggravated assault.

[3] Property crime is offenses of burglary, larceny, and auto theft.

Source: Federal Bureau of Investigation, *Uniform Crime Reports—1973* (Washington, D.C.: U.S. Government Printing Office, 1974), p. 126.

Western Germany, have not led to a decline in the juvenile delinquency volume. This discrepancy has been explained by some observers in terms of improvement of the material conditions of life without a parallel improvement in discipline, moral values, and social responsibility. Without the latter, little can be done, they claim, to control, prevent, or reduce the increase in these new juvenile delinquency forms.

While poverty appears to be closely related to acts of delinquency, an examination of the diversity of juvenile legal violations of higher status youth reveals that poverty does not cause all youthful deviant acts. The growth of industrialization has also stimulated many new offense forms. Urban growth and industrial expansion appear to serve as criminogenic agents. The absence of economic industrial, urban, and social integration has permitted by default the continued evolution of delinquency. The deemphasis of moral values and the disintegration of the traditional family ties are also factors contributing to the present shape of juvenile delinquency. Growing materialism, contradictory value systems, distrust and insecurity, and general social corruption similarly take their toll. Youths, particularly those in highly developed countries, enjoy material and economic advantages never before available to their age group, yet their delinquency continues to increase.

Preventing Delinquency • Prevention, an almost impossible task, appears, nevertheless, as the best method for eventual control of delinquency.[12] In order to promote this end, the President's Crime Commission in 1967 recommended that unemployment be reduced, a minimum family income be provided, and regulations be revised so that family integration will be enhanced. Further suggestions included improvement in the dispensing of family planning assistance information, a provision for domestic management and child care assistance, and the creation of counseling and therapy outlets for the whole family. Advice has also been given to involve young people in community activities, train and employ youth as subprofessional aids, establish youth services, offer community residential centers, and increase the involvement of religious institutions, private social agencies, fraternal groups, and other community organizations in youth programs. In other words, prevention has been viewed primarily in terms of physical environment improvement, family membership, and whatever generally helps a person to live in a better, cleaner, and safer manner. Solutions of this type, proponents presume, will solve the social problem of juvenile delinquency, which in turn will effect the resolution of other problems as well. But community involvement alone does not guarantee a solution to the delinquency problem.[13]

Efforts to Prevent Youth Offenses • The first community attempt to help the unfortunate or potential delinquent, a Judeo-Christian approach to the poor, took the form of aid to orphans and destitute children. In succeeding generations, voluntary organizations, schools, social service agencies, and individual philanthropists added their gifts to the rehabilitation of children exposed to delinquency pressures. Despite these efforts the problem still continues and manages to increase.

When juvenile delinquency was recognized at the turn of this century as a separate social and legal problem, the attempt to uncover its causes stimulated a world-wide movement to prevent delinquency and aid delinquents. As interest in the problem of delinquency grew, new organizations offered voluntary assistance to the search for solutions. But it was not until after World War II that the American public's full interest in juvenile delinquency became evident, especially as new forms of delinquency grew. Before that time, the problem had been left almost entirely to the sometimes unskilled, semiskilled, and skilled staffs of numerous agencies which often worked with little or no cooperation and with different and sometimes sharply divergent service orientations.

In the last two decades the public has become increasingly concerned about the growth of delinquency, leading to the hope that constructive and coordinated preventive activities will bring order to the somewhat chaotic contemporary approach to the problem. However, any attempt at delinquency control is frustrated by arguments among practitioners, researchers, sociologists, psychologists, jurists, policemen and lawyers over precisely what should be controlled. While nearly every group agrees that prevention is a noble goal, the prescriptions offered to prevent delinquent acts range from a delegislation of the problem to the full infliction of bodily harm. Most advocates of a particular position fall somewhere in between. Too often, in their ideological commitment to method, they fail to recognize the different types of delinquent offenders involved in the problem.

The Analysis of Delinquent Conduct ● The delinquent and criminal acts of youth are varied and somewhat individualized. *Occasional* and *casual* delinquents deviate at certain times, spontaneously and irregularly, whenever they face pressures favoring delinquency or have an opportunity to commit a deviant act. In the occasional delinquency, the opportunity uses the child; in the casual violation, the young person uses the opportunity. Early drinking, sexual aberrations, petty theft, periodic shoplifting, minor fraud, borrowing a car, infrequent truancy, violations of city regulations, acts of anger, and similar conduct are frequently carried out by occasional or casual delinquents. *Professional* delinquents, as their adult counterparts, are motivated by a profit motive. Theft, burglary, robbery, larceny, juvenile prostitution, and other crimes against property are committed by this type offender. *Youthful* or *young adult offenders,* a further variant, are commonly between the ages of 18 and 21, although this arbitrary age limit varies from country to country. They, like their younger equivalents, may be occasional, casual, or professional offenders. They differ only in terms of maturity. Sometimes called *postdelinquents,* they are above the usual upper age limit of those under the jurisdiction of juvenile courts. What makes them a different or somewhat independent category is their special personality set which develops as a result of their being more mature than children or juveniles but less mature than adults.

Contemporary delinquency is also expressed frequently in the form of gang offenses. The gang is not merely a group of young people who band together for common activities but may also be an association of youth organized for deviant goals. Its members have a "moral" commitment to the group and to disciplined leadership, which directs the functioning organization. Although middle-class gangs are not unknown, the overwhelming majority of gangs known to the police are composed of children from lower social class families. Because they are mostly products of big cities or metropolitan areas (*e.g.,* New York, Chicago, London and Paris), their activities take place primarily in urban rather than rural areas. Although the technical aspects of the ganging process are still being studied, some evidence suggests that the delinquent juvenile gang has its origin in a conforming social clique. As outside competition emerges, the clique, in order to defend itself or attack its competition, modifies its conceptual structure to become an "opposition group," and ultimately reaches the developmental stage of a gang whose members hold needs, aspirations, and deviant goals in common. A special formation of the clique may be the so-called "street-corner group," named after the location of its meeting place.[14]

An early ecological evaluation of gang behavior, initiated by Frederic M. Thrasher, revealed that the origins of delinquency rest within the *physical environment* shared by the juveniles composing the gang. Adolescents are encouraged to participate in delinquent acts and to ignore controls that normally constrain most juveniles. Thrasher hypothesized that individual choices and free will count for little when weighed against predetermined and innate delinquency factors. According to his classical ecological orientation, gangs and delinquents arise spontaneously only if conditions within the environment favor their emergence. The gang area, the birthplace of delinquency, is a geographically and socially interstitial area of the city. Therefore, American delinquency, Thrasher argues, is a product of social disorganization, largely resulting from the nation's rapid economic development and the unequal acculturation and assimilation of vast numbers of alien workers.[15]

A more recent approach to delinquency, suggested by Albert K. Cohen, visualizes the problem in terms of a *lower-class delinquent subculture.* He argues that the delinquent subculture can be identified from official statistics which support the finding that delinquency is predominantly a work-class phenomenon. Delinquency differs from adult crime in that it is nonutilitarian, malicious, and negativistic. It is nonutilitarian because a "valuable" item provides little monetary value to those who have stolen; malicious because delinquency is an apparent form of malice, an enjoyment of the discomfiture of others and a delight in the defiance of taboos; and negativistic because the realistic motivation of the delinquent act is not easily recognizable. According to Cohen, delinquency is characterized by versatility, short-run hedonism, and group autonomy. The delinquent subcultural defense mechanism, which provides juveniles with ways to cope with failure, provides youth with status and answers to problems of adjustment. Because many children are excluded from the higher statuses, the delinquent subculture provides status criteria that excluded youth can meet. Therefore, the delinquent subculture permits the delinquent youth to compete successfully with those in similar social positions and mitigates, and even eliminates, status inferiority.[16]

Herbert A. Bloch and Arthur Neiderhoffer focus their attention upon *personality development* and its accompanying drives rather than upon the antagonistic attitudes of lower-class boys to middle-class institutions. Disagreeing with the common assumption that delinquency is an exclusive product of slum areas, they contend that as adolescents strive for the attainment of adult status, they engage in new experiences which provoke reactions of the public. In their judgment, adolescent striving is a cultural universal; the degree to which this phase is socially disruptive depends upon a variety of factors, especially upon the extent to which a society provides rites of passage through emotional and intellectual preparation and supportive rituals to facilitate juvenile entrance into adulthood.[17]

Whereas the delinquent subculture approach sees the gang as a product of lower-class protest against the middle-class, the personality development approach believes it to be an adolescent revolt against adult society, a reaction that can be understood in terms of the emotional and psychological needs of youth. While the delinquent subculture theory supports the nonutilitarian concept of juvenile delinquency, the adolescent revolt orientation maintains that money and valuable property are often sought in burglaries and robberies by lower-class gangs, an assumption supported by police records.

Viewing juvenile delinquency as an essential factor in conformity to *lower-class values,* Walter B. Miller suggests, on the other hand, that the role of the lower-class in gang delinquency is an independent variable and attempts to demonstrate that the dominant motivational component underlying human conduct is a direct effort by the human actor to adhere to forms of designated behavior and to achieve value standards defined within his community. In this theory, the most influential cultural system in gang behavior is the lower-class community, which is a generating milieu of delinquency.

According to Miller, the lower-class way of life is characterized by a set of focal concerns, which together with the total lower-class culture become stabilized as the numbers of their adherents increase. Among the focal concerns are toughness, smartness, trouble, excitement, fate, and autonomy. *Trouble* represents a situation which results in unwelcome or complicating involvement with officials or agencies of middle-class society. The personal status of the young person in the lower-class culture is often measured in these terms. *Toughness* refers to a combination of qualities, the most important of which are strength and endurance. The so-called "tough-boy," a hard, fearless, and skilled physical fighter, enjoys a reputation in the lower-class. *Smartness* is the capacity to achieve one's objectives with maximum mental agility and minimum physical effort. Considerable prestige is attached to persons possessing this quality. *Excitement,* a focal concern of another type, is often identified with a "thrill" or "kick," found in alcohol, gambling, dice-throwing, and sexual adventure. Concern with *fate* reflects a wide-spread lower-class fatalistic belief in luck.

Although members of the lower-class feel that their lives are subject to forces over which they have little control, they are nevertheless concerned with *autonomy*, the extent and nature of control over the behavior of their person.

These adolescent and adult focal concerns, focused around the central concerns of belonging and status, represent, according to Miller, the essence of lower-class culture. Satisfying them automatically involves the actor in the violation of various legal norms. Even when alternative action is possible, non-law-abiding avenues provide greater and more immediate returns. Because the desire of lower-class youths to conform to their own culture inevitably brings them into conflict with the larger society, lower-class practices in and of themselves lead to legal violations.[18]

But Richard A. Cloward and Lloyd E. Ohlin believe that delinquency and gang behavior can best be explained in terms of society's *differential opportunity structure*. They answer the question of how the relative availability of illegitimate opportunities effects the resolution of adjustment problems leading to deviant behavior. Believing that differential support for one or another type of illegitimate activity is available at different points in the social structure, the type and strength of this support determines how individuals will resolve adjustment problems. According to their hypothesis, each individual is located in both legitimate and illegitimate opportunity structures. When legitimate access to success goals is limited, the nature of the resultant delinquent response will vary according to the availability of various illegitimate means. Although this orientation accepts the general conception of a delinquent subculture, it really consists, Cloward and Ohlin argue, of three subcultures that form the principle orientations of the dominant groups of the urban lower-class. The socialization of potential criminals takes place primarily within a *criminal* subculture, which stimulates crimes for profit. In the *conflict* subculture of the lower-class, the transient, unstable, and weak middle-class social controls of the slums are expressed in delinquency. This encourages status aspirations. The *retreatist* subculture, which provides the milieu that produces drug dependency, is partially the result of a breakdown of interpersonal relations, which occurs when a boy is rejected by the legitimate, criminal and conflict subcultures.[19]

Stephen Schafer understands delinquent gangs and juvenile delinquency in terms of the degree and direction of *socialization of youth*. He notes three types of juvenile gangs: the social, antisocial and asocial. The *social gang* accepts and abides by social norms; its members, orientated toward conforming activities, are a norm-accepting gang. The *antisocial gang,* or norm-attacking group, engages in various forms of nonconformist and delinquent activity that threaten and challenge social norms. The *asocial gang,* a norm-denying unit, is midway between the social and antisocial types and consists of socially indifferent youths who indulge in only certain kinds of nonconforming and delinquent behavior. Although the antisocial gang leans toward conduct characteristic to adult criminality, the asocial gang is guided in its deviant acts by a desire for excitement, kick, or thrill. Whether the juvenile joins the norm-accepting group of other juveniles or moves from membership in one of the other two types of gangs in which social norms are attacked or refused depends upon the kind of socialization the juvenile receives.[20]

The emphasis upon socialization implied in Schafer's conception is also expounded forcefully in terms of the juvenile's self-concept, actually a product of socialization, by Simon Dinitz, Frank R. Scarpitti, and Walter C. Reckless. They view the problem as one of *delinquency vulnerability*, in which a good self-concept serves to insulate the juvenile from deviance and a weak to make the juvenile susceptible to delinquency.[21] While Richard D. Knudten agrees that socialization plays a major function in delinquency formation, he nevertheless argues that *relative cultural, social organizational, peer group,* and *personality interaction* is also involved in different combinations for each juvenile offender. Delinquency is a form of "conspicuous masculinity or feminity" and delinquent youth are commonly unable to defer their desires for gratification.[22]

Sociocultural Influences in Delinquency

The Family ● Juvenile delinquency and youth crime evaluators largely agree that certain family characteristics and functions are among the primary causes of delinquency. Although the family normally assumes the task of constructing and integrating social life, not all families are able to fulfill this function. The destructive and disorganizing impact of delinquency and crime is especially strong when family functioning is deficient. While the inadequacy of familial socialization may encourage delinquent conduct by failing to develop adequate socioethical personalities, the exact contribution of families to an increase or decrease in delinquency is open to question.

Since the nineteenth century, nearly all criminological theorists have maintained that delinquency is a product of family inadequacy or malfunctioning. Although available data do not unconditionally support this belief, it is logical to assume that the family is of central importance to the formation or nonformation of delinquent patterns. It is the first social group to which the child belongs and, despite his gradual participation in other associations, remains his basic group during his juvenile years. Although the child is also influenced by other groups or agencies during his adolescence, the family provides the foundation from which he either resists or accedes to delinquency pressures. As an agency for transmitting the fundamental social value system, the family influences the development of personality from helpless infancy to maturity, maintaining this capability as long as it remains the child's primary group. While the family is charged with the responsibility of socializing its members to the prevailing value system, it may not succeed in this task because of its own inability to receive or transmit these values or to overcome contrary extra-familial influences.

The six types of homes or family relationships that frequently encourage delinquency are those in which 1) immoral, alcoholic, or criminal members live;

2) one or both parents are absent; 3) parental control is lacking; 4) favoritism, extreme severity, neglect, crowded conditions, or interference by relatives prevails; 5) racial or religious differences or foster parent relationships receive emphasis; and 6) economic pressures exist.[23] Sheldon and Eleanor Glueck generalize the sociocultural meaning of home atmosphere as a delinquency factor, mentioning "homes of little understanding, affection, stability or moral fibre" in which children "readily give expression to their untamed impulses and their self-centered desires by means of various forms of delinquent behavior."[24] Naturally, the influences of the home environment on delinquency operate selectively, according to the juvenile's constitutional traits and his sociocultural conditioning.

Although a long list of family features that may cause delinquency can be readily compiled, three main factors are generally recognized as major familial stimulants to juvenile delinquency: a) Parental deviation from socioethical values that almost necessarily encourage the future deviance of the child; b) Parental inability to resist delinquency pressures that hinders the defense of children against external delinquency pressures; and c) Disharmony in the home which may resemble the tensions of so-called broken homes and which are present even without the divorce, separation, or death of one or both parents.

Immigration as a Cause • Another sociocultural influence in delinquency is immigration, which takes the form of unavoidable culture conflict brought about by movement to a new country or territory. Problems of immigrant entry are not always mitigated or assisted by the attitudes of the receiving population. The old saying that emigration is the last recourse of those afflicted by misery still seems valid. In fact, its meaning has been greatly enhanced by events of the 1930's, 1950's, and 1960's when the last resource of those afflicted by political oppression was emigration. To the desire to escape from want was added the desire to escape from fear. Emigration became for many a "weapon of survival."[25]

The greatest difficulty for the immigrant is his need to make a socioethical readjustment to his new environment. Whereas the juvenile and adult immigrants want generally to adapt themselves to their new surroundings, they are often hesitant, cautious, timid, and bewildered by their circumstances. The immigrant in conflict, unless aided in overcoming this problem, may turn to delinquency or crime. Because the host population commonly believes that an entrance permit, preliminary assistance with charity dollars, and formal suggestions concerning work opportunities and procedures will solve his basic problems, the immigrant's conflict is frequently misinterpreted or dismissed as unimportant. However, emigration stimulated many conflicts that are neither easily classified nor readily resolved. Variations in cultural and socioethical values hinder adjustment and make the immigrant susceptible to hostile forces.

Because immigration is not unilateral, it calls for mutual understanding. While the receiving country rightly expects the acculturation of the immigrant, little success is achieved until his original conflicts are resolved. Some immigrants, not content with the hospitality of their new country, seek to gain unfair advantages through challenges of law and order. These "failures" among the general mass of immigrants, however, have not proved to be more frequent than those among the native-born population. Although obvious socioeconomic difficulties suggest the probability of immigrant delinquency and crime, the inhibiting force of physical relocation and new cultural orientation may actually limit such deviance.

Sporadic studies of the relationship between immigration and delinquency or crime reveal several insights. The criminality of immigrants has generally been higher among people under thirty, comparable to that of the native-born population between the ages of 30 to 35, and lower among those over 35.[26] Although some studies suggest that immigrants have a higher crime rate upon their arrival in the receiving country, others conclude that the so-called "second generation," the native-born children of immigrants, evidence a higher crime rate than that of the original immigrants. The immigrant's children, they believe, are peculiarly subject to cultural conflict since they are both socialized to "Old World" mores by parents and to "New World" patterns by schools, churches, peers, neighbors, and mass communications media. Immigration seems to have more visible effects upon delinquency than upon the crime.

Ecology and Delinquency • Ecological patterns, actually environmental, social and institutional relations of human beings in geographical areas, also influence the problem of delinquency. The social group in which an individual participates is not only an association of individuals and subgroups but also a "local area" representative that has a marked influence upon both individuals and subgroups. Geographical influence on human life is not simply a fact but is also an element in social functioning. In nearly all metropolitan areas, professional crime, delinquency and vice are centered in well-defined districts. New York, Chicago, London, Paris and Rome have their "badlands" where crime prospers. Their development has been attributed to the moral isolation of pariahs from modern society and the establishment of an area for survival by parasitic social elements.[27] While criminological interest in ecology is not new, Gabriel Tarde's "Laws of Imitation" offering the original theoretical foundation,[28] criminal ecologists have been unable to guarantee the reliability of their crime and delinquency distribution maps due to the incompleteness of statistics concerning these problems and the hidden character of much of middle- and upper-class crime.

Social workers Sophonisba P. Breckenridge and Edith Abbott, who investigated increasing juvenile delinquency in Chicago during the ten-year period from 1899 to 1909 and developed the "delinquent neighborhood" concept,[29] pioneered studies of the ecology of delinquency. Between the two world wars, the most significant ecological investigations were carried out in Chicago by the probation officer Clifford R. Shaw and subsequently by Henry D. McKay in a series of other cities.[30] As a result of their work, Shaw and McKay concluded that delinquency is functional to an area and does not result from the interaction of its inhabitants. Although their discoveries were significant, their conclusions were open to criticism. While ecological interpreters of the delinquency problem still publish their findings, this element no longer is the only one used to explain the rise in delinquency.[31]

Economic Aspects of Delinquency • Even though economic conditions are significant influences in the development of juvenile delinquency, empirical evidence does not support the statement that economic conditions have a decisive effect on the formation of delinquent conduct. Actually, no other delinquency factor is as strongly interwoven with other causal factors as the economic. Culture conflicts, class mobility, role constellations, poor living conditions, community disorganization, poverty, white-collar delinquency, black-marketing, immigration, prostitution, and other factors or problems, often held to be independent variables in delinquency, are ultimately related to economic conditions.

The balance of economic supply and demand depends not only upon the gratification or restraint of aspirations but also upon crude factors that may shape a number of social situations conducive to delinquency. The nature of the family, the home, labor, statuses, roles, aspirations, the power structure, and other such dimensions are shaped by variations in economic conditions. The economic matrix of delinquency rests not so much upon the disparities in economic distribution as upon the effects of these disparities upon social institutions. The family and home, religious attachments, education, neighborhoods, mass communications, collective behavior and health may exert differing influences upon the prevailing economic power and the socialization process. Because the economic order is a system characterized by periodic conflicts, delinquency, a form of conflict, may issue from it. The exact etiological importance of independent effects of economic values on the shape and incidence of delinquency are still incompletely understood.

A socialist point of view, essentially embodied in theories of economic determinism and social materialism, maintains that the capitalistic system, not its conditions, is the major and possibly only cause of delinquency and crime. Adherents to this viewpoint argue that crime is a product of existing capitalist organization and economic structure and that delinquency and crime rates will decrease if private property and the tools of production are socialized. However, this theoretical orientation cannot be correlated with human practice. Delinquency and crime rates are not consistently less in those countries with socialized economies.

Delinquency and Education • Education or lack of educational response is a most significant sociocultural influence in delinquency. Based upon the principle of universal education, the American system requires school attendance of all youth until a designated age. Although the school is only one of several agencies that serve a socialization function, it is one of the most important. The school system is charged with transmitting prevailing cultural norms that may help the child to avoid deviance. The content, scope, and manner in which courses are offered may in themselves operate to help prevent delinquency. Some contend that the structure and operations of the school system, however, in themselves guarantee the development of delinquent personalities. The fact that many youths commit crimes and are judged delinquent without really knowing what the consequences of their actions will be suggests the need for a primer on law for youth and the failure of school and society to delineate and teach fundamental social values and norms to their charges.

One of the most frequent scholastic conflicts occurs between the educational approach of the school and parental attitudes and values. Whereas parents previously dominated socialization and in some cases encouraged nonconforming values and attitudes often in conflict with those of schools, parental socialization has faltered with the increased employment of mothers outside the home, parental disinterest in socialization responsibilities, and the disintegration of the family through divorce, separation, or other home tensions. Consequently, the socializing tasks of the school have become greater. As traditional familial responsibilities have been shifted to the school, the former conflict between parent and school values has been replaced by a three-way conflict when parent substitutes, whether grandparents, relatives, neighbors or domestic employees, assume daytime responsibility for juvenile socialization. The patriarchal or matriarchal attitudes of the parent substitutes, the parent-school socialization conflict, and socialization by other social agencies often undermines the overall success of common socialization to group norms. Peer group influences also frequently undermine the socializing goals of the school. The peer, another youth with whom a juvenile is in close association, is a nonadult teacher. If peers support opposing values, they may ultimately isolate the child from constructive adult influences and disturb or prevent the full transmission of cultural norms and knowledge.

Walter E. Schafer and Kenneth Polk contend that schools may promote delinquency as they offer irrevelant curriculums, reinforce students' tendencies toward failure, and rely on inappropriate teaching methods.[32] The failure to offer adequate compensatory and remedial education and the tendency to provide inferior teachers and facilities to schools in low income areas often demolish any potential of student achievement. The tendency of schools to label and dismiss those who misbehave only enhances the negative processes already set in process. Education and delinquency are not only two interrelated social problems, but the school itself is also a representative of many complex social problems. Efforts to prevent delinquency within the schools are largely oriented to provisions for counseling and some social work assistance. Integrated delinquency prevention programs are almost nonexistent.[33]

Religion and Delinquency • Religion possesses a significant relationship to the state of delinquency, although observations on its influence in the formation and volume of deviant behavior are scattered and inconclusive. And yet, if religious devotion is a moral expression and if morality and conforming behavior represent the same social phenomenon, religion should have a marked effect upon the delinquency problem. Emile Durkheim argued that religion is central to social life and has the force to unite people in a single "moral community."[34] Others have held that the "potential role" of religion in preventing delinquency "is tremendous"[35] or that "by adding a divine sanction to human values, religion can effectively win compliance with the norms of society."[36]

Although many juvenile courts and treatment institutions place major significance upon religious affiliation and practices, they put little emphasis on the development and importance of religious life practices. The religious atmosphere of the home, the attitude of the school toward religion, religious orientations of peer groups, organizational activities of the church, personal experiences tending to support or undermine religious belief, the religious character of the local culture, and the peculiar requirements and patterns of different denominations strongly influence attachment to religion and cannot be ignored in any assessment of religion's effect upon deliquency.

Even though several American and European studies have attempted to discover whether or not delinquency and criminality are denominationally oriented, their conclusions have been limited. Several have attempted to prove that Roman Catholics are more deviant than Protestants and that Jews are less delinquent than Protestants. Others reverse the order. But most of these studies are based upon analyses of institutional populations which cannot represent the whole world of criminals or delinquents. Neither can they provide the basis for answers to any questions about the influence of religion in delinquency or for analysis of all factors affecting individual religious beliefs.[37]

Mass Media and Delinquency • The sociocultural influence of mass communications media in the shaping of juvenile delinquency and youth crime is a controversial question. Since the advent of television, the focal point of most argumentation, the debate over the relationship between mass communications media and delinquency and crime has continued without conclusive results. Along with television, newspapers, movies, radio, and certain periodicals, particularly the "comics," have all come under attack. The issue is neither new nor even a product of the television age. As early as 1892 Enrico Ferri, for example, called attention to the relationship between popular literature, the daily newspapers, illustrated journals and crime.[38] The attack did not center upon the use of criminal themes in the arts, but rather upon the influence of "sensational" or "popular" presentations in the stimulation of deviant conduct. Since then, mass media have broadened the scope of modern communications and have extended the influence of actions and ideas.

Delinquency and crime problems are closely related to the effects of mass media. They often serve to disseminate deviant ideas; however, they may also be dynamic cultural weapons against delinquency. The mass media may favorably or unfavorably influence young people either by reinforcing their socioethical resistance or by undermining their normal evaluative powers, thereby exposing their "free will" to delinquency and criminal pressures. Actually, mass media offer the cheapest nourishment source of both culture and crime. One or more, even in the lowest strata, enter nearly every home. The Bible, which is the world's continuing best seller, newspapers, films, radio, television, and the comics are the media most readily available to the public.

A fundamental charge leveled against mass media is that they treat delinquency not as a social problem or from the point of view of informing the public but rather as a form of entertainment. Modern society seems unable to dispense with the experience of adventure, thrill, sexual excitement, shooting, violence, crime, and sensation. The media seek to satisfy these demands by presenting coverage of delinquent and criminal events. Although they formally preach the slogan "crime doesn't pay," the media ignore its implications in their quest for new subscribers and advertising markets. Whether the story is true or fictional is of little consequence. The more dramatic, exciting, sensational, thrilling or incredible, the more it is likely to be accepted. Mere entertainment, which omits consideration of the problem and does not stimulate constructive thinking, serves only to arouse emotion and fails to create understanding.

Many critics of mass media express anxiety over the moral well-being of children and youth. Arguing that the sight of hanging, flogging, shooting, and acid throwing cannot help but influence the adolescent, they seek control of "televiolence," the crime influence delivered to the home. This concern seems to be justified, for media evaluators now recognize that "the mass media penetrate more layers of consciousness in less time than any other systems of communication."[39] Although it may not be possible to gather direct evidence about the actual role of media in delinquency causation, it is questionable that such statistical proof is even necessary.[40]

The Control of Delinquency

The confusing uncertainty about which factors cause delinquency and to what extent they influence adolescent deviance make the efficient prevention and control of delinquent conduct extremely difficult. While law enforcement agencies, juvenile courts, and treatment institutions are charged by society with the responsibility of preventing and controlling delinquency, current statisitical information does not reveal success in this endeavor.

The Police and Juvenile Delinquency ● Police activity is the front line defense of law and order. How the police officer conducts this defense, carries out his duties, and behaves toward juveniles and the youth depends largely upon his interpretation of his function. Although the policeman does not dispense eventual justice, he is the first and most crucial evaluator of delinquency. He may use or abuse his power, according to his understanding of his role, his frustrations, and his general definition of modern law enforcement tasks.

The police have a delegated power to safeguard the security of group members, but the prevention of delinquency and the rehabilitation of delinquents partially depend upon the responsible use of this power. Because police cannot avoid administrative and suppressive duties, they will necessarily arouse antagonism and even hostility among those whose illegal conduct they suppress. While the suppression of deviant behavior may protect society, prevent delinquency and crime, win respect for the police, and encourage the public to assist in law enforcement, unjustifiable or unreasonable suppression leads to a disrespect and public distrust of the police.[41]

The recognition that juvenile delinquency is a special crime area is providing a new impetus for the development of specialized juvenile branches in many law enforcement agencies. The majority of police forces now realize that law and order are most effectively furthered by assigning competent youth officers to deal with delinquent children rather than by continuing the older view that these children are violators of the law. Special branches, units, or departments with such names as Crime Prevention Bureau, Juvenile Bureau, Juvenile Division, or Youth Aid Bureau have been created by many police departments in order to differentiate the problems of delinquency and crime. Because their organization has been determined by local needs and resources, they differ in size, staff, administrative structure, and even in division of labor and responsibility between male and female police officers.

The first women were attached to police forces in the United States in 1900, a time when a large number of women entered business life. However, many years elapsed between the recognition of the special problem of juvenile delinquency and the use of policewomen to handle youth problems. In recent years female police personnel have been assigned in many jurisdictions to work with boys and girls under the age of puberty. Although the reasons why women seem to be better at juvenile work than men are not clear, they perhaps have some natural aptitude to which adolescents are more willing to respond.

The Fourth Congress of the International Association of Children's Judges, meeting in Brussels in 1954, was impressed with the record of policewomen and recommended that they be assigned to cases that require effective surveillance and detection, especially when children are witnesses or victims of sexual crimes. Even Interpol (The International Criminal Police Organization) strongly believes that inasmuch as juvenile treatment philosophy assumes that police work in delinquency cases should incorporate a sort of social work approach, the use of policewomen is preferable.

Nevertheless, special qualifications and training should be required of both male and female officers responsible for the prevention and investigation of delinquency. While a few universities offer special training and diplomas in juvenile police work and juvenile corrections, current trends suggest that such programs will become more widespread in the future. The answer to the social problem of juvenile delinquency and youth crime depends significantly upon the work of well-trained and qualified law enforcement officers who are aware of their role, know how to play it, and are devoted to its primary task.

The Juvenile Court • A relatively new institution, the juvenile court, represents a revolutionary departure from common law principles of equality of all offenders before the law regardless of age. Not until the middle of the nineteenth century were juvenile delinquents differentiated from adults within the system of criminal justice, then processed and treated differently. England, which pioneered this reform in 1847, empowered justices to deal summarily with children accused of simple larceny instead of committing them for trial at the so-called "quarter sessions of assizes."[42] Provisions for such summary trials were extended in 1879 to all cases involving children. Although this English breakthrough in treatment of juvenile offenders opened the way to the development of specialized juvenile courts, such modified courts only first opened in South Australia in 1890.

The first totally separate children's court in the United States was created by law in Chicago on July 1, 1899 as a result of the efforts of the Chicago Women's Club, the Catholic Visitation and Aid Society, and the Chicago Bar Association. A second juvenile court was established in 1903 in Denver, Colorado. England, Canada, Hungary, and Switzerland began to treat children in separate juvenile courts during the first decade of this century. Today, most legal systems operate juvenile courts, having adapted the English legal doctrine of "parens patriae," which presumes that the juvenile offender is a child in need of care, education and protection rather than a criminal punishment.[43]

In view of the essential philosophy of the juvenile court, special terminology was soon created in the attempt to eliminate the stigma attached to adult court appearances. As a result, terms common to adult criminal court operations were either modified or eliminated from the juvenile courts' terminology in an attempt to help the public distinguish between the juvenile's act and the court's judgment. The concept of guilt was replaced by adjudication, indicating that the child is not a criminal, but a dependent or delinquent. Arrest gave way to custody; jail to detention; charge to petition; sentencing to commitment; and trial to hearing.

Although court reformers had hoped that these distinctions would gain public acceptance, they unfortunately did not. The public identified the new terms with their adult criminal counterparts and continued to view the juvenile system in criminal terms. This was especially true when an increase in delinquency rates alarmed the public and they equated an increase in adolescent offenses as evidence of a crime wave, despite accurate knowledge whether the offenders were merely delinquent children or were criminal personalities. As a result, juvenile-court terminology has been unable to soften the delinquency stigma and the child, therefore, receives both the serious punishment of public opinion, a social consequence of being delinquent, and the additional corrective judgment of the juvenile court judge.

Although the juvenile court is a court, it is supposed to function, according to its original design, in the interest of the child. However, the original conception of the court has now been clouded by both the public's reluctance to accept the differentiation of delinquents and criminals and recent Supreme Court decisions. Probably the most important legal decisions relating to the delinquency problem since the development of the juvenile court have been the Supreme Court's decisions of *Kent v. United States* (1966) and *Gault v. Arizona* (1967). As legal judgments, they clearly modified the boundaries of earlier juvenile court philosophy. While efforts to achieve the goal of effective juvenile treatment and rehabilitation continue, the Kent decision, affecting federal jurisdiction, and the Gault judgment, oriented to the states, redefine juvenile court procedure and guarantee children many rights accorded to adults under criminal law. As a consequence, these decisions have limited to some extent the judge's right to intervene in juvenile family affairs without adequate cause. For example, the youthfulness and vulnerability of the defendant, the Gault decision states, "does not justify a kangaroo court."

Although the exact implications of the legal decisions are not fully evident, it is apparent already that juvenile deliquent cases will have to be prepared with greater thoroughness in the future and that the judge cannot exercise indiscriminately the often beneficial flexibility and freedom of the court in the interest of the child. Inasmuch as adjudication in the juvenile court is sometimes a first step to a life of crime, it is possible that the increased demands of due process, collateral costs for legal services, and the increased rigidity of the juvenile court atmosphere may encourage the delinquent's career toward criminality. At the same time, it is possible that these new limitations will lessen the intrusion of the court into family affairs. The 1974 Juvenile Delinquency and Delinquency Prevention Act, establishing an Office of Juvenile Delinquency and an Institute to support research, evaluation studies, and other projects, promises to invigorate work in this field. The earlier Youthful Offenders Act previously corrected some of the evident abuses in the processing and treatment of delinquent youth.

Probation and Delinquency ● Most changes have not affected probation, the successful outside-the-institution treatment method. The early development of probation and conditional sentencing, related to such thirteenth century concepts and procedures as "benefit of clergy," "treuga dei," and "sanctuary," was due to the initiative of John Augustus, a Boston shoemaker, who posted bail for drunken offenders in 1841 and subsequently offered them a wide range of personal assistance. The success of his initiatives led to the 1878 passage of the first American probation law, an act repeated in England in 1879. Under its provisions, the sentence of an offender was suspended for a designated period of time under specified conditions. As currently applied, the system of probation tests the juvenile delinquent to see if he can overcome his deviant tendencies without institutional treatment. If so, no sentence will be executed, and he will remain outside the formal system of institutional confinement.

The probation system is a treatment method rather than a system of total supervision and control. Although a conditional sentence offers the delinquent juvenile an opportunity to readjust to the community without having legal sanctions applied against his person, probation officials aid and guide their reform and rehabilitation within the community. Even though the deviating youth is supervised and assisted by a probation officer, an officer of the court, his own resolve to reform ultimately determines the success of probation. Statistics on the success or failure of probation are filled with shortcomings. However, data from most countries testify to its great value. The conditional sentence and probation seem to be most useful alternatives to institutionalization. Failure on probation usually results in the institutionalization of the adolescent offender.

Throughout history, many creative and experimental institutions have been designed to benefit youths. In Amsterdam, the Dutch Houses of Correction in 1596 cared for up to 12 youths who would today be described as juvenile delinquents. In the middle of the seventeenth century, the Hospice of San Filippo de Neri in Florence opened for the correction of vagrant and wayward children. In 1704 Pope Clement XI erected the Hospice of San Michale in Rome to assist the reformation of "bad" boys. The London Society for the Improvement of Prison Discipline and for the Reformation of Juvenile Offenders established an asylum in 1815 for young lawbreakers, while a similar institution was opened in 1874 in Budapest. The influence of John Griscon, a New Jersey Quaker, led the Society for the Reformation of Juvenile Delinquents in 1823 to advocate the establishment of a juvenile "house of refuge" which would emphasize education rather than punishment.

Juvenile correctional institutions today are concerned both with socialization, the sensitazation of the juvenile to his expected role and conduct, and with resocialization, the redirection of the youth from deviance to conformity. These goals are somewhat hampered, because institutions still isolate deviant youths from normal society. Although many of these correctional centers were founded upon a belief that rehabilitation can best be accomplished in a custodial setting, correctional workers are now questioning whether deprivation of freedom and removal from the larger society does not actually create a false environment for the resocialization of the juvenile offender. Such a unilateral strategy, they increasingly believe, may be at the foundation of the community's rejection of the juvenile deviant. A survey of training schools for the President's National Crime Commission in 1967 revealed that these institutions house a nonselective population and are operated in a manner which makes their theoretical ability to change adolescent behavior marginal. Nevertheless, the study disclosed that the other purposes of the typical training facility are being met.

The development of new treatment programs has been stimulated by the increasing delinquency rate. Community-based treatment services with their various methods of handling juveniles in a community setting instead of committing them to institutions have achieved new status. Massachusetts and some other states have taken rather dramatic steps to close down juvenile institutions and replace them with group homes.[44] Group treatment methods which offer many of the values of a one-to-one counseling relationship at a lower cost for more persons have been extended. In the attempt to diversify treatment alternatives, small camp programs, halfway houses, treatment centers, reception and screening units, short-term treatment programs, and vocational training centers have received new support.[45] However, much still needs to be done to improve law enforcement, the juvenile court system, and the field of treatment in order to lessen the social problem of delinquency.

Recommendations of the National Advisory Commission ● The 1973 Report of the National Advisory Commission on Criminal Justice Standards and Goals contended that "the highest attention must be given to preventing juvenile delinquency, to minimizing the involvement of young offenders in the juvenile and criminal justice system, and to reintegrating delinquents and young offenders into the community."[46] It proposed, rather optimistically, that such action should lead to a 50 percent decrease in delinquency cases by 1983. The Commission proposed further that youth should be diverted from the normal channels of correctional institution recruitment and kept away from the concentration of delinquent offenders which institutionalization requires. Problematic youth should be diverted, if this may be done safely, to a youth services bureau for work assistance or counseling, a drug abuse program for treatment, or some other diversionary outlet which would allow public response to the event without the application of the label of "delinquent."

Further, the Commission strongly suggested that the present system of juvenile justice is an inadequate method for handling adolescent offenses. Recognizing that 510,000 delinquency cases were disposed of through the juvenile courts in 1960 and 1,125,000 in 1970, it questioned whether the present system effectively controls juvenile violations. While the Commission supported the idea of special treatment for juveniles, it concluded that the juvenile courts, as presently conceived and operated, do not provide adequate, fair, or equitable treatment to juveniles. The jurisdiction of juvenile courts must be narrowed, the courts themselves must be integrated, and relationships between the courts and service agencies must be strengthened. Reforms must be undertaken in intake proceedings, detention of juveniles, disposition of youth, and transfer of youth to the adult system. The Comission recommended that youths should be detained no longer than 24 hours while a family (or juvenile) court awaits its intake unit's evaluation of thier care; be transferred to an adult court for prosecution only if they are above a designated age, have had a full and fair hearing, and such action is in the best interest of the public; and have all the rights of an adult criminal defendant, excepting trial by jury, during adjudicatory hearings to evaluate guilt or innocence. In accord with the *McKeiver v. Pennsylvania* decision,[47] the State, as a matter of policy, should provide nonjury trials for juveniles.[48]

References

1. Stephen *Schafer and Richard D. Knudten,* Juvenile Delinquency: An Introduction (New York, 1970), pp. xiii-xvii. ,
2. United Nations Department of Economic and Social Affairs, *New Forms of Juvenile Delinquency: Their Origin, Prevention and Treatment* (New York, 1960), p. 64.
3. Austin L. Porterfield, *Youth in Trouble* (Austin, Tex., 1946).
4. James F. Short, Jr. and Ivan F. Nye, "Extent of Unrecorded Juvenile Delinquency: Tentative Conclusion," *Journal of Criminal Law, Criminology and Police Science,* 29 (Nov.-Dec., 1958), pp. 296-302.
5. Robert H. Hardt and George E. Bodine, *Development of Self Report Instruments in Delinquency Research* (Syracuse, 1965), pp. 1-12.
6. Sophia M. Robison, *Juvenile Delinquency: Its Nature and Control* (New York, 1960), p. 7.
7. The idea that delinquency is a legal concept and not a clinical symptom leads to the conclusion that the term "predelinquent" should be eliminated. See J. V. Fornataro, "It's Time to Abolish the Notion of Pre-Delinquency," *The Canadian Journal of Corrections,* (April, 1965), VII, 189-192.
8. *New Forms of Juvenile Delinquency,* p. 62.
9. *The Challenge of Crime in a Free Society,* A Report by the President's Commission on Law Enforcement and Administration of Justice (Washington, D.C., February 1967), p. 55.
10. Jack D. Douglas, *Youth in Turmoil,* NIMH, Crime and Delinquency Issues: A Monograph Series (Chevy Chase, Maryland, 1970), pp. 2-3.
11. *New Forms of Juvenile Delinquency,* p. 33-35.
12. Task Force Report: *Juvenile Delinquency and Youth Crime,* The President's commission on Law Enforcement and Administration of Justice (Washington, D.C., 1967), pp. 41-56.
13. See Schafer and Knudten, *Juvenile Delinquency,* pp. 349-350.
14. *Ibid.,* pp. 128-155; As suggested readings see Frederic M. Thraser, *The Gang* (Chicago, 1927); Albert K. Cohen, *Delinquent Boys: The Culture of the Gang* (New York, 1955); William C. Kvaraceus and Walter B. Miller, *Delinquent Behavior, Culture and the Individual* (Washington, D.C., 1959); Walter B. Miller, "Lower Class Culture as a Generating Milieu of Gang Delinquency," *Journal of Social Issues,*[14] (1958); Richard A. Cloward and Lloyd E. Ohlin, *Delinquency and Opportunity: A Theory of Delinquent Gangs* (New York, 1960); David J. Bordua, "Delinquent Subcultures: Sociological Interpretations of Gang Delinquency," *The Annals of the American Academy of Political and Social Science,* 338 (Nov., 1961) 120-136; James F. Short, Jr. and Fred L. Strodtback, *Group Process and Gang Delinquency* (Chicago, 1965).
15. Thrasher, *The Gang.*
16. Cohen, *Delinquent Boys.*
17. Herbert A. Bloch and Arthur Niederhoffer, *The Gang: A Study in Adolescent Behavior* (New York, 1958).
18. Miller, *Delinquent Behavior.*
19. Cloward and Ohlin, *Delinquency and Opportunity.*
20. Schafer and Knudten, *Juvenile Delinquency,* pp. 138-139.
21. Simon Dinitz, Frank R. Scarpitti, and Walter, C. Reckless, "Delinquency Vulnerability:

A Cross Group and Longitudinal Analysis," *American Sociological Review,* (Aug., 1962), XXVII, 515-517.

22. Richard D. Knudten, *Crime in a Complex Society* (Homewood, Ill., Dorsey Press, 1970).

23. Edwin H. Sutherland and Donald R. Cressey, *Principles of Criminology* (6th ed.), (New York, 1960), p. 172.

24. Sheldon and Eleanor Glueck, *Unraveling Juvenile Delinquency* (New York, 1950), pp. 281-282.

25. Hans von Hentig, *The Criminal and His Victim: Studies in the Socio-biology of Crime* (New Haven, 1948), p. 259.

26. C. C. Van Vechten, "The Criminality of the Foreign-Born," *Journal of Criminal Law, Criminology and Police Science,* (July-Aug., 1941), XXXII, 139-147.

27. Walter C. Reckless, *The Crime Problem* (3rd ed)., (New York, 1961), pp. 53-54.

28. Gabriel Tarde, *La Criminalite Comparee* (Paris, 1886).

29. Sophonisba P. Breckenridge and Edith Abbott, *The Delinquent Child and the Home* (New York, 1912).

30. Bernard Lander, *Towards an Understanding of Juvenile Delinquency* (New York, 1954).

31. Clifford R. Shaw and Henry D. McKay, "Social Factors in Juvenile Delinquency," *Report on the Causes of Crime,* II (Washington, D.C., 1931); *Juvenile Delinquency and Urban Areas* (Chicago, 1942).

32. Walter E. Schafer and Kenneth Polk, "Delinquency and the Schools," *Task Force Report: Juvenile Delinquency and Youth Crime,* pp. 222-277.

33. Stanley Brodsky and Richard D. Knudten, *Strategies for Delinquency Prevention in the Schools* (Tuscaloosa, Alabama: The University of Alabama, 1973).

34. Emile Durkheim, *The Elementary Forms of the Religious Life* (New York, 1947), p. 47.

35. Paul W. Tappan, *Juvenile Delinquency,* (New York, 1949), p. 514.

36. Leonard Broom and Philip Selznick, *Sociology* (3rd ed), (New York, 1963), p. 397.

37. Richard D. Knudten and Mary S. Knudten, "Juvenile Delinquency, Crime and Religion," *Review of Religious Research,* Vol. 2 (Spring, 1971), pp. 130-152.

38. Enrico Ferri, "Les microbes du monde criminel et L'art populaire," *Les Criminels dans l'art et la litterature,* trans. Eugene Laurent (2nd ed), (Paris, 1902).

39. Joseph Bensman and Bernard Rosenberg, *Mass, Class, and Bureaucracy* (Englewood Cliffs, N.J., 1963), p. 337.

40. Some of the better known studies on the influence of mass communication media on delinquency are Herbert Blumer and Philip M. Hauser, *Movies, Delinquency and Crime* (New York, 1933); Estes Kefauver, "Television and Juvenile Delinquency," *U.S. Senate Subcommittee Report* (Washington, D.C., 1956); Hilde T. Himmelweit, A. N. Oppenheim, and Pamela Vince, *Television and the Child* (London, 1958).

41. Schafer and Knudten, *Juvenile Delinquency,* pp. 271-273.

42. Home Office, *Report of the Committee on Children and Young Persons* (London, 1960), p. 22.

43. Herbert H. Lou, *Juvenile Courts in the United States* (Chapel Hill, N.C., 1927), p. 18.

44. Brodsky and Knudten, *Strategies.*

45. See *The Challenge of Crime in a Free Society,* and *Juvenile Delinquency and Youth Crime.*

46. National Advisory Commission on Criminal Justice Standards and Goals, *A National Strategy to Reduce Crime* (Washington, D.C.: U.S. Government Printing Office, 1973), pp. 23-24.

47. *McKeiver v. Pennsylvania,* 403 U.S. 528 (1971).

48. National Advisory Commission, *Crime,* pp. 108-111.

CHAPTER 10

Racial and Ethnic Problems

American racial and ethnic problems have been dominated by attitudes of prejudice and the heritage of English and Colonial law which supported slavery and dehumanized the black slave, putting him into a legal category similar to a chattel or some other economic element that could be bought or sold.[1] While the first blacks in the Colonies after 1619 were largely free men, the legalization of slavery in Virginia in 1661 encouraged their later victimization.[2] Only 300 blacks resided in that colony in 1650; but by 1756, after slavery had been made legitimate, their numbers reached nearly 120,000.[3] Once established, the growth of slavery led eventually to the enactment of slave codes designed to forestall slave voting and to reduce threats against slave owners.

Although the debate over slavery continued during the eighteenth and nineteenth centuries, even as the agricultural reason for slavery was losing validity and many midwestern and northern states outlawed its practice, the development of the cotton gin by Eli Whitney and the application of mass production techniques to the textile industry reversed this decline and once again stimulated the growth of the slave trade. The less than one million slaves in the United States in 1800 increased to nearly four million by 1869, becoming a factor in the conflict leading to the Civil War.[4] However, an estimated 500,000 additional free blacks in 1860 lived throughout the United States; nearly one half resided in the North.[5]

The Rise of Segregation • The system of segregation which eventually came to dominate the South did not emerge until the late 1800's.[6] Previous to that date, a degree of integration had been achieved during the post-Civil War period of reconstruction. However, as the segregationist movement in the last quarter of the nineteenth century came to fear the possible coalescence of black and poor white voting power in opposition to the dominant political and social elite, it moved to recapture legislative and judicial power. In the last decade of the nineteenth and first of the twentieth century, therefore, segregation became the norm in most of the South. The principles invoked in the *Plessey v. Ferguson* (1896) decision, which resulted from a case involving a black youth riding in a railroad car restricted to whites, were extended to include the maintenance of segregated facilities and hasten the emergence of dual segregated school systems. With the adoption of new legislation, segregationist goals hardened and blacks were restricted increasingly from sharing lunch counter, waiting room, toilet and other public facilities. The main thrust of the Plessey decision stood until May, 1954, when the U.S. Supreme Court ruled that the *de jure* (by law) segregation of public schools is an effective denial of the requirements of equality guaranteed by the American Constitution.[7]

Racial and Ethnic Population Trends ● In 1910, 2.6 million (27 percent) of the 9.8 million blacks in the United States lived in cities. By 1968, the percentages had increased to 15 million (69 percent) of a 21.5 million black population total. While some 800,000 blacks (9 percent) in 1910 lived outside the South, nearly ten million (45 percent) some 58 years later lived in the North or Northwest. During those decades, the size of the black population increased rapidly. Blacks migrated heavily from southern rural areas to large southern, northern, and western cities and to densely populated large metropolitan areas, which were soon identifiable as racially segregated neighborhoods. By 1970, 16,186,000 blacks as opposed to 112,445,000 whites lived in Standard Metropolitan Statistical Areas (SMSA's) with 12,941,000 blacks and 47,520,000 whites residing in central cities alone.[8] In 1966, blacks composed approximately 11 percent of the American population, up from ten percent in 1950. While they numbered over 23.4 million in 1972 as opposed to over 182.2 million whites, Spanish-speaking Americans totaled around three million. American Indians, Chinese-Americans, Japanese-Americans and Filipinos at the same time accounted for less than one percent of the total American population.

About 75 percent of the five million or more Jews within this country live in a dozen major metropolitan centers. Nearly one half reside in New York City.[9] About 75 percent of all blacks live in urban areas today as opposed to 25 percent in 1910. While the black migration to the cities from rural areas was stimulated by the many social changes introduced following the World Wars, the increased demand for new laborers, and the gradual decline of southern argicultural profitability, Jews have historically resided in cities. By 1969, the black population in the North and West alone totalled nearly 6 million persons. However, 52 percent of all blacks in 1972 still resided in the South.[10]

According to current projections, the black population, which numbered more than 22 million persons in 1969, will probably increase to as high as 33 million by the middle 1980's, an increase from 11 to 12 percent of the total population. Already, the black population has increased from 18,916,000 in 1960 to 22,698,000 in 1970, an increase of 3,782,000 persons. At the same time, the white population grew from 159,467,000 to 178,716,000 in the same ten year period, a change of 19,249,000 individuals. Given these mobility and growth trends, it is highly probable that somewhere between 75 and 85 percent of all blacks in the United States will live outside the traditional southern states by the 1980 period.[11] Existing black majorities in Washington, D.C., Gary, and Newark will then be joined by new black majorities in such cities as Cleveland, Detroit, Philadelphia, St. Louis, Baltimore, New Orleans, Richmond, Atlanta and Memphis.

The Economic Problem of Minority Group Members • Despite their urban concentration, blacks and other minority groups face major economic problems. While six out of every ten black families had incomes of less than $4,000 per year in 1961, six out of every ten white families received an amount over $4,000.[12] Blacks were paid an average of $1,000 less per year than whites for the same work. As automation and the increased mechanization of agriculture cause a decrease in the number of unskilled jobs, which blacks and other minority group members could occupy, their employment problem became even more acute. In 1971, the ratio of black and other racial group income to white income was .63 to 1.0. Median black and other race family income was $6,714 as opposed to $10,672 for whites. When headed by males, median family income was $8,067 for blacks and $11,143 for whites; when headed by females, it reached only $3,645 for blacks and $5,842 for whites in 1971.[13]

In 1968, one out of every three black youths was unemployed and about one half of all black families had annual incomes of less than $4,500 per year.[14] The median black family income in that year was approximately 60 percent of that received by whites. In 1971, 29.2 percent of all blacks earned less than $4,000 per year as opposed to 11.2 percent of whites. Those earning between $4,000 and $6,999 per year were 24.8 percent blacks and 15.8 percent whites.[15] The situation was little better for Chicanoes, Indians, or other minority groups. The black adult unemployment rate ran close to seven percent, while remaining approximately four percent for the total population. At the same time, between 25 and 30 percent of all black youth between 16 and 21 were unemployed.[16] By 1972, total unemployment by blacks and other non-whites reached ten percent and whites five percent. However, when adjusted for age and race, female unemployment among those 16 to 19 years was 38.5 percent for blacks and 14.2 percent for whites. For males in the same age group, it reached 29.7 percent for blacks and others and 14.2 percent for whites. Among those 20 years and older, the black female rate dropped to 8.8 percent and white female to 4.9 percent; the comparable male rates were 6.8 percent for blacks and 3.6 percent for whites.[17]

Prejudice and Inequality • The economic disparity of racial and ethnic groups in income and unemployment did not just happen by chance. For decades, attitudes and practices of prejudice and discrimination have continued to take their toll in status inequality. Prejudice, an attitude, opinion, or judgment about a person or group based upon inadequate information which could possibly change if a person knew more about the individual or group in question, has provided the foundation for discriminatory acts against those victimized. While generally conceived as a rigid attitude toward a person or group which may be based upon value differences or emotional attitudes,[18] prejudice often includes the fear that the object of the prejudice may destroy one's assets or harm one's person. Discrimination, however, refers to a denigrating act or practice against a person or group.

Prejudice includes historical, sociocultural, situational, personality, phenomenological, or stimulus-object dimensions. From an historical perspective, prejudice involves ethnic conflict and sociocultural differences which give birth to prejudicial attitudes. Situationally, it contains peculiar patterns characteristic of interaction, a situation, or a region. From a personality and psychodynamic standpoint, prejudice encompasses personal hostility and interaction which give birth to eventual conflict and prejudicial stress. From a phenomenological point of view, the problem of prejudice is one of an individual definition of world reality. From a highly specific stimulus-object approach, it refers to interactional patterns between individuals and groups that lead to dislike and hostility.[19]

Whatever the dimensions involved, Gunnar Myrdal recognized in his classic study of race relations in America that while American citizens are committed to individual liberty, freedom, and the concept of equality, prejudice, racism, segregation, and discrimination affect profoundly the body politic.[20] Because such practices tend to be dehumanizing and often crude, victims of prejudice and discrimination tend to oversocialize their children to community norm conformity and to cause them to develop stereotypes of the white world that may be detrimental of their future conduct.[21] But these are not their only individual and social costs.

Prejudice and the Authoritarian Personality • A pioneering study of the authoritarian personality by T. W. Adorno and his colleagues uncovered that persons scoring high in anti-Semitism tend not only to be rather rigid conformists but also to come from families that possess high anxiety patterns. Even though older people tend to be more authoritarian, the better educated are generally less so. Highly anti-Semitic persons tend to be socially isolated.[22] Other analysts have also found that prejudice, disproportionately common among lower class members, is also disproportionately related to downward social mobility.[23]

Although prejudice may functionally assist the prejudiced person to reduce anxiety and to free him from a sense of guilt, thereby protecting him from a potential psychotic breakdown, the prejudiced person's functional prejudice, if carried out to an extreme, may become so dysfunctional that it may encourage the onset of paranoia.[24] Typically, the reduction of prejudice is related to more accurate knowledge of the other group, status equality, cooperative dependency, goal commonality, and social support. However, greater contact in one area does not necessarily mean a complete transfer of prejudice reduction to another.[25] For example, even though segregation in the army was theoretically terminated by Presidential directive after World War II, the level of integration accomplished by the military's authoritarian power structure did not carry over to the same degree to civilian life.[26]

Popular myths and attitudes continue to feed the fires of prejudice. An in-depth study by William Brink and Louis Harris in 1966 disclosed that between 43 and 66 percent of the white American population interviewed, depending upon the question asked, believed that blacks either laugh a lot, smell different, have loose morals, or want to live off of a handout.[27] While popular attitudes continue to suggest that blacks and other selected minority members are intellectually inferior to whites, most reputable scientists examining the matter believe that those differences that do exist between the races are due to differential opportunities of both blacks and whites rather than to heredity. Such findings as that although the mental disqualification of white draftees by the Selective Service in 1965 was 14.7 as opposed to 59.6 for blacks,[28] 48 percent of the South Carolina males called failed as opposed to 5 percent of those called in Iowa seem to support strongly this conclusion.[29]

The Move Toward Greater Opportunities for Minorities ● These and other findings have given stimulus to efforts to enhance black and other minority group educational opportunities. The 1954 U.S. Supreme Court decision of *Brown v. Board of Education* reasoned, for example, that racially separate public schools are inherently inequal, all schools should be maintained at the same level of support and integrated, and *de jure* segregation of public schools is unacceptable.[30] In this decision the Court overturned the previous assumptions of *Plessey v. Ferguson* (1896) which gave birth to the "separate but equal" concept.

The enactment of the Civil Rights Act of 1964, however, marked the turning point in the legislative attempt to lessen and eliminate discrimination against racial minorities. Undercutting the legality of *de jure* (by law) and *de facto* (in practice) methods of segregation, the Act enjoined under threat of federal fund termination the desegregation of public accomodations, employing organizations, eating places, and other organizations or practices which had served to keep blacks and other minority members in a position of inferiority. As further laws and/or interpretations were extended in the next four years to guarantee greater minority group freedom in housing, voting, due process, employment, union membership, use of public facilities, and even marriage judgments, public resistance to many of these decisions heightened.[31] However, by withdrawing the legal supports of segregation and by enacting the Civil Rights Act of 1964 and the other ensuring legislation, blacks were given new political strength and voting power. By 1968, approximately 62 percent of the black voting age population of the South was registered to vote. By 1974, strong black political representation was evident, especially in the South.

Although the Supreme Court has moved to eliminate *de jure* segregation (segregation by law), it has not been fully able to completely disrupt *de facto* segregation (segregation in fact or practice). The move to break existing housing patterns which densely concentrate blacks in the central city areas of most metropolitan communities, for example, has been met with strong resistance by both blacks and whites. Cries that property values will decrease, community security will be threatened, and educational quality will decline have prompted whites to oppose the creation of low-income housing in suburban communities and the mass integration of urban areas. Even though nearly three quarters of the black urban residents within a sample studied by Angus Campbell and Howard Schuman preferred integration as a long-term national goal,[32] they too were hesitant to leave their friends and neighbors. The greater number of blacks even now are unable or unwilling to move to the more costly suburbs to live. When coupled with an unofficial federal policy of "benign neglect," the issues become even more acute. As ghetto housing has become increasingly overextended, frustrations and economic discontent have increased and the seeds of distrust have given birth to periodic riots and other forms of expressed conflict.

Riots and Violence ● Although riots have occurred periodically throughout the history of the United States, the ghetto riots in American cities during the 1960's provoked great concern and a series of inquiries into the reasons for their development. The Kerner Commission, one such presidential group, concluded that while riots are threats to community order, those actually rioting desire to participate within the normal economic system and to receive its material benefits. However, others disagree, maintaining that a riot action is more indicative of the alienation of the poor and not-so-poor blacks from this system rather than an expression of their interest in participating within it.[33] Despite these differences of interpretation, it is fairly clear that the high black arrest rate reflects the push of blacks to fulfill aspirations and the determined resistance of the police to maintain their traditional control of society. The subdued warfare engaged in by ghetto youth, other residents, and the police is a natural product of this conflict.[34] While some analysts find that rioting and violence do little to help the black cause, and their occurrence leads to voter pressure to cut off assistance to such communities,[35] the nationally publicized riots of Harlem in 1964 (112 stores), Watts in 1965 (600 stores) and Detroit in 1967 (about 2,700 stores) did force civil and political leaders to examine the sources of these problems and to take some ameliorative action.[36] Even the efforts of the Symbionese Liberation Army in 1974 to influence public opinion and support for improved welfare assistance plans resulted in a short-term food distribution plan.

Causes of Rioting and Violence ● The causes of riots and violence are many. They, as well as crime, vandalism, non-cooperation and other political protest forms, occur commonly when economic and social institutions do not provide a substantial part of the population with adequate life opportunities and when aspirations are acted out in unacceptable and illegitimate ways.[37] The increasing resort to urban civil disobedience merely indicates that the former accommodation between blacks and whites in the United States has given way to a new process of "collective marketing" concerning the rights and responsibilities of the various groups within their communities.

Looting represents an index of social change.[38] When individuals in structural positions are prevented from gaining access to legitimate and even to criminal and illegitimate channels, they may engage in violence as a means by which to attain achievement goals. Not only does an act of violence tie the participant symbolically to a revolutionary movement, but it also disrupts his previous life and commitment ties. Violence equalizes the relationships of all actors and enables the violent actor to gain access to previously restricted areas of life. Consequently, violence not only signals the existence of major social maladjustment, but it also serves as a catalyst for change.[39]

In the ghetto, violence is a reaction to conditions of poverty, unemployment, hopelessness and hunger. Blacks, unlike the earlier European immigrants to the United States, have been unable to escape poverty due to the general maturity of the American economy which demands a highly skilled rather than unskilled labor force, discrimination which permits black employment opportunities, the political naivete of the black population, the lack of savings necessary to move to new locations, and the difficulty of the predominantly rural black to succeed in the urban complex.[40] Even so, blacks on welfare have become increasingly hostile to the traditional welfare solutions to their problems and have moved to secure major changes in the total welfare system and an adequate income for their families.[41] If such changes are not effected and present policies are continued indefinitely, the probability of even larger disorders or violence by ghetto or central city dwellers is high.[42]

Black Power and the Electoral Process ● One early effort to overcome the dependency status traditionally relegated to blacks was founded upon a call for black power. When Stokeley Charmichael and Charles V. Hamilton urged blacks to close their ranks and to enter into partnership within the pluralistic society from a position of strength, they stimulated the imaginations of the younger blacks and frightened a large portion of the white population.[43] They encouraged each black to control his own destiny and to make the central decisions which affect his life.[44] In their call for black power, they sought to broaden the base of the protest movement and to take it beyond the simple goals of integrating schools, desegregating lunch counters, and securing jobs. White reaction to their proposal, however, was immediate and produced a temporary, if not longer, polarization of the races.[45]

Despite this reaction of whites, black power has been growing in recent years. The percentage of blacks participating in the electoral process, for example, increased sharply between the years of 1952 and 1960[46] and has continued to grow to the present day. In several cities and regions of the country, the black vote has now become a pivotal and decisive factor. Proportionately, more lower class blacks have become politically active than lower class whites.[47] While these trends continue, the mere exercise of black power will not solve all the problems which blacks face. Whether due to white racism,[48] interinstitutional conflicts,[49] the absence of male role models in matriarchal one-parent households, or an occupational structure which provides black women with greater opportunity than black men, blacks have only had limited success in bringing about major changes in housing, employment, and education patterns.[50] Black power can hardly be black power, for example, when 285 (2.6 percent) of the 10,997 policy-making positions in major Cook County (Chicago) institutions and 29 (8 percent) of the 364 Cook County elected posts have been occupied at one time by blacks. Even then, the actual power of blacks was only about one third as great as the percentage of posts they held.[51]

Housing and Minority Groups • Members of the black community have been forced to a great extent to reside in central city ghetto areas. Despite laws promoting integration, segregation in housing patterns remains due to the continuance of racial discrimination in subtle and even blatant forms, the limited availability of low-income housing, zoning restrictions that inflate building costs, governmental housing policies, tendencies of ethnic groups to remain within their own communities, and inflation, which makes downpayments more difficult to gather. While earlier incoming immigrant groups were able to enter a metropolitan settlement and disperse from there as their economic condition improved, the black population has never been able to disperse randomly throughout the suburbs and surrounding territories in the same manner. Therefore, black families have remained disproportionately in black neighborhoods. If they did move, they did so mostly by traveling to the edges of their old neighborhoods and by occupying vacant houses formerly housing whites who had moved to other locations.[52]

Although the restricted covenant, which limited housing choices for blacks and other minorities, was declared unenforceable in 1948 by the Supreme Court on the grounds of serious economic injustice and probable violation of an individual's civil rights, informal social and real estate practices still support its continuance. Even the 1968 Federal Fair Housing Act, which prohibits discrimination in the sale or rental of housing as a means of eliminating separate black and white housing markets, has not been fully able to overcome this practice. As with many programs designed to lessen discrimination and to foster greater freedom of living for the black population, enforcement of the law has been rather spotty. In many instances, the implementation of its provisions has aggravated rather than reduced the housing problems blacks have to face.

Although a study of white Kalamazoo residents disclosed about half of those surveyed were indifferent to mixed housing, 50 percent of those possessing less than a high school education were clearly hostile and only 31 percent neutral to mixed housing. Among professional and business persons, six percent were hostile and 75 percent neutral.[53] Some of this hostility was due to fear and hatred; another portion was due to fear of economic loss through a decline in property values.[54] But other elements have entered into the housing problem as well. In many instances, black ghetto families, which have economic potential to move to white suburbs, have been slow to accept this opportunity and have chosen to remain where they are.[55] In remaining, many have sought, however, to convert their ghetto from an isolated racial prison to an ethnic area of their choice.[56]

Education and Minority Group Problems ● For years, inner city schools have been notorious for their failure to provide their students with the same quality of education made available to students by suburban schools. For example, the percentage of youth above or below the average achievement of all 17 year olds on reading achievement in 1970 was 2.2 *above* for whites and 16.4 *below* for blacks.[57] Inner city schools have also been noted for their racial homogeneity and lack of population representativeness. Nearly 87 percent of all black first grade and 66 percent of all black twelfth grade public school students, for example, attended predominantly black schools in 1965. At the same time, close to 80 percent of white children in both grades attended predominantly white schools.[58] Efforts to close the distance between the two and to make them more reflective of the population have led to the gradual integration of the dual school system of the South, open enrollment, re-districting of school boundaries and the bussing of students to achieve racial balance within the schools. Most have been supported by the courts as a means by which blacks and whites may be brought into closer contact in order to overcome the traditional handicaps carried by black children as a result of their ghetto life and to make both parties more aware of each other's problems.[59] While desegregation of the school system has been widespread in the South, progress has been slower in northern cities.

The search for solutions to the problem of racial imbalance in the schools has led to the redefinition of school districts in order to achieve maximum racial balance, the building of new schools in locations outside the ghetto, the pairing of black and white schools bordering black housing areas, the replacement of general educational institutions with specialized ones, and the rearrangement of grade promotional and school feeder procedures to bring about greater racial balance.[60] Although some supporters of greater racial balance in education further propose the development of metropolitan educational parks to serve approximately 15,000 elementary, junior high and high school students, critics find this approach to be excessively costly, bureuacratic and insensitive to the significant role that a school system can and does play within its more localized community.

Although racial desegregation in the last decades has been opposed to a large extent by lower middle-class members, the upper middle class, until recently, has generally supported racial desegregation of schools in larger numbers. Seventy-four percent of the whites in a 1966 Gallup sample indicated their willingness to send their children to a school with a few black children. However, only 44 percent were willing to do so if half the children were black.[61] While lower-class black mothers in the study of a small city near New York were more ready to have their children bussed to predominantly white schools than were black middle-class parents,[62] the especially strong support of George C. Wallace as a 1972 Democratic presidential primary candidate and more recently in other elections suggests that white parents are unwilling to proceed in the same direction.

While the enactment of many of these educational programs was based upon the earlier findings that black children reach a higher level of achievement in predominantly white rather than in predominantly black schools,[63] a more recent controversial study of education by Christopher Jencks, *et al* suggests the need to modify this finding. While racial desegregation raises the test score of black elementary school children by a couple of points, the test score gap between blacks and whites continues even when they are in the same schools. Consequently, school reform, they conclude, is unlikely to have any significant effect upon the degree of inequality among adults. Bussing should be justified on political and moral grounds rather than in terms of the probability of higher achievement of minorities. If the goal of society is the integration of society, integrated schools, they maintain, are a necessary component of that goal.[64] Their conclusions are not shared, however, by a significant proportion of the public.[65] Even their methodology has been subject to extensive criticism.

Some steps taken to overcome the problems of isolation and inadequate educational opportunities in urban areas have not always been successful in bringing about desegregation. In many instances, they have actually encouraged its maintenance and even expansion. For example, segregation has become more pronounced as the number of private schools has increased, boundaries in the many school systems have been modified, black and white mobility patterns have changed, and the more than 25,000 school districts have expanded operations. As of 1972, the percentage of youth 20 or older finishing four years of high school was 43.7 for blacks and other races and 63.6 for whites. Of those 20 to 24, the percentage reached 67.9 and 84.9 percents respectively. Percentages of those completing four or more years of college was 6.9 for blacks and others and 12.6 for whites.[66]

Finding a Solution • The solution to the racial and ethnic relations problem in America ultimately depends upon the termination of segregationist trends in major central cities and the restructuring of central city ghettoes. Not only is greater metropolitan cooperation needed, but more realistic economic and educational programs must be inaugurated and supported within the ghetto. Shortcomings in present housing patterns, leading to segregation, must be overcome by the extension of public housing authority to the total metropolitan areas, the development of land banks and housing development corporations, the allocation of large amounts of state and federal aid to low-income families, and the enforcement of the provisions of the 1964 Civil Rights Act. As long as the unemployment rate of those normally in low-income groups remains high, the ability of blacks and other limited income persons to rise above their problems will remain rather low. A greater diversity of jobs must be created to employ the marginally employable.

Three basic policy choices regarding racial and ethnic problems appear to be possible alternatives. Under the *present policies choice,* the proportion of resources currently allocated to programs of assistance to the poor, unemployed, and disadvantaged would be continued, growing at a moderate but probably inadequate pace to meet the basic needs of the areas. If the *enrichment choice* is enacted, the effects of continued black segregation and deprivation in large city ghettoes must be lessened insofar as possible through increased spending in education, housing, employment, job training, and social services within the disadvantaged central city neighborhood. Steps also must be taken to raise the status and subsistence level of both whites and blacks within that area. If the *integration choice,* on the other hand, is decided upon, the movement toward two separate and unequal societies must be reversed, and strong incentives for the enlarged freedom of choice in employment, housing and schools must be created. Even then, however, the integration choice is not likely to result in full integration, but rather a degree of integration and some voluntary segregation of participants.[67]

References

1. Frank Tannenbaum, *Slave and Citizen* (New York: Knopf, 1947).
2. Thomas F. Pettigrew, "Race Relations," *Contemporary Social Problems,* eds. Robert K. Merton and Robert Nisbet (New York: Harcourt, Brace and Jovanovich, 1971), p. 141.
3. John Hope Franklin, *From Slavery to Freedom* (New York: Knopf, 1961), p. 72.
4. Bureau of the Census, *Negro Population—1790-1915* (Washington, D.C.: U.S. Government Printing Office, 1918), pp. 52-53.
5. *Ibid.,* p. 53.
6. C. Van Woodward, *The Strange Career of Jim Crow* (New York: Oxford University Press, 1966).
7. *Plessey v. Ferguson,* 163 U.S. 537 (1896).
8. Report of the National Advisory Commission on Civil Disorders, *The Formation of Racial Ghettoes* (Washington, D.C.: U.S. Government Printing Office, 1968), pp. 236-237; and Executive Office of the President, Office of Management and Budget, *Social Indicators, 1973* (Washington, D.C.: U.S. Government Printing Office, 1973), p. 258.
9. Fred Massarik, "Jewish Community," *Social Problems: Persistent Challenges,* eds.

Edward C. McDonagh and Jon E. Simpson (New York: Holt, Rinehart and Winston, 1969), p. 33.

10. U.S. Departments of Labor and Commerce, *The Social and Economic Status of Negroes in the United States, 1969* (Washington, D.C.: U.S. Government Printing Office, 1969), pp. 3-5, and U.S. Department of Commerce, *USA Statistics in Brief, 1973* (Washington, D.C.: U.S. Bureau of Census, 1974), p. 1.

11. Horace C. Hamilton, "The Negro Leaves the South," *Demography,* (1964), I, 294; and Executive Office, *Social Indicators,* p. 256.

12. St. Clair Drake, "The Social and Economic Status of the Negro in the United States," *Daedalus,* (Spring, 1967), XCVI, 776-785.

13. Paul M. Siegel, "On the Cost of Being a Negro," *Sociological Inquiry,* (Winter, 1965), XXXV, 41-57; and Executive Office, *Social Indicators,* pp. 175, 177.

14. Julius Jacobson, "Union Conservatism: A Barrier to Racial Equality," *The Negro and the American Labor Movement* (New York: Doubleday and Co., 1968).

15. U.S. Departments of Labor and Commerce, *Status of Negroes,* pp. 14-41; and Executive Office, *Social Indicators,* p. 180.

16. Pettigrew, *Social Problems,* p. 435.

17. Executive Office, *Social Indicators,* pp. 135, 137.

18. See Gordon Allport and D. M. Kramer, "Some Roots of Prejudice," *Journal of Psychology,* (July, 1946), XXII, 21-22; Robin Williams, Jr., *The Reduction of Intergroup Tensions* (New York: Social Sciences Research Council, 1947), pp. 37-38; and George E. Simpson and Milton J. Yinger, *Racial and Cultural Minorities* (New York: Harper and Row, 1965), pp. 9-11.

19. Gordon W. Allport, *The Nature of Prejudice* (Garden City: Doubleday and Co., 1958), pp. 202-211.

20. Gunnar Myrdal, *An American Dilemma* (New York: Harper and Row, 1944).

21. Robin M. Williams, Jr.; *Stranger Next Door* (Englewood Cliffs, N.J.: Prentice-Hall, 1964).

22. T. W. Adorno, Else Frenkel-Brunswick, D. J. Levinson and R. N. Sanford, *The Authoritarian Personality* (New York: Harper and Row, 1950).

23. See Seymour M. Lipset, "Democracy and Working-Class Authoritarianism," *American Sociological Review,* (August, 1959), XXIV, 487-489; and Bruno Bettelheim and Morris Janowitz, *Dynamics of Prejudice* (New York: Harper and Bros., 1950), pp. 57-60.

24. Robert W. Winslow, *Society in Transition* (New York: Free Press, 1970), p. 327.

25. Allport, *Prejudice,* pp. 250-267.

26. Charles C. Moskos, "Racial Integration in the Armed Forces," *American Journal of Sociology,* (September, 1966), XXXII, 145-148.

27 William Brink and Louis Harris, *Black and White: A Study of U.S. Racial Attitudes Today* (New York: Simon and Schuster, 1967), pp. 136-137.

28. Howard E. Freeman and Wyatt C. Jones, *Social Problems: Causes and Controls* (Chicago: Rand-McNally and Co., 1970), p. 157.

29. Daniel P. Moynihan, "Urban Conditions," *Social Problems: Persistent Challenges,* p. 10.

30. *Brown v. Board* of Education, 347 U.S. 483 (1954).

31. Leon Mayhew, *Law and Equality* (Cambridge: Harvard University Press, 1968).

32. Angus Campbell and Howard Schuman, "Racial Attitudes in Fifteen American Cities," *Supplementary Studies* (Washington, D.C.: U.S. Government Printing Office, 1968), pp. 4-6.

33. Robert Blauner, "Internal Colonialism and Chetto Revolt," *Social Problems,* (Spring, 1969), XVI, 393-408.

34. David Boesel, Richard Berk, W. Eugene Graves, Betty E. Eidson and Peter H. Rossi, "White Institutions and Black Rage," *Trans-Action,* (March, 1969), VI, 29-31.

35. Paul Feldman, "The Pathos of 'Black Power'," *Dissent,* (January-Feburary, 1967), XIV, 78-79.
36. E. L. Quarantelli and Russell R. Dynes, "Looting in Civil Disorders: An Index of Social Change," *American Behavioral Scientist* (March-April, 1968), II, 7-8.
37. Boesel, Berk, Graves, Eidson and Rossi, *Trans-Action,* pp. 24-29.
38. Quarantelli and Dynes, *Behavioral Scientist,* pp. 7-10.
39. Lewis A. Coser, "Some Social Functions of Violence," *Annals,* (March, 1966), CCCLXIV, 9-17.
40. Report of the National Advisory Commission on Civil Disorders, *Comparing the Immigrant and Negro Experience* (Washington, D.C.: U.S. Government Printing Office, 1968), pp. 278-282.
41. Boesel, Berk, Graves, Edison and Rossi, *Trans-Action,* pp. 25-27.
42. Moynihan, *Social Probelms,* p. 25.
43. Stokeley Charmichael and Charles V. Hamilton, *Black Power* (New York: Random House, 1967), pp. 43-45.
44. Charles E. Silverman, "The Deepening Crisis in Metropolis," *Journal of Intergroup Relations,* (Summer, 1965), IV, 120-123.
45. Freeman and Jones, *Social Problems,* p. 179.
46. Anthony M. Orum, "A Reappraisal of the Social and Political Participation of Negroes," *American Journal of Sociology,* (July, 1966), LXXII, 39-42.
47. *Ibid.,* pp. 34-46.
48. National Advisory Commission on Civil Disorders, *Report of the National Advisory Commission on Civil Disorders* (New York: Bantam Books, 1968).
49. See Daniel P. Moynihan, *The Negro Family: The Case for National Action* (Washington, D.C.: U.S. Government Printing Office, 1965); and Charles A. Valentine, *Culture and Poverty: Critique and Counter-Proposals* (Chicago: University of Chicago Press, 1968).
50. Harold M. Baron, "Black Powerlessness in Chicago," *Crisis in American Institutions,* eds. Jerome H. Skolnick and Elliot Currie (Boston: Little, Brown and Co., 1970), p. 74.
51. *Ibid.,* p. 81.
52. National Advisory Commission of Civil Disorders, *Civil Disorders,* pp. 240-243.
53. Chester L. Hunt, "Private Integrated Housing," *Social Problems,* (Spring, 1960), VII, 206-207.
54. St. Clair Drake, *Daedalus,* pp. 771-777.
55. Louis G. Watts, Howard E. Freeman, Helen M. Hughes, Robert Morris and Thomas Pettigrew, *The Middle-Income Negro Family Faces Urban Renewal* (Washington, D.C.: Department of Housing and Urban Development, 1965).
56. Pettigrew, "Race Relations," pp. 432-433.
57. Executive Office, *Social Indicators,* p. 103.
58. James S. Coleman, *Equality of Educational Opportunity* (Washington, D.C.: U.S. Government Printing Office, 1966), pp. 477-478.
59. William Sewell, "Review Symposium," *American Sociological Review,* (June, 1967), XXXII, 477-478.
60. Pettigrew, "Race Relations," *Social Problems,* p. 443.
61. Gallup Political Index, *Report No. 12* (May, 1966), p. 16.
62. Elmer Luchterhand and Leonard Weller, "Social Class and the Desegregation Movement: A Study of Parents; Decisions in a Negro Ghetto," *Social Problems,* (September, 1965), XII, 83-88.
63. Coleman, *Equality,,* pp. 1-8; and Thomas F. Pettigrew, "The Negro and Education: Problems and Proposals," *Race and the Social Sciences,* eds. Edwin Karz and Patricia Gurin (New York: Basic Books, 1969), pp. 49-112.
64. *The Milwaukee Journal* (September 24, 1972).

65. See Rudi Tretten, "Black Power and Education," *School and Society*, (November, 1968), XCVI, 428-430.
66. Executive Office, *Social Indicators*, pp. 100, 107.
67. Daniel P. Moynihan, *Social Problems: Persistent Challenges*, p. 24.

CHAPTER 11

The Population Question

Public concern for the costs of population increase has mounted in recent years as scientists have made the world more aware of the problems involved in excessive population growth. If the rate of increase evident between 1959 and 1970 were to continue unchecked into the future, and if the level of resource availability remained the same, no resources would be available to support the world population within 1,750 years.[1] Only if modern technology provides large supplies of substitute materials and if nations possessing an abundance of resources maintain close cooperation in the interim can such a dire forecast be countered.[2]

The Rate of Population Growth

Between the Neolithic Period and the Modern Period of the 1970's, world population increased from an estimated ten million in the early period to one billion in 1820, two billion in 1930, three billion in 1960, and 3.6 billion in 1970. Today the total is approaching four billion. If 1963 fertility levels continue, world population will reach 4.5 billion by 1980 and 7.5 billion by the year 2000.[3] While such large numbers may sound ominous, the impact of this rate of growth, about two percent a year, becomes more meaningful when thought of as *adding* two more persons each second, 200,000 more a day, over six million more a month, and about 74 million a year. Of course, each additional person pushes all those numbers a little higher.

The sharpest annual population growth rate has been 3.4 percent in Latin America, 2.4 percent in Asia, 2.1 percent in Africa, 1.2 percent in Europe, and 1.7 percent in North America. If the present rate of population growth continues unchecked, the world population will double every 37 years. If the annual growth rate in the United States is simply stabilized at 0.8 percent, the American population alone would reach 400 million persons by the year 2070.[4]

In 1970, 6.2 percent of the world's population lived in North America, 7.8 in South and Central America, 19.4 in Europe, 56.5 in Asia, 0.5 in Oceania and 9.5 in Africa.[5] A 1960 estimate placed two thirds of the total population on about seven percent of the available land mass[6] and/or in developing or poorly industrialized areas of the world.[7] By the year 2000, 60 percent of the world's population, some scholars estimate, will reside in Asia, 13 percent in Europe and the U.S.S.R., 10 percent in Latin America, 5 percent in North America (above Mexico), 11 percent in Africa, and 0.4 percent in Oceania.[8]

The Relationship of Birth, Death, and Migration Factors ● The actual rate of population growth is determined by a unique interplay of birth, death, and migration factors. However, laws governing the age of marriage, public attitudes towards the institution of marriage, economic conditions, social expectations concerning child maturation and training, prevailing standards of living, and trends in infant birth or mortality also influence the rate of population increase.[9] In the United States, the 15 million women in 1970 in the age range (20 to 29 years) of highest productivity are expected to increase to 22 million by 1990; the 43 million women between the ages of 15 and 44 (fecund or able to produce) should likewise grow to 70 million during the same period. Although the larger group of women may eventually produce more children simply because more women are in the group than ever before, its actual birth rate can remain stable, increase, or even decrease, depending upon the social circumstances. Whatever the rate, however, its impact is extensive. The number of children being born leads eventually to larger or smaller school age populations, numbers of persons in the labor force, and so on.[10] The size of birth and death rates today determines the size of the labor force in 1995.

An excessive population increase may cause a decline in the standard of living, a greater acceptance of totalitarianism, an undermining of the economic support system, and an imbalance within the labor force.[11] High illiteracy rates, an increasingly unskilled labor force, and a general social unwillingness to use new methods to solve the problems at hand are also likely to occur.[12]

Decline in the Death Rate ● The dramatic drop in the crude death rate from 40 to 45 per 1,000 population in the seventeenth and eighteenth centuries to between ten and 15 per 1,000 in recent decades has been due to the widespread usage of immunization, antibiotics, and wonder drugs, a major emphasis upon personal hygiene, an increase in economic productivity, and rises in the general standard of living.[13] Mortality rates of 15 or lower are now found in most European countries, the United States, Japan, the Soviet Union and Oceania, but the crude death rates still range between 25 to 30 per 1,000 in Africa and many other underdeveloped countries.[14] In the United States, the life span by the year 2000 will probably by 69 to 74 years for males and 75 to 79 years for females.[15]

Migration as a Factor ● In some countries, the population question has been exacerbated by immigration from other nations. In colonial America, immigrants, coming primarily from England, Scotland, and Northern Ireland, freely entered the country until 1830. As their arrival in larger numbers began to cause problems, local and state political units began to enact legislation designed to restrict the entrance of criminals, paupers, undesirables, and other socially dependent people into the country. The Federal government entered into this field in 1882, although it was not until 1917, when the incoming population composition shifted from northern and northwestern Europe to southern and eastern Europe, that it legislated a literacy entrance test. In 1921 Congress enacted a national origins quota system, revised in 1924, which permitted the entrance into the United States of only two percent of what an ethnic population in this country had been in 1890. Not until 1965, when priority was given to the reuniting of families, the entrance of skilled workers, and an annual immigration of 170,000 persons from nations outside and 120,000 from nations within the Western Hemisphere, was the basic quota system revised.

However, before restrictions cut off the flow of immigrants, population movement was a major source of population growth in the United States. Between 1815 and 1914, 35 million people immigrated from all over the world to the United States. These incoming populations tended to come in waves. The Celtic Wave (1830-1860), so called because of the preponderance of immigrants from Ireland, also included many from the Highlands of Scotland, the mountains of Wales, the upper Rhine Valley, Belgium, Holland, and Norway. The Teutonic Wave (1860-1890) included immigrants from England, Saxons and Prussians from Germany, Austrians, Danes, Swedes, and Norwegians. The Mediterranean-Slavic Wave (1890-1914) included immigrants from Italy, Greece and other countries of the Balkan Peninsula, as well as Finland, Latvia, Lithuania, Poland, Austria-Hungary, Russia, and others.

It is estimated that between 250,000 and 500,000 Chinese entered the United States between 1850 and 1882 when the Chinese Exclusion Act was enacted. Many of these returned to China, however, and approximately 100,000 descendants of these immigrants remain. Most Japanese immigrants, some 200,000, came after 1880.

Another major source of population growth was created by forced immigration, namely the estimated 400,000 Africans who were brought to the United States as slaves before 1808 when the slave trade was officially abolished. Estimates vary widely on how many more were smuggled in between 1808 and 1860. By 1970, the black population constituted 11 percent of the total in the United States.[16]

Although some analysts propose to solve the population problem through a planned program of migration to underdeveloped areas, it is highly questionable whether the mere movement of people from one hemisphere to another offers a true solution due to the vast differences in cultural conditions, the tendency of remaining populations to fill the void, and the greater likelihood of the younger and better educated to migrate and the older and less vital to remain at home.[17] For migration to have any major impact, the total annual volume of migration would have to equal that which occurred worldwide between 1846 and 1932.[18] In only a few instances, most notably in Ireland during the potato famine, has intercontinental migration proved to be a useful means of solving problems related to population size.[19]

In the United States at the present time, most migration tends to be internal rather than international. Population mobility in recent decades has been from rural, especially rural-farm, to metropolitan and other urban areas of the country, from low-income to high-income areas, from the northeast by middle- and upper-income persons, to the south and southwest where the climate is warmer, to the Pacific coast, and from core metropolitan communities to suburban areas. Despite these patterns, the black population has been increasingly concentrated in deteriorated ghetto districts of large metropolitan cities.[20] Overall, the population which lived to a great extent on farms (75%) in the 1880's resided primarily in other places, including cities (95%), by 1970. In the 52 years after 1917, the farm population dropped from 32 million to less than 11 million.[21]

Although the United States has successfully met the challenge of migration to urban areas, Latin American countries have not been as lucky. While the birth rate in those countries has been increasing even as the death rate has been declining, the sharp increase in Latin American urban migration has caused major problems in employment, housing, and education.[22] These urban pressures would be even greater if three Latin American abortions did not occur for every five live births.[23]

Population Growth in the United States

The Birth Rate in the United States ● The annual American birth rate has ranged from 55 or more per 1,000 inhabitants during colonial days to 30.1 in 1910, 18.4 during the Depression, 26.6 shortly after World War II, 19.4 in 1965, and 15.6 in 1972.[24] As encouragement has been given to abstinence, later marriage, legalization of abortion and to coitus interruptus, nonvaginal coitus, intercourse only during safe periods, and the utilization of various contraceptive devices or aids,[25] the birth rate has varied widely.[26] Non-white fertility in the United States has been generally higher than white because the non-Caucasian population places less emphasis on the limitation of fertility, is less likely to use contraceptives before it is too late, is less inclined to employ the most effective contraceptive methods when they are used, and is more likely to be less consistent in contraceptive usage.[27]

The Death Rate in the United States ● As explained earlier, population growth is not contingent only on the birth rate, but depends as well on the death rate. Modern understanding of sanitation and disease control and the development of many new drugs has led to a decrease in the death rate over a period of years. While the death rate in 1910 was 14.7 per 1,000 persons, it dropped to 10.8 by 1940 and to a low of 9.2 in 1954. Between 1950 and the present, the rate has ranged between 9.2 and 9.7, reflecting the fact that no dramatic breakthroughs in medical care have been achieved during this period.[28]

Because of the fact that the death rate has gradually declined and for a considerable period remained fairly stable, the rate of population growth in the United States is primarily affected by the birth rate at the present time. Declining from a high of 1.8 percent in 1947, the rate of population growth in 1972 was 0.8 percent.[29] This is the rate at which zero population growth occurs. Whether such a rate will continue in the future depends on many factors. Public attitudes and social expectations regarding population growth are particularly important in this regard.

Problems in Reducing the Population Growth Rate

The high population growth rate in underdeveloped countries is due to a decline in mortality and a failure to decrease fertility. When a declining death rate is combined with economic stagnation, the number of poor within a country, as in Ceylon, is likely to increase sharply. If unrestricted population growth is permitted to continue unchecked, democratic values may be undermined and totalitarian values reinforced.[30]

Although the movement from an agrarian-based to an industrial economic system has usually been accompanied by the lowering of mortality and fertility rates,[31] it is not automatic and does not usually occur without the rise of social and economic tensions. As a result, Western countries, which have already developed supportive technology and cultural patterns, are likely to have greater per capita income, higher nutritional food consumption per capita, greater agricultural productivity, and lower fertility rates than nations only now seeking to break free of their agrarian past.[32] The increase in life expectancy in industrialized countries is due partially to their successful exploitation of raw materials, expansion of commerce, application of mass technology to agriculture, and ability to control disease better.[33]

Somewhere between 12 to 20 percent of the national income must be reinvested each year in order to secure an increasingly higher standard of living for a population growing at a rate of 3 percent per year. In Latin America, where the problem is especially acute, more than 50 percent of its annual economic productivity goes merely to maintain the existing and increasing population without any real economic expansion and with a strictly limited increase in per capita income.[34] As a general rule, each newborn child decreases the resource allocation alternatives available to the family as well as the state.[35]

Ironically, those nations most needing fertility (the desire to reproduce) control are often least likely to accept programs designed to limit the number of live births. Their unwillingness to modify values which tend to support large families and their desire to have the necessary labor force available for economic expansion tends to support a high birth rate. In many of these countries, Islamic and Roman Catholic belief systems support maximum fertility and negate attempts to lessen population growth.[36]

While the lowering of a nation's fertility rate is likely to accelerate the growth of income, encourage the creation of new jobs, stimulate the expansion of universal education, and cause female withdrawal from a wide range of tasks associated with pregnancy and infant care,[37] none of these may occur if cultural and religious values support the continuance of high birth rates.

Attempts to Explain Population Patterns

Malthus and Population Questions ● According to the theory of Thomas Malthus, population size is limited by an interplay of the means of subsistence and of such positive or preventive checks as moral restraint, vice, or misery.[38] Because human population tends to increase faster than the availability of the food supply required to sustain it, some form of conflict, including such positive checks as war, infanticide, famine, plague, vice, or misery, is inevitable. Population increase can be lessened, Malthus believed, by the enactment of preventive checks which take the form of deferrment of marriage, postponement of reproduction, abstinence, or even dependency upon moral restraint.[39] Population growth, he argued, grows in a geometric ratio (2, 4, 8, 16) which doubles nearly every 25 years. At the same time, the food supply increases only in an arithmetic (1, 2, 3, 4, 5) progression. The population, therefore, cannot help but outrun the food supply.

Although Malthus opened the discussion of theoretical principles underlying population issues, he oversimplified the relationship of food supply and birth rate and failed to take the infinite variety of social and economic conditions into account.[40] Even though he was largely supported by Michael T. Sadler, Thomas Doubleday questioned Malthus' assumptions and postulated that population decrease (rather than increase) is inversely related to food supply and directly related to a state of affluence.[41] Karl Marx, however, saw the problem in other terms. Population increase, Marx proposed, is not a product of food supply, but rather a consequence of economic and technical dislocations caused by a capitalism which requires a surplus population.[42]

Other Explanations of Population Growth and Decline ● Population development, according to some analysts, passes through three or more historical stages. Both birth and death rates are high during *Stage One*. In *State Two,* death rates fall sharply while the birth rate remains largely the same. At *Stage Three,* the final stage, birth rates decline dramatically and population growth rates either slowly increase or decline.[43] According to a second formulation, however, population passes through four developmental stages. In the *first,* birth and death rates remain high and population growth occurs rather slowly. During the *second,* the death rate falls sharply and the birth rate remains rather high, causing the population to increase rapidly. As the *third* stage is reached, the birth rate falls sharply and population increase slows. Only in the *fourth* stage do birth and death rates begin to stabilize at a lower rate and does population increase occur only as new ideas, developments, or food sources make it possible.[44]

Despite these explanations of how population expands or declines, each nation or region of the world responds differently to the problem of population. The relationships of birth and death rates vary from country to country and region to region. In *Type One* population areas, largely in Central Africa, high birth rates and high death rates are common. In *Type Two* regions, Northern Africa and most of Asia (except Japan), high but declining birth rates and rather high death rates are evident. In *Type Three* territories, including Southern Africa and Latin America, high birth and fairly low death rates are reported. In *Type Four* districts, including Chile, Argentina, Brazil, Uruguay, Japan, and the Balkan Peninsula, declining birth and fairly low death rates are dominant. In the *Type Five* populations, found especially in most of Europe, the Soviet Union, most of North America, New Zealand and Australia, low or fluctuating birth rates and low death rates are common.[45]

Movements to Control Population Trends

Population Control Movements ● Because of the fear of what might occur if population size should exceed the resources, the Planned Parenthood Association, the Population Reference Bureau, the Federal government and other interested organizations or agencies have moved in recent years to support birth control and family planning efforts. The United Nations Children's Fund (UNICEF) and the World Health Organization (WHO) have encouraged international family planning programs. Even the Roman Catholic Church, which opposes abortion as a denial of the rights of the unborn to life, encourages a degree of population control through sexual abstinence or through the use of a rhythm-type method while still refusing officially to support artificial means of contraception. However, its members have even gone further. As early as 1959, 30 percent of the Roman Catholics surveyed and nearly one half of those married 10 years or more indicated that they use artificial means of contraception.[46] In recent years, the support of birth control by Roman Catholic laymen and women has become even more pronounced despite the reaffirmation by Pope Paul of the traditional Catholic prohibition against artificial birth control techniques.[47] Nearly 60 percent of the Roman Catholics questioned in a recent study disagreed openly with their church's position on contraception.[48] Such attitudes appear to be world-wide. Only in Ireland and possibly in Spain has the Church's position against artificial contraceptive means received constant support.[49]

Zero Population Growth • The movement to achieve zero population growth (ZPG) has gained strength in recent years, especially as the American public has become aware of the impending fuel crisis. Based on a premise that an excessive expansion of the population is detrimental to the standard of living, the movement encourages the replacement of parents by the birth of only two children per couple. While this goal has received increasing acceptance, already affecting the actual United States birth rate, too quick a movement from earlier birth rate patterns to new lower ones will probably cause major dislocations in a variety of social and economic areas, including the labor supply, housing starts, educational system planning and economic expansion. The drop in the birth rate in the United States, for example, has already led to a revision of the earlier projection that college enrollment would increase by 4 million between 1970 and 1980 and continue at even a higher level into the future.

Efforts to Restrict Population Growth • As the concern for excessive population growth has intensified internationally, many developed and under-developed nations have adopted official population policies in an effort to retard population growth. India, one of the first to adopt such a policy, moved quickly in the 1950's to establish family planning and birth control clinics throughout the country. Pakistan recruited village midwives to provide contraceptive information to women of child-bearing age. Taiwan, Korea, Japan, the United Arab Republic, Tunisia, Morocco, Turkey, Kenya, Algeria, and many other underdeveloped countries made significant moves to encourage population control. The United States government began to provide its welfare recipients with family planning information.[50]

Abortion • While abortion as a means of population control has been given legitimization in some countries, for instance, Japan, where there are more abortions than live births, it has not received such ready acceptance in the United States. Although estimates place the annual number of abortions in the United States at between 700,000 and 2,000,000, its use as a means of population control has met steadfast opposition from various private groups as well as the Roman Catholic Church. However, the 1973 decision of the United States Supreme Court, which held that decisions concerning abortion should be made privately by the woman and her doctor in consultation, especially during the first six month period of pregnancy, has to a great extent limited the effect of opposition of the Roman Catholic Church. Despite such moral and religious opposition, American doctors are now free to treat abortions as they would any other operation. Most Protestant churches, which disagree with the Roman Catholic position, support the recent Supreme Court decision.

In some countries, sterilization has received some support as a population control measure, although such laws have been used very sparingly and then usually in cases involving hereditary defectives, epileptics, deaf-mutes, blind persons, or others with real or presumed hereditary problems.[51] Although the

American public overwhelmingly supports female sterilization if a woman's health is in danger or if her physical or mental health require it,[52] its support for a general government sterilization program is not nearly as strong. Public interest in the voluntary sterilization of males through vasectomy has increased in the last decade, although recent publicity concerning its possible adverse effects has caused many men to proceed with greater caution.

Sterilization has not only been conceived as a means of population control, but also as a means of improving population quality. At the same time that the world-wide eugenics movement is encouraging the sterilization of the biologically unfit in order to raise the physical and mental quality of the population, it is working to promote the greater production of children by the most fit.[53] In Japan, the Eugenic Protection Law of 1948-1949 legalized sterilization, abortion, and contraception as means of regulating hereditary deficiencies and of protecting mothers against excessive childbearing.[54] In the United States, 26 states legally permitted eugenic sterilization in 1969.[55]

Solving the Population Problem

The solution of the population problem depends upon the ability of primarily rural or agrarian areas to acquire not only a capacity for modern technology, but also the values and institutions supportive of urban life which place greater emphasis upon mobility and less upon having children. This transition is not easily made and becomes even harder to accomplish when significant social institutions are opposed to such changes. In agrarian countries, traditions and attitudes die slowly. Those techonolgically strong countries that have succeeded in lowering their birth rates have had to negate the influence of many groups and institutions to reach that goal.

That various moral and religious groups have lost much influence in the debate concerning birth control and family planning in mass industrial societies is well documented. Even in countries where the Roman Church is especially strong, its power to determine the sexual practices of married couples is lessening. Consequently, despite such opposition, most countries are adopting some birth control and family planning programs as they become aware of the threat that excessive population poses. Couples themselves are also moving voluntarily to limit the number of their children, a decision based upon greater knowledge as to the costs and benefits of population control. A 1972 survey of 15,000 American wives disclosed that married women in the age categories of 18 to 24 expect to give birth to 2.3 children, a number close to the 2.11 figure necessary to produce zero population growth by the year 2042. Although more women than ever before are now within the childbearing age group, if this level of expectation continues, the birth rate will continue at its present low level.[56]

Any attempt to increase the death rate, which itself contradicts the international tendency to prolong life, is an unacceptable solution to the population problem. Therefore, if the population question is to be solved, it will have to be through a reduction in the number of live births. Ultimately, the success of any family planning effort depends heavily upon the willingness of each couple to accept its premises. If major institutions continue to encourage unrestricted birth patterns, the reduction in birth rate may only be achieved slowly. On the other hand, if a legal government adopts a national policy of population control, it may assist those in the reproductive categories to establish more quickly a more favorable reproduction pattern.[57]

References

1. Kingsley Davis, "The World's Population Crisis," *Contemporary Social Problems,* eds. Robert K. Merton and Robert Nisbet (New York: Harcourt, Brace and Jovanovich, 1971), p. 364.
2. Edward A. Ackerman, "Population, National Resources and Technology," *Annals,* (January, 1967), CCCLXIX, 84-97; and Joseph L. Fisher and Neil Potter, "Resources in the United States and the World," *The Population Dilemma,* ed. Philip M. Hauser (Englewood Cliffs, N.J.: Prentice-Hall, 1963), pp. 122-123.
3. *New York Times,* August 14, 1974.
4. Philip M. Hauser, "Demographic Dimensions of World Politics," *Science* Vol. 431 (1960), pp. 1641-1645.
5. *New York Times,* August 14, 1974.
6. Harold F. Dorn, "World Population Growth," *The Population Dilemma*, ed. Philip Hauser (Englewood Cliffs, N.J.: Prentice-Hall, 1970), p. 15.
7. Dudley Kirk, "Population Control in the Underdeveloped World," *Annals,* (January, 1967), CCCLXIX, 49-56.
8. William Petersen, *Population* (New York: Macmillan, 1961), pp. 500-501.
9. Edward G. Stockwell, *Population and People* (Chicago: Quadrangle Press, 1968), p. 19.
10. Donald Bogue, "Population Growth in the United States," *Social Problems: Persistent Challenges,* pp. 400-403.
11. Joseph J. Spengler, "Population and Economic Growth," *Population: The Vital Revolution,* pp. 66-67; and Richard A. Easterlin, "Effects of Population Growth on the Economic Development of Developing Countries," *Annals,* (January, 1967), CCCLXIX, 98-108.
12. Davis, "The World's Population Crisis," *Contemporary Social Problems,* p. 368.
13. Ralph Thomlinson, *Demographic Problems* (Belmont, Calif.: Dickenson Publishing Co., 1967), pp. 75-77.
14. Stockwell, *Population and People,* p. 37.
15. Mortimer Spiegelman, "Longevity and Mortality in the American Population," *Population: The Vital Revolution,* p. 108.
16. *The Milwaukee Journal,* December 24, 1972.
17. Harold F. Dorn, *The Population Dilemma,* p. 27.
18. Davis, *Contemporary Social Problems,* p. 396.
19. Dennis Wrong, *Population and Society* (New York: Random House, 1961), p. 99.
20. Bogue, *Persistent Challenges,* p. 405.
21. Davis, *Contemporary Social Problems,* p. 379.
22. Kingsley Davis, *Human Society* (New York: Macmillan, 1948), p. 380.
23. Edward C. McDonagh and Jon E. Simpson, *Social Problems: Persistent Challenges* (New York: Holt, Rinehart and Winston, 1969), p. 382.
24. *Social Indicators, 1973* (Washington, D.C., U.S. Government Printing Office, 1973), p. 250.

25. Bogue, *Persistent Challenges,* pp. 400-403.
26. Davis, *Contemporary Social Problems,* p. 401.
27. F. James Davis, *Social Problems* (New York: Free Press, 1970), p. 290.
28. *Social Indicators, 1973,* p. 250.
29. *Social Indicators, 1973,* p. 249.
30. Lincoln H. Day and Alice T. Day, *Too Many Americans* (Boston: Houghton-Mifflin, 1964), p. 246.
31. George J. Stolnitz, "Demographic Transition: From High to Low Birth Rates and Death Rates," *Population: The Vital Revolution,* ed. Ronald Freedman (New York: Anchor Books, 1964), pp. 29-30.
32. Wrong, *Population and Society,* p. 393.
33. Dorn, *The Population Dilemma,* pp. 8-9.
34. Davis, *Contemporary Social Problems,* pp. 371-372.
35. Davis, *Social Problems,* p. 289.
36. Irene B. Taeuber, "Population Growth in Underdeveloped Areas," *The Population Dilemma,* p. 43.
37. Ainsley J. Coale, "Population and Economic Development," *The Population Dilemma,* p. 69.
38. Thomas R. Malthus, *An Essay on Population* (New York: E. P. Dutton, 1914), I, 18-19.
39. Thomas R. Malthus, "A Summary View of the Principle of Population," *On Population: Three Essays* (New York: Mentor Books, 1960), pp. 13-59; and Warren S. Thompson and Davis T. Lewis, *Population Problems* (New York: McGraw-Hill, 1965), p. 18.
40. *Ibid.,* pp. 28-29.
41. *Ibid.,* pp. 39-40.
42. James M. Beshers, *Population Processes in Social Systems* (New York: Free Press, 1967), p. 164.
43. *Ibid.,* p. 12.
44. Julian Huxley, "World Population," *On Population: Three Essays* (New York: The New American Library of World Literature, Inc., 1960), p. 65.
45. Wrong, *Population and Society,* pp. 15-16.
46. Ronald Freedman, Pascal K. Whelpton and Arthur A. Campbell, *Family Planning, Sterility and Population Growth* (New York: McGraw-Hill, 1959), pp. 182-183.
47. The Population Council, "American Attitudes on Population Policy," *Studies in Family Planning—No. 9* (January, 1966), pp. 5-7.
48. Davis, *Contemporary Social Problems,* p. 392.
49. William Petersen, "The Population of the Earth," *Population: The Vital Revolution,* p. 261.
50. Kirk, *Annals,* pp. 54-60.
51. Paul H. Landis and Paul K. Hatt, *Population Problems* (New York: American Book Co., 1954), pp. 502-504.
52. Gallup Political Index, *Report No. 11* (April, 1966), pp. 14-15.
53. Davis, *Social Problems,* pp. 295-296.
54. Taeuber, *The Population Dilemma,* p. 222.
55. Michael Katz, "Legal Dimensions of Population Policy," *Planned Social Intervention,* eds. Louis A. Zurcher, Jr. and Charles M. Bonjean (San Francisco: Chandler Publishing Co., 1970), p. 201.
56. *Social Indicators, 1973* p. 254.
57. Davis, *Contemporary Social Problems,* p. 401.

CHAPTRER 12

Urban Problems

The Urban Revolution

The city is the locus of two modern day revolutions. The first is one brought about by the rise of an urban way of life. The second involves the outward explosion of existing urban centers.[1] As urban communities have grown in number and size, their problems have become more complex and obvious. Common urban issues include an inadequate tax base, an excessively high crime rate, real estate deterioration, the inability of metropolitan government to provide the same level of services that suburban communities offer their citizens, educational tensions, racial hatreds, a shrinking job market, a debate over the use and abuse of welfare, ecological pollution, substandard housing, and decreasing transportation services. Despite the seemingly endless scope of the urban problem, four basic issues underlie the organization and operation of American cities. Fewer tax dollars are being received by cities as large numbers of middle-income taxpayers depart from central city areas and business and property values decline; an increasing number of tax dollars are required to provide essential public services and facilities and to meet the welfare needs of expanded lower-income groups; each tax dollar buys less due to increasing costs; and citizen dissatisfaction with municipal services increases as need expectations and standards of living rise throughout the community.[2] A U.S. Senate committee looking into the problems of urban areas in 1969 concluded that no less than one trillion dollars would be necessary if city problems were to be attacked effectively.[3]

Historical and Geographic Trends

Although cities have existed for thousands of years, early cities were quite small by modern standards. The ancient city of Ur had a population of 20,000,

228

Babylon an estimated 85,000, Syracuse 150,000, Athens 150,000, Thebes 225,000, and Rome 1,000,000. The modern city contrasts sharply with its early predecessors. Greater Tokyo alone has a minimum population of 11,350,000, while New York claims more than 7,700,000, London about 7,750,000, Shanghai nearly 7,000,000, Moscow slightly less than 7,000,000 and Bombay above 5,525,000.[4] Whereas only seven cities of 500,000 or more existed in 1800, more than 200 are found in the world today.[5] In the years between 1920 and 1960, the world urban population in localities of 20,000 or more inhabitants grew from 253 million to 753 million, almost a 200 percent increase.[6] At the same time, the rural and small town population increased from 1,607 million in 1920 to 2,241 million in 1960, only a 40 percent increase.

American Cities • The number of American cities having populations in excess of 250,000 increased between 1950 and 1960 from 41 to 51 with another five added between 1960 and 1970.[7] Some 263 Standard Metropolitan Statistical Areas (SMSA) are now recognized in the United States. A SMSA is composed of a city of 50,000 inhabitants or more (the central city) or two or three cities with combined population of 50,000 or more together with the county or counties they are in, plus adjoining counties if their business and services are an expansion of the central city. SMSA's are considered more valid units to indicate urban trends because many cities are decreasing in size even as urban areas are growing. The Census Bureau found in 1970 that 73.5 percent of the American population lived in urban areas as compared to 69.9 percent in 1960, yet many central cities had declining populations.[8] More than 74.2 million people now live in the suburbs of big American cities.[9] By 1985, with an expected population of 178 million persons, 90 percent of all American citizens will be living in urban areas.[10] While 79 percent of the growth between 1960 and 1985 will occur in suburbs, only 10 percent of the overall increase will take place in central cities. If these projections are correct, the central city metropolitan population by 1985 will drop from 52 to 37 percent even as the suburban population increases from 48 to 63 percent. This means that suburban increases will triple while the total population increases by about 50 percent.[11] By 1985 the core area of New York City will have one third of the population and one half of the jobs, a drop from an earlier projection of one half the population and two thirds of the jobs.[12]

The Move From the Central City • During the pedestrian or horse-drawn era, a population of 200,000 was largely limited in mobility to four square miles. No longer is this true. The mass production and purchase of the automobile has extended citizen mobility up to 100 square miles or more and made the city population less dependent upon the services provided within their immediate community.[13] The extension of power lines, telephone cables and sewer and septic systems has made it possible for people to leave the metropolitan center and yet to receive these services usually associated with urban centers.[14] The

Federal Housing Authority (FHA) and other government agencies or programs have made it easier for low-income families to purchase homes in outlying areas with a limited or no down payment.[15] With the full development of the installment easy-purchase credit system, underwritten in part by the government, persons who normally would have remained in low-income areas in past decades have made their move to other sections of the city. As the leisure time available to the working man has increased, the rise of the Riviera syndrome has stimulated the development of recreational areas. Warmer climates and sandy beaches have drawn people like magnets. Even those unable to afford these more costly alternatives have turned to suburban areas to secure the good life with more open space and greater community security.

Not all urban dwellers have shared in this suburban movement to the same degree, however, The black population has not shared equally in the quest for the good life. In New York State, for example, less than five percent of the suburban inhabitants in 1968 were non-white.[16] Nation-wide, almost 55 percent of white urban residents live in suburbs, but barely 20 percent of black urban residents are found in suburban areas.[17] In Chicago, where the black population is expected to increase by more than one million by 1990, bringing the total to 2.5 million, growth will occur largely in the inner city.[18] Although these figures portend the development of the predominantly black city, its emergence is still far off. Because it would in itself be a form of metropolitan apartheid and probably result in a poorer city less able to provide needed public services, the development of an all black city is not only highly unlikely but is also socially undesirable.[19]

The Problem of Political Realignment ● Although the United States has successfully made the change from an agricultural to an industrial society, it has had difficulty coping with the urban revolution that has continued as a result of this change.[20] Central city congressional representation in Congress, if current trends persist, will decline from an estimated 31 percent in 1960 to 27 percent in 1985. The representation of suburban and outlying electorates will increase during the same period from 33 percent to 41 percent.[21] Within urban areas, a multiplicity of governmental units attempt to deal with the variety of issues which arise.

Cities commonly must deal with special problems of municipal wastes, inadequate funding, poor administration, political or public agency corruptions, and deficiencies. They also must face the challenge to urban social and political coherence which the development of separate suburban communities creates. In the Chicago metropolitan community, which is composed of about six counties, 114 townships, 50 municipalities, 327 school districts and 501 special purpose districts, problems of discontinuity and inefficient use of public services abound. The increased costs of fire and police protection, garbage disposal, parks and recreation programs, and sanitation and snow removal services have made the need for integration of services more obvious even while the economic and political foundation of the area is under attack.

The increasing costs of municipal services and the relatively few additional sources of income available to municipal governments have created havoc in urban areas. Costs have increased at a faster rate than the ability of the property tax to produce revenues. During the period in the 1930's when population was evenly divided between urban and rural communities, most tax revenues flowed to the cities. State and federal governments received proportionately less. By the 1960's, however, the trend was reversed. Whereas $4.3, $1.9 and $1.8 billion, respectively, went to city, state and federal governments in the 1930's, $21.0, $20.6 and $82.3 billion went to the same units in the 1960's.[22] As a consequence, local government debt increased after 1946 at a rate of 40 times faster than that of the national government.[23] Approximately 40 percent of the local government operating budget in the years 1947 to 1967 was expended on education. During that 20-year period, the per pupil day costs of public schools in the United States increased at a rate of 6.7 percent per year compounded, nearly doubling every ten years.[24]

Business and industrial shifts to the suburbs and outlying areas have been instrumental in creating even greater problems for the city. Their leaving has caused a decline in the tax base. Already faced with depreciating housing and the movement of the more affluent to suburban and outlying areas, the city has had to cut expenses or tax those remaining to make up for the loss of revenue. Unfortunately, the poor, who are heavily concentrated in the city rather than in the suburbs, are not able to carry the increased tax burden.[25] As taxes increase even while the tax base shrinks, those industries and businesses that do remain are tempted to relocate to other lower tax areas. Every increase in the real estate tax necessary to maintain the municipal budget becomes, in fact, a penalty placed upon the physical resources and property of the city.[26] When, as in Boston, a citizen who owns a house for 50 years has to pay five times its appraised worth in taxes during his period of ownership, the scope of the problem becomes quite clear. Given this situation, therefore, some municipalities have sought a solution by annexing newly developed surrounding communities and incorporating their tax incomes into the general city budget. But even this is not a permanent answer to the problem. Cities which annex nearby communities must ultimately assume responsibility for public services to its new citizens. In most instances, annexation merely allows the city to postpone the day when it will have to face up to its problems.

Although critics have argued that the flight of urbanites to the suburbs has had the effect of reducing the tax base, lessening the quality of leadership talent available, and providing a class of people who use city services and property without supporting their operations, they fail to consider the other side of the issue. If they had stayed, many would have demanded higher quality schools and services, which would have placed an even greater strain upon an inadequate budget. As for leadership, even now, many suburbanites are actually too involved in metropolitan affairs, making political, business, and policy decisions which effect the lives of ghetto and core city dwellers. Despite these qualifications, however, there is little doubt that many criticisms do ring true. Suburbanization does tend to increase racial and class polarization, restrict the mobility of the poor and non-whites to other residential areas, create financial problems for metropolitan communities, and establish a base of interests which often oppose efforts to assist the poor.[27]

Ability to handle the problems of the urban complex depends in the long run upon the cooperation of the city and its suburbs, probably upon even the eventual political realignment of these units and the willingness of the political community to attack the core city problems on a metropolitan-wide basis.[28] Many urban analysts believe that metropolitan area government provides a solution to the inefficiency of current government practices and the need to secure economies of scale. But securing this form of political approach to the problem is neither automatic nor easy. The bringing together of many political, municipal, or county units into a working group can be accomplished only if some political leaders are willing to resign their posts. Not all agree that moves in this direction are desirable. However, long-term urban change is unlikely to come about unless the artificial boundaries separating suburb from city are replaced with more realistic ecological-social units.

The mere enlargement of boundaries, whether through annexation or some other means, is not an automotic solution to the urban problems.[29] While legislative action may serve to lessen political fragmentation and to encourage the coordination and integration of police forces, fire departments, public health services and garbage disposal departments into one workable political entity, this may not be the only answer to the problem. Some analysts propose that neighborhood boards, which bring the community into greater contact with the city government, and regional governmental units designed to foster a higher degree of cooperative planning be developed.[30]

Economic Trends

A major impetus to urban growth is the continual evolution of the economy and the nature of occupations available. The increased rate, frequency, and penetration of economic and technological change has caused many critical personal and societal dislocations. The application of technology to agriculture has contributed to unemployment and the movement of the population to the cities. Between 1910 and 1954, farm output increased 77 percent and land use for crops increased by 15 percent. During the same period, farm labor man-hours decreased by 30 percent.[31] Although agricultural employment rose nearly ten percent between 1957 and 1965, employment in the largest industrial companies increased by 15 percent during the same period, and employment by government, excluding the military, rose by 25 percent. Between 1950 and 1972 the United States labor force, consisting of those persons who hold or make a specific effort to find a job during the four-week period preceeding their being surveyed by a representative of the Bureau of the Census, increased by about 25 million to 89 million persons. Blue collar employment, except for service workers who increased by almost three percent, actually declined during this peak period of labor force development.[32] While white collar employment increased sharply, the number of workers employed in many basic and collateral industries declined markedly. Between 1953 and 1960, the automobile industry eliminated 172,000 workers from its payrolls while still producing the same number of trucks and buses and 500,000 more passenger cars.[33] Even so, General Motors employed by the late 1960's more than 600,000 persons.[34] By 1970, factory workers accounted for about 20 percent of the non-farm labor force.[35] These trends in employment have an impact on urban areas in that decreases in industrial employment and increases in service occupations cause dislocation of the worker from available job opportunities. Other dislocations occur because of the changing composition of the labor force.

Women and Men in the Labor Force ● Even as these changes were occurring between 1900 and 1972, the percentage of women in the labor force more than doubled from 20 to over 40 percent. During the same period, the proportion of men employed declined slightly. Female employees now provide over 95 percent of all nursing staffs and approximately 70 percent of elementary and secondary school teaching personnel. Women are overly represented in clerical occupations, including bookkeepers, secretaries, cashiers; other service workers, including janitors, hairdressers, waiters, barbers, policewomen; and private household workers, including cooks, maids, and servants.[36] At the same time they are underrepresented in the census categories of managers, officials, and proprietors, including executives, retail tradesmen, government inspectors; craftsmen and foremen, including bankers, carpenters, machinists, and plumbers; and non-farm laborers including stevedores, fishermen, or lumbermen. Because the 1969 median income for primary and secondary school teachers, usually female, was $8,241 and for self-employed physicians, usually males, was $24,512,[37] women's liberation groups, including the National Organization for Women (NOW), are now lobbying not only for equal wages for equal work, but also for equal opportunity of access to higher paying occupations. Typically, women have earned less than men both because the jobs they occupy have lower incomes and because they are often paid less for the same work.

Blacks in the Labor Force ● Only about one fourth of the black labor force, as opposed to one half of the white, is employed in some white collar job. Blacks who have jobs are disproportionately concentrated in the blue collar occupations. While more black than white women, who tend to withdraw between the ages of 25 to 44 to raise their families, are likely to remain in the labor force, they have often had a higher rate of unemployment than black males. For the better educated blacks, however, the situation is not as bleak.

As black employability has increased, the trend toward the recruitment of blacks for better paying occupations has accelerated. Between 1960 and 1969 alone, the number of blacks in clerical jobs doubled and in health professions tripled.[38] Due to increased governmental requirements to hire minority group members and the lack of trained persons within the group, a qualified black may receive several thousand dollars more per year than his white counterpart. Those not as qualified, however, may remain unemployed or employed in marginal jobs. Because the largest proportion of blacks are still employed in lesser-paying jobs, there has been an *increase* in the gap between the median income of black and white families even though some blacks are employed in higher paying positions.[39]

Participation in the labor force varies markedly with age. The percentage of older persons in the labor force drops precipitously at age 65. Not only are most employees forced to retire at 65, but many do so voluntarily for health and other reasons. Once an older person is terminated from employment, he finds it increasingly difficult to find another job. Although nearly 70 percent of those over 65 were part of the United States labor force in 1900, only about 44 percent were in 1960. By 1972 the percentage dropped even lower, to 33.4[40]

Costs of the Urban Revolution

One part of the urban revolution is the rise of an urban way of life. More and more technological advancements of modern society have had a vast impact upon social organization and operations. In the field of agriculture, technology has fostered the development of new farm machinery, fertilizers, insecticides, better crops, and new livestock strains. Correspondingly, it has also stimulated an increase in productivity which has forced a decrease in the number of farm-employed from a level of 4.9 million in 1963 to four million by 1975. The development of the electronic computer, originally created for warfare but now applied to domestic and business problems, has had similar effects in old-type job shrinkage and new-type job creation. As other advances have occurred in the fields of instrumentation and automatic control, of communication technology, of transportation systems, and of power production, the modern day unskilled worker, a major component of the urban population, has become increasingly uncompetitive.[41] The impact of this trend on urban areas has been vast.

Technology and the Worker • In the early development of technology, man remained at the center of all activity. However, as technological development proceeded from the first stage of mechanization to the second of mass production and finally to the third of automation, the need for workers to do many of the tasks assumed by machines lessened.[42] With the advent of automation, man lost much of his centrality in the economic process and now serves more as a supervisor than a laborer.[43] As automation has required the conversion of industrial material into a flow, the setting of uniform standards so that output can be treated in such a manner, the use of electronic computers with built-in feedbacks which permit the exercise of automatic control, and the application of new energy sources to the total process, the need for manpower, especially unskilled, has decreased.

Part of the economic problem involves the nature and character of the labor force in relation to changes brought about by technological advances and automation. The modern nonprofessional skilled and unskilled labor force is largely distributed over craft, assembly line, or continuous process work units. The *craft worker* occupies a predominantly skilled position. By working on a more individualized basis, he dominates the technical system and determines the work pace and the quality and quantity of output. Able to identify with his product, he receives a strong sense of self-fulfillment. Typically, he works in small shops rather than large plants. The *assembly line worker,* who passes along a project through a plant by way of a conveyor belt at a predetermined rate of speed, participates in an extreme division of labor. His work methods are predetermined; his work speed is constant. Requiring little training or skill, the average assembly worker completes only a few operations in the product creation process. His only relief from the pressures of the conveyor belt comes when he is relieved, stops to eat, or ends his shift. Because he completes a productive but rather meaningless job, he is likely to become highly alienated. The *continuous process worker,* characteristically found in the oil and chemical industries, completes the designated tasks in relationship to the flow of product he deals with. He usually monitors control consoles or gauges and makes necessary adjustments. Even though he does not touch the final product, he maintains responsibility for its eventual output. In this technological form, he controls the speed of development and the quality of the product. When a breakdown occurs, he is responsible for re-establishing the process.[44]

Automation and the Labor Force • Automation has brought about many changes. In some instances, automation has reduced the worker to a mere functionary doing a monotonous task. In others, it has necessitated the giving of great responsibility to the worker. Automation frequently replaces physical fatigue with mental tension and forces the worker to make adjustments to new methods and operations. Because the four fundamental principles of mechanization, continuous process, automatic control, and rationalization characterize the process of automation, the worker has to learn to function within the context of these characteristics. Most important is rationalization, which requires that the worker be able to use reason, a product of education, to solve involved problems.[45]

The acceptance of automation has resulted in a decline in the importance of manual skills, an increase in employee responsibility, a lessening of the requirement of physical strength for certain jobs, a demand for a cleaner work environment, an enlargement of jobs, and an encouragement of worker idea cross-fertilization.[46] Automation has blurred the distinction between physical and mental work and threatens the employment future of the typical male middle management employee. At the same time, it has created a parallel demand for better educated white collar personnel and has made many blue collar workers obsolete.[47] The advantages of automation, according to one advocate, are "(Machines) don't call in sick; they don't talk back; they work early and late and without overtime; they don't get tired; and last, but far from least, they don't line up at the cashier's window every week for a slice of the operating funds."[48] As an example of the effect which automation may have, at the Census Bureau, the work accomplished by 4,000 statisticians in 1950 was completed by 50 technicians in 1960.[49]

Alienation and Economic Life • With the adoption of mechanization and automation has come a sense of work alienation, especially among younger workers. Many workers see themselves as powerless, isolated, fragmented and self-estranged from their work; they feel they are mere objects in a vast economic system, without power or ability to control circumstances. Many consider themselves isolated from a network of community and personal relations even as they complete a specialized role for a highly impersonal organization.[50]

Attitudes of alienation, although considered now to be a problem, are not new. Karl Marx, for example, early observed that the technology which necessitates the building of factories and the employment of workers in routine and rather monotonous jobs also gives rise to worker estrangement. The former mastery of the worker over his craft and materials is replaced by the dominance of the machine which has taken away much of the job satisfaction his work normally provides. As the worker is increasingly separated from the problem-solving and decision-making process, he becomes, Marx theorized, susceptible to alienation, itself a by-product of the new economic form. Because he now has to depend upon the owner of the means of production and not upon himself, he no longer is able or willing to accept responsibility for what he produces. In turn, his sense of isolation is made greater, and the likelihood of his supporting the corporation for which he works lessens. Because he works for another, he becomes, Marx believed, his employer's victim.[51]

Following Marx's lead, other critics contend that the technological system causes the repression of true human needs, while creating false needs in individuals, and produces changes in human character.[52] According to Jacques Ellul, the problem of modern technological society is centered in the fact that efficiency and technique have replaced purpose and participation. As a consequence, the individual worker is often made subservient to the demands of the economic organization and his self-esteem made victim of corporate profits. While employers attempt to create the illusion that work is becoming more humane, corporate managers in fact strive for greater economic production and efficiency.[53]

The Reality of Alienation • That technological change produces both positive and negative effects, usually at the same time and as a result of each other, cannot be denied. The advancement of technology creates new opportunities which in turn require alterations in social organization if the new opportunities are to be maximized. This, then, requires the redefinition of many social functions and the realignment of earlier goals. When existing social structures are unable to exploit technological opportunities, or when new technologies cause detrimental latent social effects, social dislocation caused by technological change can be costly.[54]

Alienation in the form of disenchantment over mass production line jobs has been increasing. In some factories, for example, an automobile manufacturing plant in Lordstown, Ohio, alienation has become so acute that absenteeism and work stoppage have undermined many of the economic incentives introduced by management. Worker and management conflict has become intense. However, in other industries, management's awareness of worker job dissatisfaction has sometimes caused it to redefine work tasks more broadly in order to permit variety and worker pride.

The Labor Union Movement • As mechanization and automation have advanced, the role and function of labor unions in economic life have changed. Unions which fought to secure job security, changes in unsatisfactory working conditions, and wage increases during the Depression are now forced to vie for members, fight labor force cutbacks due to automation, secure shorter work weeks, and gain better pensions.[55] Of the between 3,500 and 5,000 strikes which have occurred in the United States since 1945, most have been over questions of wages, fringe benefits, job security, and working conditions. Recently, shorter work weeks, defiance of required overtime and other issues relating to job satisfaction have been important issues. Future strikes are likely to be over union recognition in the agriculture and textile industries. Although most strikes have been shortlived, a few have come close to crippling parts of the economy.[56] While economic conflict in the past was conceived in terms of a class struggle between the poor and the rich, it now takes the form of a struggle between the educated and the un- or poorly educated.[57] Craft and trade unions, which have had only limited success to date in organizing white collar and middle management workers, have been slow to accept blacks and other minority persons into membership.[58]

Extension of Alienation • Because the occupational role is usually the most significant role for adults, alienation created in the work setting may extend to other areas of the individual's life. Particularly within the urban setting is this true. The disenchantment and isolation a worker feels on the assembly line may be transfered to the human interrelationships in which the urban dweller engages. Although cities have a high population density, they are characterized by a high degree of impersonality and indifference. Georg Simmel theorized that because urban dwellers come into contact with a large number of persons each day, they conserve their psychic energy by limiting their relationships to a far smaller proportion of people than their rural counterparts and by maintaining superficial relations.[59] Others suggest that when an urban dweller is exposed to an overload of social relations, he allocates less time to each input and disregards low-priority inputs. In order to save time and energy, he responds selectively to defined inputs and at times redraws the boundaries of certain social transactions in order to lighten his burden. The urban dweller moves to block off many contacts which might normally flow to him by having an unlisted telephone number or by keeping his receiver off the hook. In using filtering devices and other techniques, he permits only weak and superficial forms of involvement to engulf him.

In order to handle other inputs which might overcome him, the urban dweller creates specialized institutions. As he does this, he limits seriously the sense of direct contact and spontaneous integration which usually characterize small community life. In turn, he expresses a lessened sense of social responsibility, an unwillingness to trust and assist strangers, an inability or unwillingness to act courteously, a desire for anonymity, and a tendency to differentiate and segment roles.[60] If he is a commuter, he may refuse to join a motor pool and continue to drive himself in order to isolate himself within his automobile from the pressures of his work as well as his home.

The City and the Minority American

The mechanization of agriculture, government programs limiting agricultural production, the harm done to agriculture by the boll weevil, the shift of cotton cultivation from the South and Southeast to the Southwest and West, and the high rural South black birth rate have each influenced the movement of blacks to the cities.[61] Between 1960 and 1970 alone, 3.5 million blacks moved to urban central cities, replacing two million whites who moved to outlying areas. By the late 1960's, approximately 12.5 million blacks lived in ghettoes, a trend which, if continued, would leave 21 million blacks, an increase of 72 percent, in the same areas by 1985. By 1969, 55 percent of all blacks resided in metropolitan cities. Of the central city population, 21 percent were black, living in the highest concentrations in larger cities. If the above expected increases occur, the percentage of blacks within central cities would expand to between 31 and 35.6 percent of the total central city population. About 40 percent of the black American population lived in approximately 20 metropolitan areas.[62] The President's Commission on Civil Disorders predicted in 1968 that the projected increases would mean that all cities, in addition to Washington, D.C. and Newark, which were already more than 50 percent black, would become over 50 percent black by the following dates: New Orleans (1971), Richmond (1971), Baltimore (1972), Jacksonville (1972), Gary (1973), Cleveland (1975),

St. Louis (1978), Detroit (1979), Philadelphia (1981), Oakland (1983) and Chicago (1984). In fact, Gary was 52.8 percent black by 1970.[63] The lack of a census since then means the status of other cities is not known for sure. Black students, the Commission suggested, will probably comprise a school majority by 1986 in Dallas, Pittsburgh, Buffalo, Cincinnati, Harrisburg, Atlanta, Louisville, Indianapolis, Kansas City (Missouri), Hartford, and New Haven, because the black population in central cities tends to be younger and large numbers of white parents send their children to private schools.[64]

The Problem of Unemployment ● Unemployment, a perennial problem of labor and a particular problem for minorities, continues to plague the union and nonunion worker. The high point of unemployment was reached in 1946 when 7.5 percent of the labor force was unemployed. In 1953 unemployment reached a level of 2.9 percent but rose to 5.5 percent by 1954.[65] Fluctuating between these high and low points ever since, in early 1974 the rate was closer to 5.2 percent. For specific groups, however, these figures may be misleading. Due to the higher employment rate of the upper and middle occupational classes, a five percent average unemployment rate means a ten percent lower-class and 20 percent ghetto or other hard-core urban area unemployment rate. Among minority group youth or women, the rate may reach as high as 30 percent.[66] The non-white unemployment rate in 1967 was about three times the white unemployment rate in eight of the worst slums in twenty American cities, two times the rate in six or more, and half the rate in two others.[67] Today, black unemployment tends on the average to be approximately twice that of whites.[68]

While it is generally true that the black and other minority populations are the last hired and the first fired, discrimination provides only part of the reason. Their unemployment is partially due to their failure to learn necessary skills and the failure of the educational system to prepare them for a particular job. The importance of educational attainment for job security is evident in a study released earlier. In the spring of 1962, persons having four years of schooling or less had an unemployment rate of 7.2 percent; those with 5-7 years, 12.2 percent; and those with 16 years of schooling or more, only 1.4 percent.[69] However, even this pattern in the past five years has not remained steady. The mass lay-offs in the aerospace industry, the oversupply of personnel in the teaching profession and the cutbacks in the service professions have led to a higher than normal unemployment rate among the better educated.

Employment and unemployment trends make it obvious that new unskilled workers entering the labor force are at a distinct disadvantage. Technological development and automation require a better skilled and trained labor force. As scientific and engineering knowledge has been brought to bear on production, distribution and other economic operations, the unskilled worker, whether young or old, is at a competitive disadvantage.[70] Even the security offered by the professions is no longer definitive. Shifts in the economy have rendered temporarily perhaps, certain occupational categories, such as engineering and teaching, unemployment disaster areas. At the same, the undersupply of personnel in health services, plumbing, and general electrical and other repair fields continues.

Poverty

While unemployment is not the single cause of poverty, those persons who are either unemployed or underemployed usually find themselves in a poverty situation. The definition of poverty and the estimation of those in poverty depends to a great extent upon what definition is used to differentiate those in that state from those who are not. The Social Security Administration in an attempt to solve this problem developed a poverty line separation of the two groups in terms of the amount of money necessary for a family to maintain a minimum standard of living in an urban or rural area. Taking into consideration such factors as sex of the household head, number of persons in the family, farm or non-farm status, and ages of family members, and calculating the cost of a nutritionally adequate food plan, a Federal Interagency committee concluded that an urban family of four with a male head needs an estimated $4,217 per year to live. In 1971, an estimated 25.6 million persons fell beneath this minimum standard of living. Whereas approximately ten percent of the population is black, 28.9 percent of the persons below the low-income level are black.[71]

Who Are in Poverty? • Poverty disproportionately affects minority groups, children, youth, the unemployed, ruralities, female heads of families, and the elderly. Supported by ecological and demographic trends, poverty is largely a product of the limited economic opportunities available to the poor, the inability of the poor to sell their skills in a highly technological economy, the continuance of racial discrimination, and a tendency for welfare institutions to maintain a large number of its clients in enduring dependency.[72] The problems faced by those in poverty are revealed in a Citizen's Board of Inquiry into Hunger and Malnutrition study which disclosed in 1968 that an estimated one fifth of the country's households have poor diets, conditions in 280 United States counties necessitate a presidential declaration naming them as hunger areas, migrant labor and some Indian reservations have the worst health conditions possible, early childhood diet deficiencies cause irreversible organic and psychological brain damage, and federal food programs often fail to serve the needy.[73]

Nearly all cycles of poverty begin and end with being poor. Being poor means living in a poor neighborhood in deficient housing; going to a second-rate school, having an inadequate education, and failing to learn as much; working at a low-paying job, if any; eating poor food and having poor health; and continuing to be poor. In another sense, it means that the person in poverty realizes that he is not like others, perceives himself as a failure, lacks self-confidence, gives up, and reinforces his probability of remaining poor.[74]

Although such cycles exist, the poor may be differentiated into several sub-categories. David Matza differentiates among the *disreputable poor* who remain permanently on welfare and assume all the effects of its demoralizing stigma, the *welfare poor* (poor who occupy welfare roles) who are not necessarily disreputable in themselves. While the welfare poor simply are unable to support themselves and tend to include disabled, blind, aged or dependent persons, the disreputable poor, Matza believes, include those who remain unemployed even when prosperity and full employment exist. The latter category in turn is further subdivided into the *dregs,* who either are spawned in poverty or are representatives of families which have been left behind in ethnic mobility; *newcomers* who settle in slum or ghetto areas and possess few or no marketable skills or financial resources; *skidders,* who face a decline in social status because of their alcoholism, addiction, or some other problematic conduct; and the *infirm,* who have either moved to a disreputable neighborhood or have been forced to stay there as the neighborhood changed.[75]

Those whom Matza defines as "disreputable poor" have sometimes been thought to be part of a "culture of poverty." This concept which designates those who persist generation after generation in an impoverished condition stresses the feelings of deprivation, frustration and alienation which such individuals experience. Although the concept has been widely used and accepted, recent findings suggest that it is an improper designation. A survey by the University of Michigan's Institute for Social Research finds that an individual's own hopes and sense of competence have very little to do with his ability to rise above or fall below a poverty level. Being strongly or weakly motivated toward success explains virtually nothing about the family's movement up or down the economic ladder.[76]

Problems of the Ghetto • Minority urban ghetto dwellers are beset by a wide variety of problems. In addition to high illness and social disorder rates, lack of training or education, high unemployment rates, and inadequate incomes, they have a deficiency in political power.[77] Whereas the Irish, Italians, Poles, and other ethnic groups were generally able to maintain control over their own ethnic areas during their one or two generation lifetime in the ghetto area, blacks have secured what influence they do have in urban areas only recently.[78] Because they have been unable to move and disperse to suburban areas as easily as the white ethnic groups did in the past, blacks have been near captives of the ghetto.

The restrictions upon black mobility in the United States have caused the creation of two increasingly separate Americas in which whites live in suburbs, smaller central cities, and the peripheral parts of large central cities and the blacks and other selected minorities remain concentrated within the core of large central cities. This, of course, relegates blacks to future status similar to their present state, regardless of the amount of money spent in an attempt to change the situation.[79] Because of these limitations, the President's Commission on Civil Disorders concluded that the divided society faces the possibility of sustained urban violence and the eventual denial of the traditional American ideals of freedom, individual dignity, and equality of opportunity.[80]

Urban Housing and Development ● In order to counteract the trends leading to ghettoization, the federal government designed programs to solve urban housing and development problems. During the 1930's and 1940's, early housing and urban development acts emphasized public housing and low interest rate mortgage assistance to low-income groups. However, the 1949 Housing Act, which promised a decent standard dwelling unit for every American, gave birth to an urban renewal program which eventually destroyed more than 350,000 low rental housing units.[81] By March, 1961, 126,000 dwelling units had been demolished and only about 28,000 new ones built. Even though the program had largely been created to assist the poor living in slums, the median monthly rental for new housing built between 1960 and 1962 ranged from $158 to $192.[82] As the public became aware of the weaknesses of these programs, their focus began to shift slightly to the renewal of the central business district. When the thrust of urban renewal was redirected from a concern for slum clearance to general urban regeneration, attempts were made to reclaim downtown store areas, induce industries to return or remain in cities, and build middle and high-rent housing.[83] By 1968, some 2,326 urban renewal projects, involving grants of more than $6 million, existed in 954 communities.[84]

By the time of the 1965 and 1968 passages of the Housing and Urban Development Acts, greater emphasis was being placed upon private initiative in the development of municipalities and housing. Unfortunately, many of these programs did little to assist the poor for whom they were supposedly designed and instead became boons to middle and upper class developers and investors.[85] Even the 1966 Federal Demonstration Cities and Metropolitan Act, which became the foundation of the experimental Model Cities program, did not solve the urban problem.

Criticisms of Housing and Urban Renewal Programs ● While proponents of urban renewal at one time believed that urban life could be restored through this approach, it now appears unlikely. Urban renewal critics, such as Jane Jacobs and Martin Anderson, maintain that the displacement caused by urban renewal undermines social organization and forces hardships upon those least able to bear them, despite urban renewal regulations which now require that those displaced be provided replacement housing even as the program proceeds. Too often, those who are supposed to live in the new housing cannot pay the rent charged, do not like the architectural form or find that an overdensity of problem families makes the situation worse. Consequently, less than 25 percent of those being dislocated ever eventually transfer to the substitute housing provided for in urban renewal regulations.[86]

In too many cases urban renewal has undermined ethnic and community solidarity and left little social organization in its place. Operating on the assumption that many slums, often the prime targets for renewal, have little or no social or moral organization, urban renewal proponents have moved without qualms to break up physically run-down neighborhoods. But their assumptions are gross oversimplifications. In his study of one Chicago slum, for example, Gerald D. Suttles found that the attempt to develop a moral order is realized.[87] Even Herbert Gans discovered in a study of a Boston Italian-American community that the area often called a slum by some is better described as an urban village through which its inhabitants make the adaptation to urban life. People live in such areas of low-cost housing because they are poor. Consequently, their urban village differs markedly from a slum, characterized by rapid disease infestation, condemnable housing, or other clearly deficient standards, and meets a definite social need. Once community unity is broken, however, it is difficult to re-establish. In Boston, only ten percent of the urban villagers ousted by renewal were actually rehoused in the same district despite the Redevelopment Commission's Pledge to relocate 60 percent there.[88]

The Costs of Urban Renewal • Urban renewal costs are not limited to the breakup of ethnic communities. Many of the problems existing in the community before the development of the high-rise apartment houses have simply been made more severe. Crime, drug abuse, and despair have become even more pronounced. The displacement caused by urban renewal has not only forced the relocation of many community members but has broken up important relationships of relatives and friends. Small businessmen have lost their clientele and in many instances have been put out of business altogether.[89] Overall, urban renewal programs have detrimentally reduced the supply of low-cost housing in urban cities at an especially exorbitant cost.[90]

Lewis Mumford considers urban renewal to be a costly mistake. From the outset, it has done little more, he argues, than to continue the inadequate characteristics of the city. Not only does it fail to face up to the desire of people to have open space and recreational outlets or to the need to anticipate regional goals, but it also reproduces the same urban designs which failed in the past[91] and forces higher rents upon those displaced from their homes.[92] Even those buying homes are required to pay a higher cost for a new house. If they are older persons. these costs may be unbearable.

Critics of urban renewal have had their effect. In order to offset some of the undesired consequences of former urban renewal programs and to meet the arguments of program critics, the government has redirected its efforts to the gradual development of selected neighborhoods. Rent subsidy and rent supplement legislation now provide the needy with funds with which they can secure decent housing on the open market.[93] However, despite these efforts, attempts to reintegrate the core city by encouraging the return of whites and programs to allow minority members to purchase in the suburbs have generally been unsuccessful. Present policies anticipate a continuation of the limited mobility of the more affluent members of the black population to areas on the periphery of poor black neighborhoods. They recognize that although the federal government may invest some public funds within the ghetto, funds alone will not provide the leadership for the solving of urban problems. An enrichment policy encourages government to share in the development of more jobs, black businesses, better training and education programs, and innovative self-help efforts. While this approach holds some promise and involves a high degree of government funding, it may also hasten the separation of the black middle class from its lower class members. A more radical policy, integration, passes well beyond the previous accepted alternatives. If such a policy were activated, stronger efforts to provide blacks with housing in suburbs where jobs are being created would be necessary. The government would need to guarantee publicly the opportunity of blacks to compete openly and freely with others for employment.[94] Whether this choice will dominate the urban scene for the next decade is still an open question.

While the breakdown of urban segregation is difficult to accomplish under the best of circumstances, it may become even more difficult to achieve if those determining the future fail to take it into consideration. Too often, economic and political rather than social decisions are likely to shape the future of the city. A metropolitan Washington planning agency which designed a plan anticipating the fundamental needs of a doubled population by the year 2000, adequately considered the need for urban transit, service and commerce areas, and open recreation areas but failed to make provision for the potential integration of the population in its new creation. Although its plan for the year 2000 encouraged the future growth of the city along six radial corridors which would permit the coordination of highway and transit lines and the preservation of as many parks and recreation areas as possible, its engineers failed to take the major element of race into account, a weakness which probably made the plan unfeasible even before it was implemented.[95]

Not all planners have been this naive, however. Some community and business leaders on occasion have taken the racial factor, often indirectly, into account. A few companies in cooperation with the government have moved to hire many unskilled and marginal members of the labor force in ghetto areas despite the fact that to do so violates a fundamental business principle of not hiring the least productive members of the work force.[96] They do so anyway in the hope that they may develop future markets in the urban complex. Others, especially in the furniture, food, lumber, textile and clothing industries, stay in the central city and provide jobs because they need to remain close to the services and the cheaper labor force which they need in order to operate.[97]

The Future of American Cities

Despite these many problems, the city, identified in the past in terms of unrelieved residential density, distinguished boundaries and a static political form, is giving way to the city of the future which has a national urban culture, is fluid at its boundaries, is capable of indefinite reproduction and reflects an intricate urban way of life. Because of its dynamic character, it may be difficult to plan and order its design. In fact, what is now called suburbs actually may be the prototype of the urban form to come. Once political power is gained by those already dominating urban culture numerically, the central city may become subordinate to "a new super-urbia community."[98] In the future, therefore, the scope and direction of urban life may be determined by the character and rate of growth of its population, a quality of its leadership, and the willingness of the metropolitan public to build for its urban future.

The social isolation and poverty of minority groups must ultimately be recognized if the problems of the city are to be attacked. Public policy must attempt to maintain community stability while still striving to bring about constructive social change. Local government must respond to urban problems with insight and decisive action even if it means the reorganization of traditional forms of urban policy. The Federal government must encourage, possibly through incentives, local governments to assume responsibility for their problems rather than to look to national categorical aid programs for leverage to act. Public services must be equalized even as people move in patterns which disrupt the neat urban packaging of yesteryear. Only when local, state and federal authorities work in concert toward the solution of urban problems will realistic solutions emerge.[99]

Bigness in itself is no automatic solution. When a metropolitan community becomes too large, many of its problems may center in its very bigness. One urbanologist, for example, has recently encouraged New York City to decentralize and permit communities to levy taxes and control the schools in their areas on the ground that only then will they become more responsive to the clients and be able to overcome the inadequacies brought about by excessive size.[100] Whichever approaches are devised, concern for the problems of poverty are at the heart of solutions to urban problems.

Toward the Solution of the Poverty Problem • Recognizing the many cycles of poverty and the various classifications of the poor, many proposals have been submitted in the quest for the solution of the poverty problem. Among the more meaningful are the extension of short-term employment benefits to those looking for new jobs, the provision of a pension or mustering-out pay to an individual displaced in employment by technological change, the authorization for housing subsidies to individuals rather than to structures, the development of income guarantees that are suitable for modern life, and a more progressive modification of the graduated Social Security Tax. As a solution to the poverty problem, the A. Philip Randolph Institute seeks a "freedom budget" which will restore full employment, assure adequate incomes for those employed, guarantee a minimum adequacy level of income, eliminate slum ghettoes, provide for medical care and educational opportunity, give greater attention to those areas neglected in the public sector, and sustain full production and high economic growth.[101]

Although the solving of the poverty problem involves many complex dimensions and programs, the single most important action towards a solution appears to involve the full employment for all persons desiring work. Unless men and women are permitted to earn adequate incomes, the poverty problem will never be fully solved. The mere re-distribution of incomes to the poor through some forms of assistance does not truly solve the question in the long run. If individuals are given opportunity for employment and some support through income maintenance programs, meaningful steps may be taken to solve the poverty problem. A significant program of education must be enacted, Lee Rainwater believes, in order to overcome the "trained incapacity" of the lower class, especially members of the black population, to function adequately in a heavily industrialized and bureaucratized world. Opportunities for the pursuit of self-interest and strong sanctions against those who are indifferent or callous in providing services to the slum must be enacted, he concludes, if lower class members are to overcome their existing sense of powerlessness and stigmatization.[102]

The War on Poverty ● The War on Poverty proposed by President Lyndon B. Johnson in March, 1964 unleashed a massive governmental attempt to solve the poverty problem. Requiring the maximum feasible participation of the poor, the War sought to bring economic and political power to those in this condition. However, it soon became a target of political attack because it provided new power bases from which to challenge the traditional powers of mayors and other politicians. Despite its good intentions, the War on Poverty by the late 1960's underwent a series of cutbacks and reorganizations which lessened its revolutionary aims and practices.[103] A later revelation that only one fourth or thereabouts of the money expended for the solution of poverty actually reached the poverty group did serve to reinforce the earlier criticisms. Nearly one out of every five dollars spent for welfare, some argued, went largely for the mere determination of the eligibility of an applicant for assistance.[104]

The Nixon Approach ● The Nixon Administration introduced its plan to solve the poverty problem in 1969. Calling for a major restructuring of the welfare system and the enactment of a family assistance program, the Nixon proposal combined the concepts of family assistance and guaranteed annual income in a proposal which guaranteed annually $500 per person for the first two members and $300 for each additional family member. Under its provisions, a family of four with no other sources of income would receive up to $1,600 per year. If other income were available to the family, the first $720 would be disregarded but all payments on earnings above the first $720 would be reduced by $.50 on each dollar. If a family of four had an annual income of $2,000, it would receive $960 in benefits in addition to its basic $2,000 income. The amount would vary for other families depending upon family income and the number of persons within the family. Even though it represented a radical departure from the traditional American welfare approach, the program failed to provide even a poverty level standard of living to those marginally employed or unemployed. Emphasizing work incentives, the Nixon approach sought to keep welfare from being attractive as a life economic pattern[105] and to encourage recipients to assume work responsibilities. While many European countries have provided family assistance allowances in relationship to some state national formula for some years, such a program is somewhat revolutionary for the United States. Nevertheless, family assistance in France is given in relationship to the total average wages paid in manufacturing. Monthly allowances of between six dollars and ten dollars are given Canadian families for each child, depending upon age.[106]

The Negative Income Tax • Another approach to the problem provides for the development of a negative income tax program. In one of two forms, the negative income tax would permit families with incomes of less than the value of tax exemptions and nonstandard deductions provided within the present tax system to receive a negative income tax payment of a stated percentage of the shortage. In its second form, each eligible family would be provided an annual supplement in relationship to an established tax rate and a formula pertaining to family income. In both cases a break-even point in income at which the family would not receive any outside or governmental support would be included. The amount granted to those eligible for the program would vary in relationship to family size, monies earned, and taxes paid.[107] While the negative income tax approach may be less stigmatizing to those receiving aid, it still does not permit a ready solution to the poverty problem or provide an adequate level of economic support so that the family may avoid poverty status.

Education and Economic Status • What one learns in school in preparation for eventual employment has a pronounced effect upon one's economic success. For the average man, education for education's sake, however, is a luxury. Most of his training efforts are directed toward specific vocational goals. Consequently, when the schools focus excessively upon middle-class educational achievements, children from lower-class and minority families frequently find the schools do not provide adequate training for the life occupations realistically open to them. When this occurs, lower-class youth may conclude that schools are irrelevant and may be alienated from both the educational and work system. Despite the increase in support for vocational education, the problems caused by alienation and irrelevant curricula have not been overcome.

Many youths who have dropped out of school have been unsuccessful in securing employment due to their lack of employable skills. Nearly twice as many youth who drop out are likely to be unemployed in any year as opposed to ten percent of those who finished high school.[108] Many lower-class youth who do secure employment unfortunately take dead-end jobs due to their lack of knowledge concerning the prerequisites and procedures for entering the better fields of employment. Not all youth face this problem, however. Those who have been willing to defer their desire for immediate economic gratification in order to complete their education have generally been able to find meaningful positions. In 1969 and 1970, the youth unemployment rate ran as high as 17.5 percent for 18 and 19 year olds with one to three years of high school and 15.7 percent for those with only an eighth grade education.[109] For all persons over 18 years of age, in 1972, those with less than 12 years education had an unemployment rate of 7.3 percent, while those with more than 12 years education were unemployed at a 3.7 percent rate.[110]

At the same time, too much education may result in the future underemployment of many, in the sense that individuals are capable of more difficult jobs than they perform. U.S. Bureau of Labor Statistics indicate that 28 percent of today's college graduates are making less than the median income of those with only high school diplomas.[111]

Solutions to the Unemployment Problem ● Because the number of unskilled jobs continues to decline even while positions in banking, health, insurance, education, and public service increase, the solution to the unemployment problem is especially difficult. The flight of manufacturing and retailing organizations from the central city to outlying suburbs and other areas makes the minority group unemployment problem all the more serious. After reviewing the causes leading to urban rioting, the President's Commission on Civil Disorders concluded that the growing number of black ghetto unemployed should be provided jobs by encouraging industry through an incentive system to create new employment centers near black residential areas. Blacks should be encouraged to move closer to suburban residential and industrial centers, and ghetto dwellers should have available better transportation to potential job locations. Although the Commission did not go so far as to recommend a minority employment quota system, others have. However, their recommendation has been resisted by Jews and other more qualified groups which stand to lose employment in certain occupations and professions if such a system is invoked indiscriminately. Although this approach would benefit the Negro, Puerto Rican and native American populations, it can work against the successes achieved by other groups.

While black militants and many other black spokesmen demand greater employment opportunity for blacks in the skilled labor categories, the eventual hiring of a proportionate number of blacks in these occupations depends in large degree upon the retirement of current employees, the creation of new jobs to utilize their services, or the preparation of minority members to assume job responsibilities in occupations most have not been trained for. Over 80 percent of the overall employment increase in 1968 occurred within white collar occupations, a category of work which demands higher educational accomplishment.[112] Given this trend, it will be some time before a large number of those from the lower-class will be able to qualify for white collar employment.

As employment has increased, workers have increasingly sought the assistance offered by unemployment insurance. The inadequacy of unemployment benefits in many states, however, has let many unions, such as the United Auto Workers, to negotiate supplementary unemployment benefits in union contracts with management. In such contracts, employers not only augment the unemployment insurance provided by the state, which at one time averaged $35.56 per week for slightly more than 12 weeks, but also extend the period of coverage for many additional weeks.[113] But even this program is generally a stop-gap answer to the problem.

Other Answers to Poverty Problems ● Recognizing that the goal of full employment, a sustained condition in which only about two percent of the civilian labor force is unemployed full-time, has rarely been reached, critics suggest full employment should not be a goal. John K. Galbraith maintains that the idea of a national policy of full employment should be abandoned on the ground that it is no longer necessary to stimulate rapid promotion and economic growth. High employment can be inflationary and can disturb the social balance. Therefore, rather than seeking total employment, the state should provide adequate unemployment benefits for jobless workers. In any case, if unemployment is a structural problem, its solution rests in the retraining of those out of work. But if it is a problem tied to shortage of demand, then increases in spending or reductions in taxes will aid in its resolution. However, unemployment is more than this. Due to inadequate demand, it is both a structural problem and a product of variable and specialized demand. At the same time that fewer jobs are available to the unskilled, a variety of openings are available for those having the necessary job qualifications. If unemployment opportunities are to be maximized and unemployment minimized, the needs of the industrial system must be more closely coordinated with the cultural and educational systems.[114]

References

1. York Willbern, *The Withering Away of the City* (Tuscaloosa, Ala: University of Alabama Press, 1964), pp. 9-33.
2. Daniel P. Moynihan, "Urban Conditions," *Social Problems: Persistent Challenges*, eds. Edward C. McDonagh and Jon E. Simpson (New York: Holt, Rinehart and Winston, 1969), p. 26.
3. Lloyd Saxton and Walter Kaufmann, *The American Scene: Social Problems of the Seventies* (Belmont, Calif.: Wadsworth Publishing Co., 1971), p. 67.

4. Albert W. Stewart, *The Troubled Land* (New York: McGraw-Hill, 1972).
5. Jean Gottman, *Planning for a Nation of Cities* (Cambridge, Mass.: MIT Press, 1966), pp. 163-164.
6. United Nations Population Division, "World Urbanization Trends, 1920-1960," *Cities in Change,* ed. John Walton and Donald E. Carns (Boston: Allyn and Bacon, 1973), p. 67.
7. U.S. Bureau of the Census, *Statistical Abstract of the United States, 1973* (Washington, D.C.: U.S. Government Printing Office, 1973), p. 22.
8. James R. McIntosh, "The Urban Fringe," *Cities in Change,* p. 303.
9. Gresham M. Sykes, *Social Problems in America* (Glenview, Ill.: Scott, Foresman and Co., 1971), p. 38.
10. Patricia L. Hodge and Philip M. Hauser, *The Challenge of America's Metropolitan Population Outlook, 1960 to 1985* (New York: Praeger, 1968).
11. Mitchell Gordon, *Sick Cities* (Baltimore: Penguin B ooks, 1963), pp. 15-17.
12. Willbern, *The Withering Away,* p. 33.
13. *Ibid.,* p. 27.
14. Gottman, *Nation of Cities,* pp. 163-177.
15 See Ashley A. Foard and Hilbert Fefferman, "Federal Urban Renewal Legislation," *Law and Contemporary Problems,* Vol. 25 (Fall, 1960), pp. 635-647.
16. Herbert J. Gans, "The White Exodus to Suburbia Steps Up," *Cities in Change,* pp. 296-298.
17. U.S. Department of Commerce, Bureau of the Census, *Our Cities and Suburbs* (Washington, D.C., 1973), p. 5.
18. Bernard Weissbourd, "Are Cities Obsolete?" *The Saturday Review* (December 19, 1964), pp. 12-13.
19. Gans, *Cities in Change,* p. 297.
20. Charles Abrams, "Housing Policy—1937-1967," *Shaping an American Future: Essays in Honor of Catherine Bauer Wurster,* eds. Bernard J. Frieden and William W. Nash, Jr., (Cambridge, Mass,: MIT Press, 1969), p. 39.
21. Moynihan, *Social Problems,* p. 3-20.
22. Sykes, *Social Problems in America,* pp. 40-42.
23. Gordon, *Sick Cities,* p. 257.
24. Moynihan, *Social Problems,* p. 23.
25. Patricia C. Sexton, "City Schools," *Annals,* (March, 1964), CCCLII, 95-106.
26. Edward Higbee, *The Squeeze* (New York: Morrow and Co., 1960), pp. 31-32.
27. Gans, *Cities in Change,* pp. 296-297.
28. Charles R. Adrian, "Metropology: Folklore and Field Research," *Public Administration Review,* (Summer, 1961), XXI, 155.
29. Gordon, *Sick Cities,* pp. 365-370.
30. Victor Jones, "Representative Local Government from Neighborhood to Region," *Public Affairs Report,* (April, 1970), XI, 1-6.
31. Ben B. Seligman, "Man, Work and the Automated Feast," *Commentary* (July, 1962), pp. 18-19.
32. Executive Office of the President, Office of Management and Budget, *Social Indicators 1973* (Washington, D.C., 1973), pp. 140, 143.
33. John K. Galbraith, *The New Industrial State* (Boston: Houghton-Mifflin, 1967), pp. 233-240.
34. Andrew Hacker, "A Country Called Corporate America," *Social Profile: U.S.A. Today* (Princeton, N.J.: Van Nostrand, 1970), pp. 354-365.
35. U.S. Bureau of Labor Statistics, *Employment and Earnings Statistics for the United States, 1909-1968* (Washington, D.C.: U.S. Government Printing Office, 1968), pp. 47-48.

36. U.S. Bureau of Labor Statistics, *Employment and Earnings, Vol. 16* (Washington, D.C.: U.S. Government Printing Office, 1969), p. 125.
37. U.S. Bureau of the Census, *Current Population Reports, No. 66* (Washington, D.C.: U.S. Government Printing Office, 1969), p. 103.
38. Robert S. Weiss, Edwin Harwood and David Reisman, "Work and Automation: Problems and Prospects," *Contemporary Social Problems*, eds. Robert K. Merton and Robert Nisbet (New York: Harcourt, Brace and Jovanovich, 1971), p. 556.
39. *New York Times,* July 24, 1974.
40. *Social Indicators 1973,* p. 141.
41. Seymour L. Wolfbein, *Manpower Implications of Automation* (Washington, D.C.: U.S. Department of Labor, 1965), pp. 15-28.
42. Walter Buckingham, *Automation: Its Impact on Business and People* (New York: Harper and Row, 1961), pp. 14-22.
43. Seligman, *Commentary*, pp. 9-12.
44. Leonard Broom and Philip Selznick, "Technology and Human Relations," *Automation, Alienation and Anomie*, ed. Simon Marcson (New York: Harper and Row, 1970), pp. 14-17.
45. Buckingham, *Automation*, pp. 16-22.
46. Broom and Selznick, *Automation, Alienation*, pp. 22.
47. George A. Miller, "Thinking Machines: Myths and Actualities," *Public Interest,* (Winter, 1966), II, 92-112.
48. Seligman, *Commentary*, pp. 9-19.
49. *Ibid.,* pp. 12-19.
50. Robert Blauner, *Alienation and Freedom: The Factory Worker and His Industry* (Chicago: University of Chicago Press, 1964), pp. 24-34.
51. Broom and Selznick, *Automation, Alienation*, pp. 12-14.
52. Herbert Marcue, *One-Dimensional Man* (Boston: Beacon Press, 1964).
53. Jacques Ellul, *The Technological Society* (New York: Knopf, 1964), pp. 120-140.
54. Emmanuel G. Mesthene, "The Role of Technology in Society," *Technology and Man's Future*, pp. 127-151.
55. H. M. Douty, "Union and Non-Union Wages," *Unions, Management and the Public*, eds. E. Wight Bakke, Clark Kerr and Charles W. Anrod (New York: Harcourt, Brace and Jovanovich, 1967), pp. 603-604.
56. Elizabeth Jager, "Why Strikes?" *Unions, Management and the Public*, pp. 273-281.
57. Galbraith, *New Industrial State*, pp. 245-246.
58. Julius Jacobson, "Union Conservatism: A Barrier to Racial Equality," *Crisis in American Institutions*, p. 97.
59. Georg Simmel, *The Sociology of Georg Simmel*, ed. K. H. Wolff (New York: MacMillian, 1950).
60. Stanley Milgram, "The Experience of Living in Cities," *Science* Vol. 167 (March, 1970), pp. 1461-1468.
61. Thomas F. Pettigrew, "Issues in America," *Shaping An American Future*, pp. 46-47.
62. *Ibid.,* p. 48.
63. *Statistical Abstract 1973,* pp. 13-14.
64. President's Commission on Civil Disorders, *Report of the National Advisory Commission on Civil Disorders* (New York: Bantam Books, 1968), pp. 389-408.
65. *Social Indicators 1973,* p. 136.
66. Elliott Liebow, "No Man Can Live With the Terrible Knowledge That He Is Not Needed," *New York Times Magazine* (April 5, 1970), pp. 28-29.
67. U.S. Department of Labor, "A Sharper Look at Unemployment in U.S. Cities and Slums," *Summary Report to the President* (Washington, D.C.: U.S. Government Printing Office, 1967), pp. 1-2.

68. U.S. Bureau of Labor Statistics, *Employment and Earnings*, pp. 113-116.
69. Galbraith, *New Industrial State*, pp. 235-238.
70. Wolfbein, *Implications of Automation*, pp. 15-20.
71. *Social Indicators 1973*, pp. 183, 187.
72. Louis A. Ferman, Joyce L. Kornbluh and Alan Haber, *Poverty in America* (Ann Arbor: University of Michigan Press, 1968), pp. vi-vii.
73. Citizens' Board of Inquiry into Hunger and Malnutrition in the United States, *Hunger, U.S.A.* (Boston: Beacon Press, 1968), pp. 84-85.
74. Thomas Gladwin, *Poverty, U.S.A.* (Boston: Little, Brown and Co., 1967), pp. 76-77.
75. David Matza, "Poverty and Disrepute," *Contemporary Social Problems*, eds. Robert K. Merton and Robert Nisbet (New York, 1971), pp. 606-640.
76. *Milwaukee Journal*, May 9, 1974.
77. Eunice Grier and George Grier, "Equality and Beyond: Housing and Segregation in the Great Society," *Daedalus*, Vol. 95 (Winter, 1966), pp. 85-88.
78. Robert Blauner, "Internal Colonialism and Ghetto Revolt," *Social Problems*, (Spring, 1969), XVI, 393-408.
79. Moynihan, *Social Problems*, p. 31.
80. President's Commission on Civil Disorders, pp. 406-408.
81. Francis Fox Piven and Richard A. Cloward, "What Chance for Black Power?" *Social Problems: Persistent Challenges*, p. 365.
82. Herbert J. Gans, "The Failure of Urban Renewal," *Commentary*, (April, 1965), XXXIX, 29-30.
83. Abrams, *American Future*, pp. 37-38.
84. Sykes, *Social Problems in America*, p. 47.
85. Gans, *Commentary*, pp. 29-30.
86. Nathan Glazer, "The Renewal of Cities," *Scientific American*, (September, 1965), CCXIII, 194-204.
87. Gerald D. Suttles, *The Social Order of the Slum: Ethnicity and Territoriality in the Inner City* (Chicago: University of Chicago Press, 1968).
88. Herbert J. Gans, *The Urban Villagers* (New York: Free Press, 1965), pp. 1-3.
89. Marc Fried, "Grieving for a Lost Home," *The Urban Condition: People and Policy in the Metropolis*, ed. Leonard J. Duhl (New York: Basic Books, 1963).
90. Moynihan, *Social Problems*, pp. 3-10.
91. Lewis Mumford, *The Urban Prospect* (New York: Harcourt, Brace and Jovanovich, 1968), pp. 217-220.
92. J. Allen Williams, Jr., "The Effects of Urban Renewal upon the Black Community: Evaluation and Recommendations," *Social Science Quarterly*, Vol. 50 (December, 1969), pp. 703-712.
93. See Nathan Glazer, "Housing Policy and the Family," *Journal of Marriage and the Family*, (February, 1967), XXIX, 153-155.
94. President's Commission on Civil Disorders, pp. 406-408.
95. Grier and Grier, *Daedalus*, pp. 77-89.
96. Peter Wiley and Beverly Leman, "The Business of Urban Reform," *Leviathan*, (March, 1969), I, 11-54.
97. Mark Reinsberg, *Growth and Change in Metropolitan Areas and Their Relation to Metropolitan Transportation: A Research Summary* (Evanston, Ill.: Northwestern University, 1961), pp. 9-10.
98. Paul N. Ylvisaker, "The Shape of the Future," *The Urban Future*, ed. Eli Chinoy (New York: Lieber-Atherton, 1972), pp. 112-113.
99. Daniel P. Moynihan, "Toward a National Urban Policy," *The Public Interest*, (Fall, 1969), XVII, 3-20.
100. *New York Times* (February 13, 1973).

101. A. Philip Randolph Institute, "A Freedom Budget for All Americans," *Poverty in America*, ed. Margaret S. Gordon (San Francisco: Chandler, 1965), pp. 631-632.

102. Lee Rainwater, "Crucible of Identity: The Negro Lower-Class Family," *Daedalus*, (Winter, 1965), XCV, 172-261.

103. Daniel P. Moynihan, "Poverty and Progress," *American Scholar*, (Autumn, 1964), XXXIII, 594-606.

104. Richard A. Cloward and Francis Fox Piven, "The Weight of the Poor: A Strategy to End Poverty," *The Nation*, (May, 1966), CCII, 510-517.

105. Richard M. Nixon, "Address to the Nation on Social Reform," (August 8, 1969); and Sar S. Levitan, *Programs in Aid of the Poor in the 1970's* (Baltimore: Johns Hopkins Press, 1969), p. 47.

106. Levitan, *Programs*, p. 11.

107. Christopher Green, "Income Guarantee Alternatives," *Poverty in Affluence*, p. 200; Milton Freedman, *Capitalism and Freedom* (Chicago: University of Chicago Press, 1962); and Levitan, *Programs*, p. 42.

108. Herbert Bienstock, "The Transition to Work Here and Abroad: Do U.S. Youth Fare Worse?" *New Generations*, (Winter, 1969), LI, 2-6.

109. William Deuterman, "Educational Attainment of Workers, March 1969 and 1970," *Monthly Labor Review* (October, 1970), pp. 12-13.

110. *Social Indicators 1973*, p. 137.

111. *Milwaukee Journal*, May 5, 1974.

112. Ben Wattenberg and Richard Scammon, *This U.S.A.* (Garden City: Doubleday, 1965), pp. 280-295.

113. F. James Davis, *Social Problems* (New York: Free Press, 1970), p. 97.

114. Galbraith, *New Industrial State*, pp. 238-242.

Name Index

254

Subject Index